Andrew Greet

play the
Queen's Indian

EVERYMAN CHESS

Gloucester Publishers plc   www.everymanchess.com

First published in 2009 by Gloucester Publishers plc (formerly Everyman Publishers plc), Northburgh House, 10 Northburgh Street, London EC1V 0AT

British Library Cataloguing-in-Publication Data

A catalogue record for this book is available from the British Library.

ISBN: 978 1 85744 580 0

Distributed in North America by The Globe Pequot Press, P.O Box 480, 246 Goose Lane, Guilford, CT 06437-0480.

All other sales enquiries should be directed to Everyman Chess, Northburgh House, 10 Northburgh Street, London EC1V 0AT
tel: 020 7253 7887 fax: 020 7490 3708
email: info@everymanchess.com; website: www.everymanchess.com

To my grandmother, Mavis

EVERYMAN CHESS SERIES
Chief advisor: Byron Jacobs
Commissioning editor: John Emms
Assistant editor: Richard Palliser

Typeset and edited by First Rank Publishing, Brighton.
Cover design by Horatio Monteverde.
Printed and bound in the UK by Clays, Bungay, Suffolk.

Contents

Bibliography

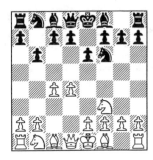

Books

Chess Explained: The Queen's Indian, Peter Wells (Gambit 2006)
Grandmaster Repertoire: 1.d4: Volume 1, Boris Avrukh (Quality Chess 2008)
How To Play The Queen's Indian, Dimitrij Oleinikov (ChessBase CD 2006)
Opening For Black According To Karpov, Alexander Khalifman (Chess Stars 2001)
Play 1 d4!, Richard Palliser (Batsford 2003)
Starting Out: The Queen's Indian, John Emms (Everyman Chess 2004)
The Queen's Indian, Jouni Yrjölä and Jussi Tella (Gambit 2003)
The Queen's Indian Defence, Jacob Aagaard (Everyman Chess 2002)
The Queen's Indian – The Easy Way, Jacob Aagaard (ChessBase DVD 2006)

Databases, Periodicals and Websites

Britbase, ChessPublishing.com, MegaBase 2008, Mega Correspondence 2006, New In Chess Yearbooks 1-88, and *The Week In Chess* 1-734.

Preface

Greetings, dear reader, and thank you for taking the time to read this book. The aim of this brief introduction is to set the scene for the remainder of the work by providing some relevant background information to our subject, as well explaining the ethos behind the proposed repertoire.

Whilst I hope and, indeed, expect this book to prove useful for players of a wide range of abilities, I would expect most readers to possess some basic knowledge of the fundamental principles underlying this opening. Therefore I have no intention to waste time by expounding such concepts as 'controlling the central squares with pieces rather than pawns', and so on. Countless other authors have elucidated the principles and historical development of hypermodern chess theory and I will say no more about the subject here.

As is customary for the '*Play the ...*' series, the primary aim of the present book is to provide a complete repertoire that will enable the reader to employ the Queen's Indian Defence with confidence. It is common knowledge that, along with its close relative the Nimzo-Indian, the Queen's Indian enjoys a reputation as one of Black's most dependable answers to 1 d4. His pieces can quickly emerge on to active squares, and his pawn structure is both unblemished and extremely flexible in the early stages of the game.

Despite its ongoing popularity amongst players of varying abilities, there are many who regard one of this opening's foremost strengths – its extreme solidity – as something of a drawback. Simply put, there are several major lines in which it can prove difficult for Black to generate realistic winning chances. This may not represent a problem at the lofty heights of Wijk aan Zee or Linares, but there is no doubting the fact that most of us would prefer to combine solidity with genuine prospects to play for a full point with the black pieces. *Therefore one of my primary goals in writing this book was to present a repertoire which would enable Black to unbalance the game in order to play for a win, without compromising on soundness.*

Overall, I believe that I have succeeded in finding a suitable balance, although ultimately this is something that the reader will have to judge for himself. On that note, let me once again thank you for reading. I sincerely hope that you will enjoy this book, and that the ideas contained herewith will play a role in improving your understanding, enjoyment and – most importantly of all – your results when playing the Queen's Indian.

Andrew Greet
Edinburgh,
January 2009

Chapter One

Early Bishop Developments

1 d4 ♘f6 2 c4 e6 3 ♘f3 b6

We will begin by examining variations in which White develops his dark-squared bishop without delay:

A: 4 ♗f4
B: 4 ♗g5

A) 4 ♗f4

This variation is named after the late Tony Miles, who utilized it with great success during the 1970s and 80s. Several other Grandmasters have also played it on a regular basis, including Akopian, Bareev, Gretarsson and Lputian.

4...♗b7

The bishop takes up its usual post.

5 e3

If White changes his move order with 5 ♘c3 then Black can obtain an improved version of Chapter 6 with 5...♗b4, as the white bishop would be better off on g5. After the logical 6 ♕b3 (others can be met by 6...♘e4) it looks interesting for Black to play 6...♗a5!? when Y.Seirawan-R.Dzindzichashvili, USA 1984, continued 7 e3 ♘e4 8 ♗d3 ♗xc3+ 9 bxc3 d6 10 ♕c2 f5 11 d5! (the only move to put pressure on Black).

(see following diagram)

We've reached a very similar position to those found in Chapter 6. Now instead of the game's 11...exd5, I suggest that Black continues in a similar vein to Chapter 6 with 11...♘d7!?, heading for the newly created hole on c5.

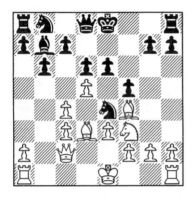

Play may continue 12 ♗xe4 (12 ♘d4 would be met by 12...♘dc5) 12...fxe4 13 ♘g5 (13 ♕xe4?! ♘c5 works well for Black after 14 ♕c2 exd5 or 14 ♕d4 e5 15 ♘xe5 dxe5 16 ♕xe5+ ♕e7, while 13 ♘d4 ♘c5 14 ♘xe6 ♘xe6 15 ♕xe4 ♕e7 16 ♕xe6 ♕xe6 17 dxe6 ♔e7 is equal, as shown by the plausible continuation 18 ♔d2 ♔xe6 19 f3 ♗a6) 13...♘c5 (13...exd5 14 ♘e6 ♕c8 is highly unclear) 14 ♘xe4 exd5 15 ♘xc5 bxc5 16 ♖b1 ♗c6 17 cxd5 ♗xd5 18 ♕f5 ♗c6 with roughly equal chances. Note that here 11...♘c5!? is also interesting after 12 dxe6 ♘xd3+ 13 ♕xd3 0-0 14 c5 (otherwise there would follow ...♘a6-c5) 14...bxc5, or even 12...♗e4!? 13 ♗xe4 fxe4 14 ♘g5 0-0.

5...♗e7!

This is Black's most solid move. For the time being he refrains from any central activity, preferring to develop a piece while conveniently preparing ...♘h5, forcing the exchange of the enemy bishop. Black should definitely take care to avoid 5...c5?! 6 d5! exd5 7 ♘c3 which is dangerous, as shown by 7...dxc4 8 ♘b5! ♘a6 9 ♗xc4 with excellent compensation for the pawn.

6 h3

Safeguarding the bishop, although White can also ignore the so-called threat with 6 ♘c3 ♘h5 7 ♗g3. This is not much of a try for a theoretical advantage, but Black should certainly be prepared for a complex middlegame. A sensible continuation would be 7...d6 8 ♗d3 ♘d7 9 ♕c2 g6

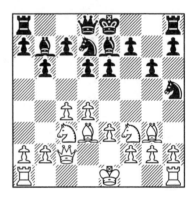

10 ♗e4 c6! (10...♗xe4 has been played, but with the text Black can retain a great deal more dynamic potential by keeping both his bishops) with a choice for White:

a) 11 d5 yields a slight advantage according to Yrjölä and Tella, but 11...cxd5 12 cxd5 e5 looks fine to me: for example, 13 ♘d2 f5 14 ♗f3 0-0!? (14...♘g7) 15 ♗xh5 gxh5 16 f3 ♖c8 17 e4 b5!? with excellent counterplay.

b) In L.Javakhishvili-M.Lomineishvili, Batumi 2002, White preferred 11 ♘d2 ♘xg3 12 hxg3 and now 12...♕c7 13 0-0-0 0-0-0 looks sensible with approximately equal chances. White controls slightly more space, but the power of the bishop-pair should not be underestimated.

6...c5

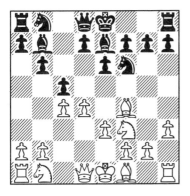

Now that White has spent a tempo on a non-developing move, it is fine for Black to strike in the centre. It should be noted that 6...0-0 7 ♘c3 d5 is equally playable: for example, 8 cxd5 ♘xd5 9 ♘xd5 ♕xd5! when the greedy 10 ♗xc7?! ♗b4+ 11 ♘d2 ♘c6 gave Black a lot of activity for the pawn in J.Dybowski-J.Adamski, Bytom 1986.

7 ♘c3

Alternatives are not worrying:

a) 7 ♗d3 cxd4 8 exd4 d5 should lead to a very comfortable IQP position for Black.

b) 7 ♗e2 cxd4 8 ♘xd4 0-0 9 0-0 (I.Farago-A.Adorjan, Sarajevo 1983) 9...d5 10 ♗f3 ♘bd7 11 cxd5 ♘xd5 is already slightly easier for the second player.

c) The sacrifice 7 d5?! exd5 8 ♘c3 is no longer viable thanks to the inclusion of the moves ...♗e7 and h3. In P.Nikolic-J.Lautier, Moscow 2001, Black scored an easy win after 8...dxc4

9 ♘b5 0-0 10 ♘c7 d5 11 ♘xa8 ♗xa8 (Black has two pawns for the exchange and a hugely powerful pawn phalanx) 12 ♗e2 ♘c6 13 0-0 b5 14 a4 b4 15 ♕b1 ♘e4 16 ♖d1 ♘a5 17 ♘e5 ♘b3 18 ♗xc4 ♘ed2 19 ♕c2 dxc4 0-1.

d) 7 dxc5 has actually been the most frequently played move, but I will not consider it in detail here as the positions which arise after 7...bxc5 are conceptually almost identical to those found in Line B of Chapter 10. For instance, after the further 8 ♘c3 0-0 9 ♗e2 d6 10 0-0 ♕b6 11 ♕c2 ♖d8 12 ♖ad1 ♘bd7, the position is almost identical to that reached after 4 a3 ♗a6 5 ♕c2 ♗b7 6 ♘c3 c5 7 dxc5 bxc5 8 ♗f4 ♗e7 9 ♖d1 0-0 10 e3 ♕b6 11 ♗e2 d6 12 0-0 ♖d8 13 ♖d2 ♘bd7, except that White has substituted the move h3 for ♖d2 whilst his a-pawn stands on a2 instead of a3. Neither of these factors alters the character of the position in any meaningful way, so rather than go over the same ground twice I instead invite the reader to turn to page 137 for a discussion of the relevant positions.

7...cxd4 8 ♘xd4

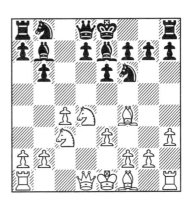

This is White's most promising re-capture – he fails to achieve anything with either of the alternatives:

a) After 8 ♕xd4 ♘c6 9 ♕d2 (H.Gretarsson-J.Jurek, Pardubice 1998) it looks interesting to try 9...♗b4!? 10 ♗d3 d5 with an active game.

b) 8 exd4 0-0 9 ♗d3 (after 9 d5?! exd5 10 cxd5 ♖e8 11 ♗e2 ♗b4 White is likely to lose material for insufficient compensation; here neither is White helped by 10 ♘xd5?! ♘xd5 11 cxd5 ♗b4+ 12 ♗d2 ♖e8+ 13 ♗e2 ♗a6) 9...d5 10 0-0 (10 cxd5 ♘xd5 11 ♘xd5 ♗xd5 12 0-0 ♘c6 was no better for White in the game F.Gonzalez Alvarez-A.Magallon Minguez, correspondence 2000) 10...dxc4 11 ♗xc4 ♘c6 12 ♖c1 ♖c8 was the course of M.Rivas Pastor-R.Hübner, Linares 1985; Black has achieved a comfortable IQP position in which the moves h3 and ♗f4 appear somewhat out of place.

8...0-0

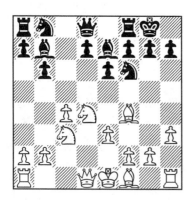

A decent alternative is 8...a6, but there is no real need to prevent the following.

9 ♘db5 ♘e8

White must now make an important choice.

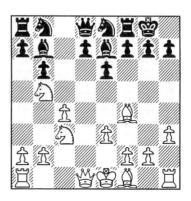

10 ♘d6

With this move White aims to keep control and stifle the opponent's counterplay, although we will see that Black's position is not without its resources. The alternatives also deserve attention, especially variation 'b':

a) 10 ♗xb8?! is a slightly cheeky pawn grab which enables Black to obtain full compensation after 10...♕xb8 11 ♕xd7 ♗c5 12 ♖d1 a6 13 ♘d4 ♘f6 14 ♕a4 (P.De Jong-H.Newton, correspondence 1997) 14...♖d8, as well as with the untested 10...♖xb8!? 11 ♘xa7 ♘f6 12 ♘ab5 d5 13 cxd5 ♘xd5.

b) 10 ♕d2 is a bit more challenging. Now after 10...a6 11 ♘d6 (11 ♘d4 d6 12 ♘f3 ♘d7 13 ♗e2 was P.Dunn-R.Vujnovic, correspondence 2000, and here 13...♕c7 would have given Black a very comfortable Hedgehog set-up) 11...♘xd6 12 ♗xd6 ♗xd6 13 ♕xd6 it may seem that by comparison with the main line White has lost a tempo with his queen, but the flip side of the coin is that Black can no longer develop his knight on a6. However, in A.Miles-V.Kupreichik, Reykjavik 1980, Black made full use of the additional pawn move to offer an interesting pawn sacrifice with 13...b5!?.

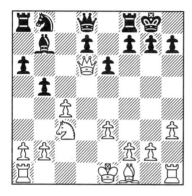

Now White has a choice:

b1) If he accepts the pawn with 14 cxb5 axb5 (14...♛a5?! 15 ♗d3! axb5 16 ♗xh7+! ♚xh7 17 ♛xf8 leaves Black with insufficient compensation) there may follow 15 ♗xb5 (15 ♘xb5 ♘c6 should give Black enough activity) 15...♛g5 (after 15...♗xg2 16 ♖g1 White may be able to utilize the g-file to his advantage) 16 ♛g3 ♛xg3 17 fxg3 ♗xg2 18 ♖h2 ♗c6 with approximate equality.

b2) In the game Miles declined the offer with 14 a3 bxc4 15 ♖d1 (15 ♗xc4 can be met by 15...♛g5 or 15...♛h4) when Kupreichik chose 15...♘c6 and eventually triumphed, although at this stage I would be tempted to try 15...♛g5!?.

10...♘xd6 11 ♗xd6 ♘a6

This is the best square for the knight, eyeing the c5-square while keeping the long diagonal clear for the bishop.

12 ♛d2

The alternatives are no better:

a) 12 ♘b5 (M.Dlugy-G.Ligterink, London 1981) 12...♗c6 13 ♗e2 ♗xd6 14 ♘xd6 ♛g5! is slightly awkward for White.

b) 12 ♗xe7 ♛xe7 13 ♛d2 ♖fd8 14 ♖d1 d5 15 cxd5 ♗xd5! gave Black a strong initiative in S.Djuric-A.Ornstein, Pamporovo 1981. Our main line was suggested as an improvement by Ornstein in his annotations.

12...♗xd6 13 ♛xd6 ♛f6

Ornstein's analysis ended here with an evaluation of unclear, which seems reasonable enough after something like 14 ♖d1 ♖fd8 15 ♖d4 ♛g6 when White still has some problems connected with the development of his kingside pieces. If, on the other hand, he gets greedy with 14 ♛xd7?! then he risks coming under pressure after 14...♘c5 15 ♛d4 ♛e7!.

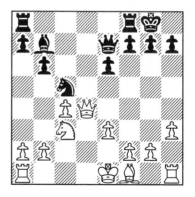

A possible continuation would be 16 ♗e2 ♖ad8 17 ♛g4 ♘e4! 18 ♘xe4 ♛b4+! 19 ♘c3 (or 19 ♚f1 ♛xb2 20 ♖e1 f5!) 19...♛xb2 20 0-0 ♛xc3 with a clear advantage, while another runs 16 0-0-0

罩fd8 17 ♕f4 (after 17 ♕g4 f5! 18 ♕e2 ♗e4! 19 ♘xe4 ♘xe4 White has serious problems developing his kingside pieces) 17...罩xd1+ 18 ♔xd1 (18 ♘xd1 ♗xg2!) 18...罩d8+ 19 ♔c2 e5 20 ♕g4 ♕f6 21 f3 (21 ♕e2? ♕g6+!) 21...♕h6!

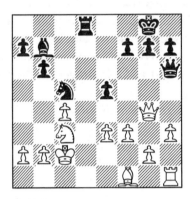

when White has serious problems, as shown by 22 ♗e2 (22 f4 ♘e4!) 22...♕xe3 23 罩d1 罩xd1 24 ♗xd1 (24 ♔xd1 ♘e6!) 24...♗a6 25 ♗e2 ♘e6 with a near decisive advantage.

B) 4 ♗g5

Despite being relatively uncommon, the text is eminently playable and actually poses something of a move order dilemma with respect to our proposed repertoire. Later in the book you will find that, in the majority of cases, I recommend that the development of a white knight on c3 be met with the pinning ...♗b4 in the style of the Nimzo-Indian Defence. If, however, we continue with the natural 4...♗b7, intending to meet 5 ♘c3 with 5...♗b4, we end up in a position usually reached via the move order 4 ♘c3 ♗b4 5 ♗g5 ♗b7. Here White has at his disposal a highly venomous and fashionable continuation in 6 ♘d2!?. Thus in Chapter 6 following 4 ♘c3 ♗b4 5 ♗g5 I recommend the move 5...h6 which is specifically intended to avoid this very possibility.

Are there any other ways in which we can aim for a transposition to Chapter 6? One obvious attempt is 4...♗b4+ when 5 ♘c3 h6 leads to our target position. However, in that case we must also worry about the quite common response 5 ♘bd2, while in D.Spence-R.Martyn, Amsterdam 2005, White tried the novel 5 ♘fd2!? which led to very interesting play. Neither possibility is terrifying for Black, but both require considerable attention and in the end I did not feel that 4...♗b4+ was an ideal solution. Thus it transpires that 4 ♗g5 demands very careful consideration, if only as a tricky transpositional device.

For a while I thought that the ideal solution might lie in 4...h6 5 ♗h4 ♗e7 6 ♘c3 c5!?, as used successfully by Ivanchuk and later Carlsen. The critical variation continues 7 e4! (7 e3 is less challenging, although this also requires care from Black) 7...cxd4 8 ♘xd4 d6 9 ♘db5 a6 and now:

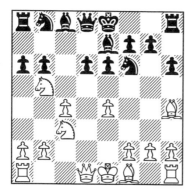

a) In B.Jobava-V.Ivanchuk, Havana 2005, Black was able to sacrifice a pawn with 10 ♗xf6 ♗xf6! 11 ♘xd6+ ♔e7 12 ♘xc8+ ♕xc8 13 ♘a4 (13 ♗e2 ♖d8 14 ♕c1 ♕c5 15 0-0 ♘c6 gave Black good compensation in L.Pantsulaia-A.Volokitin, Beersheba 2005) 13...♖d8 14 ♕b3 ♘d7 15 ♕a3+ ♘c5! 16 ♗e2 (16 ♘xb6 ♕c6 17 ♘xa8 ♗xb2! 18 ♕xb2 ♕xe4+ 19 ♕e2 ♘d3+ is winning for Black) 16...♕c6 17 ♘xc5 ♕xc5, which supplied more than enough compensation.

b) In B.Jobava-M.Carlsen, Skanderborg 2005, the talented Georgian improved with 10 e5!? dxe5 11 ♗xf6 ♗xf6 12 ♕f3!, winning the exchange. The game continued 12...axb5 13 ♕xa8 b4 14 ♘e4 ♗d7 15 ♘xf6+ gxf6 16 c5!? bxc5 17 ♕a7 ♘c6 18 ♕xc5 ♘d4 with decent compensation for Black who eventually went on to win. While this may seem very encouraging, a closer inspection casts doubt on the viability of Black's sacrifice. Several improvements have

been suggested for White, including 15 ♘d6+!? ♔f8 16 0-0-0 ♕c7 17 ♕e4 and 16 ♕f3 ♗c6 17 ♕e2 ♘d7 18 f3, both of which ought to bring the first player an advantage as far as I can see.

Despite this conclusion, I can easily imagine the above variations causing considerable practical difficulties for many White players, so if you like the look of this sort of thing then please do go ahead and give Ivanchuk's move order a try.

When writing a book of this type I believe that an author's recommendations should, above all else, be fundamentally sound. Thus although my heart tells me that the aforementioned system would be terrific fun to play and analyse, my head has finally ruled that my final recommendation must go to a more reliable, if somewhat drier approach. We begin with the standard bishop development:

4...♗b7

We have learned from the above analysis that if Black delays this move then a subsequent e4-e5 advance could cause problems.

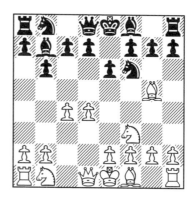

5 ♘c3

5 e3 h6 6 ♗h4 ♗e7 will almost certainly lead to a transposition after a subsequent ♘c3, as the knight can hardly have a better square.

5...h6

I will briefly remind the reader that 5...♗b4 would reach the line 4 ♘c3 ♗b4 5 ♗g5 ♗b7. In Chapter 6 I suggest that Black avoids this position with 5...h6 6 ♗h4 g5 on account of the dangerous 6 ♘d2!?.

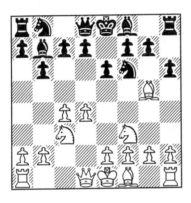

6 ♗h4

White gains nothing from 6 ♗xf6 ♕xf6: for example, 7 e3 ♗b4 8 ♗e2 ♗xc3+ 9 bxc3 0-0 10 0-0 d6, or 7 e4 ♗b4 8 ♗d3 ♗xc3+ 9 bxc3 d6 10 0-0 ♘d7 11 ♕a4 ♕e7 when Black enjoyed a solid position with the superior pawn structure in B.Lalic-B.Kohlweyer, Bad Wörishofen 1989.

6...♗e7!

This is the solid, no nonsense approach that I finally decided to recommend. Developing the bishop to the less active e7-square may seem like a concession, though, and it is true that we are unlikely to reach such interesting and double-edged middlegames as in Chapter 6. On the other hand, when playing with the black pieces we must face the reality that there will be times when we just have to play solidly. In this particular position Black's main resources include the typical ...c5 thrust, as well as a timely ...♘e4 to exchange some minor pieces.

7 e3

In case of 7 ♕c2 Black should definitely play 7...c5!, preventing the opponent from establishing a classic central pawn trio. There might follow either 8 e4 cxd4 9 ♘xd4 ♘c6 10 ♘xc6 ♗xc6 or 8 dxc5 bxc5 9 e3 0-0 10 ♗e2 d6 11 0-0 ♘bd7 12 ♖fd1 ♕b6 13 ♖d2 ♖fd8 with equality in both cases. Following the latter course, the game Seirawan-L.Portisch, Montpellier 1985, was soon agreed drawn after 14 ♖ad1 ♘f8 15 ♘e1 ♖d7 16 ♗f3 ♖ad8 17 ♗xb7 ♕xb7 18 h3 ♘g6 and ½-½.

7...c5

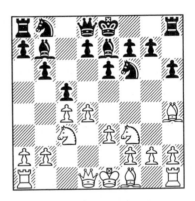

The other main move is 7...♘e4. This has a solid reputation, although White may be able to claim a slight edge after 8 ♘xe4 ♗xe4 9 ♗g3!? 0-0 10

♗d3 ♗xd3 11 ♕xd3 d6 12 0-0 ♘d7 13 e4 with a space advantage. After the text White usually develops his light-squared bishop to one of two squares:

B1: 8 ♗d3
B2: 8 ♗e2

These two moves lead to markedly different types of position, both of which present their own unique challenges to the two combatants.

The alternatives do not require much attention:

a) 8 d5? has seen White embarrassed more than once after 8...♘xd5! 9 cxd5 ♗xh4, winning a clear pawn.

b) I will not discuss 8 dxc5 bxc5 in any depth here, for the same reason as with variation 'd' in the note to White's 7th in Line A: the resulting positions are so closely related to those found in Line B of Chapter 10 that there would be little point in conducting a detailed investigation here. For example, after the natural moves 9 ♗e2 0-0 10 0-0 d6 11 ♕c2 ♘bd7 we reach an identical position except for the position of the white a-pawn on a2 instead of a3 and the inclusion of the moves ...h6 and ♗h4, neither of which are likely to alter the nature of the subsequent play in any drastic way.

B1) 8 ♗d3 cxd4 9 exd4

9 ♘xd4 looks inconsistent with the bishop on d3, and after 9...0-0 10 0-0 ♘c6 11 ♘xc6 ♗xc6 Black was fine in W.Uhlmann-L.Portisch, Mar del Plata 1966.

9...0-0

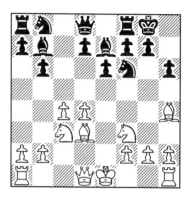

10 0-0

In Z.Azmaiparashvili-L.Aronian, Saint Vincent 2005, White attempted to prepare a kingside attack with 10 ♗c2 intending ♕d3; a creative approach which, unfortunately for Azmaiparashvili, was exposed as overly optimistic by the leading Armenian's expert handling. The game continued 10...d5 11 cxd5 (11 ♗xf6 ♗xf6 12 cxd5 ♗xd5! 13 ♕d3 g6 14 ♘xd5 ♕xd5 15 ♕e3 ♕a5+ 16 ♕c3 ♘c6 17 ♗e4 ♖ac8 is better for Black – Ftacnik) 11...♘xd5 12 ♕d3 g6 13 ♘xd5?! (13 ♗xe7 would have been better, although even then Black maintains a healthy position after 13...♕xe7 14 ♕d2 ♔h7 15 ♗e4 ♘d7 16 0-0 ♘7f6, as analysed by Ftacnik) 13...♗xd5 14 ♗xe7 ♕xe7 15 ♗b3 ♕b4+ 16 ♕c3 ♕xc3+ 17 bxc3 ♗xf3! 18 gxf3 ♘c6, reaching an ending in which Black successfully exploited his opponent's pawn weaknesses.

10...d5

White is at an important crossroads. He can either allow his opponent to reach a comfortable IQP position or relinquish the bishop-pair in order to reduce his opponent's control over d5.

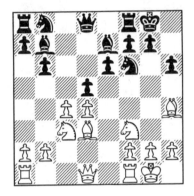

11 ♗xf6

I consider this to be the most consistent move. Instead 11 cxd5 ♘xd5 gives Black a pleasant IQP position, as an exchange of minor pieces would diminish White's dynamic possibilities, while 12 ♗g3 ♘d7 intending ...♘7f6 gives Black a firm grip over the key d5-square. Other moves such as 11 ♖e1 allow 11...dxc4, forcing White to move his bishop for a second time and leaving Black with a comfortable position after 12 ♗xc4 ♘c6.

11...♗xf6 12 cxd5 exd5

Now Black's dark-squared bishop enjoys tremendous potential, although it is true that its brother on b7 may have a harder time becoming active.

13 ♖e1 ♘c6 14 ♗c2

In B.Spassky-L.Portisch, Geneva 1977, White preferred 14 ♗b5. Here I see no reason for Black to fear the exchange of minor pieces and would recommend 14...♛d6 as a sensible developing move. Now Witkowski claims a clear advantage for White after 15

♗xc6 ♗xc6 16 ♘e5 ♖fe8 17 f4 ♗d7 18 ♛f3, but I don't buy this assessment. One possible improvement is 17...♖e7 intending to double on the e- or perhaps even c-file, while later Black may consider expanding on the queenside.

14...♛d6

Black improves his most powerful piece while preventing the enemy knight from occupying e5.

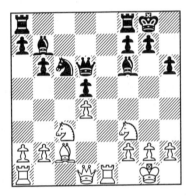

15 ♛d3 g6 16 a3

Preventing ...♘b4. After 16 ♗b3 ♘a5 17 ♘e5 ♗g7 18 ♖e2 ♘xb3 19 axb3 a6 Black eventually capitalized on his superior structure and bishop-pair in Zhao Zong Yuan-M.Carlsen, Khanty-Mansiysk 2007.

16...♖fe8

Black enjoys a healthy position. His unopposed dark-squared bishop is a long-term asset and although it may not be hurting White too severely at present, the pressure against d4 will at least help to restrict a few of his pieces to defensive duties. A sensible plan for the next few moves will be to improve Black's position on the queenside. L.Gostisa-O.Orel, Slovenia 1992, continued 17 b4 (17 h3 ♗g7 18 b4 a5! 19 b5 ♘e7 20 ♘e5 ♘f5 was similar in I.Sokolov-M.Rivas Pastor, Leon 1995) 17...a5! 18 b5 ♘e7 19 ♕d2 ♖ac8 20 ♗d3 ♖c7 21 ♘e2 ♔g7 22 ♘f4 ♗c8 23 g3 ♗g4 24 ♘e5 ♗f5 25 ♖e2 ♖ec8 26 a4 ♗g5 (26...♕b4!?) 27 h4 ♗xd3 28 ♘exd3 and here 28...♗xf4 would have left Black with the more active position.

B2) 8 ♗e2

This is the more common of the two bishop moves. White keeps the d-file clear, intending to meet ...cxd4 by recapturing with the knight.

8...0-0 9 0-0 ♘e4!

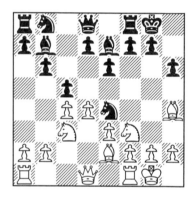

This typical exchanging manoeuvre helps to relieve any congestion in the black position. 9...d6 is sometimes seen, but White should maintain a slight edge after 10 ♕c2 or the more ambitious 10 d5!?. The difference between playing ...♘e4 here rather than on move 7 is that White is denied certain options such as the set-up involving ♗f1-d3 as noted earlier.

10 ♘xe4

10 ♗xe7 ♕xe7 11 ♖c1 (for 11 ♘xe4 ♗xe4 see the note to White's 11th move, below) 11...d6 12 ♘xe4 ♗xe4 13 ♘d2 ♗b7 was equal in J.Lechtynsky-J.Adamski, Halle 1981.

10...♗xe4 11 ♗g3

This is White's best chance for an edge. 11 ♗xe7 ♕xe7 12 ♘d2 (most other moves can be met by ...d6 and ...♘d7) 12...♗b7 13 ♗f3 d6 is equal, while if Black is looking to unbalance the game he can try 13...♘c6!? 14 dxc5 bxc5 15 ♘e4 ♘e5 16 b3 d5! 17 cxd5 exd5 18 ♘g3 ♖ad8 19 ♗e2 d4 20 exd4 cxd4 and his energetic play had yielded a distinct advantage in S.Bilsel-L.Papakosmas, correspondence 1996.

11...d6

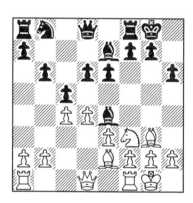

12 ♕b3

Instead 12 ♕d2 (W.Uhlmann-B.Parma, Zagreb 1965) should probably be met by 12...♗f6.

The text was seen in Wang Yue-S.Tiviakov, Khanty-Mansiysk 2007. In that game Tiviakov chose 12...♘d7, but fell short of equality after 13 ♘d2 ♗b7 14 d5! exd5 15 cxd5.

Instead I would propose 12...♘c6!? as a more active and promising alternative, with the following sample variations:

a) 13 d5 exd5 14 cxd5 ♘b4 targets the d-pawn, and 15 ♖fd1? allows 15...♗c2.

b) 13 ♘d2 ♗g6 14 ♗f3 ♕c7 15 d5 ♘a5! 16 ♕a4 e5 is similar to variation 'c'.

c) After 13 ♖fd1 ♕c7 (13...cxd4 14 ♘xd4! is slightly awkward) 14 d5 (14 ♖ac1 cxd4 15 exd4 e5! gives Black good chances) 14...♘a5 15 ♕a4 e5

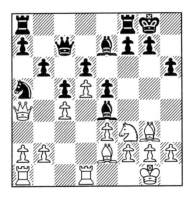

Black has good prospects: for example, 16 a3 ♗g6 (16...h5!?) 17 b4 ♘b7 and the knight on b7 is perfectly placed to fortify the queenside. Meanwhile the

opposite flank is ripe for a pawn expansion. Note too that 18 ♕c6 achieves little for White after 18...♖fc8 19 ♕xc7 ♖xc7.

Summary

The Miles variation, 4 ♗f4, is mainly used by players wishing to avoid too much heavy theory. There is nothing much wrong with it, but nor should Black have any difficulty in securing a satisfactory game. On the other hand, I wouldn't like to guess how many hours I spent working out a suitable antidote to 4 ♗g5. In fact, when judged on a time-per-page ratio, the present chapter must rank as one of the most time-intensive in the entire book.

I am happy with the finished repertoire against 4 ♗g5 and believe that the recommendations presented here will stand the reader in good stead in the event that he encounters this variation. Furthermore, I hope that the brief discussion of the move order 4...h6 5 ♗h4 ♗e7 6 ♘c3 c5!? will have proved stimulating to those readers who may seek a more experimental approach.

Chapter Two

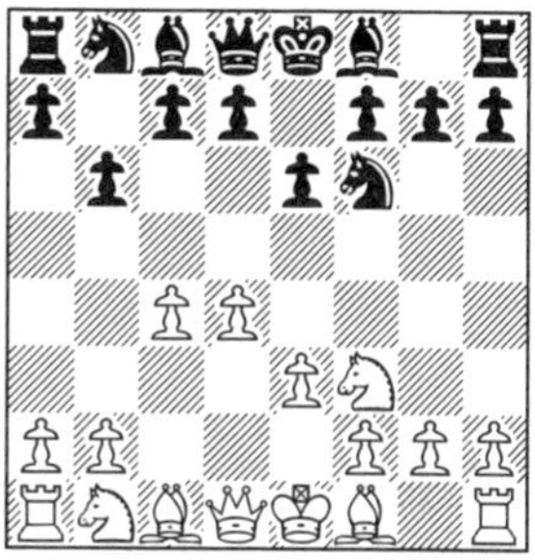

The Straightforward 4 e3

1 d4 ♘f6 2 c4 e6 3 ♘f3 b6 4 e3

This unpretentious move remains a popular choice. White's idea is to complete the development of his kingside with ♗d3 and 0-0 before bringing his remaining pieces into play. His system is not overly ambitious, but it is eminently sensible and in keeping with the classical principles of opening play. Black can react in a variety of ways, but the system with arguably the best reputation involves placing his queen's pawn on d5 and king's bishop on d6.

4...♗b7

Now White must make a choice:

A) 5 ♘c3
B) 5 ♗d3

Line B can be considered the main line, while the rare 5 ♗e2 should be met by 5...d5 intending to continue in similar vein to Line B, safe in the knowledge that the enemy bishop will be less actively placed.

A) 5 ♘c3 d5

Black can, of course, transpose to a Nimzo-Indian with 5...♗b4, although compared with the move order 4 ♘c3 ♗b4 5 e3, which allows Black to obtain a good game with 5...♘e4! as seen in Chapter 4, the present position allows White to pose slightly more difficult problems with 6 ♗d3 ♘e4 7 0-0! f5 (capturing the gambit pawn would allow White to obtain a dangerous lead in development) 8 d5!? or 8 ♘e2. Nevertheless these positions are quite playable for Black, and if the reader's repertoire already includes the 4 e3 b6 variation of the Nimzo-Indian then he is more than welcome to follow this route.

6 cxd5

This is the independent path, with which White plans what he hopes will be a disruptive check.

6...exd5 7 ♗b5+!?

Others such as 7 ♗d3 would almost certainly transpose to Line B2 below.

7...c6

7...♘bd7?! is less accurate in view of the sequence 8 ♘e5 ♗d6 (L.Bregadze-E.Shaposhnikov, Internet 2006) 9 ♗c6! ♗xc6 10 ♘xc6 ♕c8 11 ♕f3!, winning a pawn.

8 ♗d3

This is the point of White's play; he hopes that the move ...c6 will prove to be a liability by blocking the b7-bishop. On the other hand the pawn provides d5 with additional protection while also preventing any ♘b5 ideas, by contrast with the main line (B) in which Black must frequently expend a tempo on ...a7-a6.

8...♗e7!

The development of the bishop to d6 does not work so well here: for example, 8...♘bd7 9 0-0 ♗d6 10 e4!? dxe4 11 ♘xe4 ♘xe4 12 ♗xe4 ♘f6 13 ♗g5 may give White a slight edge, as the bishop is not so well placed on d6.

9 0-0 0-0

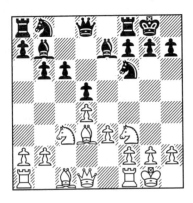

10 b3

Alternatively:

a) 10 e4 turns out to be less suitable against a bishop on e7 after 10...dxe4 11 ♘xe4 ♘bd7 12 ♖e1 ♘xe4 13 ♗xe4 ♘f6 14 ♗d3 ♖e8 (14...c5 is equal) 15 ♘e5 ♗b4 16 ♖e2 (H.Hummeling-R.Mueller, correspondence 2004) 16...c5! 17 a3 ♗a5 18 dxc5 bxc5 when Black's active pieces more than offset his isolated c-pawn.

b) 10 ♘e5 is the main alternative. Now instead of 10...♘bd7 11 f4, I prefer 10...c5, intending to develop the knight on c6 where it exerts a greater influence over the centre. There may follow 11 ♕f3 (11 f4 and 11 b3 should both be met by 11...♘c6 with equal chances) 11...♘c6 and now:

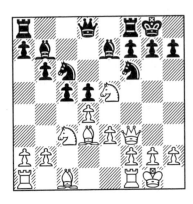

b1) 12 ♖d1 ♕d6! 13 ♘g4 ♘xg4 14 ♕xg4 ♖ad8 15 b3 (White lands up in trouble after 15 dxc5 bxc5 16 ♘xd5? ♘e5! – Kragelj) 15...♗c8 16 ♕e2 cxd4 17 ♘b5 ♕e6 18 exd4 ♕xe2 19 ♗xe2 was G.Dizdar-I.Kragelj, Slovenia 2005, and here Black could have obtained at least equal chances with Kragelj's 19...a6 20 ♘c3 (20 ♘c7?! ♖d7 21 ♘xa6 ♖a7 does not help White) 20...b5 (20...♖fe8!?) 21 ♗e3 ♗e6 22 a4 b4 23 ♘b1 a5, when 24 ♖c1 ♖c8 25 ♗a6? runs into 25...♘xd4!.

b2) In P.Gnusarev-D.Sadvakasov, Astana 2007, the aggressive 12 ♕h3 was easily defused by 12...♘xe5 13 dxe5 ♘e4 14 ♖d1 ♕c8 15 ♕xc8 ♖fxc8! (15...♖axc8?? 16 ♗xe4 dxe4 17 ♖d7 wins) 16 ♘xe4 (now 16 ♗xe4? dxe4 17 ♖d7?! can be met by 17...♗c6! 18 ♖xe7 ♔f8 19 ♘d5 – there is no other way to save the rook – 19...♗xd5 20 ♖d7 ♖d8 21 ♖xd8+ ♖xd8 with a big advantage) 16...dxe4 17 ♗e2 ♗c6 with at least equal chances in the endgame and 17...♖d8! might have been even more accurate.

10...♘bd7 11 ♗b2 ♗d6

Even though Black has lost a tempo by moving the bishop twice, that time was well spent as he no longer has to worry about the e4-advance which does not combine well with the bishop on b2.

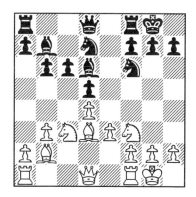

12 ♖c1

This has been White's most popular choice. A few other moves have been tried, although the general character of the position is unlikely to change very much.

12...♕e7

Black has also done well with 12...♖e8, but I rather like the idea of

keeping the rook on f8 in anticipation of a subsequent ...♘e4 and ...f5.

13 ♕e2 ♖ae8

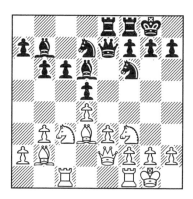

13...♘e4 also looks okay, although in this case White could at least exchange the light-squared bishops with 14 ♗a6.

14 ♗a6

14 ♘d2 is not dangerous after 14...c5 (14...♕e6!?) 15 ♘b5 ♗b8 16 ♗a3 (V.Raceanu-M.Parligras, Sovata 2000) 16...a6 17 ♘c3 ♗d6 with a promising position for Black. After the text, we will follow the game F.Levin-T.Nyback, German League 2004:

14...♗a8

14...♗xa6!? also looks fine after 15 ♕xa6 ♘b8 followed by ...♘e4.

15 ♖fd1 b5!?

15...♘e4 is fine, but Nyback is playing even more ambitiously.

16 a4

White must extricate his bishop.

16...b4 17 ♘a2

17 ♘b1 would also be met by 17...♘e4.

17...♘e4 18 ♖c2 f5!

Black stands clearly better. The

backward c-pawn is hard to attack, while White's minor pieces suffer from a serious lack of coordination. Meanwhile it's full steam ahead for Black's kingside attack.

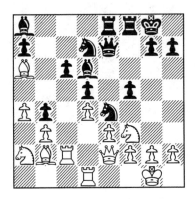

19 ♘c1 f4 20 ♘d3?

A mistake under pressure. 20 exf4 was better, although Black retains a strong initiative after 20...♖xf4 (20...♕f7!?) 21 ♘d3 ♖f5 when apart from the kingside attack White must also watch out for ...♘b8 ideas which could embarrass his bishop.

20...fxe3 21 ♕xe3?

White collapses. 21 fxe3 was the last chance, although 21...♘b8 22 ♘de5 ♗xe5 23 dxe5 (23 ♘xe5? ♖f2 wins) 23...♘xa6 24 ♕xa6 c5 leaves Black firmly in control.

21...♘b8! 0-1

White resigned as he is losing his bishop for nothing.

B) 5 ♗d3

This is White's most popular move, intending to castle before determining the position of the queenside pieces.

5...d5

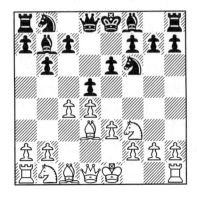

This is viewed by the majority of experts as the most reliable antidote to White's system. The general idea is to follow up with ...♗d6, ...0-0, ...♘bd7 and perhaps a timely ...♘e4 with active prospects in the centre and on the kingside.

5...♗e7 6 ♘c3 d5 is also popular, but I prefer to deploy the bishop on the more active d6-square. Here 6...c5 is the other main line, after which there can follow 7 0-0 cxd4 (7...0-0?! allows White to obtain a clear advantage with 8 d5! exd5 9 cxd5 ♘xd5 – otherwise e3-e4 would give White a vastly improved Benoni in which the b7-bishop is badly misplaced – 10 ♘xd5 ♗xd5 11 ♗xh7+ ♔xh7 12 ♕xd5 ♘c6 13 e4 followed by pressure against the kingside and along the d-file) 8 exd4 d5 (8...0-0 9 d5! is known to be good for White) 9 cxd5 ♘xd5 10 ♘e5 0-0 and now 11 ♕h5 or 11 ♕g4 gives White dangerous attacking prospects. Theoretically Black is probably okay here, but I would not expect many players to relish the task of defending such a position. Furthermore, there are certain lines in which

White can force a repetition of moves, thus rendering this variation an unsuitable choice when facing weaker opposition.

6 0-0

White often plays 6 b3, 6 cxd5 or 6 ♘bd2 before castling, but as a rule these will always end up transposing to one of the main lines as the king is hardly likely to go anywhere else.

6...♗d6

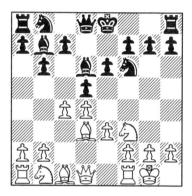

From here White will usually fianchetto his queen's bishop. His main decision concerns his queen's knight which can be deployed on either d2 or c3. Thus we will divide the material in the following way:

B1: Lines with ♘bd2
B2: Lines with ♘c3

Naturally White can trade a pair of pawns on d5 at any moment of his choosing. Here 7 cxd5 exd5 followed by 8 ♘c3 reaches Line B21. Note that in this case 8 ♘bd2?! does not combine so well with the pawn exchange.

Instead 7 b4!? is an interesting

move, but one which promises no advantage after 7...dxc4! (7...♗xb4?? loses a piece after 8 ♕a4+ ♘c6 9 ♘e5 ♕d6 10 c5! bxc5 11 ♗b5) 8 ♗xc4 0-0 (once again 8...♗xb4?? is inadvisable due to 9 ♕a4+ ♘c6 10 ♘e5 ♕d6 11 ♗b5, as pointed out by Emms) 9 a3 (9 b5 allows Black to choose between 9...a6 and 9...♘bd7 intending a subsequent ...e5, with equal chances in both cases) 9...♘bd7 10 ♗b2 ♕e7 11 ♘c3 c5 (11...a6 12 b5 a5 13 ♘e2 ♖ad8 14 ♘g3 g6 15 ♕c2 e5 16 dxe5 ♘xe5 17 ♘xe5 ♗xe5 18 ♗xe5 ♕xe5 was also fine for Black in E.Ubilava-J.Hjartarson, Linares 1996) 12 dxc5 bxc5 13 b5 ♖fd8 14 ♕e2 ♘b6 15 e4 ♘xc4 16 ♕xc4 ♘d7! gave Black an excellent position in N.Rashkovsky-A.Sultanov, Samara 2000; his bishop-pair and active pieces were far more relevant than the theoretical inferiority of his queenside structure.

B1) 7 b3

I will take this as the standard move order, although 7 ♘bd2 0-0 8 b3 is equally plausible.

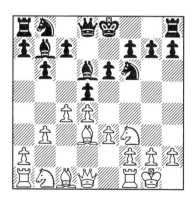

7...0-0 8 ♗b2 ♘bd7 9 ♘bd2

White can, of course, head for Line B2 with the alternate knight development.

9...♘e4

This knight thrust often forms an integral part of Black's plans. From e4 the steed exerts an influence across the board and may in particular be used as a spearhead for a kingside attack after a subsequent ...f5.

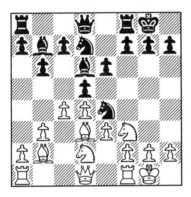

10 ♕c2

This is White's most popular and highest-scoring move, although many sensible alternatives have been tried too. Here are some examples:

a) 10 cxd5 releases the tension prematurely and after 10...exd5 11 ♘e5 ♕e7 12 f4 (D.Kosic-K.Szabo, Budapest 2007) 12...♘xd2 13 ♕xd2 ♘f6 Black stands slightly better. He can gradually aim to expel the enemy knight with ...f6, whereas the corresponding hole on e4 cannot be similarly plugged.

b) 10 ♘e5 should be met by 10...♗xe5! 11 dxe5 ♘dc5. Usually one would be ill-advised to exchange a bishop for a knight so, but in this position Black's active pieces justify the decision as you can see from the following variations:

b1) 12 ♗xe4 dxe4 13 ♗a3 ♕g5 14 ♕c2 ♕xe5 15 ♗xc5 bxc5 left White with little to show for the lost pawn in J.Curtis-T.Nixon, British League 2003.

b2) 12 ♘xe4 dxe4 13 ♗e2 (N.Sprotte-I.Jelen, Bled 1995) can be strongly met by 13...♕g5! with an excellent position.

b3) 12 ♗e2 ♘xd2 13 ♕xd2 dxc4 14 ♕xd8 ♖fxd8 15 ♗xc4 ♗a6 gave Black a pleasant endgame in E.Colle-G.Thomas, Hastings 1926, much as in note 'b' to White's 11th in the main line.

c) 10 ♕e2 can be met by 10...f5, as shown by 11 cxd5 exd5 12 ♗a6 ♗xa6 13 ♕xa6 ♕c8 with a fine position. Here Black has also done well with 10...a5!?, for example:

c1) 11 a4?! left a permanent hole on b4 in H.Dobosz-J.Howell, Wuerzburg 1988, after which 11...f5 would have left Black clearly for choice.

c2) 11 a3 f5 is comfortable enough for Black. In N.Zahariou-L.Aroshidze, Nikaia 2005, White now faltered with 12 ♘e5? ♗xe5 13 dxe5 ♘xd2 (13...♘dc5 also looks strong) 14 ♕xd2 ♘c5 15 ♗c2?! dxc4 16 ♕xd8 ♖axd8 17 bxc4 ♖d2 18 ♖ac1 ♗e4 19 ♗xe4, and here 19...fxe4 20 ♗c3 (20 ♗d4 ♘d3) 20...♖a2 or 20...♖dxf2 would have been winning for Black.

d) Finally, there is 10 ♖c1 f5 (the more restrained 10...♕e7 is also a good move) 11 ♘e5 ♗xe5 (11...c5 is also fine, as shown by 12 f3 ♘xd2 13 ♕xd2 cxd4 14 exd4 ♘xe5 15 dxe5 ♗c5+ 16 ♔h1 dxc4 17 bxc4 ♗c6 with the better chances in M.Berta-M.Vesovic, correspondence 1977, and here 12 f4 should probably be met by 12...♘xe5 13 fxe5 ♗e7) 12 dxe5 ♘dc5 and now:

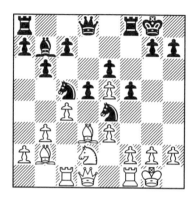

d1) 13 ♗b1 ♘xd2 14 ♕xd2 dxc4 15 ♕xd8 ♖fxd8 16 ♖xc4? (16 bxc4 was the only chance, although White's pawn weaknesses are likely to tell eventually) 16...♗a6 17 ♖xc5 bxc5 18 ♖c1 ♖d7 was winning for Black in N.Jasnogrodsky-E.Delmar, New York 1893.

d2) 13 ♗e2 ♘xd2 14 ♕xd2 dxc4 15 ♕xd8 ♖fxd8 16 ♗xc4 ♗a6 17 ♗d4 ♗xc4 18 ♖xc4 ♘a6 19 ♖c6 ♖ac8 20 ♖fc1 ♔f7 21 b4 ♖d7 was approximately equal in G.Laketic-V.Ikonnikov, Cheliabinsk 1991. Here Black has the superior structure, but compared with some other versions of this endgame White's active pieces should enable him to maintain the balance. That said, in this particular game he went wrong with 22 b5? (22 a3 was better) 22...♘b8 23 ♖6c4 c5! 24 bxc6 ♖dc7 25 ♔f1 ♖xc6 26 ♖xc6 ♖xc6 27 ♖xc6 ♘xc6 and Black successfully converted his advantage.

Returning to 10 ♕c2:

10...f5

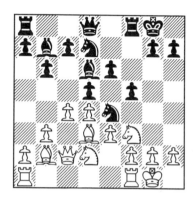

White must already be very careful here. His safest continuation is probably...

11 cxd5

...to ensure that the b7-bishop remains blocked in for the time being. If White fails to do this then he risks falling under a devastating attack, as illustrated by the first of the following examples:

a) 11 ♖ad1? has been played several times, but in the model game E.Dizdarevic-A.Miles, Biel 1985, Britain's first Grandmaster provided a brilliant demonstration of Black's attacking potential after 11...♘xd2! 12 ♘xd2 (12 ♖xd2 dxc4 13 ♗xc4 ♗xf3 14 gxf3 ♗xh2+! 15 ♔h1 ♕h4 16 ♗xe6+ ♔h8 17 ♖c1 ♕h3! wins thanks to the lethal threat of ...♗d6+ followed by ...♖f6, as analysed by Emms, who points out too that here 15 ♔xh2 ♕h4+ 16 ♔g2 ♕g5+ 17 ♔h1 ♖f6 also wins) 12...dxc4 13 ♘xc4 (13 ♗xc4 would have been relatively better, although even here Emms indicates the line 13...♗xh2+! 14 ♔xh2

♕h4+ 15 ♔g1 ♗xg2 16 f3 – 16 ♔xg2
♕g4+ 17 ♔h1 ♖f6 18 ♗xe6+ ♖xe6 19
♕c4 ♖ae8 20 ♕d5 ♕h5+ 21 ♔g1 c6 is
winning for Black – 16...♖f6 17 ♘e4!
fxe4 18 ♕xg2 ♖g6 19 ♕xg6 hxg6 20
♗xe6+ ♔f8! when Black is clearly better, as 21 ♗xd7? ♕g3+ 22 ♔h1 ♔e7
wins easily) 13...♗xh2+! 14 ♔xh2 ♕h4+
15 ♔g1 ♗f3!! (this beautiful move deserves a diagram; instead 15...♗xg2?
would have allowed White to fight on
with 16 f3 or 16 f4)

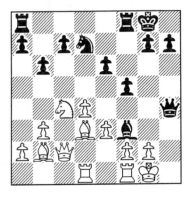

16 ♘d2 (the alternatives are no better:
for example, 16 ♖fe1 ♖f6 17 gxf3 ♕h3!
or 16 ♗e2 ♗xg2! when Emms analyses
17 f3 ♕g3 18 ♖f2 ♗h3+ 19 ♔h1 ♕xf2
and 17 ♔xg2 ♕g5+ 18 ♔h2 ♖f6, winning easily in both cases) 16...♗xg2!
(now this works as the knight blocks
the white queen's path along the second rank!) 17 f3 (17 ♔xg2 ♕g4+ 18 ♔h1
♖f6 19 ♕xc7 e5! wins – Emms) 17...♖f6
(17...♕g3?? 18 ♘e4! turns the tables) 18
♘c4 (18 ♘e4 fxe4 19 ♕xg2 exd3 is also
decisive) 18...♗h3! and White resigned.
More than twenty years later this remains one of the finest examples of
Black's attacking potential in the entire
4 e3 variation.

b) 11 ♘e5?! may block Black's
bishop from sacrificing itself on h2, but
it allows Black to swap down to a superior and by now familiar endgame
with 11...♘xd2 12 ♕xd2 ♗xe5 13 dxe5
♘c5 14 ♗e2 dxc4 15 ♕xd8 ♖fxd8 16
♗xc4 ♗a6!.

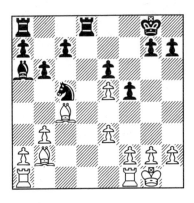

This occurred in C.Hoi-P.Sjodahl,
Copenhagen 1995, which continued 17
♖fc1 ♗xc4 18 ♖xc4 ♘d3 19 ♗c3 c5 20
♖a4 a5 21 a3 ♖d5 22 f4, at which point
Black was able to seal the win with the
simple but attractive combination
22...♘b2! 23 ♗xb2 b5 24 ♖xa5 ♖xa5.

We must now return to the prudent
exchange on d5:

11...exd5

Now Black's pawn structure is
slightly the more favourable, but at
least White no longer has to worry
about ...dxc4 ideas to unleash the
power of the Queen's Indian bishop.

12 ♘e5 c5!

This active move should ensure an
excellent game. Moreover, the white
queen may start to feel uncomfortable
on the c-file.

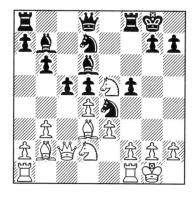

13 f3

The alternatives are no better:

a) 13 ♘xd7 ♕xd7 14 f3 ♘xd2 15 ♕xd2 ♖ae8 16 ♖ae1 ♕c7 17 f4?! was J.Cardenas Valero-J.Baron Rodriguez, St Feliu 1994, and now 17...c4 followed by ...b5 would have given Black a near-decisive positional advantage.

b) 13 ♗b5 ♘xe5 14 dxe5 ♗e7 15 ♖ad1 ♕c8 16 f3 (K.Kretschmer-D.Puppendahl, correspondence 1989) 16...♘xd2 17 ♕xd2 a6 18 ♗d3 b5 with a full share of the chances.

13...cxd4!

Probably the most accurate, although there is nothing wrong with 13...♘xd2 14 ♕xd2 ♕e7 15 f4 ♕e6 16 ♖ad1 at which point a draw was agreed in N.Ristic-Z.Mijailovic, Kladovo 1992. In the final position Black is at least equal after 16...♘f6.

14 ♘xd7

14 exd4?? ♘xe5 15 dxe5 ♗c5+ 16 ♔h1 ♘g3+! 17 hxg3 ♕g5 wins beautifully. After the text, we will follow the game M.Hammes-I.Farago, Boeblingen 2003:

14...♕xd7 15 ♗xd4

Farago analyses 15 fxe4 fxe4! 16 ♗xd4 (16 ♗e2 does not help White after 16...dxe3 17 ♖xf8+ ♖xf8 18 ♘f1 ♕f5) 16...exd3 17 ♕xd3 ♕c7 when Black maintains the advantage.

15...♖ac8 16 ♕b2 ♘c5 17 ♕b1

17 ♗e2 ♘e6 is also pleasant for the second player.

17...♘xd3 18 ♕xd3 ♕c7! 19 f4 ♕c2! 20 ♕xc2 ♖xc2 21 ♘f3 ♖fc8

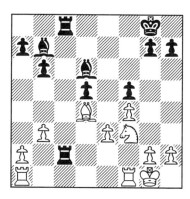

White's well-placed minor pieces are outweighed by Black's dominant rooks as well as his pair of bishops, and in the game Farago went on to convert his advantage.

B2) 7 ♘c3

If White intends to place the knight here then I will assume that he will do so immediately, although alternative move orders such as 7 cxd5 exd5 8 ♘c3 and 7 b3 0-0 8 ♗b2 ♘bd7 9 ♘c3 are equally valid ways of reaching the positions considered below.

7...0-0 8 b3

White can exchange on d5 any time, but the bishop will almost always come to b2 regardless.

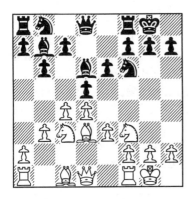

8...♞bd7 9 ♗b2 a6

Sooner or later the threat of ♞c3-b5 will force this move. I will now divide the material for a final time between the following:

B21: White exchanges on d5
B22: White maintains the central tension.

B21) 10 cxd5

Of course, White could have employed this capture any time from move 6 onwards.

10...exd5

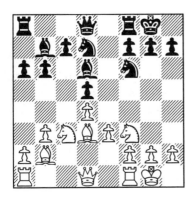

The pawn exchange brings certain

pros and cons for both sides. Black's inability to open the long diagonal with ...dxc4 diminishes the potential for the kind of swashbuckling kingside attack that we witnessed in Dizdarevic-Miles, but on the other hand, the open e-file could prove useful in transferring the heavy pieces to the kingside, as well as for supporting a knight on e4. From White's point of view, he can look to press on the open c-file, but must also forgo any ideas of a queen-side advance with c4-c5 which can sometimes be a useful option in Line B22.

11 ♖c1

White has tried a multitude of different move orders, but I doubt that he has anything to gain from postponing this useful move.

11...♞e4

11...♕e7 has been the most popular move when the usual result has been a transposition to the main line after 12 ♞e2 ♞e4. White does, however, have at his disposal the interesting and quite high-scoring possibility of 12 ♗f5!?. I do not believe that this line represents a major problem for Black, but why allow it at all when the text enables us to avoid it without making any concession at all?

12 ♞e2

This is White's standard reaction to the arrival of an enemy steed on e4. His typical plan will involve repositioning this knight on g3 to bolster the king-side, followed by ♕e2 and doubling rooks on the c-file.

12...♕e7

I think that Black should prevent ♘e5 before expanding with ...f5.

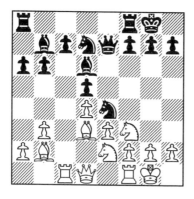

13 ♘g3

Several alternatives have been tried here, but in most cases the overall character of the position remains quite similar. The most noteworthy alternative is probably 13 ♕c2 intending to meet 13...f5 with 14 ♘e5!, although even here 14...♗xe5 15 dxe5 c5 looks quite acceptable for Black. Still, in general I think that it makes more sense to prevent the knight from occupying e5 altogether. One possible solution is 13...c6!? 14 ♘g3 f5, although this has the disadvantage of restricting the b7-bishop and so most analysts have recommended 13...♖ac8 as the most appropriate reaction. Play then continues 14 ♘g3 f5 15 ♕e2 ♖a8 16 ♖c2 when compared with the main line below White has gained a tempo. In his well-written book *Play 1 d4!* Richard Palliser mentions the game I.Sokolov-S.Kindermann, Austrian League 1995, which saw 16...♖f7 17 ♖fc1 c5 18 ♖e1! a5 19 ♗b5 with an edge for White. Black can, however, do much better

with 16...c6!.

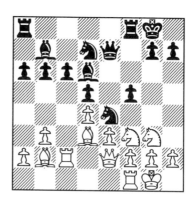

From here the game M.Sher-S.Hansen, Copenhagen 1996, continued 17 ♖fc1 ♖f6!, indirectly guarding against the exchange sacrifice on c6. The remainder of this game serves as a fine example of Black's attacking potential; Hansen patiently transfers all of his pieces to the kingside before brutally bludgeoning his way through White's flimsy defences: 18 ♕f1 (the defensive value of Black's last is illustrated by the variation 18 ♖xc6?? ♗xc6 19 ♖xc6 ♗xg3!) 18...a5 19 a4 ♖af8 20 ♖a1 ♖h6 21 ♕c1 ♖f7 22 ♗a3 c5! (preventing the exchange of a valuable attacking piece) 23 ♗b5 ♘f8! (transferring another piece to a prime attacking position) 24 ♕e1 ♘g6 (24...♘e6! looks even better; from this square the knight facilitates an advance of the f-pawn, while additionally supporting c5 and providing the option of ...♘6g5) 25 dxc5 bxc5 26 ♕xa5 (White grabs a pawn but is swiftly annihilated on the kingside) 26...f4 27 ♘f1 fxe3 28 fxe3 ♘e5 29 ♗b2 ♘xf3+ 30 gxf3 ♖g6+ 0-1.

13...f5 14 ♖c2

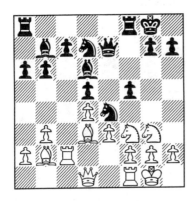

Continuing with his plan, White prepares to double on the c-file. It is worth mentioning once again the possibility of 14 ♕c2 in order to prepare the positional threat of ♘f3-e5, after which Black will no longer be able to win a pawn due to the pressure against c7. One sensible response is 14...♖f7 and another is 14...♖ac8!?, which transposes to the previous note. Finally, the computer even suggests 14...c6!? followed by ...♖ae8.

14...♖f7

This has been almost an automatic choice, although I see no particular reason why this should be the case. If one is looking for an alternative approach then 14...♖f6!?, 14...♕e6!? and 14...♖ae8!? are all obvious candidates. Even 14...a5!? looks quite sensible, with the possibility of softening up the enemy queenside. This may appear counterintuitive, but when one considers that White has just expended two tempi transferring a knight to the opposite side of the board, the idea begins to make a bit more sense. In any case, it is clear that the position is open to mul-

tiple interpretations and I see no value in attempting an exhaustive analysis. Instead we will restrict our attention to a few particularly instructive examples.

15 ♖e1

The analysis of the following two alternatives should help to demonstrate some of the resources available to both sides:

a) 15 ♕a1? decentralizes the queen in order to prepare a knight invasion on e5, so in J.Adler-F.Jenni, Swiss League 2003, Black wisely opted for 15...♖e8!, combining prophylaxis with his own active ideas. The game continued 16 ♖fc1 c6! (preventing an exchange sacrifice on c7 – Black must always be on the lookout for this!) 17 ♖e1 (Black was threatening a pseudo-sacrifice on g3; please also note that 17 ♖xc6? ♗xg3 18 hxg3 ♗xc6 19 ♖xc6 is refuted by 19...♘xf2!, as pointed out by Emms) 17...g6 18 ♖ee2 h5! (White's set-up involving the queen on a1 has been exposed as faulty, and he now faces a powerful attack) 19 ♘f1 h4 20 ♘e1 (20 h3 g5 21 ♘1h2 ♖g7 sees Black preparing ...g4) 20...♖h7 21 f3 ♘g3 22 hxg3? (Emms points out that 22 ♘xg3 hxg3 23 h3 was the last chance) 22...hxg3 23 f4 ♕h4 24 ♘xg3 ♕h2+! 25 ♔f2 ♘f6 26 ♘f1 ♘g4+ 27 ♔f3 ♕g1 28 ♖f2 (28 ♔g3 is refuted by 28...♘h2! 29 ♘xh2 ♖xe3+ 30 ♘hf3 – 30 ♖xe3 ♕xe3+ 31 ♘ef3 ♗xf4 is mate – 30...♖h3+!! 31 ♔xh3 ♗xf4 32 ♖xe3 ♕h1+, as found by Emms) 28...♕xf1 29 e4 (29 ♖xf1 ♖xe3 is mate) 29...dxe4+ 0-1.

b) 15 ♕e2 is perhaps the most significant alternative to the main line, tying the a8-rook down to the defence of a6 while preparing ♖fc1 and a possible exchange sacrifice on c7. In this case it looks quite interesting for Black to change tack with 15...a5!?.

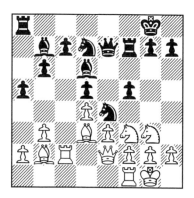

As mentioned previously, the plan of ...a5-a4 to soften up the enemy queenside makes a certain amount of sense following the transfer of the enemy knight from c3 to g3. The game D.Kosic-M.Krivokapic, Bar 2006, continued 16 ♗b5 (16 ♖fc1 should be met by 16...c5) at which point 16...♘b8!? looks quite promising: for example, 17 ♖fc1 c6 18 ♗d3 a4 or 17 ♘e5 ♗xe5 18 dxe5 c6 19 ♗d3 ♘a6 20 a3 ♘ac5 with good play in both cases.

15...g5!?

This works to perfection in the present game although 15...g6!? (A.Shestoperov-R.Siegmund, Lignano Sabbiadoro 2005) also deserves consideration, with the idea of ...h5-h4. We now follow N.Borne-S.Tiviakov, Banyoles 2006:

16 ♕e2 g4 17 ♘d2 ♕e6 18 ♘df1 ♘df6 19 f3?

This backfires badly. 19 ♖ec1 would

have been better.

19...h5!

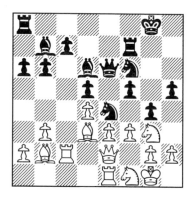

In less than twenty moves Black has whipped up a formidable attack.

20 ♕d1 h4 21 ♘h1 gxf3 22 ♕xf3 ♖g7 23 ♘f2 ♘g5! 24 ♕e2 ♘fe4 25 ♔h1 b5!?

Shielding the a6-pawn before transferring the rook to the main battleground.

26 a4 c6 27 ♖ec1 ♖f8 28 ♖e1

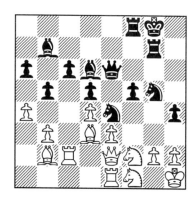

28...♕g6

Perhaps even more convincing would have been 28...♘g3+! 29 hxg3 hxg3 30 ♘xg3 (neither do the alternatives help White: 30 ♘d1? ♕h6+ 31 ♔g1 ♖h7 or 30 ♘h3 ♘xh3 31 gxh3 g2+)

30...♗xg3 31 ♔g1 ♕h6 with a decisive attack.

29 ♗xe4?!

This does not help White's cause, although it is doubtful that he could have survived even with correct defence.

29...fxe4 30 ♘d1 ♘f3 0-1

According to *MegaBase* the final move was 30...♘f7, but this appears a slightly strange choice, so I suspect a data error. In any case, whichever move was played was enough to force resignation.

B22) 10 ♖c1

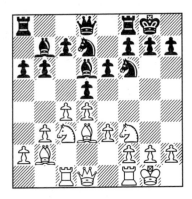

Just as in the previous variation, this is the best square for the rook. White may yet wish to open the c-file with cxd5, while in other cases the rook might be used to support an advance with c4-c5.

10...♕e7!

In Line B21 we encountered the exact same position but with the exchange of pawns on d5. It is possible for Black to continue analogously with 10...♘e4, although the slight change in the position does introduce certain nuances as seen after 11 ♘e2 ♕e7 12 ♘e5!, which is only possible with a black pawn still on e6. The game L.Portisch-I.Csom, Hungary 1984, continued 12...♖fd8 (12...♗xe5 may be better, although I am not convinced that Black can equalize here either) 13 cxd5! exd5 14 ♘c6 ♗xc6 15 ♖xc6 when White's bishop-pair assured him of a lasting advantage which he subsequently converted to victory.

11 ♘a4

Several alternatives have been tried, but I think that by now the reader will have seen enough of these positions to be able to react sensibly and appropriately. Here are a few examples:

a) 11 cxd5 exd5 is likely to lead to Line B21 after a subsequent ...♘e4.

b) The most important alternative is probably 11 ♘e2 when, just as in the main line, 11...dxc4!? looks like a good way to equalize. Now:

b1) 12 ♗xc4 ♖fd8 13 ♘g3 c5 gives Black no problems whatsoever after either 14 ♗e2 ♖ac8 (V.Malaniuk-G.Dizdar, Amantea 1992) or 14 ♕e2 cxd4 15 ♘xd4 ♘e5 (B.Avrukh-A.Kunte, Zagan 1997).

b2) 12 bxc4 e5 (12...c5!? is a valid alternative) 13 c5 (13 dxe5 ♘xe5 14 ♘xe5 ♗xe5 15 ♗xe5 ♕xe5 leaves Black with the healthier structure, so White should probably continue 16 c5 when 16...bxc5 transposes back to the game) 13...bxc5 14 dxe5 ♘xe5 15 ♘xe5 ♗xe5 16 ♗xe5 ♕xe5 17 ♕c2 ♖ad8 18 ♖fd1 was Su.Polgar-T.Utasi, Stary Smokovec 1984, and here 18...♗e4 looks like the simplest route to an equal position, as shown by 19 ♘g3 ♗xd3 20 ♖xd3 ♖xd3 21 ♕xd3 ♕d6 22 ♕c3 ♖b8.

11...dxc4!?

It is time for Black to start thinking independently. 11...♘e4 is also playable, but Black must not fall into the trap of assuming that he can blindly repeat the same moves as in Line B21. Once again 12 ♘e5! gives White good chances of an edge: for example, 12...dxc4 13 ♘xc4 ♖fc8 (in G.Flear-A.Harley, British League 2001, Black was unsuccessful with the creative but ultimately unsound 13...♗xh2+? 14 ♔xh2 ♕h4+ 15 ♔g1 ♘g5 16 ♘d2 f5 17 d5! ♗xd5 18 ♗e2 ♘f6 19 ♗e5 and Black was unable to justify his sacrifice) 14 ♕e2 (14 f3!?) when Black had yet to equalize in L.Portisch-A.Miles, Tunis 1985.

12 bxc4 ♘e4!

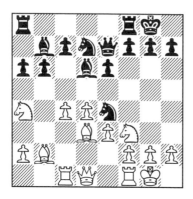

On the face of it Black has made a major concession in exchanging a valuable central pawn for a less worthy counterpart. Needless to say, I would never advocate such a concession unless we were gaining something in return, in this case the activation of the b7-bishop. This approach has been vindicated by several grandmaster games and is now considered the most reliable plan at Black's disposal. Before moving on I will briefly mention that 12...c5 is a fully playable alternative, but I have chosen to focus on the text.

13 c5!?

This seems to be White's most challenging course of action, although the main line seems to have been more or less analysed out to a draw. Instead 13 ♘c3 should be met by 13...f5, while the quieter 13 ♕e2 f5 also gives Black a comfortable game: for example, 14 ♘c3 ♖f6! 15 g3 ♖h6 16 ♗b1 ♘df6 17 ♘xe4 ♘xe4 18 ♖fd1 ♕e8 19 ♗xe4 fxe4 20 ♘e5 (G.Danner-Z.Almasi, Budapest 1993) 20...♗xe5 21 dxe5 ♗c6 with advantage to Black, or 14 ♖fd1 ♘g5 (14...♕e8!?) 15 ♘xg5 ♕xg5 16 f4 ♕e7 and here a draw was agreed in Su.Polgar-R.Dautov, Brno 1991.

13...bxc5 14 ♘e5!

This is the only move to have been played – others would see White struggling to justify his pawn sacrifice.

14...♖fd8!

A few weaker alternatives have been analysed, but we need not concern ourselves with such distractions. The text has proven to be perfectly reliable, although players looking for something completely different may wish to investigate the computer's suggestion of 14...♕h4!? .

15 ♘xd7

Dautov mentions the inferior 15 f3?! ♘ef6 16 ♘xd7 ♘xd7 17 dxc5 ♘xc5 18

♘xc5 ♗xc5 19 ♗xh7+ ♔h8! 20 ♕e2 ♕g5 with advantage. White has a better chance of holding the balance with 20 ♕e1!?, although even here 20...♔xh7 21 ♕c3 ♗xe3+ 22 ♕xe3 f6 leaves Black with some chances to convert his extra pawn.

15...♖xd7

15...♕xd7?! 16 ♗xe4 ♗xe4 17 ♘xc5 ♗xc5 18 ♖xc5 should be tenable for Black, but his inferior structure would consign him to a purely defensive existence with no realistic hope of a win.

16 dxc5

Instead 16 ♗xe4 ♗xe4 17 ♘xc5 ♗xc5 18 ♖xc5 ♕xc5 19 dxc5 ♖xd1 20 ♖xd1 f6 soon led to a handshake in A.Yusupov-A.Khalifman, German League 1994, and to be honest I see no particular reason why White should aspire to anything more here.

16...♘xc5

This leads by force to a drawish position, but if Black is looking for more then he may wish to investigate the untested 16...♗xh2+!? 17 ♔xh2 ♗c6.

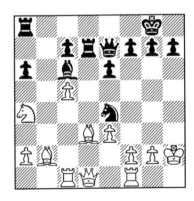

This seems to have been underestimated and now some plausible con-

tinuations include:

a) Dautov recommends 18 ♕c2? ♗xa4 19 ♕xa4 ♕h4+ 20 ♔g1 ♖xd3 21 ♖c4 f5 22 ♕c6 ♖f8 23 ♕xe6+ ♔h8 with a clear advantage to White, but overlooks the superior 18...♕h4+! 19 ♔g1 ♘g5! when Black stands well.

b) 18 ♗e5 ♖ad8 19 ♘b2 ♗b5 20 ♕f3 ♗xd3 21 ♖fd1 f5 is, once again, at least equal for Black.

c) 18 ♖c4 ♖ad8 19 ♖d4 e5 20 ♗xe4! (20 ♖xd7 ♖xd7 is unclear according to Dautov, but Black is probably better here) 20...♕h4+ 21 ♔g1 ♖xd4 is rather messy. One sensible line of play continues 22 ♗xh7+ ♕xh7 23 exd4 ♕e4 24 f3 ♕e3+ 25 ♖f2 ♗xa4 26 ♕xa4 ♕e1+ 27 ♖f1 ♕e3+ with a draw by perpetual.

d) 18 ♕g4!? leads to complications after 18...f5 19 ♗xe4! fxg4 20 ♗xc6 ♖f8 21 ♗xd7 ♕xd7 22 ♖c4 (White should avoid both 22 c6? ♕d6+ 23 ♔g1 ♕b4 and 22 ♘c3?! ♕d2 23 ♘d1 ♖b8) 22...e5!, reaching a position that is hard to evaluate. White has a lot of material for the queen but his pieces are badly coordinated and the computer goes so far as to prefer Black.

Summing up, I have been unable to find anything wrong with 16...♗xh2+!? so if the reader is dissatisfied with the drawish positions found in the main line, I would strongly urge him to investigate this further.

17 ♘xc5

17 ♗xh7+ ♔xh7 18 ♕h5+ ♔g8 19 ♘xc5 ♗xc5 is an equally valid route to the same position.

17...♗xc5 18 ♗xh7+ ♔xh7 19 ♕h5+ ♔g8

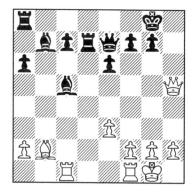

The dust has more or less settled. White will recapture his bishop on the following move, leaving a simplified position with equal material and opposite-coloured bishops. The asymmetry of the pawns offers some potential for either combatant to strive for a win, but so long as both sides play reasonably accurately, one would expect the great majority of games to end in a draw. Indeed, 20 ♕xc5 ♕xc5 21 ♖xc5 f6 was equal in L.Portisch-R.Dautov, Ter Apel 1994, while 20 ♖xc5 ♖d5 (20...f6 should

also be fine for Black) 21 ♖xd5 ♗xd5 22 ♕g4 f6 23 a3 ♖b8 was a similar story in Z.Franco Ocampos-L.Bruzon Bautista, Turin Olympiad 2006.

Summary

4 e3 will always be a popular choice, although we have seen that the recommended set-up involving 4...♗b7 followed by ...d5 and ...♗d6 should ensure Black of a comfortable game. In some cases there may even be an opportunity for a stunning sacrificial attack as we saw in the game Dizdarevic-Miles.

The line with ♘c3 and cxd5 (B21) is quite promising for Black, although the position remains quite tense and complex. In the event that White retains the central tension (B22), a plan involving a timely ...dxc4 seems to ensure a satisfactory game as well, although the reader will certainly benefit from a decent level of theoretical knowledge if he wishes to follow this path.

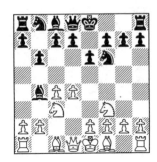

Chapter Three

The Hybrid System: 4 ♘c3 ♗b4

1 d4 ♘f6 2 c4 e6 3 ♘f3 b6 4 ♘c3 ♗b4

The choice between this and the equally reliable 4...♗b7 is largely a matter of taste, although I must concede that the latter is slightly more popular amongst the world's elite. The text leads to a kind of hybrid between the Nimzo-Indian and the Queen's Indian. I feel that this should suit the vast majority of Queen's Indian players very well, as the two openings are closely related. Indeed, it has been my experience that virtually all Queen's Indian players also play the Nimzo-Indian.

White's two most popular and challenging tries here are 5 ♗g5 and 5 ♕b3, both of which will be considered in dedicated chapters along with the slightly less critical move 5 e3. Before moving on to those lofty subjects, however, we must first deal with the following rarer, though still quite respectable moves:

A: 5 ♗d2
B: 5 g3
C: 5 ♕c2

White's remaining alternatives are unpromising and barely warrant our attention:

a) 5 a3?! ♗xc3+ 6 bxc3 is a bad choice for White. In the Sämisch variation of the Nimzo-Indian (3 ♘c3 ♗b4 4 a3 ♗xc3+ 5 bxc3) he will typically aim to construct a strong pawn centre with f3 and e4, but in the present position the knight on f3 obstructs this plan and Black's chances may already be viewed as preferable. Any sensible move should lead to a fine game with 6...♘e4!? being one promising idea, after which 7 ♕c2 ♗b7 8 e3 0-0 9 ♗d3 f5 leaves Black effectively a tempo up on our next chapter as White's a2-a3 is completely useless in this position.

b) 5 ♗f4 is not very logical, and after 5...♘e4 6 ♕c2 ♗b7 7 e3 f5 8 ♗d3 0-0

9 0-0 ♗xc3 10 bxc3 d6 11 ♘d2 ♘xd2 12 ♕xd2 ♘d7 13 f3 e5 14 ♗g3 ♕e7 Black was very comfortably placed in P.Petran-P.Lukacs, Budapest 1978.

A) 5 ♗d2

This is hardly the most ambitious approach, but there is nothing particularly wrong with it. Black can react in a number of different ways, but perhaps the most straightforward involves a quick ...♗xc3 followed by ...♘e4. Depending on how the game develops, as well as on individual preference, he can proceed in one of two ways:

1) Simplification with ...♘xc3, ...d6, ...♘d7, etc with a very solid position.

2) Maintain the knight on e4 and play more aggressively with ...f5.

5...♗b7

Before doing anything else, Black develops the bishop to its usual square.

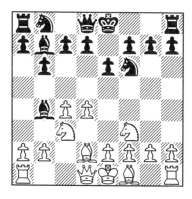

6 e3

The alternative is to opt for a kingside fianchetto, either before or after attacking the enemy bishop:

a) 6 a3 ♗xc3 7 ♗xc3 ♘e4 8 ♕c2 0-0 9 g3 (9 e3 d6 gives Black an easy game –

compared with the main line White has wasted a tempo on a3) 9...♘xc3 10 ♕xc3 d6 11 ♗g2 ♘d7 12 0-0 ♕e7...

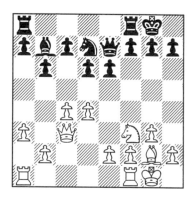

...with equality, as seen in several games.

b) In case of an immediate 6 g3 Black may be tempted to try 6...♗xf3!? 7 exf3 0-0, leading to a double-edged battle of bishops versus pawn structure. If this does not appeal then there is also nothing much wrong with 6...♗xc3 7 ♗xc3 ♘e4. Compared with variation 'a' White has saved a tempo by omitting a3, but on the other hand this is unlikely to make much difference to the overall assessment of the position.

6...♗xc3 7 ♗xc3 ♘e4 8 ♖c1

White does best to avoid doubled c-pawns as, unlike most variations of the Nimzo, in the present position he would not be compensated by the advantage of the bishop-pair. 8 ♗b4 has been played a few times, but after 8...d6 the bishop is less than ideally placed and one could make the argument that the knight on e4 remains a more useful piece in any case.

8...d6 9 ♗e2

9 ♗d3 is possible, although the drawback is that after 9...♘d7 10 0-0 ♘xc3 11 ♖xc3 (A.Brazda-V.Ruzicka, Klatovy 2005) 11...0-0 the mobility of White's queen may be restricted by the spectre of a damaged pawn structure that could result from an exchange on f3. Furthermore, in the event of a subsequent ...e5 White's minor pieces will be threatened with a fork.

9...♘d7 10 0-0

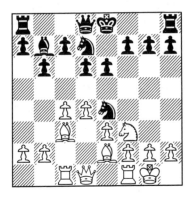

10...0-0

This is the most popular move, leading to a position that has occurred numerous times via several slightly different move orders. If Black wishes to avoid the following note then he can also play 10...♘xc3 11 ♖xc3 0-0 with equality, as in R.Franck-E.Oldach, Gladenbach 1999. With two pairs of minor pieces already exchanged, Black's slight spatial disadvantage is of no consequence whatsoever.

11 ♘d2

The main alternative is 11 ♗e1, hoping to make a real asset out of the bishop-pair. Then 11...f5 12 ♘d2 ♕e7

13 f3 ♘xd2 14 ♕xd2 e5 was roughly equal in A.Graf-A.Horvath, Dresden 2001, although there remains plenty of scope for either side to play for the win.

11...♕g5!?

An ambitious approach. White is unlikely to suffer a mating attack any time soon, but sometimes the mere presence of enemy forces within close proximity to one's king can prove psychologically unpleasant. The more prosaic 11...♘xc3 12 ♖xc3 is equal, just as in the note to Black's 10th.

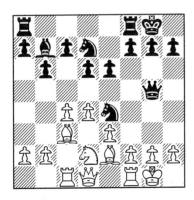

12 ♘xe4 ♗xe4 13 ♗f3

13 g3 ♗b7 14 ♗d2 f5 15 f3 ♕g6 16 ♖f2 ♘f6 also worked out well for Black in R.Stern-N.Vitiugov, Dresden 2007. After the further 17 ♗f1 Black was successful with the ultra-aggressive 17...h5!?, although a calmer move such as 17...e5 or 17...c5 might have been my own choice.

13...f5 14 ♕e2

In S.Sarsam-O.Annageldyev, Istanbul 2000, White gained nothing by weakening his kingside with 14 g3 ♘f6 15 ♗g2 ♖ae8.

14...♖f6 15 b4 ♖af8 16 g3

We have been following the game J.Novacek-Z.Choleva, Czech League 1998. At this point I rather like the look of...

16...♖h6!

Black intends ...♘f6-g4 with good attacking chances.

B) 5 g3

I would tend to regard this as a somewhat less dangerous cousin of the Fianchetto system versus the Nimzo-Indian (3 ♘c3 ♗b4 4 g3). In the present variation White's bishop on g2 can be effectively neutralized by its opposite number on b7.

5...♗b7

Creative souls looking for something less well studied might wish to investigate 5...♗a6!?.

6 ♗g2 0-0 7 0-0

7 d5?! is a dubious sacrifice and after 7...exd5 8 ♘h4 c6 9 cxd5 ♘xd5 10 ♗xd5 cxd5 11 0-0 ♗xc3 12 bxc3 (R.Polaczek-T.Rrhioua, Internet 2004) 12...♖e8 Black is a pawn up for nothing.

7...♗xc3 8 bxc3 d6

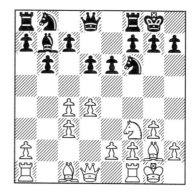

Black's position is a picture of harmony with ideally-placed pieces and an extremely elastic pawn structure. White's doubled c-pawns are in no immediate danger, but their weakness could begin to tell later in the middlegame or ending. Before moving on I would like to share what I hope will be prove a useful set of guidelines relating to the diagram position:

1) The b8-knight can, according to circumstances, be developed on d7 or perhaps c6 and subsequently a5 in order to attack the vulnerable pawn on c4. If necessary, this weakness can be fixed by a timely ...c5, after which the pressure can be further augmented by ...♖c8 and/or ...♕c7.

2) To repeat an earlier point, one of the most attractive features of Black's position is its flexibility. Depending on circumstances, one or any combination of the c-, d-, e- or even f-pawns might be employed in the battle for the central squares.

3) White would like to construct a powerful pawn centre with e2-e4, but at the moment this is easier said than

done. First he will need to retreat his knight to e1 or d2, although not everyone would be happy to allow the exchange of light-squared bishops. He might consider vacating the long diagonal with ♗h3 or ♗f1 (after ♖e1), but this will cost additional time.

4) White can attempt to play on the queenside in two principal ways:

4a) The first is with a2-a4, intending a4-a5 and later either a5-a6, cramping the enemy queenside, or axb6 to open the a-file while conveniently exchanging off one of White's long-term weaknesses. Black should almost always prevent this either with ...a5, or ...♘c6-a5 as in the main line below.

4b) The second is with the pawn sacrifice c4-c5. This will usually be played with the intention of opening a file (such as after ...bxc5), compromising Black's structure, and perhaps opening some lines for the white bishops. *The second player should constantly be on his guard against this idea.* In certain positions he might even prefer to refrain from taking on c5 in order to avoid falling in with White's plans.

9 a4

A great variety of alternatives have been tried here. It is impossible to determine which, if any, is objectively best, but the text has been the most common so I will treat it as the main line. There is little point in covering all of White's possible deviations exhaustively, but the following assortment will provide a good illustration of the different plans and resources available to both sides:

a) 9 ♗a3? c5! just makes the bishop look stupid.

b) The immediate sacrifice with 9 c5 is not dangerous after 9...dxc5 10 ♗a3 ♘bd7 11 dxc5 (J.Mont Reynaud-T.Shaked, Hawaii 1998) 11...♘xc5 12 ♗xc5 bxc5 when it seems to me that the most White can hope for is to equalize by regaining his sacrificed pawn.

c) 9 ♕c2 is well met by 9...♗e4!, intending 10 ♕b3 ♘c6 or 10 ♕a4 ♕d7 11 ♕xd7 ♘bxd7.

d) 9 ♗g5 ♘bd7 is unpromising for White who, following a subsequent ...h6 and exchange on f6, will no longer have a pair of bishops to compensate for his doubled c-pawns.

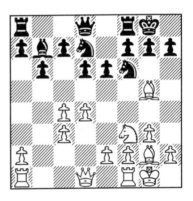

For example, after 10 ♘d2 ♗xg2 11 ♔xg2 h6 12 ♗xf6 ♘xf6 Black's superior structure enables him to claim the tiniest of advantages in a near-equal position.

e) 9 ♘e1 ♗xg2 10 ♘xg2 ♘bd7 (10...♘c6 is also possible) 11 ♕d3 c5 12 e4 ♕c7 13 ♗a3?! misplaced the bishop in G.Khokhlov-N.Shutemov, Dagomys 2004, after which 13...♕c6 14 ♖fe1 ♖fc8 would have given Black an edge.

f) In J. Hebert-F.Caire, Quebec 2004, White preferred to preserve his bishop with 9 ♗h3 ♘bd7 (9...♘c6!? also looks interesting: for example, 10 d5 – otherwise ...♘a5 comes anyway – 10...♘a5! 11 dxe6 fxe6 12 ♗xe6+ ♔h8 with compensation), only now opting for 10 ♘d2 c5 11 f3, intending to expand with e2-e4. Black sensibly decided to nip this in the bud with 11...d5, and after the further 12 cxd5 exd5 13 ♘b3 ♖e8 14 ♗g5 ♕c7 15 ♗f4 ♕c6 16 dxc5 Caire could have obtained a fine position with 16...♗a6! followed by 17 ♖e1 bxc5 (as ♘b3-a5 will no longer fork queen and bishop), or 17 ♘d4 ♕xc5.

g) 9 ♖e1 ♘bd7 10 a4 is possible when, compared with the main line, Black no longer has the resource of ...♘c6-a5 at his disposal. Instead he should make do with the typical 10...a5, after which A.Groszpeter-H.Danielsen, Norresundby 1992, continued 11 ♕c2 ♗e4 12 ♕b3 ♖e8 13 ♗h3 ♗b7 14 ♘d2 e5 15 ♗a3 h5!?, gaining space on the kingside although the more orthodox 15...♘f8 was an equally valid course of action.

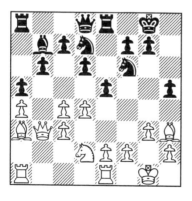

Unfortunately, after reaching a balanced and fertile middlegame with great scope for creativity on both sides, the players prematurely agreed to a draw after 16 ♖ad1 ♖b8 17 ♕c2 e4 (17...♘g4!?) 18 ♘f1 ♘g4.

We now return to 9 a4:

9...♘c6!?

9...a5 is a common and sound response, but the text also looks promising and has scored extremely well.

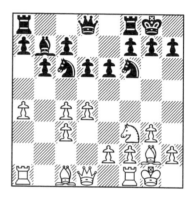

10 ♘d2

10 ♗g5 (P.Mattila-M.Harjula, Naan 1997) should be met by 10...♘a5, but we should also consider the attempted pawn sacrifice 10 c5!?. In A.Iglesias-O.Panno, Mar del Plata 1988, Black decided not to play into his opponent's hands, preferring 10...♘a5! 11 ♗f4 (11 cxd6 cxd6 would leave White with a backward c-pawn) 11...♕d7 12 ♕b1, at which point 12...♘e4 would have given Black excellent chances.

10...♘a5 11 e4

It is hard to decide whether or not White should keep the light-squared bishops on the board. In S.Tzardis-S.Logothetis, Athens 2000, he preferred

11 ♗xb7 ♘xb7 12 e4 (or 12 ♘b3 d5 13 ♗a3 ♖e8 14 ♕d3 ♕d7 15 ♗c1, as in M.Katetov-J.Foltys, Prague 1946, and now 15...♘d6 with advantage to Black) 12...♘d7 13 f4, at which point 13...c5 would have been logical, intending ...♕c7, ...♘a5, etc with a good game.

11...c5 12 d5 ♕c7 13 ♖e1

We have been following the game U.Vetter-B.Moelder, Internet 2002. Here I think that Black should have organized his pieces as follows:

13...♖ae8 14 f4 ♘d7 15 ♖b1 ♗a6 16 ♗f1 ♖e7

Black intends ...♖fe8 with a very compact and harmonious position. Note how the pressure against c4 is presently tying up two white pieces in such a way as to render the transfer of his forces to the kingside quite problematic.

C) 5 ♕c2

This system bears a close resemblance to the Classical variation of the Nimzo-Indian (3 ♘c3 ♗b4 4 ♕c2), and in some cases direct transpositions can occur.

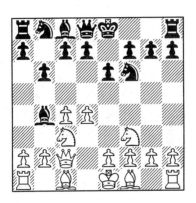

5...♗b7 6 a3

White may instead take play elsewhere: 6 ♗g5 h6 7 ♗h4 g5 8 ♗g3 ♘e4 reaches Chapter 6 (see the move order 5 ♗g5 h6 6 ♗h4 g5 7 ♗g3 ♘e4 8 ♕c2 ♗b7), while 6 e3 ♘e4 7 ♗d3 ♗xc3+ 8 bxc3 f5 leads us to Chapter 4 (5 e3 ♘e4 6 ♕c2 ♗xc3+ 7 bxc3 ♗b7 8 ♗d3 f5).

6...♗xc3+

Black gains nothing from the insertion of 6...♗e4?! 7 ♕d2 ♗xc3 8 ♕xc3, as a subsequent ♗g5 and ♘d2 would gain extra time for White.

7 ♕xc3 ♘e4!?

Preventing any ♗g5 ideas once and for all. 7...0-0 would transpose directly to the Classical Nimzo, normally reached via the move order 3 ♘c3 ♗b4 4 ♕c2 0-0 5 a3 ♗xc3+ 6 ♕xc3 b6 7 ♘f3 ♗b7. This should be quite okay for Black, who has avoided some of the more critical modern lines in which White develops with e2-e3 and ♘g1-e2. Nevertheless this is still a massive theoretical topic and, given the rarity of 5 ♕c2, for our purposes I think it makes sense to stick to an independent path. If, on the other hand, your repertoire already includes the Classical Nimzo with 4 ♕c2 0-0, then your most convenient choice may well be to accept this transposition.

8 ♕c2 0-0

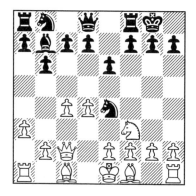

9 e3

White has a major alternative in 9 g3 f5 10 ♝g2. Now one common continuation is 10...♘f6!? 11 0-0 ♝e4 12 ♕c3 ♕e8 13 b4 d6 14 ♝b2 ♘bd7 with a decent position. Alternatively Black can try the more dynamic 10...c5!? 11 0-0 ♘c6 and now:

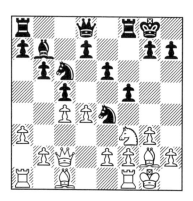

a) 12 e3 ♖c8 13 dxc5 bxc5 14 b3 ♘a5 15 ♖d1 was G.Bakalarz-R.Gasik, Trinec 1998, and now 15...♘f6!? looks good,

intending ...♝e4 followed by pressure along the b-file.

b) 12 d5 exd5 13 cxd5 ♘e7 14 ♘g5 (after 14 ♖d1 ♘xd5 15 ♕b3 ♕f6! 16 ♕a2 ♕c6! Black maintains his extra pawn) 14...♝xd5 15 ♘xe4 ♝xe4 16 ♝xe4 fxe4 17 ♕xe4 d5 18 ♕e6+ ♖f7 19 ♝g5 ♕c8 was slightly better for Black in Gambrinus-G.Kasparov, Internet 1998.

c) 12 ♖d1 (O.Stork-A.Rosskothen, German League 2004) 12...cxd4 13 ♘xd4 ♘xd4 14 ♖xd4 ♕e7 with a balanced position.

d) 12 dxc5 bxc5 13 ♖b1 ♕e7 14 b3 ♖ab8 15 ♝b2 d6 16 ♝a1 e5 17 b4 ♘d4 18 ♕d1 was W.Sapis-L.Ostrowski, Polanica Zdroj 1995, and now 18...f4! would have given Black quite a strong initiative. It is worth noting that 19 e3 does not help White in view of 19...♘xf2! 20 ♔xf2 fxe3+ 21 ♔xe3 ♝xf3 followed by ...♕g5+ with a huge attack.

9...d6 10 ♝d3

10 ♝e2 ♘d7 11 0-0 f5 leads to similar types of positions.

10...f5 11 b4

This has been less popular than castling immediately, but I will consider it as the main line because it was once played by Vladimir Kramnik. I think it makes a certain amount of sense for White to refrain from defining the position of his king, although transpositions can easily occur.

11 0-0 can be met by 11...♘d7 (some players have experimented with the more overtly aggressive 11...♖f6!?), after which 12 b4 ♕e8 13 ♝b2 ♕h5 reaches our main line. The main alternative is 12 ♘d2 ♕h4 13 f3 (Emms

points out that 13 b4? loses immediately to 13...♘xd2 14 ♗xd2 ♗xg2! 15 ♔xg2 ♕g4+ 16 ♔h1 ♕f3+ 17 ♔g1 ♖f6, while 13 g3?! ♘g5 14 d5 ♕h5 15 f4 ♘h3+ 16 ♔g2 exd5 was excellent for Black in Z.Kozul-M.Cebalo, Osijek 1992) 13...♘g5!? when Black has quite promising attacking chances.

In A.Huss-A.Kosteniuk, Silvaplana 2003, the future Women's World Champion produced a beautiful attacking miniature after 14 f4 ♘h3+!? (14...♘f7 is also quite playable) 15 gxh3 ♖f6 16 ♘f3 (16 e4 is a stronger defence when Emms' main line runs 16...♖g6+ 17 ♔h1 ♕xh3 18 ♖f2 ♘f6 19 d5 fxe4 20 ♘xe4 exd5 21 ♘xf6+ – 21 cxd5 ♖e8! 22 f5 ♖g4 23 ♗f4 ♘xd5 is good for Black – 21...♖xf6 22 ♔g1 ♖e8 23 ♗d2 d4 24 ♗f1 ♕h5 with good compensation although White is still very much in the game) 16...♖g6+ 17 ♔h1 ♕xh3 18 ♕e2 ♘c5!! 19 ♗xf5 (19 dxc5 loses to 19...♖g3!, intending 20 ♕c2 dxc5! 21 ♖f2 ♖d8! 22 ♗e2 ♗xf3+ 23 ♗xf3 ♖xf3 24 ♖xf3 ♕xf3+ 25 ♔g1 ♖d1+ winning the queen, while 19 ♗c2 leads to the same result after 19...♘e4 20 ♗xe4 ♗xe4 21 ♕f2 ♖g3!, as

analysed by Emms) 19...exf5 20 ♗d2 ♗e4! and 0-1 in view of 21 dxc5 ♖g3!.

11...♘d7 12 ♗b2 ♕e8

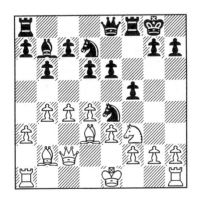

Several other moves have been tried, but I rather like the directness of the text. 12...a5 eventually led to a draw in V.Kramnik-P.Nikolic, Monaco (rapid) 1998, although White managed to obtain a slight but enduring edge after 13 0-0 axb4 14 axb4 ♕e7 15 ♘d2 ♖xa1 16 ♖xa1 ♘xd2 17 ♕xd2 ♖a8 18 ♖xa8+ ♗xa8 19 f3.

13 0-0

After the highly creative 13 ♖g1!? ♘df6 14 h3 ♕h5 15 0-0-0 a6 (15...c5!?) 16 ♖df1 ♕h6 17 ♔b1 c5 Black's attack turned out to be the faster in P.Lagowski-M.Dziuba, Chalkidiki 2001, which concluded 18 dxc5 (18 g4 can be safely met by 18...♕xh3) 18...bxc5 19 ♘e1 cxb4 20 axb4 a5 21 b5 a4 22 g4 a3 23 ♗c1 ♘d7 24 ♔a2 ♕f6 25 ♗xe4 ♗xe4 26 ♕d2 ♗b1+ 0-1.

13...♕h5

The rarely played 13...♕g6!? can also be considered.

14 d5

This seems to be the only really

critical move. The following examples demonstrate the potency of Black's attacking resources:

a) Inkiov mentions that 14 ♘d2?? loses to the now familiar 14...♘xd2 15 ♕xd2 ♗xg2! 16 ♔xg2 ♕g4+ 17 ♔h1 ♕f3+ 18 ♔g1 ♖f6 19 ♖fd1 ♕h3, just as we saw in the note to White's 11th move, above.

b) 14 ♘e1 ♖f6! 15 f3 ♖h6! 16 g4 (White cannot be satisfied with either 16 h3 ♘g3 or 16 g3 ♘xg3 17 ♖f2 f4) 16...♕h4 (16...♕g5?! 17 ♘g2! is less promising, but 16...♕h3!? may be possible) has been seen in two games:

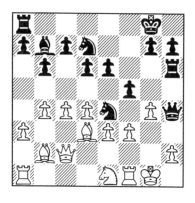

b1) In the game R.Dambravaite-A.Dambravaite, Vilkaviskis 1994, White's position soon collapsed after 17 fxe4? fxe4 18 ♗xe4 ♗xe4 19 ♕e2 ♘f6 20 ♖f4 ♖g6 21 ♘f3 ♖xg4+ 22 ♖xg4 ♕xg4+ 23 ♔f2 ♖f8 24 ♖g1 ♗xf3 0-1.

b2) In S.Semkov-V.Inkiov, Bulgaria 1985, White put up stiffer resistance with 17 gxf5 exf5 18 d5, but still came unstuck after the spectacular 18...♖e8!! 19 ♗d4 (19 fxe4 fxe4 20 ♖f2 exd3 21 ♘xd3 ♖g6+ 22 ♖g2 ♖xe3 is very good for Black according to Inkiov) 19...♘e5

(Inkiov indicates that 19...c5 may have been stronger, although I can find no fault with his play in the game) 20 fxe4 ♘xd3 21 exf5 (21 ♘xd3?? ♖g6+ 22 ♔h1 ♕xe4+ wins) 21...♘xe1 22 ♖axe1 ♖e4!

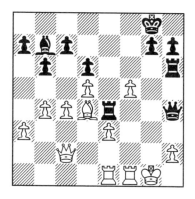

23 b5 (Black was threatening 23...c5!) 23...♗c8 24 ♕f2 (24 ♖e2 ♗xf5! 25 ♖xf5 ♕g4+ 26 ♖g2 ♕xf5 27 ♖xg7+ ♔f8 is mentioned by Inkiov, while 24 f6 can be met simply by 24...gxf6, intending 25 ♔h1 ♗h3 26 ♖g1+ ♖g4 27 ♖xg4+ ♗xg4 with a near-decisive advantage) 24...♖g4+ 25 ♔h1 ♗xf5 26 e4 ♕xf2 and White resigned.

Returning to the superior 14 d5:

14...e5!?

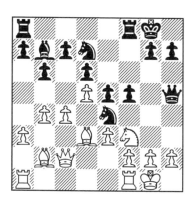

This is a very interesting and perhaps necessary pawn sacrifice. Instead 14...♖ae8?! can be strongly met by 15 ♕a4!, while 14...exd5 15 cxd5 ♗xd5 16 ♕xc7 ♘df6 17 ♗c4 ♗xc4 18 ♕xc4+ looks like a safe edge for White.

15 ♗xe4

This has been the usual choice, although in P.Gelpke-R.Douven, Hilversum 1985, White declined the offer with 15 ♘e1!?, after which 15...b5 16 f3 ♘ef6 17 ♗xf5 ♘b6?! 18 g4 ♕e8 19 g5 soon led to a convincing win for White. Instead it looks very interesting for Black to utilize a different queenside lever with 15...a5!?: for example, 16 f3 (or 16 ♗xe4 fxe4 17 ♕xe4 axb4 18 axb4 ♖xa1 19 ♗xa1 b5! with strong counterplay) 16...♕h6! 17 ♕e2 (17 fxe4 fxe4 18 ♗xe4 ♕xe3+ 19 ♖f2 ♖xf2 20 ♗xh7+ ♔h8 21 ♕xf2 ♕xf2+ 22 ♔xf2 ♔xh7 is slightly better for Black) 17...♘g5 18 f4 ♘e4 with rather an unclear situation; White has a pair of bishops, but his central position is somewhat unstable with ...b5 being a constant worry.

15...fxe4

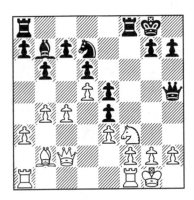

16 ♕xe4

Instead E.Grima Crespo-R.Montecatine Rios, correspondence 1997, continued 16 ♘d2 ♘f6 17 f3 (Kodinets analyses 17 ♘xe4 ♘xe4 18 ♕xe4 ♕e2! with strong counterplay based on the activity of Black's queen combined with the possibility of ...♖f4!) 17...exf3 18 ♖xf3 c6 19 dxc6 (or 19 e4 cxd5 20 cxd5 ♗a6 with the initiative) 19...♗xc6 20 e4 ♕h4 21 ♖h3 ♗xe4 when Black had won a pawn which later resulted in victory.

16...♘f6 17 ♕h4

17 ♕c2 gives Black a choice:

a) Kodinets analyses 17...♘g4 18 h3 ♖xf3! 19 gxf3 (19 hxg4? ♕xg4 20 ♕e2 ♖af8 gives Black a very strong attack, while 19 ♕e4 ♘xe3! 20 fxe3 ♖ff8! equalizes the material count while leaving Black with the easier game) 19...♕xh3 20 fxg4 (20 ♖fc1?? ♘h2! wins for Black) 20...♕xg4+ 21 ♔h2 ♕h4+ with a perpetual.

b) Black might also consider 17...c6!? to liberate his bishop, while intending to meet 18 e4 with 18...♕g6.

17...♕g6

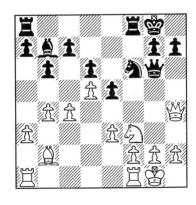

Black has fair compensation based upon the active disposition of his forces combined with the open f-file and the possibility of undermining White's centre with a timely ...b5.

18 ♘e1

White has plenty of other possibilities, but no clear-cut way to consolidate his extra pawn:

a) E.Karelin-V.Perevertkin, correspondence 1999, saw 18 ♖ac1 ♘e4!

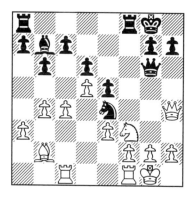

19 ♔h1 (19...♖xf3 was threatened, and White can hardly contemplate 19 ♕h3?? ♗c8 or 19 ♘e1?! ♘d2) 19...♖f6 20 ♘xe5 dxe5 21 ♗xe5 ♖f7 22 f3 ♘d6 23 e4 ♗a6 24 b5 ♘xc4 25 ♖xc4 ♗xb5 26 ♖fc1 ♗xc4 27 ♖xc4 c5 with unclear play. It may, though, have been even more promising for Black to have played 19...b5!?: for example, 20 cxb5 ♗xd5 21 ♖fd1 (21 ♖xc7?? ♘d2!) 21...♖xf3 22 gxf3 ♘d2 23 ♕g3 ♗xf3+ 24 ♔g1 ♕xg3+ 25 hxg3 ♗xd1 26 ♖xd1 ♘c4 27 ♗c1 a6 28 bxa6 ♖xa6 29 ♖d3 c6 30 e4 ♔f7 with slightly the better chances for Black.

b) 18 ♖ad1!? b5! (this move is a recurring theme in virtually all of these lines) 19 cxb5 ♘xd5 (not 19...♗xd5? 20 ♖xd5! ♘xd5 21 ♕c4 ♕f7 22 ♘g5 ♘b6 23 ♕xf7+ ♖xf7 24 ♘xf7 ♔xf7 25 ♖c1 with a

decisive advantage – Kodinets) 20 ♘e1 ♖f7 (20...♘b6!?) 21 ♕c4 ♘b6 22 ♕b3 is clearly better for White according to Kodinets, but I think that Black has decent compensation after 22...♖af8.

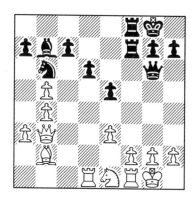

The immediate idea is to unpin with either ...♔h8 or ...♗c8-e6.

c) 18 ♘g5 should also probably be met by the undermining 18...b5!, after which the game might continue:

c1) 19 cxb5 h6! 20 ♘e6?! ♖f7 leaves the knight in jeopardy.

c2) 19 f4?! bxc4 20 f5 (or 20 e4 ♘xe4 21 ♘e6 ♖f7) 20...♕h6 21 ♕xh6 gxh6 22 ♘e6 ♖f7 leaves White unable to maintain his centre.

c3) 19 e4 might lead to a repetition after 19...♘xe4!? 20 ♘xe4 ♖f4 21 ♕e7! ♖f7! 22 ♕h4 ♖f4.

c4) 19 f3 bxc4 20 e4 c6 21 dxc6 ♗xc6 looks roughly equal.

c5) 19 ♘e6 ♖fc8 (19...bxc4?! does not quite give Black enough compensation after 20 ♘xf8 ♖xf8 21 f4 ♗xd5 22 ♕h3) 20 f4 (20 f3 bxc4 21 e4 c6 22 dxc6 ♗xc6 turns out well for Black) 20...bxc4 looks rather messy, but I think that Black should be doing okay.

Returning to the main line, 18 ♘e1, in which we have thus far been following the game A.Mazja-K.Kodinets, USSR 1991. At this point Black could have obtained excellent counterplay with Kodinets' suggestion:

18...b5!

By now this idea should have become second nature. Black's central superiority and active pieces offer full compensation for the missing pawn.

Summary

Throughout the course of this chapter we have concentrated on three options for White after 4 ♘c3 ♗b4. Here 5 ♗d2 is only seldom seen and is hardly likely to worry Black, while 5 g3 leads to positions of a greater strategic richness. That said, we have seen that in most cases Black's flexible and harmonious position combined with his superior pawn structure should assure him of a good game.

By far the most challenging of the options encountered is 5 ♕c2. This is very closely related to the Classical variation of the Nimzo-Indian, and transpositions can frequently occur. For those players whose repertoires do not include this heavily-analysed path, our recommended system involving an early ...♘e4 should ensure a sound position with plenty of opportunities to fight for the initiative.

Chapter Four

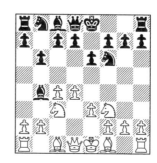

The Hybrid System: 5 e3

1 d4 ♘f6 2 c4 e6 3 ♘f3 b6 4 ♘c3 ♗b4 5 e3

According to the *ECO* classification we have officially crossed over to Nimzo territory (the diagram position being reached via the move order 3 ♘c3 ♗b4 4 e3 b6 5 ♘f3), although naturally I have no intention of using this as an excuse not to cover it here. For reasons explained earlier, I would expect most readers of this book to feel eminently comfortable with Nimzoesque positions, and many of you will already have some experience on the black side of this variation.

5...♘e4!

Black seizes the opportunity to increase the pressure against the pinned knight, immediately forcing the opponent on to the defensive. Later he can double White's c-pawns with ...♗xc3 and support his advanced stallion with the Dutch-like ...f5. It is worth noting, in passing, that the present move order actually constitutes a very real improvement for Black over the pure Nimzo sequence. The point is that after 3 ♘c3 ♗b4 4 e3 b6 White can play more accurately with 5 ♗d3! (5 ♘f3 ♘e4 would reach the present position) 5...♗b7 6 ♘f3 ♘e4 7 0-0! when taking on c3 would be very risky as White would acquire a dangerous lead in development. This variation is still quite playable for Black after 7...f5, but there can be no doubt that forcing White to spend a tempo defending c3 must improve his chances.

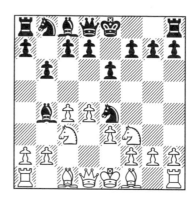

6 ♕c2 ♗xc3+

6...♗b7 is equally playable and usually leads to the same position after 7 ♗d3 f5 8 0-0 ♗xc3 9 bxc3 0-0.

7 bxc3 ♗b7 8 ♗d3 f5 9 0-0

9 ♗a3 d6 achieves very little for White, while 9 a4 ♘g5!? (9...♘c6 and 9...a5 are valid alternatives) 10 ♘xg5 ♕xg5 11 f3 ♕h4+ 12 ♕f2 ♕xf2+ 13 ♔xf2 ♘c6 14 ♗a3 ♗a6 15 ♔e2 ♘a5 16 c5 ♗xd3+ 17 ♔xd3 bxc5 18 ♗xc5 d5 reached a position in which the white bishop was no match for the black knight in S.Conquest-J.Emms, British Championship, Eastbourne 1990, which continued 19 ♖ab1 ♔d7 20 e4 ♘c4 21 ♖he1 ♖he8 22 ♖b3 ♖ab8 23 ♖eb1 ♖xb3 24 ♖xb3 a6 25 ♖b1 h5! 26 h3 h4 27 ♖b3 g5 28 ♖b1 ♖g8 29 ♖e1 fxe4+ 30 fxe4 g4 31 exd5 exd5 32 ♖e7+ ♔c6 33 ♖e6+ ♔b7 34 hxg4 ♖xg4 35 ♖e2 ♖g3+ 36 ♔c2 ♖xg2 and Black soon won the ending after 37 ♖xg2 ♘e3+ 38 ♔d2 ♘xg2 39 ♔e2 h3 40 ♔f3 ♘f4 41 ♔g3 ♘e2+ 42 ♔xh3 ♘xc3 43 a5 ♔c6 44 ♔g4 ♔b5 0-1.

9...0-0

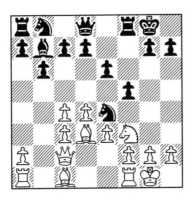

From this position Black will typically look to complete development with ...d6 and ...♘bd7, although more aggressive ideas such as ...♖f6-g6 can also be considered. White's most obvious plan is to prepare the move f2-f3 in order to exchange or expel the dangerous enemy knight. Thus at this point he normally chooses between:

A: 10 ♘e1
B: 10 ♘d2

A great variety of alternatives have been tried, but most non-forcing moves should be met by queenside development as prescribed above. Here we will consider a few of White's immediate attempts to threaten the enemy position:

a) 10 d5!? is an attempt to wrest the initiative at the cost of a pawn. Black's best reaction is probably 10...♘c5! (10...exd5 11 cxd5 ♗xd5 12 ♘d4 gives White some compensation and at least opens lines for his bishops) 11 ♗a3 ♘ba6 with good play.

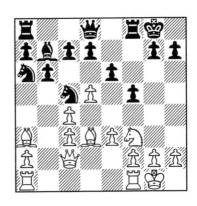

The game might continue 12 ♘d4 (J.Plachetka-J.Franzen, Trnava 1982) 12...♕h4!? intending ...♖f6 with attacking chances, or 12 e4 (J.Sadorra-T.Tukiran, Singapore 2003) 12...♘xd3 (also worth considering is 12...d6!? 13 exf5 e5!? with compensation) 13 ♕xd3 fxe4 14 ♕xe4 c5!? 15 ♖ad1 ♘c7 when Black should be fairly happy.

b) 10 ♗a3 should be met by 10...c5!, immediately shutting the bishop out of the game, whereas 10...d6 allows White to stir up some trouble with 11 c5!? or 11 d5!?. V.Korchnoi-B.Damljanovic, Plovdiv 2003, continued 11 dxc5 (otherwise ...d6 will fortify the c5-pawn, making the bishop look completely stupid on a3) 11...bxc5 12 ♖ab1 ♕c7 13 ♘d4!? (trying to complicate the game and make sense of the placement of his problem bishop) 13...cxd4 14 ♗xf8 ♔xf8 15 cxd4 ♘f6 16 f3 ♘c6 17 ♕b2, at which point 17...♖b8 looks good for Black.

c) 10 a4 ♘c6! 11 ♗a3 (11 ♗xe4?! fxe4 12 ♕xe4 ♘a5 13 d5 ♕e8 gives Black more than enough for a pawn, as White will have a hard time defending his weaknesses) 11...♖f6 12 d5 ♘a5 13 ♗xe4 fxe4 14 ♕xe4 c5! (once again we see this reaction to a white bishop on a3) 15 ♖fd1 was B.Kogan-S.Gershman, Kiev 1964, and here 15...♕f8!? looks interesting, intending ...♖e8 with good compensation.

Now 16 ♘e5 is inadvisable due to 16...exd5 intending ...♖e8, while if White tries to bring his queen out of harm's way with 16 ♕d3 there follows 16...♖xf3! 17 gxf3 ♕xf3 18 e4 ♕xd3 19 ♖xd3 ♘xc4 20 dxe6 dxe6 with fabulous positional compensation for the exchange after 21 f3 ♘e5 22 ♖e3 ♖d8.

A) 10 ♘e1 d6

Many other moves have been tried, but I have chosen to focus on the text.
11 f3 ♘g5!

11...♘f6 is also possible, but it makes sense to position the knight closer to the enemy king while keeping the third rank free for the transfer of heavy pieces.

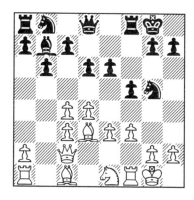

12 d5!?

This must be the critical move, attempting to break open the centre in much the same manner as we will see in Chapter 7. The alternatives can hardly threaten Black:

a) 12 e4 does not appear to have been played here. Black can choose between 12...f4, keeping the position closed, or the possibly superior 12...fxe4 13 fxe4 ♖xf1+ 14 ♔xf1 ♘d7, maintaining a fluid position in which the enemy king will have to waste time returning to g1.

b) 12 c5 is premature and after 12...bxc5 13 dxc5 ♘d7 14 cxd6 cxd6 15 ♗a3 ♕c7 16 ♗b5 (I.Piven-N.Sulava, Aschach 1996) 16...♘b6 Black stands better.

c) 12 h4?! ♘f7 just leaves the h-pawn a target, and after 13 e4 (or 13 ♕f2 ♘d7 14 ♗a3, as in G.Dishlijski-G.Georgiev, Pamporovo 2001, and now 14...c5!, keeping the bishop locked out of play) 13...♕xh4 14 exf5 e5 (also possible is 14...exf5 15 ♗xf5 ♘c6) 15 ♗e4 c6!? 16 ♗e3 d5 17 ♗d3 ♘d7 18 cxd5 cxd5 19 ♗b5 ♘f6 20 dxe5 ♘xe5 Black had an excellent position in M.Auer-P.Lamby, German League 2004.

d) 12 ♗a3 ♘d7 13 ♖b1 (E.Pontoppidan-L.Petrova, correspondence 2002) runs into the standard reaction of 13...c5! when the bishop is completely misplaced on a3.

e) 12 a4 a5 13 ♖b1 ♘d7 14 h4 ♘f7 15 g3 ♕e7 16 e4 fxe4 17 ♗xe4 ♗xe4 18 fxe4 e5 19 d5 (E.Juez Villar-P.San Segundo Carrillo, Donostia 2008) 19...♘h6! with good kingside prospects in addition to Black's superior structure. Please note that after 20 ♖xf8+ (no better is 20 ♗xh6 ♖xf1+ 21 ♔xf1 ♕f6+) 20...♖xf8 21 ♗xh6 gxh6 intending ...♕f7 Black's activity more than makes up for the slight weakness of his kingside.

12...♘a6!

Black wastes no time in exposing the drawback to White's last, while producing a pleasing forerunner to the more topical 12...♘a6!? of Line B3 of Chapter 7. No knight could dream of finding a better home than c5 in the present position. We now follow the game A.Dreev-A.Motylev, Moscow 2004:

13 h4

Now that White has started down an uncompromising path he is practically forced to continue in the same vein. It is worth noting that 13 f4?! would have been weaker in view of 13...♘e4 14 ♗xe4 fxe4 15 ♕xe4 ♘c5 16 ♕d4 e5! 17 fxe5 ♖xf1+ 18 ♗xf1 dxe5 19 ♕xe5 ♕h4! (threatening ...♕xe1+ and ...♕xc4+, as well as menacing the white kingside) 20 ♗a3 ♕xc4+ 21 ♔g1 ♘e4 when Black will soon restore material equality while maintaining a distinct positional advantage.

13...♘f7 14 dxe6 ♘h6

14...♘e5!? 15 ♗xf5 ♕xh4 was also interesting, but the text should turn out well enough.

15 e4

Once again this is the only consistent move. If White plays slowly then Black will swiftly regain the e6-pawn while maintaining all his positional trumps.

15...♕xh4 16 exf5 ♘c5 17 ♗xh6 ♕xh6 18 g4 g6!

Black must not hesitate in undermining the enemy pawn chain.

19 ♖f2 ♖ae8 20 ♖h2

We have reached a critical and highly unusual-looking position. White has an extra pawn, but he desperately needs to maintain his f5-e6 pawn wedge as otherwise his entire position could collapse. In the game Motylev played 20...♕e3+ and eventually drew a long endgame after 21 ♕f2 ♕xf2+ 22 ♔xf2 h5 23 ♖g2 ♔h8 24 ♗c2 hxg4 25 ♖xg4 gxf5 26 ♖h4+ ♔g7. For the time being Black's king is safer and his pieces are much better developed, and thus I believe a more promising course of action may have been:

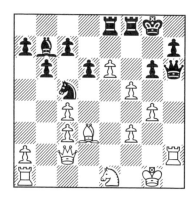

20...♕g5!

With the idea of meeting...

21 fxg6

with the stunning...

21...h5!!

My thanks to the computer for that one! This is without a doubt a visually-striking move, although once one has recovered from the initial shock the variations are not too difficult to follow.

22 ♕d2

The main tactical point of Black's last was that 22 ♖xh5 would leave f3 undefended, thus allowing 22...♕e3+ 23 ♕f2 ♕xf2+ 24 ♔xf2 ♘xd3+ 25 ♘xd3

♖xf3+ 26 ♔e2 ♖xe6+ 27 ♔d2 ♗e4 28 ♘b4 ♗xg6 when White's kingside has been decimated and his remaining weak pawns will, as the saying goes, drop like ripe fruit.

22...♖f4!

Intending to capture either on e6 or perhaps g4.

23 ♘g2

23 ♗c2? ♘xe6 does not help White.

23...♖xg4!

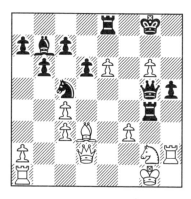

This final tactical nuance leaves White facing serious and possibly mortal difficulties as shown by the following variations:

a) 24 f4 ♕f6 25 ♗e2 (no better is 25 f5 ♘xd3 26 ♕xd3 ♗e4) 25...♖xg2+ 26 ♖xg2 ♗xg2 27 ♔xg2 ♘xe6.

b) 24 ♕xg5 ♖xg5 25 f4 (White is not helped by either 25 ♗c2 ♗xf3 or 25 ♗e2 ♖xe6) 25...♖xg2+ 26 ♖xg2 ♗xg2 27 ♔xg2 ♘xd3 28 f5 ♔g7 29 ♔g3 ♘e5 with a decisive advantage.

12 d5!? must rank as White's most principled method of handling the 10 ♘e1 variation, but the above analysis indicates that Black is more than holding his own. Let us now see if White

fares any better with the alternative knight retreat.

B) 10 ♘d2 ♕h4!

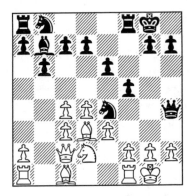

Black should definitely seize the opportunity to bring his most powerful fighting unit to within striking distance of the enemy king.

11 f3

This is White's most consistent and best continuation.

a) 11 ♗a3?? is a blunder which has cost White several games after 11...♘xd2 12 ♕xd2 ♗xg2!: for example, 13 ♔xg2 ♕g4+ 14 ♔h1 ♕f3+ 15 ♔g1 ♖f6 with unstoppable threats in T.Fuss-Schmidt, correspondence 1989.

b) 11 g3?! enables Black to obtain the upper hand with 11...♘g5! because 12 gxh4?? ♘h3 would be mate. White has nothing better than 12 f3 (he is certainly not helped by either 12 e4?! fxe4 13 gxh4 ♘h3+ 14 ♔g2 exd3+ 15 ♔xh3 dxc2 or 12 d5 ♕h5 13 h4 ♘f7 14 ♗a3 ♖e8 15 ♖ae1, as in O.Malcanek-R.Teschner, Reggio Emilia 1965, and now 15...♘a6 with a big advantage) 12...♕h5 13 ♕d1 d6 when Black has won a couple of stylish victories:

b1) 14 ♕e2 ♘d7 15 e4 fxe4 16 ♗xe4 ♗xe4 17 ♘xe4 ♘xf3+ 18 ♔h1 ♘h4! proved decisive in E.Kraemer-A.Vinke, German League 2006.

b2) 14 ♗a3 ♘d7 15 ♕e2 ♖ae8 16 h4 ♘f7 17 f4 ♕g6 18 ♔h2 ♘f6 19 ♖ae1 ♘g4+ 20 ♔h3 e5 21 e4 exf4 22 ♖xf4 ♘g5+!

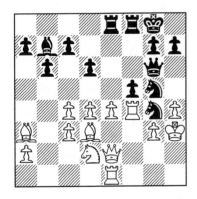

23 ♔g2 (23 hxg5 ♕h5+ 24 ♔g2 fxe4! is crushing) 23...♘xe4 24 ♗xe4 fxe4 25 ♕xg4 e3+ 26 d5 ♕xg4 27 ♖xg4 exd2 soon led to victory in M.Sipila-J.Norri, Vantaa 1988.

c) 11 f4 ♘xd2 12 ♗xd2 ♕g4! is a good move, improving the position of the queen while threatening mate.

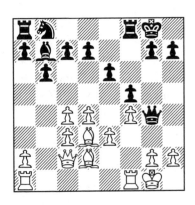

White has now tried:

c1) 13 ♖f2 ♕g6 14 ♖af1 d6 15 ♖e2 ♗e4! 16 ♗xe4 fxe4 17 g4 ♘c6 18 ♖g2 (K.Darga-L.Portisch, Oberhausen 1961) 18...♖ae8 19 f5 exf5 20 gxf5 ♕f6 intends ...♘a5 with advantage.

c2) 13 e4 fxe4 14 ♗xe4 ♗xe4 15 ♕xe4 ♘c6 16 ♖ae1 ♖ae8 was pleasant for Black in R.Schoene-Cu.Hansen, German League 1997. After the game's 17 d5 Black might have done well to consider 17...♘a5, intending 18 ♖f3 ♕f5 19 ♖fe3 ♕xe4 20 ♖xe4 ♔f7 when White's weak pawns could give him some problems in the endgame.

Returning to 11 f3:

11...♘xd2

11...♘g5?! works less well here in view of 12 f4! ♕g4 13 d5!.

12 ♗xd2 ♘c6

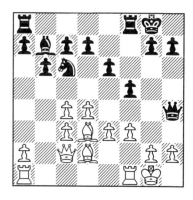

Now White must worry about the typical plan of ...♘a5 and ...♗a6, targeting c4.

13 ♖ab1

This has been White's most common choice, although the position has rather a non-forcing character and thus many different moves are playable.

Here are a few other possibilities:

a) In case of 13 ♖ae1 ♘a5 14 c5 (M.Simonsen-H.Vinagre, correspondence 1988) it looks interesting for Black to try 14...♖f6!?...

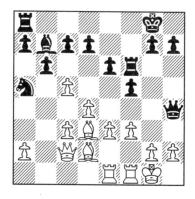

...when he has quite good chances with ...♖h6 on the agenda (but note that 14...bxc5?! is inferior due to 15 ♕a4 ♘c6 16 ♕b5 – Portisch).

b) 13 ♗e1 ♕h6 14 ♗f2 (after 14 ♕e2 e5 15 d5 ♘e7 16 g3 d6 Black's sounder and more flexible pawn structure gave him an edge in H.Hurme-S.Hamann, Aarhus 1971) 14...♘e7 15 ♖fe1 was prematurely agreed drawn in V.Neverov-V.Baklan, Alushta 2004.

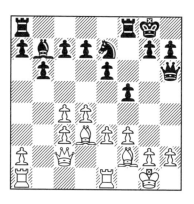

After 15...♘g6 the position looks about equal, but far from dead.

c) 13 e4 fxe4 and now:

c1) 14 fxe4 d6 15 ♗e3 ♘a5 (15...e5!?) 16 c5 dxc5 17 dxc5 ♕h5 18 ♖ae1 (J.Enevoldsen-Tan Hong Ghee, Amsterdam 1961) 18...♖ad8 looks approximately balanced.

c2) 14 ♗xe4 should be met by 14...♘a5, after which 15 ♖ae1 ♗xe4 16 ♖xe4 ♕h5 left Black with the sounder structure and excellent long-term chances in I.Rabinovich-A.Alekhine, Moscow 1920. Therefore White should retain his bishop-pair with 15 ♗d3! when L.Portisch-P.Nikolic, Niksic 1983, continued 15...♗a6 16 ♗e1 ♕h6 17 ♕e2 c6!? (17...d5 18 cxd5 ♗xd3 19 ♕xd3 exd5 20 ♗g3 c6 21 ♖ae1 may be just a little better for White) 18 ♗d2 ♕f6 19 ♖fe1 ♖fe8 20 ♕e4 g6 21 c5, at which point Black should have played 21...♗xd3 22 ♕xd3 ♕f5! 23 ♕a6 (Portisch mentions 23 ♖e4? bxc5 24 ♕a6 ♘c4! with advantage to Black) 23...♕d5 24 ♗h6 ♘c4 when his queen and knight complement one another very nicely.

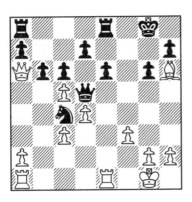

Portisch's analysis continues 25 ♖ad1! when Black must decide whether or not to snatch a pawn with 25...bxc5 26 dxc5 ♕xc5+ 27 ♔h1 when White has some compensation, although it is hard to say how much. My own choice, however, would be 25...e5! which enables Black to improve his position without ceding the initiative.

13...d6

Better than 13...♗a6?! when 14 ♕a4! forces 14...♗b7, as 14...♘a5? would leave d7 unprotected.

14 e4

This is White's most energetic continuation. Others can be met by standard moves like ...♗a6, ...♘a5 or the more aggressive ...♖f6!?.

14...fxe4 15 ♗xe4

15 fxe4 does not appear to have been tested here, but in any case 15...e5 looks like the right response.

15...♘a5

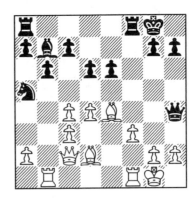

Black has no problem with a bishop exchange. White's remaining cleric will be partially restricted by the c3- and d4-pawns, and c4 will remain a chronic weakness.

16 ♗xb7

In this particular position White gains nothing with 16 ♗d3 ♗a6, while 16 ♖fe1 ♗xe4 17 ♖xe4 ♕f6 18 d5 ♕f5 19 ♕d3 e5 led to equality in P.Lukacs-R.Skrobek, Lodz 1978.

16...♘xb7 17 ♖be1

17 ♖fe1 will probably lead to the same position after 17...♖ae8 18 ♖e4 ♕h5 19 ♖be1.

17...♖ae8 18 ♖e4

Doubling on the e-file is White's most logical course of action. Instead 18 ♕a4 ♘a5 19 f4 ♕h5 20 ♖f3 e5 21 dxe5 dxe5 22 f5?! ♖d8 23 ♕c2 ♘xc4 left him a pawn down for very little in I.Sokolov-Cu.Hansen, Novi Sad Olympiad 1990.

18...♕h5 19 ♖fe1

We have been following the game

H.Banikas-T.Wippermann, Gibraltar 2008, which continued 19...♕g6 20 ♕d1 (20 ♕a4!? may also have been promising) 20...d5?! 21 ♖g4 ♕h5 22 ♗f4 ♘d6, at which point 23 ♗e5! ♖e7 24 cxd5 exd5 25 ♗xd6 ♖xe1+ 26 ♕xe1 cxd6 27 ♕e6+ ♕f7 28 ♕xd6 ♕f5 29 h3 would have left White with an extra pawn and excellent winning chances in the endgame.

Rather than be tied to the defence of e6 I think Black should have begun his own counterattack with 19...♘a5!. There might follow 20 ♖xe6 (20 ♕d3?! allows 20...♘xc4 anyway!) 20...♘xc4 21 ♖e7 ♖xe7 22 ♖xe7 ♖f7 23 ♖e8+ ♖f8 and then 24 ♖e7 repeats while 24 ♖xf8+ ♔xf8 leads to an endgame in which Black has no problems and may have some chances to be better.

Summary

5 e3 is a sensible developing move, but it fails to place the enemy position under any immediate pressure. The active 5...♘e4! combined with ...♗xc3+ and the Dutch-like ...f5 ensures Black of an active position as well as the sounder pawn structure. Throughout this chapter we have seen that these assets should provide the second player with a full share of the chances.

Chapter Five

The Hybrid System: 5 ♕b3

1 d4 ♘f6 2 c4 e6 3 ♘f3 b6 4 ♘c3 ♝b4 5 ♕b3!?

This used to be viewed as something of a sideline, but became more popular after a number of successful outings from Yasser Seirawan in the 1980s and 90s. More recently it has been championed by Ivan Sokolov. These and other players have continued to enrich the system with new ideas, and even today there remains plenty of room for creativity.

5...c5

Logically this feels like the right move; Black defends his bishop while simultaneously striking at the enemy centre. White's next task will usually be to develop his dark-squared bishop. Once this has been done he will be able to continue developing with e3 (without blocking in the queen's bishop), but he sometimes delays this in favour of an early centralization of the rook by means of ♖d1 or even long castling, which takes full advantage of the early queen excursion! Usually the dark-squared bishop will come to g5, although some players have preferred to place it on f4. White's other main decision concerns whether – and if so, when – to hit the b4-bishop with a3.

For Black the choices are just as plentiful: should his light-squared bishop go to b7 or a6? Should he castle early or instead strike in the centre with ...♘c6 and/or ...d5? Should he retreat his attacked bishop or exchange it for the knight on c3? This vast volume of variables combined with a volatile vichyssoise of interchangeable move orders can render this vivacious variation a veridically vexing one for both colours!

I hope that the analysis presented here will provide some answers, but before moving on to specifics I wish to stress one crucial point. The 5 ♕b3 variation is, in many ways, rather irregular and the resulting positions require both sides to consider the concrete implications of every move. This is most definitely not a variation in which either side can expect to succeed by following a predetermined plan of development for the first ten moves. At each turn you should ask yourself:

1) What were my opponent's options on the previous move?

2) What were the strengths and weaknesses of their chosen move compared with the alternatives?

3) What are my own candidate moves?

4) Given the specific features of this particular game, which of the above moves would best meet the demands of the position?

Over the course of this chapter I will endeavour to explain why certain moves are appropriate in some positions and not in others.

The ...♗xc3 and ...♘e4 tactic

Throughout most of this book I have refrained from presenting any themed diagrams to illustrate common positional or tactical motifs, instead preferring to explain ideas as I went along.

However, the following theme occurs so commonly, and is such a crucial resource for the player of the black pieces, that on this occasion I have decided to make an exception.

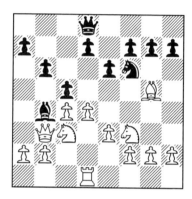

The small details may vary, though: for instance, the moves a3 and ...♗a5 may have been inserted; White's e-pawn may be back on e2 and he may have played either ♖ad1 or 0-0-0; and similarly, Black's king may be on its original square or he may have castled, while his queen's bishop may or may not have come to b7. Regardless of all that, the following possibility should be at the forefront of both players' minds.

1...♗xc3!

Normally Black would be reluctant to exchange this bishop for a knight, but here the decision is justified by the specific features of the position. If White wishes to play ambitiously then he will have to accept a serious pawn weakness with 2 bxc3; a concession which his fifth move was at least partially designed to avoid. The point of Black's play is seen after 2 ♕xc3 ♘e4! 3 ♗xd8 ♘xc3 when, due to the attack on the d1-rook, White has no choice but to play 4 bxc3 when Black responds by recapturing on d8. White will then suffer from a compromised pawn structure without the bishop-pair for compensation, meaning that Black will generally be at least equal in the resulting endgame.

For this mini-combination to work, the position must meet two principal conditions:

1) When the black knight arrives on c3 it *must* attack a white piece (in this case the rook on d1). If this were not the case then the white bishop could simply retreat from d8 when White would maintain the two bishops plus an unblemished pawn structure. Finally, please note that the vulnerable white piece does not necessarily have to be a rook on d1. Another example could be a bishop on e2, especially if White has already castled.

2) The white bishop must still be on g5. If the moves ...h6 and ♗h4 have been inserted, then White could respond to ...♘e4 simply by moving his queen. For this reason, *I strongly advise you to refrain from meeting ♗g5 with an early ...h6 in the opening*, unless there is a truly compelling reason to do so.

Theoretical Analysis

After 5 ♕b3 c5, I have decided to divide the material as follows:

A: 6 ♗f4
B: 6 a3 ♗a5 without 7 ♗g5
C: 6 ♗g5 including lines with a subsequent a3

None of White's irregular sixth moves are particularly worrying:

a) 6 d5 is hardly ever played, but I have not been able to find anything drastically wrong with it. A sensible response would be 6...♘e4!? 7 e3 (or 7 ♗d2 ♘xd2 8 ♘xd2 0-0) 7...♕f6 8 ♗d2 ♗xc3 9 bxc3 (E.Ausmins-D.Vismara, Crema 2000) 9...d6 with a decent game, as shown by 10 a4!? ♘d7 11 a5 ♘e5 12 ♗e2 ♘xf3+ 13 ♗xf3 ♘xd2 14 ♔xd2 ♖b8.

b) 6 e3 can be met by 6...♗a6 or by 6...0-0 7 ♗e2 ♘e4, which can be compared with note 'b' to White's 7th in Line B.

c) 6 ♗d2 0-0 7 e3 ♗b7 8 ♗e2 d5 9 cxd5 (or 9 dxc5 ♗xc5 10 cxd5 ♘xd5 11 0-0 ♘xc3 12 ♗xc3 ♘d7 13 ♖fd1 ♕e7 with equality) 9...cxd4 10 ♘xd4 ♗xc3 11 ♕xc3 ♘e4 12 ♕c2 ♕xd5 13 ♗f3 ♘d7 14 ♗xe4 ♕xe4 15 ♕xe4 ♗xe4 16 0-0?! (16 f3 ♗b7 would have been equal) 16...e5 was pleasant for Black in J.Jezek-P.Lehikoinen, correspondence 1986.

d) 6 dxc5 bxc5 is also not dangerous. J.Silman-W.Browne, New York 1987, continued 7 g3 (7 a3 ♗a5 reaches note 'c' to White's 7th move in Line B, to which 7 ♗g5 h6 8 ♗h4 g5 9 ♗g3 ♘e4 10 ♗e5 0-0 should also be compared) 7...♘c6 8 ♗g2 ♗a6! 9 0-0 0-0 10 ♗f4 (after 10 ♖d1?! ♘a5 11 ♕a4 ♗xc4 12 ♘e5 d5 13 e4 d4 14 ♘xc4 ♘xc4 15 a3 ♘b6 16 ♕a6 ♗xc3 17 bxc3 e5 18 a4 ♕c8 Black had consolidated his extra pawn and went on to win in S.Barbeau-I.Ivanov, Quebec 1987) 10...♘a5 11 ♕a4 ♗xc4 12 ♗d6 ♖e8 13 ♘e5 with some compensation for White. Instead Black's simplest continuation is probably 10...d5!? with a very active position.

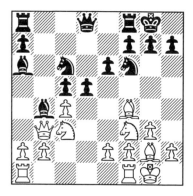

A) 6 ♗f4

The bishop comes to an active square, albeit one that is usually considered slightly less threatening than g5.

6...0-0

This looks safer than 6...♘c6 when 7 d5!? ♘a5 8 ♕c2 ♘xc4 9 e4 is an interesting pawn sacrifice.

7 e3

Instead 7 a3 ♗a5 reaches Line B, while 7 ♖d1 ♗a6! should be compared with the same lines.

7...d5 8 ♖d1

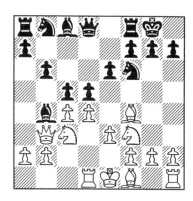

8...♘c6

The game A.Dreev-V.Ivanchuk,

Linares 1995, showed another promising route for Black in 8...♘bd7 9 cxd5?! (White should almost certainly try something else here) 9...♘xd5 10 ♗g5 (10 ♗d6?? c4! would be embarrassing for White) 10...♕c7 11 ♗c4 cxd4 12 ♗xd5 (12 exd4 ♗b7 13 0-0 ♗xc3 14 bxc3 ♖fc8 15 ♘d2 ♘xc3 16 ♕xc3 b5 and 12 ♖xd4 ♘c5 13 ♕c2 ♗b7 are both favourable for Black according to Dautov) 12...♗xc3+! 13 bxc3 exd5 14 cxd4 (or 14 ♕xd5 ♕xc3+ 15 ♘d2 dxe3 16 ♗xe3 ♖b8 with a clear advantage – Dautov) 14...♗a6 when White had problems connected with his inability to castle and was unable to save the game.

9 cxd5

Black was threatening 9...♘a5.

9...exd5 10 ♗e2 c4

Black advances his queenside majority while conveniently gaining time against the white queen. His position is already the easier to play, as White is in no position to do any harm with his central majority.

11 ♕c2 ♘e4

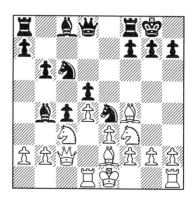

Black could also have considered 11...♘e7!? intending ...♗f5.

12 0-0?!

White should have preferred the pawn grab 12 ♗xc4! ♘xc3 13 bxc3 dxc4 14 cxb4 ♘xb4 15 ♕xc4 a5 when Black has sufficient compensation, but probably no more than that. With accurate play from both sides it seems that an equal endgame is the most likely outcome: 16 ♕c7 ♗a6 17 ♕xd8 ♖fxd8 18 ♔d2 ♖dc8 19 ♖c1 ♘xa2 (Black's activity has enabled him to regain the pawn, while White has managed to exchange queens and catch up in development) 20 ♖c7 ♘b4 21 ♖hc1 ♘d5 22 ♖xc8+ ♖xc8 23 ♖xc8+ ♗xc8 24 ♗d6 ♘f6 with approximate equality, although there is still plenty of play left in the position.

12...♗f5 13 ♕c1

13 ♘xe4 ♗xe4 14 ♕a4 ♕e8! (Dolmatov and Dvoretsky) also works out well for Black.

13...♖c8 14 ♘e1 ♘xc3 15 bxc3 ♗d6 16 ♗xd6 ♕xd6 17 ♕b2 ♖b8 18 g4 ♗g6 19 ♕b5

We have been following the game E.Bareev-S.Dolmatov, USSR Championship 1986. At this point Black could

have obtained a clear advantage with 19...a6! 20 ♕xa6 ♖a8 (20...b5!? also looks promising) 21 ♕b5 (21 ♕xb6?? ♖fb8 22 ♕c5 ♕e6 would cost White his queen after a subsequent ...♖a5) 21...♖xa2 22 ♗f3 ♖a5 23 ♕b2 ♖fa8.

B) 6 a3 ♗a5

At this point White's most common move is 7 ♗g5, after which 7...♗b7 reaches a position which we will consider under the move order 6 ♗g5 ♗b7 7 a3 ♗a5 (Line C3 or C4, depending on how White continues). Before moving on it is worth noting that Black has at his disposal a very interesting alternative in 7...h6!? 8 ♗h4 g5 9 ♗g3 g4 10 ♘d2 cxd4 winning a pawn (at least temporarily).

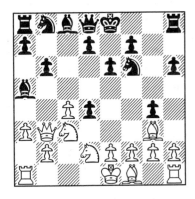

I have decided not to cover this in detail, though, partly due to my confidence in 7...♗b7, but also to conserve space as well as to reduce the reader's workload. It is all very well to prepare this line, but you would still need to find something else against the 6 ♗g5 move order. The point is that without the insertion of the moves a3 and ...♗a5 the capture ...cxd4 would leave the bishop on b4 hanging – a good example of how a seemingly minor detail can make a big difference! However, in order to provide a useful starting point for readers who are interested in broadening their repertoire to include this option I present the relatively recent game P.Wells-M.Adams, London 2006: 11 ♘b5 ♘e4 12 ♘c7+ ♔f8 13 0-0-0 ♘xd2 14 ♖xd2 ♗xd2+ 15 ♔xd2 ♗b7 16 ♗d6+ ♔g7 17 ♕g3 ♘c6 18 ♘xa8 ♗xa8 19 ♕xg4+ ♕g5+ 20 ♕xg5+ hxg5 21 b4 ♔f6 22 c5 ♘e7 23 cxb6 axb6 24 e3 dxe3+ 25 fxe3 e5 26 h3 ♘f5 27 ♗c7 ♘g3 28 ♖g1 ♘e4+ 0-1.

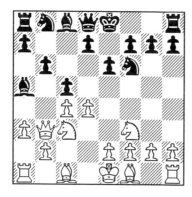

7 ♗f4

This is the chief alternative to 7 ♗g5. White's other options should not be too threatening, although your author once came unstuck against the last of these:

a) With 7 ♗d2 0-0 8 e3 White announces that he is not interested in a theoretical duel, and instead just wants to play chess. Black can play just about anything; one of the simplest responses is 8...d5 and 8...cxd4!? is also fine, followed by 9...d5 after either recapture.

b) 7 e3 is similarly unambitious, and Black can again obtain easy play with 7...0-0 (7...♗a6!? is also interesting) 8 ♗e2 (8 ♗d2 d5 returns to variation 'a' and 8 ♗d3 ♗b7 9 0-0 d5 is also fine for Black) 8...♘e4! when White has tried:

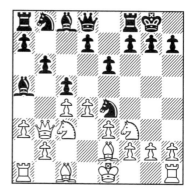

b1) 9 d5 ♗xc3+ 10 bxc3 ♗a6 gave Black comfortable play in Y.Seirawan-J.Timman, Hilversum 1990, and 10...f5!? also looks interesting.

b2) 9 0-0 ♗xc3 10 bxc3 ♘c6 11 ♘e5!? ♘xe5 12 dxe5 f5 13 exf6 ♕xf6 14 ♕c2 was V.Korchnoi-C.Lutz, Budapest 2003, and here 14...♗b7 would have been very comfortable for Black. Note that the pin 15 ♗f3 is nothing to worry about in view of 15...♕e5! or 15...♕g6! when the bishop must move again due to the threat of ...♖xf3.

c) The experimental line 7 dxc5!? bxc5 8 ♗g5 was played against me in I.Sokolov-A.Greet, Gibraltar 2007. Here Black's options include:

c1) In the game I tried 8...♕b6 9 ♕c2 ♘e4?! (a creative attempt, but unfortunately my opponent was one step ahead of me) 10 ♕xe4! ♕xb2 11 ♖b1! f5!

(otherwise Black loses material) 12 ♖xb2 fxe4 13 ♗d2 exf3 14 exf3 ♘c6 15 ♘e4 when White had a very pleasant endgame and went on to win.

c2) Today I would prefer John Emms' subsequent suggestion of 8...h6 9 ♗h4 g5!? 10 ♗g3 ♘e4

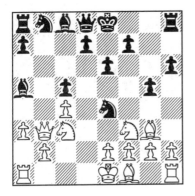

11 ♗e5 (11 ♗xb8 ♘xc3 12 bxc3 ♖xb8! is better for Black – Emms) 11...0-0 12 ♕c2 (12 e3 ♘c6 13 ♗d3!? f5! looks nice for Black) 12...♗b7 (12...d5!? may also be playable) 13 e3 d6 14 0-0-0 ♗xc3 15 ♗xc3 ♘d7 16 ♗d3 ♘xc3 17 ♕xc3 ♕f6 as presented on the ChessPublishing website.

Returning to 7 ♗f4:

7...0-0

Black should preserve the central tension for the time being, as after 7...cxd4 8 ♘xd4 d6 White might be tempted to try 9 0-0-0!?.

8 ♖d1

From time to time in the 5 ♕b3 variation White accelerates the development of his queenside pieces, hoping that the opposition of rook and queen will prove troublesome for Black. Moreover, the alternatives here are certainly nothing for Black to worry about:

a) 8 e3 has not been tested, perhaps with good reason as 8...cxd4! would highlight convincingly the major drawback of the move a3, as Black no longer has to worry about the bishop on b4. Following 9 exd4 d5 Black has easy play in the centre and the bishop on f4 looks misplaced.

b) 8 dxc5 ♘e4! 9 cxb6 axb6 10 g3 ♘c6 11 ♗g2 ♗xc3+ 12 bxc3 ♗a6 13 0-0 ♘c5 14 ♕c2 ♗xc4 15 ♘e5 ♗b3 16 ♕d2 ♘xe5 17 ♗xe5 d5 was fine for Black, whose central control and sounder pawn structure more than made up for White's bishop-pair in A.Dreev-J.Timman, Moscow 1993.

8...♗a6!

This active move should ensure an excellent game for Black.

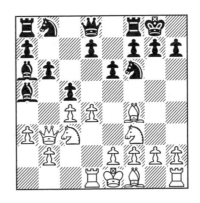

9 e3

Just as in the previous note, 9 dxc5 can be strongly met by the pawn sacrifice 9...♘e4! 10 cxb6 ♘xc3 11 bxc3 ♕xb6 with excellent play, and 9 ♗d6 ♖e8 10 dxc5 also fails to convince after 10...♘e4 (possible too is 10...bxc5!? 11

♗xc5 ♕c8) 11 cxb6 ♗xc3+ 12 bxc3 axb6, or 12...♘xd6 13 ♖xd6 ♘c6.

9...cxd4 10 ♘xd4 d5 11 ♗e2 ♗xc4

11...♕e7!? is also tempting, intending 12 ♗xb8 dxc4 13 ♗xc4 ♗xc3+ 14 ♕xc3 ♖c8 with good play.

12 ♗xc4 dxc4 13 ♕xc4 ♕d5 14 ♕xd5

At this point the game C.Garcia Palermo-V.Eingorn, Cienfuegos 1986, was agreed drawn although I would take Black after 14...♘xd5.

C) 6 ♗g5

All of the variations involving the deployment of the bishop to this square will be considered under this section.

6...♗b7

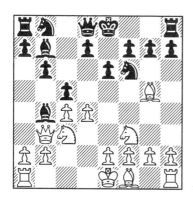

White has tried a number of different moves here. To make matters more complicated, different lines frequently transpose into one another. Thus, to render the following material as user-friendly as possible, I will divide it in the following way:

C1: 7 dxc5
C2: 7 0-0-0

C3: 7 a3 ♗a5 without 8 e3
C4: 7 a3 ♗a5 8 e3
C5: 7 e3 without a3

The last two named are, of course, very closely related, but there are certain situations in which the difference can be felt. From White's point of view, the advantage of including the moves a3 and ...♗a5 in an e3 set-up is that the black bishop will have a hard time transferring itself to the kingside in case of it being required there for defensive duties. On the other hand, the bishop is less exposed on a5, which may, for example, enable Black to play ...cxd4 without having to worry about his bishop being captured.

Finally, it should briefly be noted that 7 ♖d1 0-0 8 e3 cxd4 reaches Line C5.

C1) 7 dxc5

This is hardly the most dangerous move for Black to face, but anything that has been played by Sokolov (albeit only once) deserves some attention.

7...♗xc5

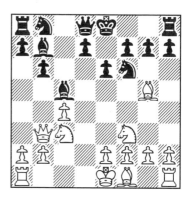

We have now transposed to a position more commonly reached via the Nimzo-Indian move order 3 ♘c3 ♗b4 4 ♕b3 c5 5 dxc5 ♗xc5 6 ♘f3 b6 7 ♗g5 ♗b7. Instead 7...bxc5 led to an eventual victory for Black in I.Sokolov-J.Hjartarson, Reykjavik 2003, but I believe the text to be a more reliable route to equality.

8 e3

White should avoid 8 e4?! as 8...h6 would force him to exchange his strong bishop for a knight. Occasionally he plays 8 ♖d1 here, but after 8...0-0 we will almost always reach something resembling the main line after 9 e3 ♗e7, etc.

8...0-0 9 ♗e2 ♗e7

It may appear strange to retreat the bishop voluntarily, but Black is planning ...♘a6-c5, hitting the queen and taking control over e4.

10 0-0 ♘a6 11 ♖fd1

11 ♖ad1 is sometimes played, but the general character of the position remains the same.

11...♘c5 12 ♕c2 ♘fe4

This typical simplifying manoeuvre assures Black of a comfortable game.

13 ♗xe7 ♕xe7 14 ♘xe4 ♘xe4 15 ♘d2 ♘f6

15...♘xd2 is perhaps even simpler, intending 16 ♕xd2 d5 or 16 ♖xd2 ♕g5 17 ♗f1 d5.

16 ♗f3 ♗xf3 17 ♘xf3 ♖fc8 18 ♕d3 ♕c5 19 b3 d5

The game is equal, and the game G.Serper-B.Gulko, Salt Lake City 1999, was agreed drawn here.

C2) 7 0-0-0

This aggressive try falls flat thanks to a standard tactical procedure.

7...♗xc3!

If White now wants to play ambitiously then he has no real choice but to compromise his pawns.

8 bxc3

The point of Black's play is that 8 ♕xc3 can, of course, be met by 8...♘e4!. White has tried two moves in this position:

a) 9 ♕e3 ♘xg5 10 ♘xg5 cxd4 11 ♖xd4 ♘c6 12 ♖g4 (or 12 ♖h4 ♕e7, maintaining the options of ...♖c8 and ...0-0-0) 12...♕e7 13 ♘f3 f5 14 ♖g3 ♖c8 15 ♕c3 0-0 16 e3 was M.Bosboom-S.Bakker, Amsterdam 2006, and here 16...b5! would have given Black an excellent position.

b) After the alternative 9 ♗xd8 ♘xc3 10 bxc3 ♔xd8 11 d5 ♔e7 12 e4 d6 we reach a semi-endgame, perhaps even minutely favourable for Black in view of the doubled c-pawns which, though not in any imminent danger, are nonetheless a permanent feature of the landscape.

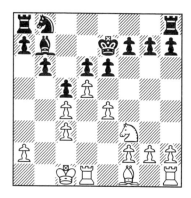

In M.Mchedlishvili-F.Kouvatsos, Rethymnon 2003, White tried to mix things up with 13 e5!? dxe5 14 ♘xe5, at which point the simplest solution looks like 14...♘d7!? as after 15 ♘xd7 ♚xd7 16 ♗e2 (with 16 dxe6+?! ♚xe6 White achieves nothing except to liberate the b7-bishop while relinquishing his only real asset, the passed d-pawn) 16...♖he8 the position of Black's king is no real cause for concern and the doubled c-pawns are not running away.

8...h6

Black should break the pin at the earliest convenience.

9 ♗h4 g5 10 ♗g3 ♘e4

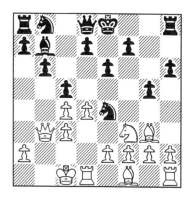

The resemblance to Chapter 7 is almost too obvious to need stating. White's queen occupies the somewhat less influential square of b3 instead of the customary c2, while the situation of his king is also far from perfect. On the other hand, there can be little doubt of the undesirability of Black's ...c5 is this position. The problem is not so much the prospect of dxc5 – which, despite opening a file for the white rook, would practically doom both c-pawns and jeopardize the safety of White's king – but rather that of d4-d5, which also improves the prospects of the rook without, crucially, ceding the magnificent c5-square to the black knights.

11 d5

This logical move has been played in both of the games which have reached this position. Aside from the points mentioned above, a further benefit for White is the blunting of the Queen's Indian bishop.

11...d6

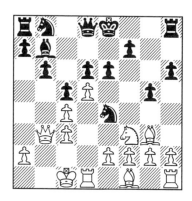

12 ♕c2

We have been following the game A.Barsov-A.Istratescu, Patras 2001, which continued 12...exd5 13 cxd5 ♕e7 14 ♗e5 ♘f6 15 ♗g3 ♘e4 and in view of the repetition a draw was agreed on the following move. In spite of this theoretical victory, I would feel distinctly uneasy about opening the centre in this way and there are plenty of ways in which a more ambitious White player might have continued the fight.

Instead I would prefer to keep my valuable e6-pawn, and thus 12...♘xg3 would seem to be the natural choice (12...f5!? may, though, also be worth investigating; Black maintains the powerful knight and prepares ...♕f6, ...♘d7 and ...0-0-0, followed by perhaps closing the position with ...e5 if a suitable moment presents itself). After the likely continuation 13 hxg3 (or 13 fxg3 ♕e7 intending ...♘d7), the move 13...♕f6!? looks very interesting, intending 14 dxe6 fxe6 (but not 14...♕xe6? 15 ♘xg5) 15 ♖xd6 ♘d7 followed by ...0-0-0 with definite compensation.

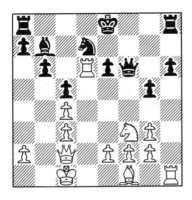

C3) 7 a3 ♗a5

7...♗xc3+!? is Black's extra option which is only available when White delays 6 a3. Following 8 ♕xc3 h6 9 ♗h4 the interesting 9...g5!? 10 ♗g3 ♘e4 11 ♕d3 ♘xg3 12 hxg3 ♕f6! 13 dxc5 bxc5 eventually led to a crushing victory for Black in L.Van Wely-V.Bologan, Wijk aan Zee 2004, but numerous improvements have been suggested for White and I am not altogether convinced that Black should follow this path.

8 dxc5!?

For many years this was considered completely harmless in view of Black's next. However, in 2002 Ivan Sokolov came up with a novelty which once again forced Black players to take it seriously. The more common 8 e3 will form the subject of Line C4, while the following two alternatives allow a familiar motif:

a) 8 0-0-0 ♗xc3! is almost identical to Line C2, the only difference being the inclusion of White's a3 which changes virtually nothing: 9 ♕xc3 ♘e4! 10 ♗xd8 (or 10 ♕e3 ♘xg5 11 ♘xg5 cxd4 12 ♖xd4 ♘c6, which should be compared with variation 'a' in the notes to White's 8th move in Line C2) 10...♘xc3 11 bxc3 ♔xd8 12 d5 ♔e7 13 e4 d6 14 ♗d3 ♘d7 was equal in H.Gretarsson-J.Hjartarson, Leeuwarden 1995.

b) 8 ♖d1 can also be met by 8...♗xc3+! 9 bxc3 (once again 9 ♕xc3 ♘e4! gives Black comfortable play) 9...♕e7 10 d5 d6 11 e3 ♘bd7 12 ♗e2 h6 13 ♗h4 e5, which led to a double-edged position resembling the Leningrad variation of the Nimzo in R.Gunawan-J.Timman, Bali 2000. Another sensible continuation would have been 13...g5 14 ♗g3 ♘e4 15 ♘d2 ♘xg3 16 hxg3 and now either 16...0-0-0 or 16...♘f6.

8...♘a6!

The strength of this pawn sacrifice was first highlighted in a game between Van Wely and Seirawan in 1995 (see note 'a2', below). Although the American's play in that game was exemplary, the move itself was first played way back in 1989 by Dzindzichashvili in a game against none other than Seirawan himself.

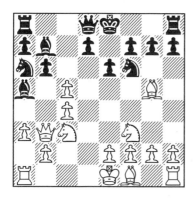

9 c6!

This was Sokolov's aforementioned innovation which breathed new life into this variation. The following variations reveal why an improvement was required:

a) The gluttonous 9 cxb6?! is asking for trouble. Black's pieces will spring into action and he can already force a serious weakening of White's queenside structure after 9...♘c5 10 ♕c2 (White had better provoke the bishop into blocking the e4-square; instead H.Ree-R.Douven, Breda 2000, saw 10 ♕d1, after which 10...♘ce4! would

have been very strong: 11 ♗d2 ♗xc3 12 ♗xc3 ♘xc3 13 bxc3 axb6, or 11 b4!? ♗xb6 12 c5 – 12 ♘xe4 ♘xe4! – 12...♘xc3 13 ♕d4 ♘ce4 14 ♗xf6 ♘xf6 15 cxb6 axb6, with a distinct advantage for Black in both cases) 10...♗e4 11 ♕d1 (White is unable to avoid the shattering of his queenside pawns in view of 11 ♕c1?? ♘b3) 11...♗xc3+ 12 bxc3 ♕xb6 when White must fight for equality:

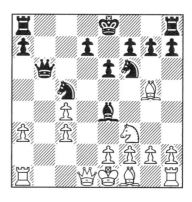

a1) 13 ♕d4? ♕b2 14 ♖d1 ♘b3 15 ♕d6 was S.Ozceviz-K.Sakai, correspondence 2001, and now 15...♘a1! looks even better than the game's 15...♕xc3+ 16 ♗d2 ♘xd2 17 ♖xd2 ♕xc4 which was, nonetheless, sufficient to bring home the full point.

a2) 13 g3? also leads to trouble after the energetic 13...♘g4! 14 ♕d4 (14 ♗g2?? ♘d3+) 14...0-0 15 ♗e7 (15 ♗e3 is well met by 15...♘b3!) 15...♕b2! 16 ♖d1 ♘b3 17 ♕xe4 ♕xc3+ 18 ♘d2 ♘xd2 19 ♖xd2 ♕a1+ 20 ♖d1 ♕c3+ 21 ♖d2 ♕c1+ 22 ♖d1 ♕xd1+ 23 ♔xd1 ♘xf2+ 24 ♔c2 ♘xe4 25 ♗xf8 ♖xf8 26 ♗g2 ♘c5, which saw Black go on to convert his extra pawn in L.Van Wely-Y.Seirawan, Wijk aan Zee 1995.

a3) In S.Marinosson-O.Coclet, correspondence 1999, White sought solace with 13 ♗xf6?! gxf6 14 ♕d4. At this point Black's strongest continuation would have been 14...♕b2 15 ♖d1 ♕xa3 16 ♕xf6 ♖f8!; the sting in the tail being the virulent threat of 17...♗c2!. White has nothing better than 17 ♕f4, after which 17...♕xc3+ 18 ♕d2 ♕xd2+ 19 ♘xd2 ♗c6 leaves Black clearly better in the endgame thanks to his superior development and strong passed a-pawn.

a4) 13 ♘d4 is probably White's best. Many moves are possible here, but perhaps the most spirited is 13...e5! when D.Scholz-R.Priebe, Internet 2003, continued 14 ♘b5 d5! 15 f3 ♖d8! (15...a6!? is also playable, but I prefer the text) 16 ♗xf6 gxf6 17 fxe4 ♘xe4.

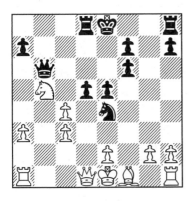

According to the game score White resigned here. This seems wildly premature, although White is certainly under some pressure after 18 e3 dxc4 19 ♕c2 ♕xe3+ 20 ♕e2 (20 ♗e2?? ♕f2 is mate) 20...♕g5, or 19 ♕g4 f5! (19...♕xb5 is less clear after 20 ♕xe4 ♕b2 21 ♕c6+ ♔f8 22 ♗e2!! ♕xa1+ 23 ♔f2 ♕xh1 24

♕xf6) 20 ♕xf5 ♕xe3+ 21 ♗e2 0-0 with an ongoing initiative in both cases.

b) Instead of digesting a toxic pawn, White is better advised to settle for the more prudent 9 ♕c2 (9 ♘d2 is likely to transpose after 9...♘xc5 10 ♕c2 ♗xc3 11 ♕xc3 a5!) 9...♗xc3+ (note that 9...bxc5?! would be a mistake as then the knight on a6 would be misplaced) 10 ♕xc3 ♘xc5 11 ♘d2 (11 ♗xf6 ♕xf6 12 ♕xf6 gxf6 should be at least equal for Black, whose doubled f-pawns are weak in no more than a symbolic sense), at which point 11...a5! looks like a good move.

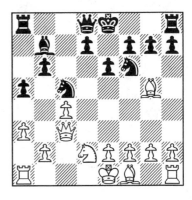

We have been following the game J.Campos Moreno-M.Adams, Spanish Team Championship 2001, in which White proceeded with the natural but overly ambitious 12 b4?! (12 f3 a4 would have been unclear according to Adams) 12...axb4 13 axb4 ♖xa1+ 14 ♕xa1 ♘a6! when White had some problems with the b4-pawn. Perhaps his relatively best option would have been 15 b5 ♘c5, although in that case the absolute stability of the knight coupled with Black's lead in development would have more than compensated for the bishop-pair. In the game White preferred 15 ♕b2?! ♕e7 16 c5!? (a creative though ultimately unsound attempt to change the course of the game) 16...bxc5 17 e4 h6 (Adams analyses 17...cxb4? 18 e5 as leading to an advantage for White) 18 ♗h4 (18 ♗xf6 ♕xf6 19 ♕xf6 gxf6 20 ♗xa6 ♗xa6 21 bxc5 ♖g8 is clearly better for Black – Adams) 18...e5 19 ♗xa6 ♗xa6 20 ♕a3 ♕e6 (20...♕d6 is also promising) 21 ♗xf6 cxb4! 22 ♕xb4 gxf6 23 f3 (23 ♕b8+ ♔e7 24 ♕xh8 ♕g4 wins) 23...♕c6 when Black was a safe pawn up and eventually converted his advantage.

We must now return to Sokolov's 9 c6:

9...♗xc6

In I.Sokolov-V.Ivanchuk, Wijk aan Zee 2006, Black was successful with 9...dxc6!? 10 ♕c2 c5 11 ♖d1 ♕c7 12 ♗xf6 (12 e3 is better according to Ftacnik, who gives 12...♘e4 13 ♗f4 ♕c8 14 ♗d3 f5 15 0-0 ♘xc3 16 bxc3 0-0 17 ♘e5 with a slight edge to White) 12...gxf6, although White missed more than one opportunity to fight for the advantage along the way.

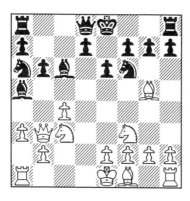

10 ♕c2 ♗xc3+ 11 ♕xc3 ♘c5 12 ♘d2

The position is identical to that reached in Campos Moreno-Adams above, except for one crucial detail: Black's light-squared bishop is on the slightly more exposed square of c6 rather than b7. This seemingly minor detail necessitates a significant change in strategy as we shall soon see.

12...0-0!

One of the main points behind White's 9th is that after 12...a5?! 13 b4! axb4 14 axb4 ♖xa1+ 15 ♕xa1, by contrast with Campos Moreno-Adams, the move 15...♘a6?? is no longer available. Instead Black would have to settle for 15...♘ce4, after which 16 ♘xe4 ♗xe4 17 f3 followed by e2-e4 gives White a pleasant advantage.

13 f3

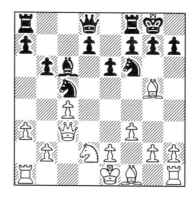

This is a critical moment at which Black has tried a few different approaches. Precision is required, as nondescript moves would allow White to catch up in development and exploit his bishop-pair. Please note that on the last move 13 ♗xf6 ♕xf6 14 ♕xf6 gxf6 is nothing for White, while 13 b4 ♘ce4 14

♘xe4 ♘xe4 15 ♗xd8 ♘xc3 16 ♗e7 ♖fe8 17 ♗d6 ♘e4 18 ♗e5 d5 is equal according to Sokolov.

13...e5!?

This active move seems to meet the demands of the position. Black gains some space in the centre and increases his influence over the dark squares while also providing a convenient retreat square on e6 for the queen's knight. It is important to note that 14 ♕xe5? is impossible due to 14...♘d3+! 15 exd3 ♖e8 winning the queen. 13...d5 is a major alternative, but having analysed both options in some detail I slightly prefer the text.

14 e4

14 b4 may be a tad premature in view of 14...♘e6 15 ♗h4 (15 ♕xe5 ♘xg5 16 ♕xg5 d5 gives Black good compensation) 15...♘e4!.

J.Gustafsson-F.Zeller, Deizisau 2003, continued 16 ♗xd8 ♘xc3 17 ♗h4 (17 ♗e7 ♖fe8 18 ♗d6 ♘d4 19 ♖c1 ♘a2! 20 ♖b1 ♘f5 is better for Black) 17...♘d4 (after 17...d5!? 18 cxd5 ♘xd5 I would prefer Black's lead in development over White's bishop-pair) 18 ♔f2 ♘f5

19 ♗g3 ♘xg3 20 hxg3 a5 21 b5 ♗b7 22 a4 d5 23 cxd5 ♗xd5 24 e4 ♗e6 25 ♗c4 ♖fd8 26 ♔e3 ♖d4 with equality.

The alternative 14 e3 is rather timid and in A.Korotylev-P.Eljanov, Moscow 2006, Black easily held the balance with the aid of a familiar tactic after 14...♖e8 15 b4 ♘e6 16 ♗h4 ♘e4! 17 ♗xd8 ♘xc3 18 ♗h4 a5 19 b5 ♗b7 20 ♖c1 ♘a4 21 ♗e2 ♘ac5 22 0-0 f5 23 ♖fd1 g5 and ½-½.

We now follow the game B.Macieja-Z.Efimenko, Khanty Mansiysk 2005:

14...♖e8!?

14...d6 also looks playable. The careless 15 ♗e2? would allow 15...♘fxe4! 16 ♘xe4 ♘xe4 17 ♗xd8 ♘xc3 18 ♗e7 ♖fe8 19 ♗xd6 ♖ad8 20 ♗b4 ♘xe2 21 ♔xe2 when only Black can be better. However, 15 b4 ♘e6 16 ♗e3 may give some chances for an edge.

15 ♗e3

Here 15 b4 ♘e6 16 ♕xe5 ♘xg5 17 ♕xg5 d5 18 cxd5 h6!? should give Black enough compensation. Instead Macieja refrains from pushing his b-pawn, apparently reasoning that this would only drive the knight to a better location.

15...d6

According to the database there have been no other games which have reached this position. The present encounter saw Black eventually emerge victorious, although there is clearly a great deal of scope for new ideas from both sides. For what it's worth, the game proceeded with:

16 ♗e2 ♘h5 17 g3 ♕d7 18 ♘b3 ♕h3 19 ♗f1 ♕e6 20 ♘xc5 dxc5

I would assess this position as approximately equal, and indeed White was doing quite okay until he self-destructed between moves 42 and 44.

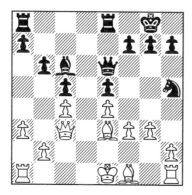

The remaining moves were: 21 0-0-0 a5 22 ♗e2 ♖ad8 23 ♖xd8 ♖xd8 24 ♖d1 ♖xd1+ 25 ♗xd1 a4 26 ♕d3 ♕e7 27 ♗c2 ♘f6 28 ♗d2 ♕d7 29 ♕e2 ♕d4 30 ♗e3 ♕d6 31 ♗d2 ♘e8 32 ♗c3 f6 33 ♕d2 ♕xd2+ 34 ♔xd2 ♔f7 35 ♔d3 ♔e6 36 h4 g6 37 ♗d2 ♘d6 38 g4 ♘f7 39 ♔c3 g5 40 hxg5 ♘xg5 41 ♗d1 ♗e8 42 b4?! axb3 43 ♔xb3 h5 44 f4? ♘xe4 45 f5+ ♔e7 46 g5 ♘xd2+ 0-1.

C4) 8 e3 0-0

If Black is content to play for equality without aspiring to anything more then 8...cxd4 9 ♘xd4 0-0 10 ♕c2 ♗xc3+ 11 ♕xc3 d5 could be worth considering. I suspect, however, that most readers would prefer to retain some tension in the position in an effort to create a few more problems for the opponent.

9 ♖d1!

This forces Black to demonstrate considerable precision. The alternatives are less dangerous:

a) 9 ♗e2 enables Black to equalize in familiar fashion with 9...cxd4 10 exd4 ♗xc3+ (Black can also delay this for a move with 10...♘c6!? 11 0-0 ♗xc3! 12 bxc3 ♖c8 or 12 ♕xc3 ♘e4) 11 ♕xc3 ♘e4 12 ♗xd8 (or 12 ♕e3 ♘xg5 13 ♘xg5 d5 14 0-0 h6 15 ♘f3 dxc4 16 ♗xc4 ½-½, F.Vallejo Pons-N.Pert, Aviles 2000) 12...♘xc3 13 ♗e7 ♖e8 14 ♗d6 ♘e4 and ½-½, A.Obukhov-V.Yemelin, Krasnoyarsk 2003.

b) 9 dxc5 meets with a similar treatment as in Line C3, viz. 9...♘a6! when D.Bocharov-E.Alekseev, Kazan 2005, continued 10 c6!? (wisely refusing the offered pawn) 10...♗xc6 11 ♕c2 ♗xc3+ 12 ♕xc3 ♘c5 13 ♗xf6 gxf6 when Black was fine and a draw was agreed twelve moves later.

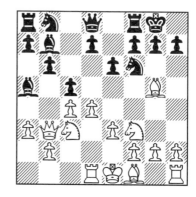

9...d5!

Despite the opposition of rook and queen along the d-file, I believe this to be the soundest response. 9...cxd4?! should definitely be avoided in view of 10 ♖xd4! when the rook may swing across to the kingside. 9...♗xc3+!? is interesting, although I think that 10 bxc3! (as usual 10 ♕xc3 ♘e4! solves all of Black's problems) may leave Black a little way short of equality. White may be able to block the centre with d4-d5 which would leave the bishop on b7 passively placed. We should also note that...h6 and ...g5 would be very risky with the black monarch already committed to the kingside.

We now follow the high-level game E.Bareev-M.Adams, Wijk aan Zee 2002:

10 ♗e2

This appears to be the only move to have been tested. However, 10 dxc5 looks like an obvious attempt when Black must justify his pawn sacrifice; 10...♘bd7! looks like the most promising way to do so: for example, 11 cxb6 dxc4 12 ♗xc4 (or 12 ♕xc4 ♖c8 with definite compensation) 12...♕xb6 13 0-0 ♕xb3 14 ♗xb3 ♗xf3 15 gxf3 ♖ab8 16 ♗a4 ♖xb2 17 ♗xd7 ♗xc3 with equality.

10...♘bd7 11 0-0 cxd4 12 ♘b5!?

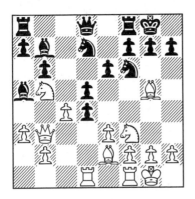

Hoping to exploit the vulnerable position of the bishop on a5. The idea is very creative, although it turns out that Black can maintain the balance quite easily. The alternatives 12 exd4 dxc4

and 12 ♘xd4 ♗xc3 13 ♕xc3 ♘e4! are certainly nothing for White to write home about, while 12 ♖xd4 could be safely met by 12...♘c5 13 ♕c2 ♗xc3 14 bxc3 ♕e7 15 cxd5 ♗xd5, or even 12...♗xc3!? 13 ♕xc3 ♕c7 with balanced chances.

12...h6 13 ♗h4 ♘c5 14 ♕c2 d3!

Returning the pawn and forcing simplification.

15 ♗xd3 ♘xd3 16 ♖xd3 a6 17 cxd5!?

White does his best to unbalance the game, as 17 ♘c3 ♗xc3 followed by ...♖c8 would be comfortable for Black.

17...axb5 18 dxe6 ♕e8 19 ♗xf6 fxe6

19...gxf6? 20 ♖d7 ♗xf3 21 exf7+ ♖xf7 22 ♕g6+ ♔f8 23 ♕xh6+ ♔g8 24 ♖xf7 works out well for White, but 19...♕xe6!? may have been playable.

20 ♗e5 ♗e4

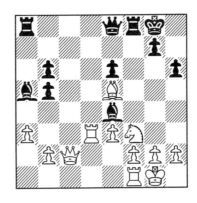

21 ♖d7

Forcing a draw. White definitely had to avoid 21 b4?? ♖xf3 22 gxf3 ♕g6+ (Aagaard), but 21 ♕d1!? might have been playable. Then 21...♗xd3 22 ♕xd3 b4 leaves White with some compensation for the exchange, although I doubt that he would be able to claim any real advantage here.

21...♗xc2

But not 21...♕xd7? 22 ♕xe4, which is winning for White as the bishop on a5 is about to be trapped.

22 ♖xg7+ ♔h8 ½-½

Finally we must consider those lines in which White refrains from nudging the enemy bishop with a3. The main difference is that a subsequent ...cxd4 will leave the black bishop on b4 *en prise*. Fortunately this is nowhere near as problematic as one might expect, and we will see several instances in which Black quite happily takes on d4 to initiate an exchange of this piece for the enemy knight on c3. The basic idea can be seen in the following diagram:

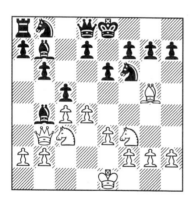

Black continues 1...cxd4, not fearing 2 ♕xb4 on account of either 2...♘a6! 3 ♕a3 dxc3 4 ♕xc3 ♘c5 or 2...♘c6! 3 ♕a3 dxc3 4 ♕xc3 ♖c8. In both cases the 'free' developing move improves his chances considerably.

C5) 7 e3 0-0 8 ♖d1

This has been the most popular choice, so I will take it as the main line, although several others have been tried:

a) 8 a3 ♗a5 transposes to Line C4.

b) 8 0-0-0 (A.Dergatschova Daus-M.Danelia, Dresden 2007) should be met by the typical 8...♗xc3, intending 9 ♕xc3 ♘e4 10 ♗xd8 ♘xc3 11 bxc3 ♖xd8 with a good position.

c) 8 dxc5 ♗xc5! illustrates one of the drawbacks of White's chosen move order: the enemy bishop can return to the centre or the kingside as required. Black's next few moves will probably involve the further retreat ...♗e7 combined with ...♘a6-c5, centralizing the knight while gaining time thanks to the enemy queen's exposed position on b3.

d) 8 ♗d3 can be met by 8...h6!? (♗d3 takes the sting out of any ...♗xc3 and ...♘e4 tricks, so there is no reason to refrain from nudging the bishop, although there is nothing wrong too with the immediate 8...cxd4) 9 ♗h4 cxd4 10 ♕xb4 (10 exd4 is well met by 10...♗e7, intending ...d5 with a fine game) 10...♘a6! illustrating the standard tempo-gaining procedure.

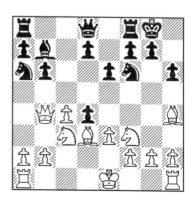

J.Yrjölä-S.B.Hansen, Reykjavik 2000, continued 11 ♕a3 (11 ♕b3? ♘c5! would gain even more time) 11...dxc3 12 ♕xc3 ♘c5 13 ♖d1 ♖c8 14 ♗e2 ♘ce4 (14...d5!?) with good counterplay for Black who went on to win.

e) 8 ♗e2 should be met by 8...cxd4 with a further split:

e1) So far no-one seems to have tried 9 ♕xb4. I would suggest 9...♘c6 (the alternative 9...♘a6 is also playable, but in the present position I slightly prefer the text) 10 ♕a3 (10 ♕b3 ♘a5! 11 ♕c2 dxc3 12 ♕xc3 ♘e4! works out well for Black after both 13 ♕xa5 f6! 14 ♗xf6 ♕xf6 15 ♕b4 ♘g5 and 13 ♗xd8 ♘xc3 14 ♗xb6 axb6 15 bxc3 ♖fc8) 10...dxc3 11 ♕xc3 ♘e4! 12 ♗xd8 ♘xc3 13 ♗c7 ♘xe2 14 ♗d6! (14 ♔xe2 ♗a6 is better for Black) 14...♘ed4!? 15 exd4 ♖fe8, intending ...♘e7-f5 with equality.

e2) 9 exd4 ♘c6 10 0-0 (10 d5?! exd5 11 cxd5 ♗xc3+ 12 bxc3 ♘a5 wins a pawn for Black) 10...♗xc3! leaves White with the usual unappealing choice:

e21) 11 ♕xc3?! ♘e4 12 ♗xd8 ♘xc3 13 bxc3 ♖fxd8 just looks better for

Black who intends ...♗a6, ...♘a5 and ...♖ac8 with intense pressure against c4, which can perhaps be augmented by ...d5 if the bishop on e2 remains unprotected.

e22) 11 ♗xf6 ♕xf6 12 ♕xc3 ♖ac8 was at least equal for the second player in G.Timoscenko-Y.Pelletier, Leon 2001. The game continued 13 ♕d2 ♘e7 14 ♖ac1 ♘g6 15 ♖c3 ♘f4 16 ♖fc1 ♘xe2+ 17 ♕xe2 ♗xf3 18 ♕xf3 ♕xd4 19 ♖d1 ♕e5 and Black was a clear pawn up.

e23) A subsequent game of Pelletier's (M.Klauser-Y.Pelletier, Leukerbad 2002) deviated with 11 bxc3, although once again the Swiss Grandmaster obtained a fine position with the simple 11...♖c8, intending ...♘a5 and ...♗a6 with strong pressure against c4.

Returning to 8 ♖d1:

8...cxd4 9 exd4

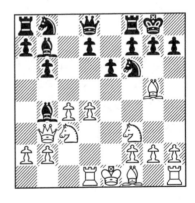

Once again 9 ♕xb4 loses time after 9...♘a6!, but 9 ♖xd4!? is not so bad, although it is nowhere near as dangerous as in the analogous position in which a3 and ...♗a5 have already been played. In P.Taboada-D.Isaacson, correspondence 1999, Black simply played 9...♗e7!, fortifying the kingside and preparing to gain time with ...♘c6 or ...♘a6-c5.

9...♗xc3+!

First played by Gelfand, this well-timed exchange should ensure Black of a full share of the chances. 9...♗xf3 10 gxf3 ♗e7 is also possible, although White's attacking chances after 11 ♖g1 should not be underestimated.

10 bxc3

10 ♕xc3 ♘e4! gives Black an easy game as usual.

10...♕c7!

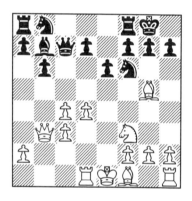

11 ♗xf6 ♗xf3!

This is the justification of Black's play. 11...gxf6 is riskier in view of 12 d5! (Alterman), although even this is not completely clear after 12...♘a6!? 13 ♖d4 f5.

12 gxf3

12 ♖d3 ♗e4 13 ♖e3 ♗g6 (Alterman) keeps things solid.

12...gxf6 13 ♕c2

We have reached a critical position. The game B.Alterman-B.Gelfand, Tel Aviv 1999 was soon agreed drawn after

13...♕f4 14 ♕e4 ♕xe4+. Alterman goes on to analyse 15 fxe4 ♘c6 16 ♖d3 ♖ac8 17 ♖g1+ ♔h8 18 ♖f3 ♘a5 19 ♖xf6 ♘xc4 20 e5 ♖g8 which he assesses as equal, although Ward suggests that White may be able to claim a slight edge with 21 ♖g3 and I have to agree. Furthermore, Yrjölä and Tella make an interesting suggestion in the shape of 14 ♖g1+!? ♔h8 15 ♖g4 ♕xh2 (15...♕xf3? 16 ♖h4 f5 17 ♖d3) 16 ♕e4 with complex play.

Although the above variations are by no means catastrophic for Black, I felt that there could be some potential for improvement and now believe that 13...♔h8!? may be the way forward.

According to my analysis Black has no need to fear the transfer of the enemy queen to the kingside:

a) 14 ♕d2 can be safely met by either 14...♖g8 15 ♕h6 ♕d8 or 14...d6 15 ♗d3 ♘d7.

b) 14 ♕e4 looks rather more threatening, but Black can utilize a tactical trick with 14...♖g8! (14...d5 is risky, since 15 ♕h4 ♘d7 16 ♗d3 f5 17 cxd5 ♕xc3+ 18 ♔f1 ♕a5 19 dxe6 fxe6 20 ♖g1

♖g8 21 ♖g3 leaves White with some initiative) 15 ♗d3 (after 15 ♕xa8 ♘c6 16 ♕xg8+ ♔xg8 Black stands better thanks to his sounder structure and safer king) 15...f5 16 ♕h4 (once again 16 ♕xa8 ♘c6 17 ♕xg8+ ♔xg8 is unappealing for White) 16...♖g6 when Black has an excellent game. The plan is ...♘c6 followed by ...♘a5, combined with ...♖ag8 or perhaps ...♖c8.

Summary

Phew! This chapter was quite variation-intensive, and I heartily salute the reader for making it this far. The positions after 5 ♕b3 can be extremely challenging for both sides, especially with so many different options and move orders available. Instead of regarding this as a negative, I prefer to view the immense variety of move orders, strategies, pawn structures and position types as a source of fascination which can hopefully inspire me to continue learning and improving.

Just remember that when you encounter the 5 ♕b3 c5 variation over the board, you will need to keep your wits about you from the outset! Take your time and think logically about the ramifications of every single move, with reference to the ideas and themes that have been discussed in the present chapter. If you can combine a reasonable level of theoretical knowledge with the correct mindset at the board, then you will have every chance of securing a fine position from the opening.

Chapter Six

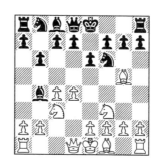

The Hybrid System: 5 ♗g5

1 d4 ♘f6 2 c4 e6 3 ♘f3 b6 4 ♘c3 ♗b4 5 ♗g5

This is sometimes referred to as the Kasparov Variation, although several of his predecessors as World Champion also utilized it from time to time. 5 ♗g5 is a rather principled, even obstinate move – White is unfazed by the pin on the c3-knight and unperturbed by the prospect of doubled c-pawns. Instead he hopes that his own pin will prove to be of greater significance. By characterizing this line as an ambitious and uncompromising one, I hope to have set the stage for what I have found to be some of the most captivating and dynamically unbalanced positions associated with the Queen's Indian.

5...h6!?

Believe it or not, this is a hugely important moment in terms of move order. 5...♗b7 has been played more frequently, after which 6 e3 h6 7 ♗h4 g5 8 ♗g3 ♘e4 9 ♕c2 would reach the main line below. So why am I recommending a different sequence? The answer is that after 5...♗b7 White has at his disposal the fashionable and quite potent 6 ♘d2!?, fighting for the crucial e4-square and intending to meet 6...c5 with 7 d5!, offering a pawn sacrifice. I will not go into detail here, suffice to say that White's system carries plenty of venom and is worth avoiding provided that we do not have to compromise ourselves in any significant way, which it appears we do not. The point of the text is to meet 6 ♗h4 with 6...g5 7 ♗g3 ♘e4 followed by a subsequent ...♗b7, angling for a transposition to the main line while bypassing this critical sub-variation.

6 ♗h4

6 ♗f4 and 6 ♗d2 should be compared with 5 ♗f4 and 5 ♗d2 respectively, while 6 ♗xf6?! senselessly cedes the bishop-pair and Black is at least equal after 6...♕xf6 or 6...♗xc3+ 7 bxc3 ♕xf6.

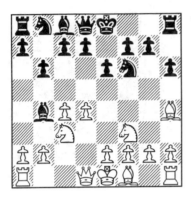

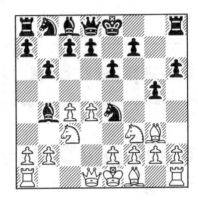

6...g5!?

This is a principled choice. Black forcefully breaks the pin in order to facilitate a knight jump into e4, thereby making full use of his fourth move. It remains to be seen whether the advancing kingside pawns will turn out to be strong or weak; obviously as Queen's Indian players we will hope for the former, and over the course of the chapter we will encounter many variations in which this indeed turns out to be the case. Before moving on it is also worth noting that the white bishop will be far from ideally placed on g3. For the time being it is sidelined away from the centre, and in some variations it may come under threat following the advance ...f5.

7 ♗g3 ♘e4

The knight leaps to an ideal central location while increasing the pressure against its counterpart on c3. For the next few moves at least the centralized stallion will become the linchpin of Black's position, and it will come as no surprise to learn that White will usually do his best to remove it.

8 ♕c2

This natural move is the usual choice, although there are a number of ways in which White may attempt to deviate. The crucial question, at least with regard to our move order choice of 5...h6!?, is whether there is any way for him to derive some benefit from the absence of the moves e3 and ...♗b7. Here is a summary of the various alternatives:

a) 8 ♖c1?! is inadvisable. The rook will end up on a blocked file and White would be much better off developing his queen to a better square (typically c2) while also defending c3. That way, the rook will be free to take up a more useful role later in the game.

b) 8 ♕b3 ♗xc3+ 9 bxc3 d6 leads to something resembling the main lines, except for the white queen's presence on b3 rather than the customary c2. After the further continuation 10 e3 (10 ♘d2 ♘xd2 11 ♔xd2 ♘c6 12 e3 ♘a5 was fine for Black in V.Shishkin-A.Stolte, German League 2000) 10...♘d7 11 0-0-0 ♗b7 (11...h5!?) 12 ♘d2 ♘xg3 13 hxg3 ♕e7 14 f3 0-0-0 the chances were ap-

proximately equal in A.Moiseenko-
V.Ivanchuk, Warsaw 2005.

c) 8 ♘d2!? has hardly ever been
played, although it is well known in
the analogous variation in which ...♗b7
and e3 have been played. Most commentators have actually condemned
this move as unplayable in view of
8...♘xc3 9 bxc3?! ♗xc3 when White will
be forced to sacrifice further material
for what must surely be considered
inadequate compensation. However, in
the game S.Bolduc-C.Malveau, Mont-
real 2005, White made things interesting with 9 ♕c2!.

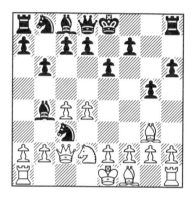

This is an easy move to miss, but it
is the only realistic way in which White
may attempt to justify his play. The
game continued 9...♘xe2 10 ♗xe2, at
which point 10...♘c6!? looks best,
commencing an immediate counterattack against the white centre. In my
view it looks even more tempting for
Black to try 9...♘xa2!?. It is true that, in
principle, it would be more desirable to
remove a central rather than a wing
pawn, but on the other hand, capturing
on e2 accelerates White's development,

whereas the text misplaces the white
rook. Moreover, it stabilizes the position of the bishop on b4 which will no
longer have to worry about being
kicked by a3. Now 10 ♖xa2 a5!? prepares ...d6 without losing the bishop to
a queen fork. A plausible continuation
might be 11 h4 d6 12 hxg5 ♕xg5 when
Black is in excellent shape.

d) 8 ♕d3!? is an interesting attempt
to deviate from the main line. White
hopes that the queen will exert a
greater influence over the centre from
d3 than c2, for instance by controlling
the third rank. The drawbacks are that
the d3-square will not be available for
the light-squared bishop, while in the
event of a subsequent d4-d5, the arrival
of a black knight on c5 would gain a
tempo against the queen. Black's most
common reaction has been the stereo-
typed 8...♗b7 and although there is
nothing especially wrong with this, I
think I would prefer the more dynamic
8...f5!?, which potentially challenges
the future of the g3-bishop. Furthermore, with the white queen committed
to the d3-square it is conceivable that
Black may wish to develop his bishop
on a6 instead of b7.

After 8...f5, the game R.Meessen-
A.Hentunen, Saint Vincent 2005, proceeded 9 ♗e5 (9 e3 h5!? looks interesting), at which point I would suggest
9...♗xc3+, taking the opportunity to
double the c-pawns before White gets a
chance to play d4-d5. Following 10
bxc3 ♖h7!? (see diagram overleaf; other
rook moves are also quite playable, but
it might be useful to swing this piece

across the second rank at some point in the future) White must worry about the future of the e5-bishop, whilst Black may seriously consider posting his own clergyman on a6.

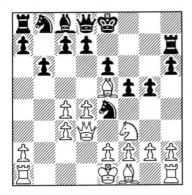

We now return to the main line, 8 ♕c2:

8...♗b7

With the white queen on c2 it seems doubtful that ...♗a6 will ever become a tempting proposition, so the text is an automatic choice.

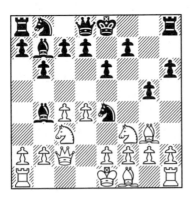

From this position White usually continues with the natural 9 e3, which will be discussed in the following dedicated chapter. White does, however,

have a number of alternatives including two which warrant special attention:

A: 9 ♗e5!?
B: 9 ♘d2!?

Here is a summary of the inferior and/or rarer options:

a) 9 a3? is senseless and after 9...♗xc3+ 10 bxc3 f5 11 e3 (11 ♘d2? ♘xd2 12 ♔xd2 f4 13 ♕g6+ ♔f8 leaves White with no real compensation for the piece) 11...d6 White is virtually a tempo down on normal lines.

b) In R.Steinhorst-A.Markgraf, Lingen 1995, White attempted to prepare d4-d5 with the somewhat artificial-looking 9 ♖d1?!. The game continued 9...f5 10 d5 and now 10...♗xc3+ 11 bxc3 ♘a6! 12 dxe6 d6 would have given Black the better game; the plan being ...♘ac5, ...♕f6 and, if permitted, ...0-0-0 combined with a timely recapturing of the e6-pawn (which will not run away). Note that 13 ♕a4+ ♔f8 does not inconvenience Black in any significant way.

c) 9 d5!? is an aggressive try which was once tested by the ever-creative Alexander Shabalov. Play continues 9...exd5 10 cxd5 and now instead of 10...♗xd5 11 0-0-0 ♘xc3 12 bxc3 ♗a3+ 13 ♔b1 ♗b7 14 h4 which gave White good compensation in A.Shabalov-*Crafty*, Internet 1996, Black should have preferred 10...♗xc3+ 11 bxc3 ♗xd5. This looks perfectly fine for the second player and should be compared with Line A1, below. Indeed, the further moves 12 ♗e5 ♖g8 would lead to a direct transposition.

d) 9 0-0-0!? is rare but not necessarily bad, and after the natural moves 9...♗xc3 10 bxc3 ♕e7 11 ♔b2 d6 White has tried two moves:

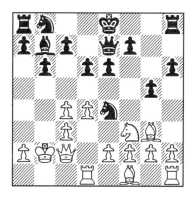

d1) 12 ♘d2 ♘xg3 13 hxg3 ♘d7 14 e4 was seen in J.Viirret-E.Hintikka, Finland 1997, and now instead of 14...e5?! which permanently weakened the f5-square, Black should have preferred the more flexible 14...0-0-0.

d2) 12 h4 ♖g8 13 hxg5 hxg5 14 ♘d2 ♘xg3 15 fxg3 ♘d7 16 e4 0-0-0 17 ♗e2 was agreed drawn in M.Krasenkow-J.Hellsten, Aghia Pelagia 2004.

A) 9 ♗e5!?

This sharp and ambitious move forces Black to tread carefully, although accurate play should see him emerge with an excellent game.

9...♗xc3+!

It is important to make this exchange and double the c-pawns before White has time for d4-d5. 9...f6 is probably playable, but the position after 10 d5! is certainly a lot more fun

for White. The text is sounder and leads to positions more in keeping with the general character of this variation.

10 bxc3 ♖g8!

This time 10...f6 can be strongly met by 11 ♘d2!. White must now decide between two radically different paths:

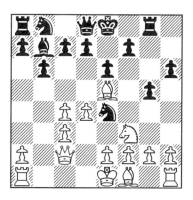

A1: 11 d5!?
A2: 11 ♘d2

The former is the aggressive choice, attempting to blast open the centre by sacrificing a pawn, while the latter is a more reserved approach. Instead the slow 11 e3? fails to make any sense of the bishop's placement on e5, and Black easily obtains a fine position after 11...d6 12 ♗d3 f5 13 ♗g3 ♘d7 or 13...h5!?.

A1) 11 d5!?

I encountered this move in the game D.Berczes-A.Greet, Budapest 2005, which we will now follow.

11...exd5

During the game I saw no reason not to accept the offer, and after three years and much analysis my opinion remains unchanged.

12 cxd5 ♗xd5 13 ♖d1 ♗b7 14 e3

Alternatively, 14 ♘d4 d6 15 f3 ♘d7! 16 ♗g3 ♘xg3 17 hxg3 ♕f6 and 14 ♘d2 ♘xd2 15 ♕h7 ♖g6 16 ♖xd2 d6 17 ♗g7 ♘d7 18 e3 ♘f6 are variations given by Emms. As a matter of fact both Emms and Ward provide useful coverage of this variation in their respective books, although I was unaware of this at the time (I was actually 'out of book' as early as 9 ♗e5), and still feel quite proud of myself for having found all the correct moves over the board.

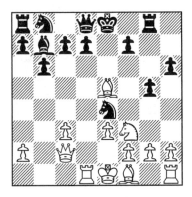

14...d6

Black plans to complete his development with ...♘d7, followed by a queen move and long castling. If he can do this without making any other concessions that he will simply be winning, and thus the onus is on White to prove something over the intervening few moves.

At this point my opponent tried 15 ♖d4?!, but the threat to the knight proved to be illusory after 15...♘d7! 16 ♗b5 (16 ♖xe4 ♗xe4 17 ♕xe4 ♘xe5 does not give White enough for the ex-

change) 16...f5! 17 h4?! (17 ♗xd6? ♘xd6 18 ♘e5 ♖g7 19 ♖xd6 cxd6 20 ♘xd7 a6! 21 ♕xf5 axb5 22 ♕f8+ ♔xd7 23 ♕xg7+ ♕e7 is given by Emms; 17 ♕b3 would have been the best try, but Black is still doing very well after 17...♔e7! 18 ♗g3 ♘dc5) 17...♕e7 18 hxg5 hxg5 19 ♗c4 and now the most efficient route to victory would have been 19...dxe5 (the game continuation of 19...♖f8 also proved sufficient for a full point) 20 ♗xg8 (no better is 20 ♖xd7 ♔xd7) 20...exd4 with a clear extra piece.

White does better with:

15 ♗d3

This appears relatively best. I believe that Black can still maintain an advantage, but he will need to show great precision. My analysis proceeds as follows:

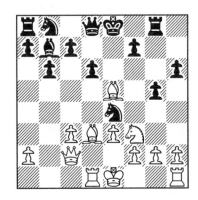

15...♘c5!

15...f5 looks natural, but it looks to me like White can gain an edge with 16 ♗c4 ♖g6 17 h4 ♕e7 18 h5 ♖e6 19 ♗xe6 ♕xe6 20 ♗h2 c5 21 ♘d2, or 20...♕c4 21 ♘d4 ♕xc3+ 22 ♕xc3 ♘xc3 23 ♖c1.

16 ♗h7

16 ♗b5+ ♘bd7 17 ♕h7 ♖g6 18 ♗d4

♔e7! 19 h4 ♘f8 20 ♕h8 ♘fe6 is clearly better for Black. The text appears more troublesome, but the second player can remain on top helped by the resolute...

16...♕e7! 17 ♗xg8 ♗e4!

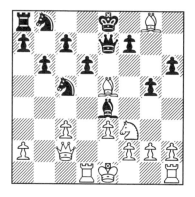

The point is that Black will pick up both bishops, leading to a position in which his two minor pieces will be stronger than the enemy rook.

18 ♗xd6 cxd6 19 ♕e2 ♔f8 20 ♗xf7 ♕xf7!

20...♔xf7 is less good, as it allows White to mobilize his knight with 21 ♘d4 when Black cannot take on g2 due to ♕h5+ and ♘f5.

21 ♖xd6 ♔e7!

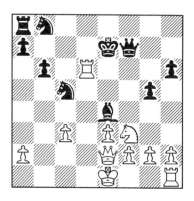

22 ♖d1

22 ♖xh6? leaves the white king too exposed after 22...♕g7! 23 ♖h5 ♕xc3+ 24 ♕d2 ♕a1+ 25 ♕d1 ♘d3+ 26 ♔e2 ♕xa2+ 27 ♘d2 ♘b2! 28 ♕a1 (or 28 ♕c1 ♕a6+) 28...♗d3+ 29 ♔f3 ♕f7+ 30 ♔g4 ♗f5+ and wins.

22...♘bd7

Despite a nominal material handicap, Black is clearly on top. His pawn structure is better and his minor pieces coordinate in perfect harmony. The game might continue 23 0-0 ♕h5 24 ♘d4 ♕xe2 25 ♘xe2 ♗d3 26 ♖fe1 ♗c4 with excellent chances in the ending.

A2) 11 ♘d2

This is a more patient and sounder approach than 11 d5!?.

11...f5!

Not only supporting the knight, but also threatening to trap the white bishop in some variations.

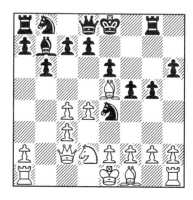

12 ♘xe4

12 f3 will usually lead to the same position after 12...♘xd2 13 ♕xd2 d6 14 ♗g3 ♘d7 15 e3. Instead 15 e4?! is an unsound sacrifice and following the

natural 15...fxe4 16 fxe4 ♗xe4 17 ♗d3 White is worse after both 17...♗xd3 18 ♕xd3 ♕f6 19 ♕e4 0-0-0 20 ♕a8+ ♘b8 21 ♕xa7 ♖gf8 and 17...♗b7 18 0-0 ♕e7 19 ♖ae1 0-0-0 20 ♕e2 ♖de8.

12...♗xe4

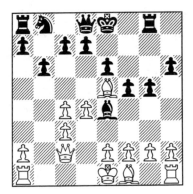

13 ♕d2

13 ♕b3 d6 14 f3 ♗b7 15 ♗g3 f4 is given by Emms, while 15...♘d7 should also be fine for Black.

13...d6 14 ♗g3 ♗b7

14...f4 does not win a piece due to 15 f3.

15 e3 ♘d7 16 f3 ♕e7

16...♕f6 or 16...h5!? are also fine.

We have been following the game T.Hillarp Persson-J.Rowson, York 1999. Although the position might reasonably be evaluated as equal, I would certainly take Black if given the choice. His pawn structure is superior, his bishop is beautifully placed on the long diagonal and his knight is likely to prove at least as useful as either of the enemy bishops in what is presently a closed position. Furthermore, the white king will have trouble finding a truly safe haven. The further course of the game illustrates these points very well:

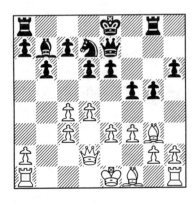

17 a4 h5 18 h3

White does not really have time for 18 a5 on account of 18...h4 19 ♗f2 h3.

18...h4 19 ♗f2 a5!

In these doubled c-pawn positions, the advance of the white a-pawn should almost always be blocked in this way. Not only does this thwart any of White's attacking ambitions, it also fixes the a4-pawn as a long-term target for the endgame. In the present game White was clearly having difficulty finding a useful plan, and Black soon took over the initiative. Play continued 20 ♗d3 0-0-0 21 0-0-0 ♔b8 22 ♔b2 ♔a7 23 ♕c2 ♗a6 24 ♖de1 c5 25 ♕b3 ♖c8 26 ♗e2 (26 e4 could have been strongly met by 26...fxe4 27 fxe4 cxd4! 28 cxd4 e5) 26...♖c7 27 ♖d1 cxd4 28 cxd4 ♖gc8 29 ♖c1 d5 and Black won easily.

B) 9 ♘d2!?

White challenges the opponent's most influential piece while making way for his f-pawn to advance.

9...♗xc3

The c3-knight is no longer pinned,

so Black should not delay its exchange.

10 bxc3 f5

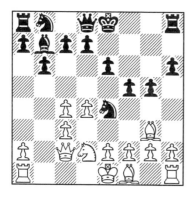

10...♘xg3 is a playable alternative, but in this instance I prefer to retain the knight for another move or two.

11 e3

This is not the only playable move, the latter of the following two warranting particular attention:

a) 11 ♗e5 ♖g8 transposes to Line A2.

b) 11 f3 forces Black to decide which enemy piece to exchange for the knight on e4.

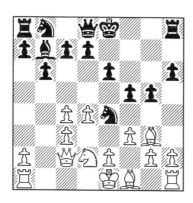

There are arguments either way and both options are playable, so I will al-

low the reader to make up his own mind:

b1) In M.Turner-A.Greet, British League 2008, I dug myself into trouble with 11...♘xd2 12 ♕xd2 d6?! (this is too slow) 13 h4 ♖g8 14 hxg5 hxg5 15 c5! dxc5 16 e3 with excellent compensation for White, but 12...♘c6 would have been better when the evaluation is not so clear.

b2) The safer course is probably 11...♘xg3 12 hxg3 ♘c6 when P.Cech-J.Parker, Berlin 1998, continued 13 g4 ♕f6 14 gxf5 ♕xf5 15 ♕xf5 exf5 16 e4 fxe4 17 fxe4 0-0-0 18 ♗d3 d6 with approximate equality.

11...h5!?

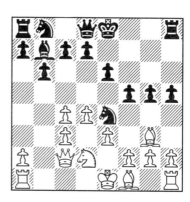

This rarely played move can lead to great complications. Instead 11...d6 leads to a position usually reached via 9 e3 d6 10 ♘d2 ♗xc3 11 bxc3 f5. This has been played many times and is acceptable enough for Black, although in the following chapter I recommend 11...♘xd2 which I slightly prefer.

12 ♘xe4!

This looks like the most dangerous continuation as far as I have been able to discern. I was only able to find a single game in which 11...h5!? was played. M.Narciso-A.Moen, correspondence 2003, continued 12 f3 ♘xg3 13 hxg3 ♕f6 with chances for both sides. It also looks quite tempting for Black to try 12...♘xd2 13 ♕xd2 h4 14 ♗f2 (14 ♗e5 ♖g8 15 h3 d6 16 ♗h2 ♘d7 is comfortable for Black) 14...d6, or even the more ambitious 14...h3!? with a promising position in both cases.

12...♗xe4 13 ♕d1

It is useful for White to eye the h5-pawn. The alternative 13 ♕d2 h4 14 ♗e5 ♖g8 (14...0-0!?) 15 f3 ♗b7 16 h3 d6 17 ♗h2 ♘d7 is quite comfortable for Black.

13...h4 14 ♗e5 ♖h6!

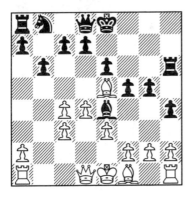

I think that this is slightly more accurate than 14...♖h7 as in some variations it can be useful to control certain squares along the third rank.

15 f3

This looks like the most natural, although 15 d5!? is an aggressive move which seeks to open the centre through a mutual trapping of bishops! Black must proceed with caution, but it

seems that he can obtain an acceptable game after 15...d6 16 f3 ♗xf3! (16...dxe5 17 fxe4 is a bit more dangerous) 17 ♕xf3 dxe5 18 dxe6 e4 19 ♕xf5 ♕f6 (this is where the rook's positioning on h6 comes in especially handy!) 20 ♕xf6 (20 ♕xe4? ♕xc3+ 21 ♔e2 ♕b2+ 22 ♔f3 ♕xa1 23 ♕xa8 ♕d1+ 24 ♔e4 ♖xe6+ 25 ♔f5 ♕d7! should win) 20...♖xf6.

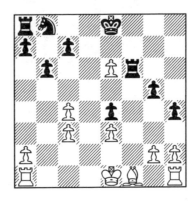

The position is roughly balanced: for example, 21 ♖d1 ♖xe6 22 ♖d5 ♘d7! (22...♘a6 allows the slightly irritating 23 ♗e2!, preventing castling) 23 ♖xg5 0-0-0 24 ♖h5 ♘c5 25 ♖xh4 ♘d3+ 26 ♗xd3 ♖xd3, regaining the material to reach what looks like an approximately equal ending.

15...♗b7 16 h3 ♘c6

16...d6 17 ♗h2 ♘d7 18 ♗d3 ♕f6 19 0-0 0-0-0 is also possible.

17 ♗h2 ♕e7 18 ♗d3 0-0-0

Black has completed his development and the stage is set for a complex struggle. This whole variation requires practical testing, but at this stage I offer the following sample continuations as possibilities of how play might now proceed:

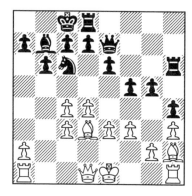

a) 19 0-0 can be met by 19...♖g8!, preparing ...g4 with an attack.

b) 19 ♕e2 ♖f8 intends ...e5 with decent play in the centre.

c) 19 c5!? is the most overtly aggressive option at White's disposal. Black should not shy away from complications and 19...e5! looks like the right response when the opponent's uncastled king could easily become a telling factor. Now 20 cxb6 axb6 21 ♗xf5 exd4 22 e4 dxc3 23 0-0 ♕c5+ 24 ♔h1 ♘d4 25 ♗g1 ♖d6 looks messy but at least okay

for Black, while 20 d5 runs into 20...e4! 21 fxe4 (21 dxc6 dxc6!) 21...♕xc5 and now 22 exf5 ♕xd5, 22 dxc6 dxc6! and 22 0-0 ♘e7 all turn out nicely for Black.

Summary

The 5 ♗g5 system abounds in strategic and tactical complexity, and I hope that the present chapter has served as a useful introduction while also whetting the reader's appetite for the following chapter in which we will consider the main lines. Of the two main options, 9 ♗e5!? contains plenty of pitfalls, but is objectively not too dangerous against accurate defence. By contrast I believe that 9 ♘d2!? is a genuinely good move, which may not be objectively any worse than the main line with 9 e3. My recommended antidote involving 11...h5!? is somewhat experimental, but as far as I can see it appears to stand up to scrutiny, although a few more practical tests will doubtless help us to formulate a more accurate evaluation.

Chapter Seven

The Main Line Hybrid: 5 ♗g5 with 9 e3

1 d4 ♘f6 2 c4 e6 3 ♘f3 b6 4 ♘c3 ♗b4 5 ♗g5 h6 6 ♗h4 g5 7 ♗g3 ♘e4 8 ♕c2 ♗b7 9 e3

We have now arrived at a position more usually reached via 5 ♗g5 ♗b7 6 e3 h6 7 ♗h4 g5 8 ♗g3 ♘e4 9 ♕c2. To recap the explanation presented at the start of the previous chapter, the main point of our move order is to bypass the dangerous possibility of 6 ♘d2!?, while as a secondary boon we have avoided having to spend time analysing such possibilities as the interesting pawn sacrifice 9 ♘d2!?.

9...d6

A lot of games have proceeded with the move order 9...♗xc3+ 10 bxc3 d6, but in my view this is slightly less accurate as White is presented with a few additional options such as the pawn sacrifice 11 c5!?, which was once played by Boris Spassky. This is only rarely seen and may not be terribly dangerous, but why allow it at all when there are no drawbacks to the recommended move order? (It is important to note that 10 ♕a4+?! can be conveniently met by 10...♘c6!.)

After 9...d6 Black intends to complete the mobilization of his forces according to the following standard recipe: over the next few moves he will exchange bishop for knight on c3 to double White's pawns, combined with ...♘d7 and ...♕e7/f6 and long castling. He may, if time permits, also consider advancing his h-pawn in order to menace the bishop on g3. The most critical – not to mention captivatingly interesting! – lines are those in which White attempts to seize the initiative in the centre before Black has completed the proposed development. There are two moves that deserve our attention, and it is surely no accident that both of them seek to challenge Black's most actively-placed piece:

A: 10 ♘d2

B: 10 ♗d3

The latter is by far the more popular, but the former is by no means bad. I will briefly mention that 10 0-0-0 has been played a few times, but after 10...♗xc3 11 bxc3 ♘d7 the white king can hardly feel confident about its long-term safety.

A) 10 ♘d2

This is a respectable alternative to the main line, although the drawback is that it is somewhat more restrained and Black will rarely come under any direct pressure in the opening phase. Still, there are plenty of players who prefer a more patient approach with which they may attempt to outplay the opponent in a more subtle way.

10...♗xc3 11 bxc3

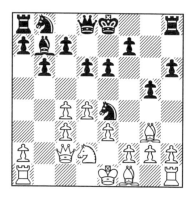

Now Black faces an important decision. It is clear that the knight on e4 will soon leave the board, but which enemy piece should it eliminate?

11...♘xd2!?

Several strong players, including Michael Adams, have preferred 11...♘xg3 12 hxg3 ♘d7. I do not claim that the text is objectively superior,

although I will admit to a slight subjective preference. There are two main arguments in favour of removing White's knight:

1) If Black exchanges on g3 then the recapture hxg3 will open the h-file for White's rook.

2) The position is relatively closed and there is no reason to believe that a bishop will necessarily prove more useful than a knight. Furthermore, the positioning of the bishop on g3 could see this piece become a target for a kingside pawn advance.

12 ♕xd2 ♘d7 13 f3

According to my database nothing else is ever played. The text blunts the a8-h1 diagonal while perhaps preparing to advance the e-pawn.

13...f5!?

13...♕e7 has been more common, but I don't think it does any harm to discourage e3-e4 while gaining some space and preparing to develop the queen on the more active f6-square.

14 ♗d3 ♕f6

I was able to find seven practical examples from this position. Not a huge sample size I realize, but a score of five wins and two draws should provide a reasonable hint of optimism about Black's chances. White has tried several different moves here, but we have reached a stage of the game in which concrete variations are of little importance next to positional understanding. Therefore I will limit the remainder of this section to a couple of examples to illustrate how Black should handle the position:

First, the game K.Stalne-K.Holmberg, Vaxjo 1992, continued 15 ♕c2 0-0-0 16 e4 (in most games White seems to play this move sooner or later) 16...f4 17 ♗f2 c5! 18 a4 a5 19 ♖b1 e5! 20 ♗e2 ♔c7.

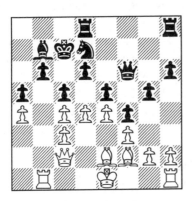

The diagram illustrates a model set-up which anybody who plays this system ought to know. Black has established a rock-solid wall of pawns on the dark squares – perfect positional strategy having exchanged the dark-squared bishop. White's bishops are doing nothing and most importantly, it is almost impossible for the first player to improve his position in any meaningful way. Even if he were in a position to triple on the b-file, Black could easily defend with ...♗a6 and ...♖b8. Meanwhile Black can look to exploit his space advantage on the kingside. This game was eventually drawn.

Our second example, M.Tunur-C.Genc, Kusadasi 2004, continued 15 0-0?! (with hindsight this may be viewed as a questionable decision) 15...0-0-0 (Black can also try the immediate 15...h5!?, as in I.Eismont-K.Thiel, Essen 2004) 16 a4 a5! 17 e4 f4 18 ♗f2 ♕e7 19 ♕e2 e5! 20 ♖fb1 c5! 21 ♖a2 ♗a6 22 ♖ab2 ♔c7.

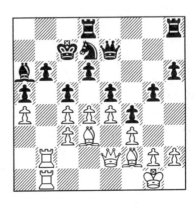

Here we see another perfect example of Black's ideal formation. When you see positions like this you can appreciate why, back on move 11, I had no qualms about allowing White to keep his bishop-pair! Once again Black is in absolutely no danger whatsoever on the queenside, while his forthcoming kingside offensive is very real and indeed proved too much for White to handle in the game. In fact, the placement of the white monarch is really the only significant difference between the last two diagrams, and probably goes a long way towards explaining the contrasting final results.

Incidentally, it is amusing to observe how computers evaluate this position. Most engines initially rate White's position as winning, perhaps because the rooks look impressive on the b-file. Of course, any knowledgeable human player would quickly see that White's queenside offensive is going nowhere. After around five minutes of thinking time *Fritz 9*'s enthusiasm has been tempered, although it still rates White's position as '+0.64'! The further course of the game, while not flawless, provides a more realistic reflection of the position. The remaining moves were 23 ♖b3 h5 24 ♕e1 ♕e6 25 ♔h1 g4 26 ♗f1 ♖dg8 27 ♖3b2 ♖g7 28 ♗e2 ♖hg8 29 ♗g1 gxf3 30 ♗xf3 ♗xc4 31 ♗xh5 ♖h7 32 ♗f3 ♖gh8 33 d5 ♕g6 34 h3 ♖xh3+ 35 gxh3 ♖xh3+ 36 ♗h2 ♖xf3 37 ♖g2 ♕h7 38 ♕d2 ♕xe4 0-1.

10 ♘d2 remains a playable move, but based on the evidence presented here I see no reason for Black to fear it.

B) 10 ♗d3 ♗xc3+ 11 bxc3 f5

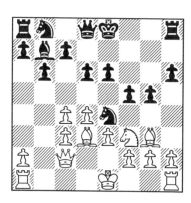

In many games Black has preferred 11...♘xg3, but while there is no doubting the viability of this approach, to me it has always seemed like a concession. I love my knight on e4 and have no wish to exchange it for such a feeble bishop.

At this point White has tried practically every remotely sensible-looking move. Most can be met by common sense replies, so I will concentrate on the following three which require a certain amount of independent thinking:

B1: 12 c5!?
B2: 12 0-0
B3: 12 d5!

The last is by far the most important, having been seen in many more games than all the other moves put together.

B1) 12 c5!?

This pawn sacrifice has only been played in eight games from a total of more than 350 on my database, but if White is looking for something obscure he could do a lot worse. I spent some time analysing the two pawn captures, both of which have been tested in practice, but was less than enthused by the resulting positions. Black should probably be okay, but in both cases White's compensation seemed quite real. Considering how rarely this line is encountered, it seems like rather a wasted effort to navigate such complications. Besides it turns out that Black has quite an attractive option in...

12...♘d7!? 13 cxd6 cxd6

As far as I am aware this position has only been reached in a single game, J.Kretz-T.Hellborg, Sweden 2000. Having managed to exchange his weakest pawn is, of course, a significant achievement for White, but the downside is that he has lost some time as well as opened the c-file for the enemy rook. Furthermore, Black now has at his disposal the rather awkward plan of ...h5, threatening to trap the bishop and effectively forcing White to move his h-pawn, thereby facilitating a favourable exchange on g3. A couple of possible continuations:

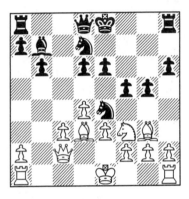

a) In the aforementioned game White continued with the inaccurate 14 ♗xe4?! ♗xe4 15 ♕b3 ♕e7 16 ♕b4, which was powerfully met by 16...e5! 17 dxe5 ♗xf3 18 exd6, at which point 18...♕e6! 19 gxf3 f4 would have won a piece for insufficient compensation.

b) It would have been better for White to delay the exchange of minor pieces with 14 ♕b3 ♕e7 15 ♕b4, although even now Black has a full share of the chances after 15...♘df6 intending ...h5, or even 15...e5!?: for example, 16 dxe5 dxe5 17 ♕xe7+ ♔xe7 18 ♗xe4 (18 ♗xe5 ♘xe5 19 ♘xe5 ♔f6 is favourable for Black) 18...♗xe4 19 ♘xe5 f4! 20 ♘xd7 (worse is 20 exf4?! ♘xe5 21 fxe5 ♗xg2 22 ♖g1 ♗f3) 20...fxg3 21 f3 ♔xd7 22 fxe4 gxh2 23 ♖xh2 ♔e6. This ending should be a draw, but Black's superior pawn structure leads me to prefer his position slightly.

B2) 12 0-0

This has been the second most popular move in the position. It is playable enough, but certainly should not worry us.

12...♘d7

Black should complete development before embarking on aggressive kingside measures. The tempting-looking 12...h5?! was shown to be premature after 13 h4! in the game W.Fronda-R.Liebich, correspondence 1986, which continued 13...♘d7 (after 13...♘xg3 14 fxg3 gxh4 15 gxh4 ♗xf3 16 ♖xf3 ♕xh4 17 ♗xf5! White has a winning attack) 14 ♗xe4! ♗xe4 15 ♕e2 when it was Black who turned out to be vulnerable on the kingside.

13 ♘d2

13 d5!? ♘dc5 14 ♘d4 reaches Line B312, below.

13...♘xd2

13...♘df6 is also possible, but the text looks to me like a slightly more accurate choice.

14 ♕xd2 h5!

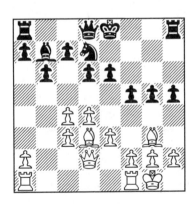

In this position Black can afford to delay castling in order to gain some kingside territory. We have been following the game F.Salzgeber-A.Huss, Neuchâtel 1996, which continued 15 f3 h4 16 ♗e1 and now it seems to me that the most logical way for Black to complete development would be 16...♕f6 17 e4 0-0-0 with a full share of the chances.

B3) 12 d5!

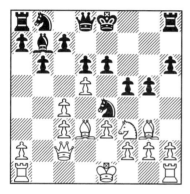

This resolute move represents the acid test of Black's chosen system. White endeavours to smash open the centre while creating threats against e4, e6 and indirectly f5; the latter two of which can be placed under further pressure by a subsequent ♘f3-d4. The main drawback to the text is that White presents the enemy knights with the use of the wonderful c5-square while seriously compromising his queenside structure.

At this crucial juncture I have chosen to recommend what might be described as a modern refinement of an established continuation. Based on the evidence of some high-level practical testing along with a bit of my own

analysis, I feel confident that the following move will come to be regarded as a reliable antidote to White's chosen system.

12...♘a6!

According to my database, the text was first played in a relatively obscure correspondence game in 1987, but in more recent times it has been used by Evgeny Alekseev, a young Russian Grandmaster whose rating broke the 2700 barrier last year, as well as Michael Adams. In order to appreciate the true value of this move we should first conduct a brief review of Black's other principal options:

a) Perhaps the most obvious response involves accepting the offer with 12...exd5 13 cxd5 ♗xd5. The problem with this is that following 14 ♘d4 White will regain the pawn by force: 14...♕f6 15 f3 ♘xg3 16 hxg3 ♘d7 17 ♗xf5 with some advantage. He has exchanged one of the problem c-pawns and obtained a strong outpost on f5. Furthermore, Black's king may have trouble finding a safe home.

b) 12...♘c5 has been played in several games, but I do not trust it. Even without the benefit of precise analysis, I cannot help but feel suspicious about moving an actively-placed knight for the third time, especially to a square within easy reach of its undeveloped brother on b8. Analysis seems to reinforce this feeling: 13 h4!? (13 ♘d4 has scored less highly, but may also give White chances for an advantage) 13...g4 14 ♘d4 ♕f6 15 0-0 ♘ba6 (15...♘xd3 16 ♕xd3 e5 has been known to be bad for

Black ever since the famous game A.Miles-A.Beliavsky, Tilburg 1986, which continued 17 ♘xf5 ♗c8 18 f4!!) 16 ♘xe6 ♘xe6 17 ♗xf5 ♘g7 18 ♗g6+ ♔d7 19 f3 ♖af8! 20 fxg4 ♕e7 21 e4. This position appears rather messy, but after analysing it in some detail I have come to the conclusion that White's chances are superior.

c) 12...♘d7 is the other main line and has been my own choice whenever I have reached this position (it was only when researching this work that I became aware of the clearly superior 12...♘a6!). For a long time I intended to recommend this move, but a thorough analysis of certain key variations revealed some difficulties for Black. The critical path continues 13 ♗xe4 (13 ♘d4 ♘c5 reaches Line B31, below) 13...fxe4 14 ♕xe4 ♕f6 15 0-0! 0-0-0 16 ♕xe6 ♕xe6 17 dxe6 ♘c5 18 ♘d4, reaching the following semi-endgame.

Black certainly has positional compensation for his material deficit, but after analysing this position in some detail I came to the conclusion that White should be able to maintain an edge.

So why is 12...♘a6! so great?

Just as with 12...♘d7, the main purpose of 12...♘a6 is to occupy the marvellous c5-square. In some cases direct transpositions can occur (most notably in Line B31). However, there are also some key differences. *The main point of the recommended move is that in certain variations involving dxe6 the knight will not be en prise on d7*, which can provide Black with certain additional opportunities. Full details can be found in Line B322, below.

We will analyse two major variations:

B31: 13 ♘d4
B32: 13 ♗xe4

B31) 13 ♘d4

This is certainly a natural-looking choice; the knight occupies an excellent central square, as facilitated by White's previous move, while augmenting the pressure against e6 and f5. The first player also gains the option of evicting the troublesome knight with f2-f3.

13...♘ac5

This is clearly the right move; the knight occupies its dream square while reinforcing its team-mates on e4 and e6. For the sake of historical accuracy, I will briefly note that almost all of the following game references reached this position via a move order involving 12...♘d7.

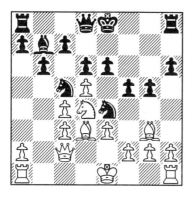

With my apologies, we arrive at a final division:

B311: 14 dxe6
B312: 14 0-0

Several other moves have been tried, but with limited success. In general, if White does not play accurately then he will more than likely end up with the inferior chances on account of his grotesque queenside structure. The following examples show how easy it can be for him to slip into a bad position:

a) After 14 ♘xe6?! ♘xe6 15 dxe6 (15 ♗xe4 fxe4 16 ♕xe4 ♕e7 reaches variation 'c', below) 15...♕f6 16 f3 ♘xg3 17 hxg3 0-0 Black's vastly superior pawn structure gave him excellent long-term chances and eventual victory in V.Ravikumar-J.Pokojowczyk, Esbjerg 1981.

b) 14 ♗e2 intends to check on h5, although it is questionable whether this small achievement is really worth the time. In any case, Black is more than okay after 14...♕f6 (14...0-0!? looks fine,

and 14...h5!? is also interesting) 15 ♗h5+ (T.Paehtz-G.Moehring, Berlin 1987) 15...♔d7 16 f3 ♘xg3 17 hxg3 ♖af8 when I prefer his position, since the black king can easily drop back to c8 if necessary while the white queenside structure is in ruins.

c) 14 ♗xe4 fxe4 15 ♘xe6 ♘xe6 16 ♕xe4 (16 dxe6 will leave Black with a clearly better structure after he regains the pawn) 16...♕e7 17 ♕g6+ ♔d8!? (also fine is 17...♕f7 18 ♕xf7+ ♔xf7 19 dxe6+ ♔xe6 when Black will regain the pawn with a better endgame; the text is even more ambitious) 18 dxe6 ♗xg2 19 ♖g1 ♗h3 20 ♕e4 ♖b8 was seen in G.Battaglini-A.Kosten, St Affrique 2003.

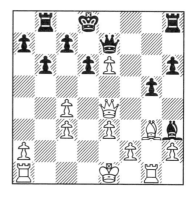

Black has the better chances, since he will soon regain the e6-pawn and it will only be a matter of time before c4 goes the same way. The only slight problem is the position of the king on d8, but White will have a hard time opening any central files and in any case his own king is far from ideally placed.

d) 14 f3?! ♘xd3+! (both sides should

keep in mind this exchange, followed by retreating the other knight to c5; in general it is more desirable for Black to remove his opponent's light-squared bishop than the one on g3, as this will accentuate the power of his own cleric on b7 as well as avoiding opening the h-file) 15 ♕xd3 ♘c5 16 ♕c2 ♕f6 reaches a comfortable position for Black, as illustrated by the following examples:

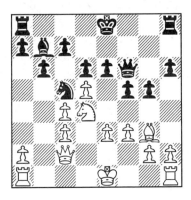

d1) 17 dxe6?! 0-0 (17...f4!?) 18 0-0 ♘xe6 leaves White without any compensation for his dire structure.

d2) In E.Porper-E.Hermansson, Holbaek 2001, White tried 17 ♘b5 to which the simplest answer would have been 17...♖h7! when Black can expel the knight with ...a6 at a moment of his choosing. Meanwhile White faces problems in the centre. His d5-pawn is insufficiently defended, while in certain variations Black may simply block the position with ...e5, obtaining a solid positional advantage. Exchanging on e6 would hardly be an attractive proposition, so I would evaluate this position as difficult for White.

d3) In P.Horvath-A.Saric, Oberwart

2004 the continuation was 17 0-0-0 f4!? (17...0-0-0 was also perfectly fine) 18 ♗f2 (18 exf4 gxf4 19 ♘xe6!? ♘xe6 20 ♖he1 ♗c8 21 ♗f2 – 21 ♖xe6+? loses to 21...♗xe6 22 ♖e1 0-0 23 ♖xe6 ♕f5 – 21...0-0 22 dxe6 ♗xe6 is unclear; Black has the far superior structure, but his king would prefer to be on the opposite flank) 18...fxe3 19 ♗xe3 0-0-0 20 ♘c6 ♗xc6 21 dxc6 ♘a6 when the c6-pawn was looking like more of a weakness than a strength.

d4) 17 0-0 0-0 18 e4 (18 dxe6?! ♘xe6 takes play back into 'd1') 18...♗a6 19 ♖fe1 f4 20 ♗f2 ♗xc4 21 ♘xe6 ♘xe6 22 dxe6 ♕xe6 left White a pawn down for nothing in H.Vinagre-P.Buj, correspondence 1980.

B311) 14 dxe6 ♕f6

A couple of other moves have been tried, but the text is clearly best. The queen takes up an active post from where she supports the f-pawn, prepares to recapture on e6 and makes way for her husband to occupy a bombproof queenside refuge.

15 f3

This is clearly the only challenging move, and nothing else has ever been played to my knowledge.

15...f4!

This is the key move for Black and one which has, to my mind at least, put the entire 13 ♘d4 variation out of business as a serious try for White.

16 exf4

16 ♗xe4!? should also work out well for Black after careful play beginning 16...♗xe4 17 fxe4 fxg3 18 hxg3.

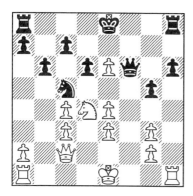

In this position White has achieved the remarkable feat of isolating all eight of his pawns! This should be more than enough to offset Black's temporary two-pawn deficit, although a certain amount of accuracy is still required. Play continues 18...0-0-0 19 ♖f1 ♛g6 (or 19...♛e5) and now:

a) In P.Horvath-D.Berczes, Budapest 2003, the continuation was 20 0-0-0 ♖de8 21 e5 ♛xc2+ 22 ♔xc2 dxe5 23 ♘b3 (23 ♘c6 is also insufficient for equality after 23...♖xe6 24 ♘xa7+ ♔b7 25 ♘b5 ♖e7 when White's extra pawn is outweighed by his chronic structural defects) 23...♘e4 24 c5 (or 24 ♘d2 ♘xd2 25 ♖xd2 ♖xe6) 24...♖xe6 25 ♖f7 ♖d8 (also strong was 25...♖f6 26 ♖dd7 ♖xf7 27 ♖xf7 ♘xg3) 26 ♖xd8+ ♔xd8 27 ♔d3 ♘xg3 28 ♔c4, and now 28...♖e7 would have left White struggling.

b) 20 e7! ♖de8 21 ♘f5 is a better attempt. The e7-pawn is annoying, and the knight on f5 not only supports it but also does a fine job of masking many of White's other weaknesses. This is the kind of position in which Black should not hesitate to offer an

exchange with 21...♛e6!.

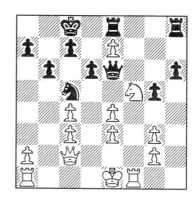

After analysing this variation the previous year, I had an opportunity to test my idea in M.Peek-A.Greet, Hastings 2006/7. That continued 22 0-0-0 (also possible is 22 ♘g7 ♛xe7 23 ♘xe8 ♖xe8 24 0-0-0 ♘xe4 when, in view of White's numerous pawn weaknesses and exposed king, I would evaluate Black's chances as superior), at which point I forgot my analysis, which had determined 22...♛xc4! to be the best move here.

However, even after the somewhat inferior 22...♛xe4 I still obtained the advantage and I think it is worth following the game for a few more moves. The problem for White is that, while there is no disputing the strength of his knight on f5 and pawn on e7, it is difficult for him to involve his other pieces in the game. On the other hand, Black can calmly gobble a pawn or two before eventually arranging to win the e-pawn, which can be achieved by a knight manoeuvre to c6 or perhaps even an exchange sacrifice if necessary. The game continued 23 ♛xe4 ♘xe4 24

♔c2 ♘c5 25 g4 (no better is 25 e4 ♘d7
26 ♖h1 ♘e5) 25...♘d7! 26 ♖d4 ♘e5 27
♖h1 ♔d7 28 ♖e4.

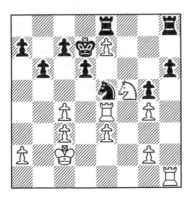

This turned out to be the pivotal
moment of the game. Had my brain
been functioning properly I would
have played the straightforward
28...♘c6, followed by capturing on e7
with excellent winning chances. Instead, thinking that I had all the time in
the world, I opted for the stupid move
28...♖h7?, allowing my opponent the
opportunity for the splendid double
sacrifice 29 c5! bxc5 30 ♖xe5! dxe5 31
♔d3 when White had full compensation and was able to draw without difficulty.

16...♘xd3+!

It is important for Black to be accurate with his move order. In
A.Shneider-J.Parker, Port Erin 1999, the
continuation was 16...gxf4 17 ♗f2
♘xd3+ 18 ♕xd3 ♘c5 19 ♕e2 0-0-0,
reaching the main line below. However
White could also have considered de-
viating with 17 ♗xe4!? ♗xe4 18 fxe4
fxg3 19 hxg3 (19 ♖f1!?) 19...0-0-0 20
0-0-0 ♖de8. The evaluation of this posi-

tion is far from clear, but as the main
line is so obviously favourable for
Black, it seems pointless to allow this
possibility.

17 ♕xd3 ♘c5! 18 ♕e2

18 ♕d2 would be pointless as after
18...gxf4 the recapture 19 ♗xf4?? is impossible thanks to the tactical trick
19...♕xf4! 20 ♕xf4 ♘d3+, regaining the
queen and keeping an extra piece.

18...gxf4 19 ♗f2

We have now transposed back to
Shneider-Parker.

19...0-0-0

In D.Komarov-R.Mantovani, Reggio
Emilia 1996, Black tried 19...♖g8!? and
soon obtained a winning position after
20 g4? (20 0-0 is better when 20...0-0-0
will probably transpose to the note to
White's 20th, below) 20...fxg3 21 hxg3
0-0-0 22 0-0-0 ♖de8 23 ♖he1, and now
23...♘xe6! (in the game Black faltered
with 23...h5? and eventually lost) 24
♘xe6 ♗xf3 wins material for Black as
pointed out by Hansen.

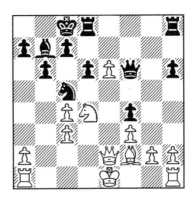

Let's take stock of the position.
White has an extra pawn, but it is hard
to think of any other positive things to

say about his situation. Besides, it is not hard to see that Black will soon restore material equality by capturing the e-pawn. After that he will enjoy a substantial and long-lasting advantage based on his vastly superior pawn structure and considerably safer king.

20 0-0-0

It is hard to determine the flank on which White should castle. The queenside is hardly likely to provide a safe refuge in the long term, but 20 0-0 places the king on an open file to which all three of Black's heavy pieces enjoy immediate access. A couple of practical examples after 20...♖de8:

a) 21 ♖fe1 ♖hg8 22 a4 ♕g6 23 ♕f1 was S.Simenon-E.Van Seben, correspondence 2002, and now 23...a5! looks simplest, stopping White's attack dead in its tracks while conveniently fixing yet another weak pawn for the endgame.

b) 21 ♖ae1 ♖hg8 22 ♔h1 was S.Ghane Gardeh-A.Bagheri, Teheran 1998, and now 22...♔b8! looks best, intending to regain the pawn with ...♘xe6 and meeting ♘xe6 with ...♗c8, just as in Shneider-Parker below.

20...♖de8 21 ♖he1 ♖hg8 22 ♗g1

22 g4? fxg3 23 hxg3 transposes to Komarov-Mantovani at which point Black could have won with 23...♘xe6! 24 ♘xe6 ♗xf3, as mentioned above in the note to Black's 19th.

22...♔b8!

Securing the king's position while preparing ...♗c8.

23 ♖d2 ♘xe6!

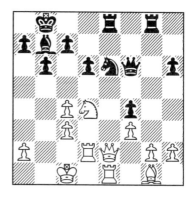

We have been following the game A.Shneider-J.Parker, Port Erin 1999 (with the exception of an important refinement in move order – see the note to Black's 16th, above). Black has conveniently regained his pawn by utilizing a simple tactical trick and now enjoys a sizeable advantage based on the factors outlined previously.

24 ♔b2

After 24 ♘xe6 ♕xc3+ 25 ♔b1 (25 ♖c2 ♕a3+ 26 ♔b1 loses to 26...♖xg2! 27 ♕xg2 ♕b4+ – Emms) 25...♗c8 26 ♗d4 ♕a5 Black will regain the piece while keeping an extra pawn as well as a positional advantage. I leave you with the remaining moves of the game; it is worth playing through them for the skilful way in which the highly talented English Grandmaster converts his advantage:

24...♘g7 25 ♕d1 ♕f7 26 ♖xe8+ ♖xe8 27 ♕a4 ♘e6 28 ♘c6+ ♗xc6 29 ♕xc6 ♘d8 30 ♕d5 ♕g6 31 ♖c2 ♖e5 32 ♕d2 ♕f7 33 ♕d3 ♘c6 34 ♖e2 ♕e6 35 ♖xe5 ♘xe5 36 ♕e4 ♘xc4+ 37 ♔c1 ♘e5 38 ♔b1 ♕g8 39 ♕e2 ♕d5 40 ♗d4 ♘c4 41 ♕e8+ ♔b7 42 ♔c2 ♕g5 43 ♕e2 d5 44

♔c1 c5 45 ♗g1 ♕e5 46 ♕xe5 ♘xe5 47 ♔d2 ♔c6 48 ♗f2 a5 49 ♗h4 b5 50 ♗f6 ♔d6 51 ♗g7 h5 52 ♗f8+ ♔c6 53 ♗h6 ♘g6 54 g3 fxg3 55 hxg3 h4 56 gxh4 ♘xh4 57 f4 ♘f5 58 ♗g5 b4 59 a4 bxa3 60 ♔c2 d4 61 cxd4 cxd4 62 ♗f6 a4 63 ♗d8 ♔b5 64 ♗f6 ♔c4 65 ♗d8 d3+ 0-1

B312) 14 0-0

This is somewhat less confrontational than 14 f3, but we have already seen that the direct approach brings problems only to White. In my view his objectively best approach may well be to play less ambitiously and aim for equality, which he can probably achieve with the aid of the text.

14...♕f6

According to my database only this move has been tested, although creative souls may wish to investigate the playable-looking 14...0-0!?.

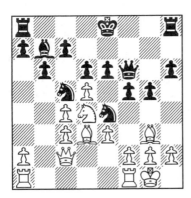

15 f3

This move was championed in the 1980s by a Russian IM (who has since become a GM) named Nukhim Rashkovsky who, according to my database, employed it four times against strong opposition, drawing on each occasion. 15 ♗xe4 fxe4 has also been seen a few times when White has tried:

a) 16 ♘xe6 ♘xe6 17 ♕a4+ (17 ♕xe4 0-0-0 18 ♕xe6+ ♕xe6 19 dxe6 ♖de8 is just a shade better for Black, who will regain both pawns while keeping a better structure) 17...♔e7 18 dxe6 ♕xe6 19 c5!? bxc5 20 ♖ab1 ♗d5 21 ♖fd1 was I.Shtern-J.Howell, San Antonio 1997, and here Black could have questioned the soundness of his opponent's pawn sacrifice with 21...♖hc8!.

b) 16 f4!? (V.Dinstuhl-M.Hackel, German League 2000) should probably be met by 16...exd5 17 cxd5 ♗xd5 18 fxg5 ♕g7!?. The position is messy but I feel that Black's chances are not worse. Instead 18...♕xg5 19 ♖f5 ♕g8 20 ♗h4 may also be playable, but for the moment Black is unable to castle and on balance I prefer the alternative.

c) In A.Peter-Z.Korpics, Hungary 2002, the continuation was 16 f3 exd5 17 fxe4 ♕g6 18 exd5 ♕xc2 19 ♘xc2 ♗a6, leading to a position that will be discussed shortly, in which Black enjoyed good compensation. The trouble with this move order is that White may have a promising deviation in 17 cxd5! when I have not been able to find a fully satisfactory continuation for Black. Instead I propose 16...♕g6!? when White may try:

c1) 17 ♖ad1 0-0-0 18 ♘b3 (18 fxe4 ♗a6 looks fine for Black, but not 18...exd5? 19 ♘f5!) can be met by the pawn sacrifice 18...♘d7!?, intending 19 ♕xe4 ♕xe4 20 fxe4 ♖de8 when I am sceptical as to whether White's extra, doubled pawn can fully compensate for his structural defects.

c2) 17 fxe4 exd5 18 exd5 ♕xc2 transposes back to the game Peter-Korpics, which continued 19 ♘xc2 ♗a6 20 ♘a3 and now 20...♘e4! (instead of the game's decentralizing 20...♘a4?! 21 e4!) should give Black full compensation.

15...♘xg3 16 hxg3 0-0

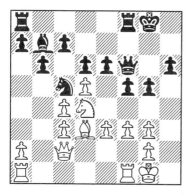

We have already seen that Black would ideally prefer to castle on the opposite flank, but the text is necessary due to the need to cover the sensitive f5-pawn, as well as to keep c8 free for the bishop, which may be required to regain a pawn on e6. Fortunately for us, it turns out that the king is not in any real danger.

17 dxe6

In N.Rashkovsky-K.Lerner, Kuibyshev 1986, White tried 17 f4?!, but soon stood worse after 17...♖ae8 (17...g4!? also looks very reasonable, as shown by 18 e4 ♘xd3 19 ♕xd3 fxe4 20 ♕xe4 exd5 21 cxd5 ♖ae8 22 ♘e6 ♗xd5 23 ♕xd5 ♕xe6 with an extra pawn) 18 g4 (18 ♖ac1 ♘xd3 19 ♕xd3 exd5 20 fxg5

♕xg5 21 ♘xf5 ♖e5 22 g4 ♗c8 is given as equal by Lerner, but 22...♗a6! is practically winning for Black), at which point the straightforward 18...fxg4 looks better for Black.

17...♘xd3 18 ♕xd3

At this point Black can choose between two fully satisfactory options:

a) If Black is looking for a simple route to a level game, then the easiest choice would be to follow the game N.Rashkovsky-K.Lerner, Kiev 1986, which continued 18...c5!? 19 ♘b5 (19 e7 ♖f7 20 ♘b5 ♖xe7 21 ♕xd6 ♖e6 22 ♕c7 ♖e7 23 ♕d6 is equal according to Rashkovsky) 19...♖ad8 20 ♘c7 ♕e7 21 ♘d5 ♕xe6 22 ♖fe1 ♗xd5 23 cxd5 ♕f6 24 a4 ½-½.

b) 18...♗c8 leads to more complex play, but again should probably peter out to equality after accurate play from both sides. The game N.Rashkovsky-A.Kremenietsky, Moscow 1984, continued 19 g4 (19 f4 ♗xe6 20 g4 reaches the same position) 19...♗xe6 20 f4 (White is doing his best to open some kingside files, but the black defences are strong enough) 20...♕f7!

21 ♕c2 (21 ♕d2?! fxg4 22 fxg5 ♕g6 achieves nothing for White, while 21 ♘xe6 ♕xe6 22 fxg5 fxg4 23 ♖f6 ♖xf6 24 gxf6 ♔h8! should also be fine for Black, as shown by 25 ♖f1 ♖f8 26 ♕d4 ♖f7 when the f-pawn seems like more of a weakness than a strength, although the game should probably end in a draw anyway) 21...c5 22 ♘xf5 ♗xf5 23 gxf5 ♕xf5 24 e4 ♕e6 (or 24...♕g4 25 ♖ad1 ♖xf4 26 e5 ♔g7 27 exd6 ♖xf1+ 28 ♖xf1 ♖d8 29 ♕d3 and a draw was agreed in N.Rashkovsky-Y.Razuvaev, USSR 1984) 25 fxg5 hxg5 26 ♕d2 ♕e7 27 ♕d5+ ♔g7 28 ♖ae1 ½-½.

Summing up, 13 ♘d4 may be good enough for equality, but as far as I can see White is unlikely to achieve anything more against accurate play. Indeed, if he plays too ambitiously as in Line B311 then he will more than likely end up worse.

B32) 13 ♗xe4

Just as after 12...♘d7, this must be the critical continuation. However, this is where the advantage of the knight's placement on a6 will be most evident.

13...fxe4 14 ♕xe4

Instead V.Akobian-J.Friedel, Chicago 2008, saw 14 ♘d2!? ♕e7 15 ♕xe4 (after 15 ♘xe4 exd5 16 cxd5 ♗xd5 17 ♕a4+ ♔f7 Black has the initiative) 15...♘c5 16 ♕g6+ with a choice for Black:

a) The game continued 16...♔d7 17 dxe6+ ♘xe6 18 f3 ♖ag8 19 ♕c2 h5 20 0-0-0 and ½-½; Black certainly enjoys full compensation here.

b) Before this game I had also ana-

lysed 16...♕f7 17 ♕xf7+ ♔xf7, which seems to bring Black an excellent game: for example, 18 e4 exd5 19 exd5 (19 cxd5 ♖ae8 regains the pawn with at least equality) 19...♖ae8+ 20 ♔d1 ♗c8! (Black can regain the pawn with 20...♘e4, but I prefer the text which places the emphasis on speedy development).

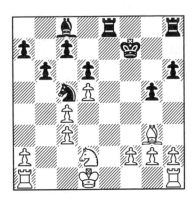

The plan is ...♗f5 when the tremendous activity of the black pieces, not to mention White's rotten queenside structure, will more than make up for the small material deficit. If White tries to improve his position with 21 ♘f1?!, the bishop can change direction with 21...♗a6! 22 ♘e3 (22 ♘d2 ♘e4 is also better for Black) 22...♖xe3! 23 fxe3 ♗xc4 with fantastic compensation for the exchange.

14...♕f6

With this multipurpose move Black defends e6 and attacks c3, while maintaining the option of castling on either side.

White had better castle here, although plenty of players have been unable to resist the temptation of grabbing a second pawn immediately. We will examine both options, beginning with the weaker one:

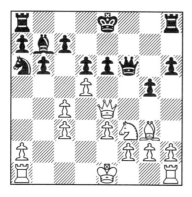

B321: 15 ♕xe6+?!

B322: 15 0-0

B321) 15 ♕xe6+?! ♕xe6 16 dxe6 ♘c5

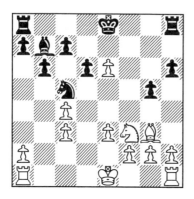

Once again we arrive at a position which has almost always been reached via the more common 12...♘d7. Black's chances in the diagram position should be evaluated as at least equal. He will soon regain the pawn on e6 and may also be able to damage White's kingside structure with a timely ....♗xf3.

Please note, however, that the immediate 16...♗xf3? would be premature as after 17 gxf3 White will be able to eradicate his weakness with a quick f3-f4.

17 h4

This is probably White's best, although a few others have been tried:

a) 17 ♘d4? has been played in a couple of games, but Black simply wins material after 17...♗xg2 18 ♖g1 ♗h3.

b) 17 0-0-0 (A.Moen-S.Brynell, Stockholm 2004) should be met simply by 17...♘xe6 (or 17...♗xf3!? 18 gxf3 ♘xe6 19 h4 ♔d7) 18 ♘e1 ♔e7 when I prefer Black.

c) 17 0-0 has been the most popular move, but it seems to me that the position after 17...♗xf3 18 gxf3 ♘xe6 is just better for Black. Computers do not see it yet, but White is in a serious positional bind. Apart from his chronic weaknesses on the queenside, his bishop is effectively trapped on the opposite flank. Black can improve his position by doubling rooks on the f-file, or perhaps swing across to the queenside via f5. There is also a simple plan of walking the king up to c5 and gobbling the weak queenside pawns. White's only good plan is to open the h-file in order to activate his rooks, but I do not believe this to be sufficient for equality.

The game C.Gokhale-R.Zhumabaev, Hyderabad 2006, continued 19 h4 (other moves have been tried, but, as noted before, White's only really useful plan is to open the h-file) 19...♔d7 (perhaps Black could consider 19...0-0!?

which slightly misplaces the king, but enables him to double on the f-file one move faster) 20 hxg5 hxg5 21 ♔g2 ♔c6 22 ♖h1 ♔c5 23 ♖xh8 ♖xh8 24 f4 gxf4 25 exf4 ♔xc4 26 ♖e1 ♘c5 27 ♖e7 when White's active pieces and powerful f-pawn proved sufficient for a draw. Instead I would recommend 21...♖h7!? 22 ♖h1 ♖f7!, intending ...♖af8 and later ...♔c6-c5, with advantage to Black.

17...♔e7!

The greedy 17...g4 18 ♘d4 ♗xg2 19 ♖g1 ♗f3 20 h5! gave Black some problems in P.Lamby-A.Litwak, Belgian League 2007. For the moment his top priority should be to improve the quality of his pieces rather than pick up pawns.

18 ♖h2

18 hxg5 hxg5 19 ♔e2 ♘e4 is equal according to Yrjölä and Tella, but I would take Black any day.

18...♘e4! 19 ♘d4

We have been following the game G.Tallaksen-T.Sammalvuo, Gausdal 2004, in which Black played 19...♗a6 and went on to win, but only after some mistakes from his opponent.

Instead I would recommend the straightforward 19...♘xg3 (19...♖ag8!? is another interesting move) 20 fxg3 g4 when Black seems fine.

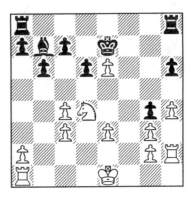

White's structure is in ruins and as long as the second player proceeds carefully, it seems likely that he will be able to pick up the e6-pawn before too long. It is worth noting briefly that after 21 h5 ♖hf8 22 ♖h4?! ♗xg2 White cannot take on g4 due to the check on f1.

B322) 15 0-0

This is much more challenging than the immediate capture. In Line B321 we saw that the black king was ideally placed in the centre following the exchange of queens. In the present position it is doubtful that Black has anything better than castling, and in some cases the delayed capture can provide White with a favourable version of the same endgame thanks to the inferior position of the enemy monarch. I should briefly mention that 15...♘c5 has occasionally been played, but after 16 ♕d4 White stands slightly better, especially when we consider that 16...e5? is refuted by 17 &xe5!.

I have stated firmly that Black should castle on the present turn, but the question of which flank should be preferred remains open to debate. My own view is that the soundest and most reliable option is 15...0-0-0, but depending on one's playing style, the opponent, tournament tactics and so on, short castling can also be considered. I will provide coverage of both continuations so that the reader may make up his own mind:

B3221: 15...0-0-0
B3222: 15...0-0!?

B3221) 15...0-0-0

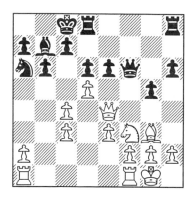

When I wrote the first draft of the present chapter in March 2008, I stated that I could see nothing wrong with this move which was then untested. Just one month later I was pleased to learn that the same conclusion had been reached by Britain's number one. The game Wang Yue-M.Adams, Baku 2008, continued:

16 &xe6+

If White refrains from this capture with, for example, 16 a4?!, there could follow 16...&c5 17 &d4 (or 17 &g4 Idg8 threatening ...b5) 17...&f5 when the threat of ...&b3 will give Black time to seal up the queenside with ...a5!.

16...&xe6 17 dxe6

It is at this moment that we see the real benefit of Black's 12th.

17...&xf3!

It is precisely this possibility which sets the modern 12...&a6! apart from the older 12...&d7. With the knight on d7 Black would have no time to exchange on f3 and would be forced to play 17...&c5, as mentioned back in the notes to Black's 12th. The idea is so simple that, in retrospect, it is quite perplexing to imagine how it took such a long time for players to notice that the knight could just as easily come to c5 via a6 as from d7 while providing this additional benefit.

18 gxf3 &c5

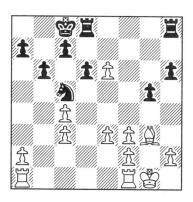

This position should be compared with note 'c' to White's 17th move in Line B321 on page 105, which I evaluated as favouring Black. The only significant difference is that in the present position Black has expended a tempo castling on the queenside, whereas in the aforementioned variation his monarch was ideally placed in the centre. This slight concession should balance out the chances, as evidenced by the following analysis.

19 h4

This is by no means the only sensible move:

a) The subsequent game E.Porper-J.Friedel, Edmonton 2008, continued 19 e4 ♘xe6 20 ♖fe1, at which point 20...♖hf8 looks like the most logical continuation. The intention is to meet 21 ♖e3 with 21...♔b7 followed by marching up and capturing on c4, or 21 ♔g2 ♘f4+ 22 ♗xf4 ♖xf4 with good play for Black in both cases.

b) 19 f4!? does not appear to have been tested, but it is eminently logical for White to exchange off one of his pawn weaknesses, so we should definitely consider the consequences of this move. Best play looks like 19...gxf4 20 ♗xf4 (20 exf4 ♘xe6 21 ♖ae1 ♔d7 leaves the f4-pawn looking vulnerable after a subsequent ...♖df8) 20...♘xe6 21 ♗g3 h5! 22 f3 (other possibilities include 22 h4 ♖dg8 intending ...♖g4, and 22 f4 ♘c5! with good compensation) 22...♖dg8 23 ♔h1 h4 24 ♗e1 h3!? 25 ♗g3 ♖h5, intending ...♖c5 followed by regaining the pawn with a good game.

19...♘xe6 20 hxg5 hxg5 21 ♔g2 ♖hf8 22 ♖ad1 ♖f5 23 ♖d5 ♖df8 24 ♖xf5 ♖xf5

The endgame can be summarized as follows.

White's queenside structure is in ruins and the black rook is ideally placed to start reaping the harvest after ...♖c5 or ...♖a5. The only problem is that as soon as the rook leaves the f-file, White will begin marching his f-pawn which can easily be supported by his rook, bishop and king. Taking everything into consideration, a draw seems like the most natural result, although if I was forced to choose a side I would marginally favour Black.

25 ♖h1 ♔d7

Perhaps Black's last realistic chance to play for a win would have been 25...♖a5!?, hoping to grab one queenside pawn before rushing the rook back to the kingside. The following sample continuation is of course far from forced, but I hope that it will provide a reasonable starting point for players who may be interested in exploring the possibilities available to both sides in the positions involving a mutual promotion race: 26 f4 gxf4 27 exf4 ♘c5! 28 f5 ♘d7 29 ♖h5 ♖xa2 30 ♗h4 ♖a5 31 ♗e7 ♖c5 32 ♖h8+ ♔b7 33 f6 ♖f5 34 ♖h6 a5 35 ♔g3 a4 36 f4 ♖c5 37 ♖h1 (37 f7

♖f5 38 f8♕ ♘xf8 39 ♔g4 ♖f7 40 ♗xf8 ♖xf8 41 f5 ♔c6 does not help White) 37...♖xc4 38 f7 ♖xc3+ 39 ♔g4 a3 40 f8♕ ♘xf8 41 ♗xf8 b5 42 f5 b4 43 f6 b3 44 f7 b2 45 ♗g7 ♖c4+ 46 ♔g5 ♖c1 47 f8♕ b1♕ 48 ♕f3+ c6 49 ♕f7+ ♔a6 50 ♕c4+! ♖xc4 51 ♖xb1 and White should probably be able to hold the draw anyway.

26 ♖h7+ ♔e8 27 f4 gxf4 28 exf4 ♖c5 29 ♔f3 ♘f8

Adams decides to settle for half a point. It is unlikely that he could have achieved anything more with 29...♖xc4 30 ♔g4 b5 31 ♔f5 ♘f8 32 ♖g7 ♖xc3 33 ♗h4 as White's passed f-pawn and active pieces will always provide enough counterplay, while Black's queenside pawns are still a long way from promoting.

30 ♖g7 ♘e6 31 ♖h7 ♘f8 32 ♖g7 ♘e6 33 ♖h7 ½-½

At the time of writing this game represents the latest word in this variation. Given the ease with which Black held the draw, it would seem fair to conclude that the ball is firmly in White's court at present.

As far as I can see, the variation 15...0-0-0 looks absolutely fine for Black from a theoretical standpoint. At the same time, there will doubtless be some players who, for whatever reason, would prefer to keep a bit more complexity in the position. If the reader falls into that category then he should definitely investigate the following option.

B3222) 15...0-0!?

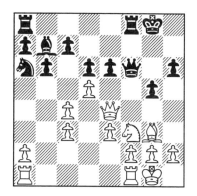

It is not too often that one sees the black monarch settling on this side of the board, but in this position the text brings a major benefit in that the added pressure against f3 discourages White from exchanging queens (see the next note for full details). At the same time Black retains his positional trumps (better structure, more active pieces) and can perhaps aim for a kingside attack later.

16 ♖ad1

This was Wang Yue's choice against Alekseev in the China-Russia match from August 2007. The much older game C.Clemens-Hofmann, correspondence 1988, continued 16 ♕xe6+?! ♕xe6 17 dxe6, and now Black should have played 17...♗xf3 18 gxf3 ♖xf3 (or even 18...♘c5!?) with slightly the better chances as the e6-pawn will soon fall, while c4 remains chronically weak. This may be compared with the positions resulting from Line B321, except that here Black has managed to bank the f3-pawn.

16...♘c5 17 ♕g4 ♗c8 18 dxe6

The computer suggests 18 ♕d4!?,

the point of which is to meet 18...e5 (if Black is worried about the following then 18...♕g6 is a perfectly valid alternative) with 19 ♘xe5!? dxe5 20 ♗xe5, although it is hard to say whether this is really a good idea for White.

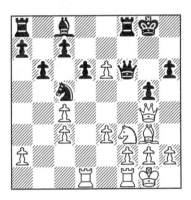

18...♗xe6

18...♕xe6!? was also playable, as Black's compensation would remain quite real in the ending, although I suppose this might be viewed as being inconsistent with his 15th move.

19 ♕d4

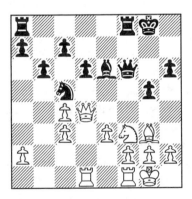

19...♕g6!

The queen is ideally placed here, monitoring several important light

squares while managing to combine both defensive and potentially attacking duties on the kingside.

20 ♘d2 ♖ae8

Also possible was the immediate 20...h5!?, intending 21 h4 gxh4 22 ♕xh4 ♖ae8 with ongoing compensation.

21 e4 h5 22 h3

22...♗c8

It also looks tempting to press on with the attack by means of 22...h4!? 23 ♗h2 g4 24 hxg4 ♗xg4 25 f3 ♗h3: for example, 26 ♖f2 (26 ♕f2 ♘xe4 27 ♘xe4 ♖xe4 regains the pawn, while if Black wishes to keep things more complex he can also try 26...♖e7) 26...♖f7 27 ♔h1 ♗c8 with complex play.

23 f3 ♗b7

Once again a more aggressive approach with 23...g4!? looks possible. In any case the position is quite delicately balanced and both sides have their trumps. Needless to say, with so few practical tests there is considerable scope for new ideas. To conclude, I would say that if Black is looking to outplay his opponent in a tense middlegame rather than simplify into a safe but relatively drawish ending, then the present variation with 15...0-0!? is an ideal choice.

Finally, I leave you with the remainder of Wang Yue-E.Alekseev, Nizhniy Novgorod 2007, which eventually ended in a hard fought draw after numerous adventures:

24 ♔h2 ♖f7 25 ♕e3 ♖g7 26 ♖de1 g4 27 fxg4 hxg4 28 h4 ♘xe4 29 ♖f4 ♖ge7 30 ♕d3 ♔h7 31 ♘xe4 ♖xe4 32 ♖exe4 ♖xe4 33 ♖f8 ♕e6 34 c5 bxc5 35 ♕b1 ♔g7 36 ♖f2 ♗d5 37 ♕b8 ♕e7 38 ♖f5 ♗f7 39 ♖g5+ ♔h7 40 ♕b1 ♗g6 41 c4 ♕f6 42 ♕b7 ♖e7 43 ♖xg4 ♕e6 44 ♖f4 ♗e4 45 ♕b2 ♖f7 46 ♕e2 ♖xf4 47 ♗xf4 ♔g8 48 ♕b2 ♔h7 49 ♕e2 ♔g8 50 ♗g3 ♔f7 51 ♕b2 ♔e8 52 ♕g7 ♕f7 53 ♕g4 ♗f5 54 ♕f3 ♔d7 55 h5 ♗e6 56 ♕xf7+ ♗xf7 57 h6 ♗g8 58 ♗e1 ♔e6 59 ♔g3 ♔f6 60 ♗a5 ½-½

Summary

We have reached the end of a long and – from my perspective at least – fascinating investigation into the 5 ♗g5 variation, which I personally consider to be one of the most enchanting in all chess theory. Whenever I play through the sharp main lines beginning with 12 d5 it always feels as though the position is balanced on a knife-edge. Both sides can claim certain advantages, but my overall impression of dynamic equilibrium seems to be borne out by both analysis and tournament practice.

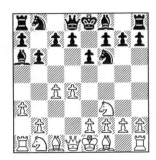

Chapter Eight

The Petrosian Variation: 4 a3 ♗a6

1 d4 ♘f6 2 c4 e6 3 ♘f3 b6 4 a3

White invests a tempo in order to prepare ♘c3 without allowing the pinning ...♗b4. This popular variation is named after Tigran Petrosian who employed it in numerous games during the 1960s, although the first example on the database dates back to 1923. Garry Kasparov went on to mould 4 a3 into a potent weapon, blazing a trail of devastation with it throughout the 1980s and suffering only a single defeat, against – of all people – Petrosian! Since then several leading Grandmasters have incorporated 4 a3 into their repertoires and it remains one of White's principal choices to the present day.

4...♗a6!?

Just as against 4 g3, this immediate attack against c4 has become one of the established main lines and is regularly used by many of the world's elite. At first glance the development of the bishop on a6 may appear peculiar and,

indeed, it is only after a detailed exploration of the various continuations that one can truly appreciate its justification.

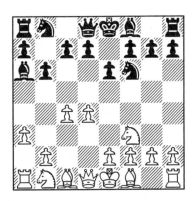

Beginning with the most rudimentary observations, we can see that Black has developed his bishop to a square from which it threatens to capture the c4-pawn. 'So what?', I hear you ask. Indeed, this may almost seem like a beginner's move until one realizes the seemingly improbable truth that *every single one of White's plausible responses is*

accompanied by a specific drawback of some kind, viz:

1) 5 b3 contributes very little towards White's development.

2) 5 e3 hampers the queen's bishop and after the standard response 5...d5 White may experience some awkward tension along the a6-f1 diagonal.

3) 5 ♘bd2 places the knight on a sub-optimal square instead of its ideal home of c3 which was, after all, the main purpose behind White's 4th.

4) Queen moves such as 5 ♕c2 (which is the main line) reduce White's control over the d5-square, thereby facilitating the thematic ...c5, undermining the centre. This is such a useful option for Black that he will quite happily lose a tempo after 5 ♕c2 with 5...♗b7! in order to prepare ...c5 on the following move. (We should briefly note that the immediate 5...c5 could still be met by 6 d5! when 6...exd5 7 cxd5 ♘xd5?? loses material after 8 ♕e4+.)

It goes without saying that, notwithstanding the above points, White has developed plenty of methods with which to fight for the advantage and we will deal with each of the above lines in detail over the course of the present and the following three chapters.

Before moving on I will briefly mention that the natural 4...♗b7 is an equally valid option, when White continues with his planned 5 ♘c3. This position can also be reached via the move order 4 ♘c3 ♗b7 (in Chapters 3-7 I instead advocate 4...♗b4) 5 a3. From

White's point of view, it seems that the choice of move order hinges on whether he is more comfortable allowing 4 ♘c3 ♗b4 or 4 a3 ♗a6.

In the present chapter we will consider after 4...♗a6 the relatively minor options:

A: 5 b3
B: 5 ♕a4
C: 5 ♕b3
D: 5 ♘bd2

The somewhat more common 5 e3 can be found in the following chapter, while the main line of 5 ♕c2 will form the subject of Chapters 10 and 11.

Others are barely worth our consideration:

a) 5 ♘e5?! (A.Mikhalevski-L.Yudasin, Beersheba 1992) 5...d6 6 ♕a4+ c6! 7 ♘f3 (7 ♘xc6 ♕d7 8 d5 ♗b7 9 ♘c3 ♘xc6 10 dxc6 ♗xc6 11 ♕c2 ♗e7 gives Black a useful lead in development) 7...♗e7 8 ♘c3 0-0 is very comfortable for Black.

b) 5 ♘fd2?! fails to impress after 5...c5 6 e4 cxd4 7 e5 ♘g8 and now 8 b4 ♗b7 9 ♗b2 a5 was better for Black in C.Lopes-R.Rodrigues, Olival Basto 2000, while after 8 ♘e4 ♘c6 9 ♗f4 f5 (9...♕b8 is also strong) 10 ♘g5 (L.Josteinsson-J.Hjartarson, Reykjavik 1986), the simplest continuation is probably 10...♘xe5 followed by 11 ♗xe5 ♕xg5 or 11 ♘xh7 ♘f7 12 ♘xf8 ♔xf8 and then ...e5.

A) 5 b3 d5 6 cxd5

White's best may well be 6 e3 c5,

leading to Chapter Nine. Others can be met by common sense replies: for example, 6 g3?! dxc4 7 ♗g2 cxb3 8 ♘e5 ♘d5 9 ♕xb3 c6 and White had less than sufficient compensation in J.Davis-W.Forster, Nelson 2007.

6...exd5

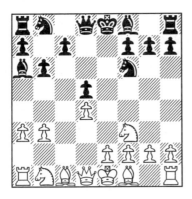

7 g3

This central pawn configuration, following a pawn exchange on d5, can be reached in several different variations of the Queen's Indian. As a general rule of thumb, I prefer to avoid it unless White has been forced to make a concession of sorts, such as prematurely blocking his queen's bishop with an early e3 or developing his queen's knight on the inferior d2-square. In the present position White has the potential to develop both of these pieces on ideal squares. However, the downside is that he has wasted valuable time on two queenside pawn moves of questionable usefulness; a significant concession which enables Black to count on a good position.

7...♗d6 8 ♗g2 0-0 9 0-0

We have been following the game

J.Leal-S.Gashimov, Cannes 1997. Although Black can play just about any sensible-looking move here, my personal favourite is...

9...♘e4!?

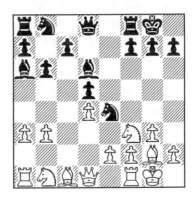

Black intends to follow up with ...c6, ...♘d7 and ...♕e7, perhaps combined with ...f5!?, leading to quite a favourable version of a Stonewall Dutch. It is always worth remembering the idea of transposing from one opening system to another when the circumstances are favourable.

B) 5 ♕a4

This is less challenging than the analogous 4 g3 ♗a6 5 ♕a4 which we will examine later in Chapter 13. Most of the time the point of the 4 g3 system is to play in the centre and on the queenside, whereas with 4 a3 White is angling more towards the centre and the kingside. Thus it stands to reason that in the present scenario the queen is more likely to be misplaced on a4.

5...c5!

Black follows the standard recipe for the Queen's Indian, striking at the centre now that d4-d5 is no longer a threat.

6 ♗f4

White develops his bishop actively, perhaps hoping for some sort of plan involving ♘c3-b5 and a quick raid on c7 or d6. Despite the earlier comment, a few players have experimented with the ambitious 6 d5!?. The idea actually works quite well after 6...exd5 7 cxd5 ♗b7 8 e4 ♕e7 9 ♗d3 ♗xd5 10 0-0 ♗c6 (E.Liebowitz-C.Van Buskirk, Berkeley 1981) when both 11 ♕d1 and 11 ♕b3 would have given White promising compensation. Instead Black should prefer 6...♗b7!, delaying the central capture so that the white queen will not be able to support e2-e4.

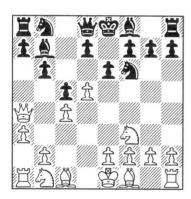

Now 7 e4 would lose the e-pawn for very little compensation and 7 dxe6 fxe6 would be an admission of theoretical defeat by White. The only consistent move is the pawn sacrifice 7 ♘c3 when V.Cmilyte-R.Tuominen, Copenhagen 2007, continued 7...exd5 8 cxd5 ♘xd5 9 ♘xd5 ♗xd5 10 e4. Compared with the 6...exd5 variation noted above, this position without knights is

a whole lot more palatable for Black, who could have gained the upper hand with 10...♗c6 11 ♕c2 ♗e7 or 11 ♗b5 ♗d6!?.

Finally before moving on, we should note that 6 ♘c3 is completely harmless after 6...cxd4 7 ♘xd4 ♗c5.

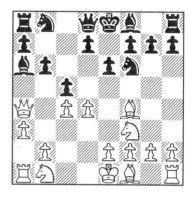

6...♗b7!

This is the most flexible move, improving the bishop before committing any of the other pieces. Black is not really losing a tempo as the white queen is probably worse placed on a4 than d1.

7 ♘c3

No-one seems to have tried 7 e3 when 7...♗xf3 8 gxf3 cxd4 9 exd4 ♘c6 may well be good. Perhaps White can consider sacrificing a pawn with 10 ♘c3!? ♘xd4 11 0-0-0 ♘c6 12 ♗d3 to obtain a lead in development, although the black position is extremely solid. Of course, a normal move like 7...cxd4 is perfectly fine as well.

7...♗e7 8 ♖d1

This looks like the best attempt to justify the fact that the queen has moved. In O.Ivanenko-N.Zdebskaja,

Odessa 2007, White preferred 8 e3 0-0 9 ♗e2 and now 9...cxd4 would have brought Black an easy game after both 10 exd4 d5 and 10 ♘xd4 d6.

8...cxd4 9 ♖xd4

9 ♘xd4 was S.Kishkurno-Erkens, correspondence 1999, and now 9...a6! looks best, covering b5 with a very pleasant Hedgehog position.

9...0-0 10 e3

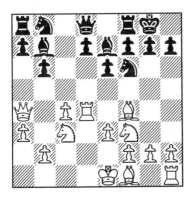

White has played the opening quite creatively, but the game I.Ganbaatar-B.Maksimovic, Cheliabinsk 1990, still saw Black seize the initiative after 10...♗xf3! 11 gxf3 e5! 12 ♗xe5 ♘c6 13 ♗xf6 ♗xf6 14 ♖g4 ♗xc3+ 15 bxc3 ♕f6 16 ♕c2 ♘e5 17 ♖f4 ♕e7 when his lead in development and superior structure gave him more than enough for the pawn.

C) 5 ♕b3 d5

I consider this to be the most straightforward method of equalizing, although just about any sensible move should lead to a playable position.

6 cxd5

6 e3 can hardly threaten Black and

after 6...♗e7 7 ♘c3 0-0 8 ♗d2 c5 9 ♖d1 ♘c6 10 ♕a4 (C.Crouch-M.Prettejohn, Brighton 1984), 10...♕c8! would have maintained the bishop's active position while conveniently sidestepping the X-ray vision of the rook on d1.

6...♕xd5

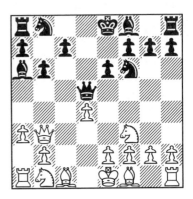

Preferable to 6...exd5 7 ♗g5 ♗e7 8 ♘c3, which gives White chances to be better after 8...c6 9 ♗xf6 ♗xf6 10 e4! ♗xf1 11 ♖xf1 dxe4 12 ♘xe4 0-0 13 0-0-0! ♘d7 14 ♘e5 ♗xe5 15 dxe5. The text makes more sense to me; Black maintains a more fluid pawn structure while forcing the white queen to move for a second time.

7 ♕c2

7 ♕xd5 is not dangerous after 7...exd5 (7...♘xd5?! 8 e4 ♗xf1 9 ♖xf1 ♘f6 10 ♘c3 is pleasant for White) and now:

a) 8 ♘c3 c6 9 ♗g5 (9 ♗f4 ♘bd7 reaches variation 'b') 9...♘bd7 10 ♗xf6?! ♘xf6 11 ♘e5 ♖c8 12 g3 ♗d6 13 ♗h3 ♖c7 14 f4 was Y.Zimmerman-L.Chachere, Budapest 1993, and now the simple 14...0-0 looks good for Black.

b) 8 ♗f4 c6 9 ♘c3 ♘bd7 10 h3 ♗e7

11 g4 0-0 12 e3 ♗xf1 13 ♔xf1 ♖fc8 was about equal in I.Sokolov-M.Adams, Groningen 1995.

7...c5 8 ♘c3 ♕d7!

This is the most accurate retreat. Instead 8...♕b7?! 9 dxc5 bxc5 (9...♗xc5?? drops a piece to 10 b4!) 10 g3! ♘bd7 11 ♗g2 ♖d8 12 0-0 gave White a pleasant advantage in M.Dzevlan-J.Hultin, Sweden 2001.

9 dxc5

9 ♘e5? loses a pawn for insufficient compensation after 9...♕xd4 10 e3 ♕xe5 11 ♗xa6 ♘xa6 12 ♕a4+ ♘d7 13 ♕xa6 ♗e7 (Karpov).

The only serious alternative is 9 ♗g5 when play continues 9...cxd4 10 ♗xf6!? (10 ♘e5? is not good after 10...♕c7! 11 ♕a4+ ♘fd7! 12 ♘xd7 ♕xd7 13 ♕xd7+ ♘xd7 when White has nothing to show for his pawn) 10...gxf6 11 ♖d1 ♘c6.

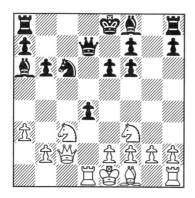

The game P.Wells-I.Farago, Budapest 1994, continued 12 ♕a4 ♗b7 13 e3 whereupon 13...0-0-0! would have been quite promising. White might also consider 12 e3!? ♗xf1 13 ♔xf1, although Black should not have too much to

worry about after 13...♗g7 followed by either 14 ♘xd4 ♘xd4 15 ♖xd4 ♕c6 or 14 exd4 ♘e7 15 d5!? exd5 16 ♘xd5 ♘xd5 17 ♕e4+ ♕e6 18 ♕xd5 0-0.

Before we move on it is worth mentioning that the actual move order of the aforementioned Wells-Farago game was 10 ♖d1 ♘c6 11 ♗xf6 gxf6. This sequence is arguably less accurate, as Black is presented with the additional option of 10...d3!? 11 exd3 ♗e7 12 d4 ♗xf1 13 ♔xf1 0-0, which led to an interesting IQP position in which White's king was less than ideally placed in I.Farago-G.Kovacs, Szentgotthard 2001.

9...♗xc5

We now follow the game A.Shirov-A.Karpov, Linares 1993:

10 g3 ♗b7 11 ♗g2 ♘c6!?

11...0-0 12 0-0 ♖c8 13 ♖d1 ♕e8 is equal (Karpov), but Black may be able to play for more.

12 0-0 ♘d4! 13 ♘xd4 ♗xg2 14 ♔xg2

14 ♘xe6? leads to disaster for White after 14...♗xf1 15 ♘xg7+ ♔f8 16 ♗h6 ♗xf2+!, as pointed out by Karpov.

14...♗xd4 15 ♖d1 ♕c6+ 16 f3

From this point the players soon

swapped down to an equal endgame after 16...♗e5 17 ♗g5 0-0 18 ♖ac1 ♖ad8 19 ♖xd8 ♖xd8 20 ♘e4 ♕xc2 21 ♖xc2 ♘d5! 22 ♘f2! f6 23 ♗d2, followed by a handshake four moves later.

Instead Black might have played more ambitiously with 16...♗xc3!?. In his notes Karpov gives the continuation 17 ♗d2 (after 17 ♕xc3?! ♕xc3 18 bxc3 ♖c8 Black's superior structure gives him a clear edge), followed by 17...♘d5?! 18 e4 ♕b5 19 exd5 ♕e2+ 20 ♔h3! or 17...♖c8 18 ♗xc3 ♘d5 19 ♖d3. Black may, however, be able to do slightly better with the immediate 17...0-0. Now 18 ♕xc3 ♕b5! could prove annoying and 18 ♗xc3 ♘d5 may also give Black a minuscule edge in an admittedly drawish position.

D) 5 ♘bd2 d5!

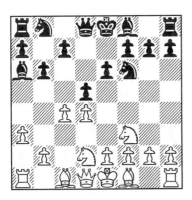

I believe this to be Black's most convenient answer, preventing e2-e4 and challenging White to justify the misplacement of his knight on d2. 5...c5 is playable, although White may now be able to put the wayward steed to some use with 6 e4! cxd4 7 e5. 5...♗b7

is the other main move, after which 6 ♕c2 d5 reaches the main line below, but 6 e3 is possible too.

6 ♕c2

6 e3 is sensible when 6...♗e7 takes play into our next chapter. Meanwhile 6 cxd5 exd5 7 ♘e5 has been played in a few games, although it is hard to believe that it can really be any good. P.Delooz-D.Grafen, Internet 2004, continued 7...♗d6 8 ♘df3 ♘e4!? (avoiding the 8...0-0 9 ♗g5 pin) 9 ♘d2 ♘xd2 10 ♗xd2, and here the simple 10...0-0 looks better for Black who enjoys a promising lead in development.

6...♗b7!

Others allow 7 e4!, which would give White some chances to be better.

7 cxd5

The alternative is 7 e3 when I rather like the look of 7...c5!?.

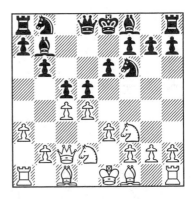

Surprisingly this move does not appear to have been tried, although I can see nothing at all wrong with it. Black plans to place his king's bishop on d6, queen's knight on d7 and rook on c8 opposite the white queen. The lost tempo associated with ...♗a6-b7 does not seem to harm Black's chances at all here, especially as the white queen is far from ideally placed on c2, and it is hard to see a way in which the move a3 is likely to prove useful.

7...exd5 8 g3

8 ♘e5 has been played, but it looks highly artificial to move this piece for a second time while so many of White's forces remain undeveloped. The game H.Grooten-V.Ikonnikov, Dieren 2006, continued 8...♗d6 9 ♘df3 0-0 10 ♗g5 c5 11 e3, and here 11...cxd4 12 exd4 ♕e8! 13 ♗e2 ♘e4 looks good for Black.

8...♗d6!

This is better than 8...♗e7, as Black would like to control e5 and keep the e-file open for a rook and/or queen.

9 ♗g2 ♘bd7 10 0-0 0-0

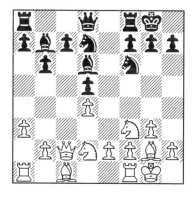

11 b4

In M.Rohde-A.Miles, USA 1989, White soon got into a mess after 11 ♘h4 ♖e8 12 ♘c4?! ♗f8 13 ♗f4 ♘e4! (with ideas of ...g5, forking two pieces, as well as ...dxc4!) 14 ♘e5 ♘xe5 15 dxe5 g5 16 ♗xe4 dxe4 17 ♖ad1 ♕e7 18 ♘f5 ♕e6 19 ♘d4 ♕h3 20 ♗xg5 (no better is .20 ♗e3 c5! 21 ♘b5 ♖xe5) 20...♖xe5 21

♗h4 ♗d6 when Black had a big plus.

11...♖e8 12 ♖e1 c5 13 bxc5 bxc5 14 dxc5 ♘xc5 15 ♗b2

We have been following H.Grooten-A.Shneider, Cappelle la Grande 2007, in which the white queen took up an active post after 15...♖c8 16 ♕f5 with an unclear position.

Instead I would suggest 15...♘fe4!.

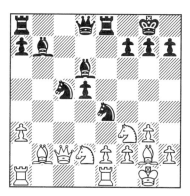

The idea is to follow up with ...♖c8 without allowing ♕f5. Later the other knight can either settle on the ideal e6-square, or perhaps even aim for c3 via a4 should the white queen move away. The tremendous activity of Black's pieces should provide ample compensation for the isolated d-pawn.

Summary

None of White's unusual fifth moves are particularly dangerous, although 5 ♕b3 and 5 ♘bd2 both carry a certain amount of potential to create problems for an unsuspecting opponent. The material presented here should enable Black to reach a fully satisfactory position, though, and with chances to take over the initiative in several variations.

Chapter Nine

The Petrosian Variation: 5 e3

1 d4 ♘f6 2 c4 e6 3 ♘f3 b6 4 a3 ♗a6 5 e3

This is not as theoretically challenging as 5 ♕c2, but it has been played in a great many games and deserves to be treated with respect, as I discovered on the single occasion on which I faced it.

5...d5

This is the most logical move, attacking c4 and exploiting the tension between the opposing bishops. Here White has four moves worthy of individual consideration:

A: 6 ♘c3
B: 6 ♘e5
C: 6 b3
D: 6 ♘bd2

The remaining alternatives are not at all dangerous:

a) 6 cxd5?! ♗xf1 7 ♔xf1 exd5 8 ♘c3 c6 9 ♕c2 ♗e7 was already slightly favourable for Black in A.Malm-A.Feinstein, correspondence 1997.

b) 6 ♕a4+ c6 7 ♕c2 (7 cxd5 ♗xf1 8 ♔xf1 – 8 dxc6?? b5 wins for Black – 8...exd5 9 ♘c3 ♗d6 10 ♕c2 0-0 11 b3 ♘bd7 was similar to variation 'a' and also favourable for Black in M.Buscher-V.Chuchelov, Porz 1991) 7...♗d6 8 b3 0-0 9 ♗d3 ♘bd7 10 ♗b2 ♖c8 11 0-0 c5 was balanced in K.Kinnunen-Y.Jouhki, Finland 1996.

c) 6 ♕c2 should be met by 6...♗e7:

c1) 7 ♘bd2 transposes to Line D.

c2) 7 b4 0-0 8 ♘bd2 c5 9 b5?! (White should probably have preferred 9 dxc5 bxc5 10 b5 ♗b7 with equal chances) 9...♗b7 10 ♗b2 ♘bd7 11 ♗e2 ♖c8 12 0-0 was N.Gaprindashvili-N.Ioseliani, 6th matchgame, Tbilisi 1980, and here the simple 12...cxd4 would have been good for Black.

c3) 7 ♗d3 0-0 8 0-0 c5 9 cxd5 ♗xd3 10 ♕xd3 ♕xd5 11 ♘c3 ♕b7 was equal in G.Izsak-P.Petran, Budapest 1995.

A) 6 ♘c3 ♗e7!

This looks better than 6...♗xc4 7

♗xc4 dxc4 8 ♕a4+ ♘bd7 9 0-0 when White stood slightly better in J.Le Roux-A.Greet, British League 2006.

7 ♘e5

7 ♕a4+ c6 8 cxd5 ♗xf1 9 ♔xf1 exd5 was already somewhat favourable for Black in J.Flesch-O.Romanishin, Lvov 1981, and 7 cxd5 ♗xf1 8 ♔xf1 exd5 also gave White nothing in J.Fedorowicz-L.Christiansen, Estes Park 1985.

7...0-0 8 ♗e2

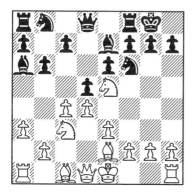

8...c6

This has been the most popular move, although I can see nothing at all wrong with the more energetic 8...c5!?.

9 0-0 ♘fd7!

Black borrows an idea from the 4 g3 ♗a6 main lines, in which he very often reacts to a knight on e5 in the same way. Indeed, you can find several examples of the same motif in Chapter 16.

10 ♘xd7

Instead F.Spenner-D.Plump, German League 1989, saw 10 cxd5 ♘xe5 11 dxe5 cxd5 (11...exd5!? was worth considering) 12 f4 ♗xe2 13 ♘xe2 ♘c6 14 ♕d3, and now 14...f6! would have brought Black a good position after both 15 exf6 ♗xf6 and 15 ♘d4 ♕d7.

10...♘xd7 11 b3 ♗d6 12 ♗b2 f5!?

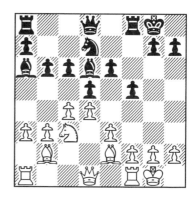

Black could have maintained equality with any sensible move, such as 12...♖c8. Instead he opts for what looks like a very comfortable version of a Stonewall Dutch. The game W.Browne-J.Benjamin, Berkeley 1984, continued:

13 ♖c1 ♘f6

Black is attempting to prepare a typical Greek gift sacrifice. Two good alternatives were 13...♖c8, improving Black's worst piece, and 13...♕h4!?, provoking a kingside weakness.

14 cxd5 ♗xe2 15 ♘xe2

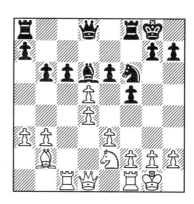

15...♗xh2+!?

15...cxd5 would have been equal, but Benjamin is unable to resist the thematic piece sacrifice. It looks quite dangerous, although according to my analysis White can emerge with a safe position and so objectively speaking I would have to recommend that Black prefers one of the many alternatives that have been suggested. The remainder of the game is of less importance to us theoretically, but you may enjoy playing over the remaining moves and light annotations as they contain some useful offensive and defensive ideas which can crop up in other Greek gift positions:

16 ♔xh2 ♘g4+ 17 ♔g3! (17 ♔g1?? ♕h4 18 ♖e1 ♕xf2+ 19 ♔h1 ♖f6 mates quickly and 17 ♔h3? ♖f6! 18 ♘f4 ♖h6+ 19 ♔g3 ♘h2! 20 ♘h3 ♕d6+ 21 f4 ♘xf1+ 22 ♕xf1 exd5 also leaves Black on top) **17...♕g5 18 f4 ♕g6 19 ♔f3 exd5** (19...♘h2+ 20 ♔f2 ♘xf1 21 ♕xf1 exd5 22 ♘g1 sees White consolidating and the knight will become a monster on e5) **20 ♖c3** (another good defence would have been 20 ♖h1!? ♖ae8 21 ♖c3 ♕e6 – threatening the queen sacrifice 22...♕xe3+ and mate! – 22 ♗c1! when it is not clear if Black has enough) **20...♖ae8 21 ♘g3 h5 22 ♖h1 ♘h2+ 23 ♔f2 ♘g4+ 24 ♔f3** (White decides not to risk the unclear 24 ♔g1!? ♘xe3 25 ♕f3 ♘g4 26 ♘f1 ♖e4 and instead settles for a repetition) **24...♘h2+ ½-½**

B) 6 ♘e5

White is planning what he hopes will be a troublesome check on a4, but Black can safely ignore the 'threat', which turns out to be illusory.

6...♗d6!

6...c6 should equalize, but it turns out that Black has no reason to fear the check.

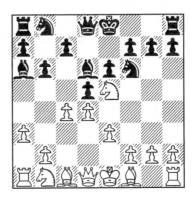

7 ♕a4+ c6! 8 ♘c3

Of course, 8 ♘xc6?? loses material after 8...♕d7; White cannot even save himself with 9 b4 ♕xc6 10 ♕xc6+ (10 b5 ♕d7 leaves the b-pawn pinned) 10...♘xc6 11 b5 on account of 11...♘a5! 12 bxa6 ♘b3.

8...♗xe5 9 dxe5 ♘fd7 10 cxd5 ♗xf1 11 dxc6

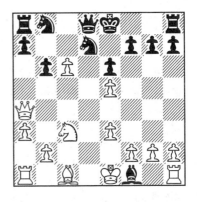

After 11 ♖xf1 exd5 12 ♕g4 0-0 13 f4

♘c5 14 ♔f2 (F.Zamecnik-J.Baranek, Slovakian League 2002), White's misplaced aggression could have best been punished by 14...f6! when the tables would have been well and truly turned.

This position was reached in S.Kalinitschew-Cu.Hansen, German League 2003, and was quickly drawn: 11...♗xg2 12 cxd7+ ♕xd7 13 ♖g1 ♕xa4 14 ♘xa4 ♗c6 15 ♘c3 ♘d7 16 f4 0-0 17 b4 b5 18 ♘e2 a6 19 ♗b2 ♘b6 ½-½.

It turns out, however, that Black could have gained the advantage with 11...♘xc6!: 12 ♕xc6 (12 ♔xf1 ♘cxe5 leaves White with nothing to compensate his misplaced king) 12...♖c8 13 ♕e4 (13 ♕f3 ♗a6 is no better) 13...♘c5 14 ♕g4 ♗a6 15 ♕xg7 ♖f8 and White's king is in grave danger.

C) 6 b3

This is a sensible move, retaining the central tension and preparing to fianchetto the queen's bishop.

6...♗e7 7 ♗d3

This is the best square for the bishop. A few other possibilities:

a) Both 7 ♘bd2 0-0 and 7 ♗b2 0-0 will almost always lead to the main line after a subsequent ♗d3.

b) 7 ♗e2 is playable if rather timid, and after 7...0-0 8 0-0 c5 9 ♗b2 ♘c6 10 cxd5 ♗xe2 11 ♕xe2 ♕xd5 12 ♘bd2 cxd4 13 ♘xd4 ♘xd4 14 ♗xd4 ♖ac8 15 ♖a2 ♖fd8 Black had already taken over the initiative in P.De Souza Haro-W.Arencibia Rodriguez, Linares 1997.

7...0-0 8 0-0

White can shuffle the order of the moves 0-0, ♗b2 and ♘bd2 in any way he pleases, but most of the time the same position will be reached.

8...c5 9 ♗b2 ♘c6

Both sides continue to develop in a logical way.

10 ♕e2 cxd4 11 exd4 ♖c8 12 ♘bd2 ♖e8

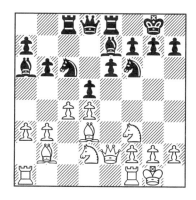

The position is approximately equal, but with plenty of possibilities for both sides to outplay the opponent. Usually in this type of structure White will attempt to build up on the kingside, while Black will look to fortify his defences with a bishop transfer to g7, all the while looking for an opportunity to exploit the potential weakness of White's c- and d-pawns. At the same time, there is plenty of room for alternative interpretations and the game Z.Kozul-G.Piesina, Olomouc 1996, took an interesting turn after 13 ♖ac1 (13 ♖ad1 ♗f8 has also been seen in a few games) 13...♗f8 14 ♖fe1 g6 when White elected to put all his eggs in the queenside basket with 15 c5!?. The game continued 15...♗xd3 16 ♕xd3 a5 17 ♕b5 bxc5 18 dxc5 ♘d7 19 b4 axb4 20 axb4 e5 and was finely balanced.

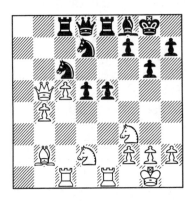

White's queenside pawns have the advantage of being passed, but Black's central pawns control more important squares. As it happens Black went on to gain the upper hand after 21 ♖ed1 ♗g7 (21...♕c7!?) 22 ♘b3?! (22 ♘f1 looks better) 22...♕c7! 23 ♖xd5 ♖b8 24 ♕e2 ♘xb4, regaining the pawn with the advantage due to the weakness of the c-pawn as well as possibilities such as ...♘a2.

D) 6 ♘bd2 ♗e7

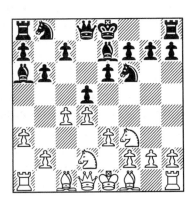

Black develops in the normal fashion. We now consider the following possibilities:

D1: 7 ♕a4+!?
D2: 7 b4

The latter is the most popular continuation and can be viewed as more ambitious than the more restrained set-up involving b3, which we've just considered. Others are not too threatening:

a) 7 cxd5 is slightly better here than on the previous move for the simple reason that after 7...♗xf1 White can play 8 ♘xf1, thus preserving the right to castle. On the other hand, after 8...♕xd5 9 ♘g3 0-0 10 0-0 ♖d8 he still had no trace of an advantage in R.Ammerlaan-A.Sewambar, Hengelo 1997.

b) 7 ♗e2 and 7 ♗d3 should both be met by 7...0-0 followed by ...c5; the likely result being a transposition to either Line C after a subsequent b2-b3 or Line D2 after b2-b4.

D1) 7 ♕a4+!?

This should not be too dangerous, although it is at least one of the few moves with which White attempts to create concrete problems for his opponent. Black's best response is...

7...c6!

Instead 7...♕d7 misplaces the queen and White should be a little better after 8 ♕c2! 0-0 9 b4. The alternative 7...♘fd7 8 cxd5 ♗xf1 9 ♘xf1 exd5 10 ♘g3 0-0 11 0-0 c5 12 ♖d1 also resulted in an edge for the first player in M.Muse-V.Stoica, Athens 1985.

8 cxd5 ♗xf1 9 ♘xf1

9 dxc6?! does not work after 9...b5! 10 ♕c2 ♗xg2 11 c7 ♕c8 12 ♖g1 ♗xf3 13

cxb8♕ ♖xb8 14 ♕xc8+ ♖xc8 15 ♘xf3 0-0 when Black enjoys the superior prospects in the endgame.

9...b5!?

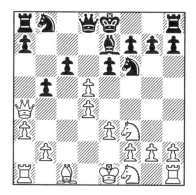

9...♕xd5 is not a bad move, but I prefer the text.

10 ♕b3

The idea of this move is that by eyeing the b5-pawn, White forces his opponent to recapture with a piece. Instead 10 ♕c2 cxd5 11 ♘g3 ♘bd7 12 ♗d2 ♖c8 13 ♕d3 ♕b6 14 0-0 a5 was perhaps slightly favourable for Black in J.Janos-S.Marek, correspondence 2004, thanks to his superior bishop.

10...♕xd5 11 ♕d3

After 11 ♕c2 Black has a pleasant choice between 11...♘bd7 12 ♘g3 c5 13 e4 ♕b7 14 ♗g5 ♖c8 and the immediate 11...c5 12 dxc5 ♕xc5 13 ♕xc5 ♗xc5 14 b4 ♗e7 15 ♘d4 a6 16 ♗b2 ♘bd7, with equality in both cases.

11...♘bd7 12 ♘1d2 ♘c5!?

Black elects to prevent e3-e4 by force. He might, however, have considered postponing this decision at least for another move with 12...0-0, as 13 e4? ♘c5! would win material.

13 ♕e2 ♘ce4 14 0-0 0-0 15 ♖d1

We have been following the game V.Eingorn-G.Vescovi, Saint Vincent 2001, which continued 15...a6 16 ♘xe4 ♘xe4 17 ♘e5 c5 18 f3 cxd4 19 fxe4 ♕xe5 20 exd4 ♕d6 with equality. In his annotations Vescovi suggests that Black might have looked for even more with...

15...♖fd8!

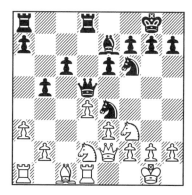

The point is that White comes under pressure after 16 ♘xe4 ♘xe4 17 ♘e5?! c5!. He dare not take on b5 due to 18...♕xe5, and 18 f3?! cxd4 19 exd4 ♘d6 also works out pretty well for Black.

D2) 7 b4 0-0

Black can also play 7...c5 immediately; an option which might well lead to a transposition.

8 ♗b2

This is almost always played and the alternatives are unsurprisingly nothing to worry about:

a) In S.Mohandesi-G.Van der Stricht, Antwerp 1999, White soon got into trouble after 8 c5? ♗xf1 9 ♔xf1 a5

10 ♗b2 ♕e8 11 ♗c3 axb4 12 axb4 ♕b5+ 13 ♔g1 ♘c6.

b) 8 ♗e2 c5 9 bxc5 bxc5 10 0-0 (A.Mirzoev-E.Berg, Soller 2006) 10...dxc4 11 ♘xc4 cxd4 12 ♘xd4 ♕c7 is equal.

8...c5

Black proceeds with the usual plan.

9 dxc5

In E.Lobron-C.Lutz, Dortmund 1993, White decided to forgo this exchange in favour of the immediate 9 b5. There followed 9...♗b7 10 ♗d3 ♘bd7 11 0-0 cxd4 12 exd4 (12 ♗xd4 ♘c5 13 ♗e2 ♖c8 was comfortable for Black in E.Matsuura-C.Sega, Sao Paulo 2001), reaching an interesting position in which Black has a choice of continuations:

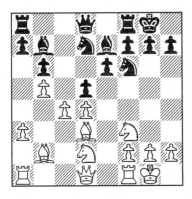

a) One safe and solid option was 12...dxc4 13 ♘xc4 ♘d5 14 ♖e1 (with equality according to Hansen) 14...a6! (one of White's main ideas is to utilize the outpost on c6, so Black begins an undermining process) 15 a4 ♘7f6 16 ♘ce5 axb5 17 axb5 ♖xa1 18 ♕xa1 ♘b4 19 ♗b1 ♕d6 20 ♕a7 ♗d5 with a good position.

b) In the game Black preferred the ambitious 12...♘e4!? and soon gained the upper hand after 13 ♗xe4?! (Hansen also mentions the variations 13 ♖e1 ♘xd2 14 ♘xd2 dxc4 15 ♗xc4 ♘f6 with an edge to Black and 13 ♕e2 ♘xd2 14 ♘xd2 ♘f6 15 ♖ac1 ♖c8 16 ♘f3 dxc4 17 ♗xc4, at which point the simple 17...♘d5 looks promising) 13...dxe4 14 ♘e1 a6! 15 a4 axb5 16 axb5 ♖xa1 17 ♗xa1 (or 17 ♕xa1 ♕c7 intending ...♖a8) 17...♕c7.

9...bxc5 10 b5 ♗b7

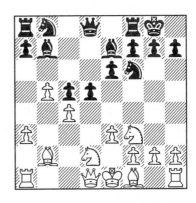

Both sides have their chances: White can point to his mobile queenside majority, while Black enjoys slightly better control over the central squares. The first player will therefore attempt to restrain the enemy centre while gradually preparing a queenside advance. The challenge facing Black will be to mobilize or otherwise make use of his central majority without creating a structural weakness.

11 ♗e2 ♘bd7 12 0-0 ♕c7 13 ♕c2

In D.Rajkovic-S.Brilla Banfalvi, correspondence 1982, White preferred 13 a4 ♗d6 14 ♕c2, at which point Black decided to initiate complications with 14...d4!?; the idea being to meet 15 exd4 cxd4 16 ♗xd4 with 16...e5 followed by ...e4 and ...♗xh2+, levelling the material and weakening the enemy king.

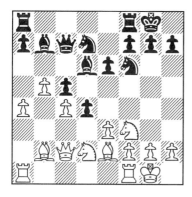

Rajkovic decided that the lesser evil was to close the centre with 15 e4, after which there followed 15...♖ad8 16 a5 ♘e5 17 ♘xe5 ♗xe5 18 g3 d3!? with complications. Black eventually won, but for a while the game was quite unclear and I believe he should be able to do better than this. Going back to the position after White's 15th, I rather like the idea of 15...a5!, preventing any further advance of the enemy pawns. True, White obtains a protected passed pawn on b5 but there are too many pieces on the board for this to be of any importance any time soon. Meanwhile Black's own passed d-pawn exerts a far greater influence by virtue of its central location, and the second player can easily utilize his considerable space advantage to prepare a kingside attack with moves like ...e5, ...g6, ...♘h5-g7 and finally ...f5!.

Returning to the main line, we now

follow the game N.Alexandria-M.Litinskaya, Vilnius 1980:

13...♗d6 14 ♗d3

White decides that the bishop will be better off on d3, although we will see that this approach suffers from a distinct drawback. In D.Rajkovic-G.Sanakoev, correspondence 1982, the continuation was 14 cxd5 exd5 15 h3 ♖fe8 16 ♖ac1 and here 16...a6! looks very sensible, exchanging off a weakness and leaving White with an isolated pawn on the queenside.

Instead of releasing the central tension, another sensible idea is 14 a4, although in that case Black may be tempted to initiate complications with 14...d4!? (if he does not wish to alter the course of the game in such a drastic way, Black can, of course, settle for a normal move like 14...a6) 15 exd4 cxd4 16 ♗xd4 (16 ♘xd4 ♗xh2+ 17 ♔h1 ♗e5 is similar) 16...e5 followed by ...e4 and ...♗xh2+. The result will then depend on the relative significance of White's powerful queenside pawns versus his weakened kingside.

14...♖fe8 15 ♖fd1 d4!?

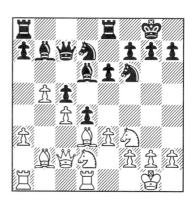

Black utilizes the tactical vulnerability of White's pieces to mobilize his central pawns. Another sensible idea would have been 15...a6 16 a4 axb5 17 axb5 ♞b6.

16 exd4

If White refuses to exchange in favour of 16 ♞e4, there follows 16...♞xe4 17 ♝xe4 ♝xe4 18 ♛xe4 ♞f6 19 ♛c2 e5 with a fine position.

16...cxd4 17 ♝xd4

If White does not take the pawn there would follow ...e5 and ...♞c5 when Black would acquire a huge positional advantage.

17...e5 18 c5!

Bishop retreats would allow 18...e4, winning a piece.

18...♞xc5 19 ♝xc5 ♛xc5 20 ♞e4 ♞xe4 21 ♝xe4 ♛xc2 22 ♝xc2 ♜ad8

Black's accurate calculation of her 15th move has been rewarded with a favourable endgame in which her two bishops are rather more important than White's potential ability to create a distant passed pawn.

Summary

5 e3 is not the most ambitious move at White's disposal, but there is nothing whatsoever intrinsically wrong with it and it is important for Black not to underestimate the opponent's set-up. 5...d5 is obviously a good move, and in most variations we have seen that a subsequent ...c5 should guarantee Black a full share of the centre and thus an equal game. One convenient factor is that in many resulting positions the move a2-a3 turns out to be of limited usefulness for White. This may explain the popularity of Line D2 with 7 b4, although we have seen that even here Black has very little to worry about.

Chapter Ten

The Petrosian Variation: 5 ♕c2

1 d4 ♘f6 2 c4 e6 3 ♘f3 b6 4 a3 ♗a6 5 ♕c2

This is White's most natural response and the undisputed main line against 4...♗a6.

5...♗b7!

To the uninitiated it may appear that the second player has simply wasted a tempo. Black's idea, however, is to strike at the enemy centre with ...c5 without allowing the response d4-d5 which will no longer benefit from the support of the white queen. Therefore White should instead concentrate on mobilizing his forces and exploiting his 'free' developing move in the most effective way possible.

Aside from the text, Black has two principal alternatives:

a) The immediate 5...c5 allows 6 d5! since 6...exd5 7 cxd5 ♘xd5?? loses a piece to 8 ♕e4+, while 7...♗b7 8 e4 ♕e7 9 ♗d3 ♘xd5 10 0-0 is a very risky pawn grab. Black's most solid continuation is 7...g6, but White should be able to

maintain an edge with precise play.

b) 5...d5 is also less than ideal as after 6 cxd5 exd5 7 ♘c3 the knight has arrived at its ideal square and the dark-squared bishop will be developed actively on f4 or g5.

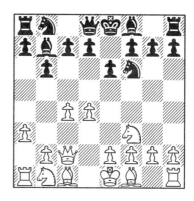

6 ♘c3

The entire point of White's fourth was to prepare this move, so the alternatives are inconsistent to say the least:

a) 6 ♘bd2 d5 takes play back into Line D of Chapter 8.

b) 6 ♗f4 c5 7 dxc5 (I.Prihastomo-Wu

Shaobin, Singapore 1997) 7...bxc5 8 ②c3 reaches Line A2, below.

c) 6 g3 leads to a strange kind of hybrid between the 4 a3 and 4 g3 systems, and Black has nothing to worry about after 6...c5 7 dxc5 bxc5 8 ♗g2 ♗e7 9 ②bd2 0-0 10 0-0 d5 11 cxd5 exd5 12 ②e5 (D.Rupel-K.Tomkins, Seattle 1984) 12...♖e8 with a good position.

d) 6 e3 c5 7 ♗e2 (7 dxc5 ♗xc5 8 ♗e2 0-0 9 0-0 ♗e7 10 ②c3 d6 11 b3 ②bd7 12 ♗b2 a6 is a comfortable Hedgehog for Black) 7...cxd4 8 exd4 ♗e7 9 0-0 0-0 10 ②c3 d5 should lead to a favourable IQP position for Black.

e) 6 ♗g5 c5 7 d5!? (others are hardly likely to threaten Black either) 7...♗e7!? (7...exd5 8 cxd5 ♗xd5 9 ②c3 ♗e6 10 e4 ②c6 11 0-0-0 might give White some compensation) 8 ♗xf6 (White should avoid both 8 e4? ②xd5 and 8 ②c3? ②xd5) 8...♗xf6 9 e4 was J.Plaskett-S.Skembris, Paris 1983, and here Plaskett's suggestion of 9...d6 looks quite satisfactory.

6...c5!

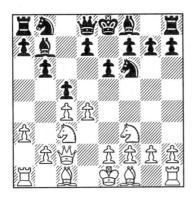

Black continues with the strategy begun on move 4. The present varia-

tion is almost unique for the Queen's Indian in that Black's counterplay will primarily be based around fighting for the dark rather than the light squares. We now consider the lines:

A: 7 d5?!
B: 7 dxc5
C: 7 e4

The alternatives are justifiably rare:

a) 7 ♗f4 cxd4 8 ②xd4 (8 ②b5? achieves nothing after 8...d6) 8...d6 9 ♗g3 a6 10 e4 was seen in V.Arbakov-D.Bunzmann, Passau 1995. Here Black should probably have secured himself the advantage of the bishop-pair with Kalinitschew and Bunzmann's suggestion of 10...②h5! 11 ♗e2 ②xg3 12 hxg3 ②d7 13 0-0-0 ♗e7.

b) 7 e3 cxd4 8 exd4 ♗e7 9 ♗e2 d5 is equal, but in L.Portisch-J.Arnason, Reykjavik 1987, White tried the provocative 9 ♗d3!?.

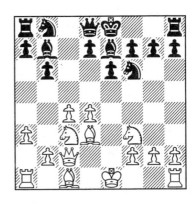

The game continued 9...♗xf3!? (this is not forced, but looks quite appealing for Black) 10 gxf3 ②c6 11 ♗e3 ♖c8 12 0-0 ②a5!? 13 ♕e2 0-0 14 ♖ac1 (14 b4?

fails to 14...♘xc4! 15 ♗xc4 d5 – Emms) 14...d5 15 cxd5 and now after 15...♘xd5 Emms prefers Black, an assessment with which I agree.

A) 7 d5?!

This type of pawn sacrifice has been tried in many different variations of the Queen's Indian (see Chapter 14 for what is presently the most topical example), but practice and analysis have demonstrated the present variation to be one of its less dangerous forms.

7...exd5 8 cxd5

The less flexible 8 ♘xd5 ♘xd5 9 cxd5 ♗xd5 reaches variation 'd' in the notes to White's 9th move.

8...♘xd5

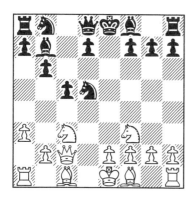

9 ♗g5

This is the most common move, although the main line demonstrates that White's attacking resources are all but exhausted. Here is a summary of his alternatives:

a) 9 e4 (J.Watson-W.Browne, Las Vegas 1994) should be met by 9...♘xc3.

b) 9 ♘b5 ♘c7 10 e4 (M.Riesen-G.Betschart, Bern 1996) 10...a6 11 ♘xc7+ ♕xc7 12 ♗c4 ♗e7 is good for Black.

c) 9 ♗d2 ♘c7 11 0-0-0 ♘d4 12 ♕d3 ♘ce6 was solid enough for Black in Y.Bayram-V.Ivanchuk, Kocaeli 2002, while the 11 ♘d5 of Y.Bayram-V.Gaprindashvili, Ankara 2002, should have been met by 11...♘xd5 12 exd5 ♘d4 13 ♘xd4 cxd4 when White's compensation is questionable.

d) 9 ♘xd5 ♗xd5 10 e4 ♗e6 11 ♗f4 ♗e7 and now:

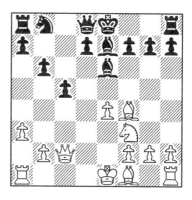

d1) 12 ♗d3 ♘c6 13 0-0 (P.Dankert-H.Behrens, German League 1988) 13...♗g4 leaves White's compensation in doubt.

d1) In J.Plaskett-I.Farago, Hastings 1982/83, White tried the more aggressive 12 0-0-0, but still fell short after 12...0-0 13 h4 ♘c6 14 ♗a6 ♘a5 15 ♕c3 d6 16 h5 h6 17 g4 b5! 18 ♗xb5 (no better is 18 g5 b4) 18...♖b8 19 a4 a6 20 g5 axb5 21 gxh6 ♗f6 22 ♘e5, at which point the quickest route to victory would have been 22...bxa4! 23 hxg7 ♔xg7 24 ♕g3+ ♔h7.

e) Finally there is 9 ♕e4+ ♕e7 with a choice for White:

e1) 10 ♕xd5? may be fun for blitz, but White has nowhere near enough for the queen after 10...♗xd5 11 ♘xd5 ♕d8, as shown by 12 ♗g5 f6 13 ♗f4 ♘c6 14 e4 (M.Bosboom-V.Anand, Wijk aan Zee (blitz) 1999) 14...♔f7!? 15 ♗c4 ♘a5! 16 ♗a2 c4.

e2) 10 ♘e5 is relatively best, but even here after 10...♕e6 11 ♗f4 (C.Ceccatelli-M.Tirabassi, Montecatini Terme 1996) 11...f6! 12 ♘c4 ♕xe4 13 ♘xe4 ♘xf4 14 ♘ed6+ ♗xd6 15 ♘xd6+ ♔d8 16 ♘xb7+ ♔c7 17 g3 ♘g6 18 ♗g2 d5! Black is winning.

9...♗e7

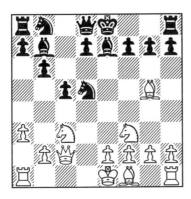

10 ♘b5

10 ♘e4 0-0 is safe enough for Black. The only other dangerous-looking alternative is 10 ♕e4?, but this is now known to lead to a practically forced loss for White after 10...♘xc3 11 ♕xb7 ♘c6 12 ♗xe7 ♔xe7 13 bxc3 (13 ♕a6 only leads to a transposition of moves after 13...b5! 14 bxc3 ♖b8, while 13 ♘e5 ♘xe5 14 bxc3 ♘c6 15 ♕a6, as in C.Santos-J.Pinheiro, Porto 2001, and now 15...♔f8 is excellent for Black) 13...♖b8 14 ♕a6 b5!, intending to trap

the queen with 15...♖b6.

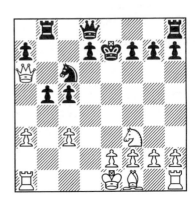

Here White has tried:

a) 15 ♘e5 ♘xe5 16 ♕xa7 ♖b6 17 0-0-0 (or 17 ♖d1 ♔e8! – Marjanovic) 17...♔e8 was winning for Black in I.Mamut-K.Aseev, Leningrad 1983.

b) 15 a4 ♖b6 16 axb5 ♖xa6 17 ♖xa6 ♕b8! is a neat tactic, indirectly protecting the knight while attacking b5 and facilitating ...♘e5. White is in deep trouble no matter how he continues:

b1) In C.Hauke-O.Melzer, Kehl 1989, White bravely or perhaps recklessly took the knight with 18 bxc6?! ♕b1+ 19 ♔d2 ♕b2+ 20 ♔e3, at which point the simplest win would have been 20...♕xc3+ 21 ♔f4 ♕f6+ 22 ♔e3 (no better are either 22 ♔e4 ♖b8 or 22 ♔g3 g5 23 ♖a4 c4 24 ♖xc4 ♕d6+ etc) 22...♖b8 23 ♖a3 c4.

b2) 18 e4 ♘e5 19 ♘h4 g6 20 c4 ♘c6! 21 ♘f3 ♘b4 22 ♖a4 ♕f4 23 ♘d2 f5 24 g3 ♕e5 led to a comfortable win for Black in A.Petrosian-G.Zaichik, Telavi 1982.

b3) In W.Schmidt-A.Marjanovic, Vrnjacka Banja 1983, White put up somewhat stiffer resistance with 18 e3 ♘e5 19 c4 (White's cause is not helped by 19 ♗e2 ♘xf3+ 20 gxf3 c4) 19...♘xf3+ 20 gxf3 ♕e5 21 ♗e2 ♕c3+ 22 ♔f1, although even here Black could have obtained a relatively certain win with 22...♖b8! 23 ♖g1 ♖b6 24 ♖xb6 axb6.

We now return to 10 ♘b5:

10...0-0 11 ♘d6

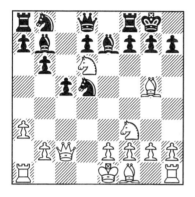

11...♘e3!

This flamboyant move has more or less put 7 d5 out of business in the eyes of most experts. It is rather old news now, having first been played in 1987, but we will still cover it for the sake of completeness.

12 fxe3

Alternatives are worse: for example, 12 ♕d3 ♗xf3 13 ♗xe3 ♗g4 14 ♕e4 ♗xd6 15 ♕xa8 ♕f6 (Gurevich) or 12 ♗xe3 ♗xd6 13 ♘g5 g6 14 0-0-0 ♗e7 followed by ...d5.

12...♗xf3 13 exf3

13 ♗xe7 ♕xe7 14 ♘f5 ♕e4 (Gurevich) is no good for White.

13...♗xg5 14 ♗c4

White has nothing better:

a) After the weak 14 f4?! Black's simplest route to an advantage is probably Aagaard's 14...♗e7 15 ♘f5 g6.

He can also obtain a fine game with 14...♗xf4 15 exf4 ♕e7+ 16 ♕e4 ♕xe4+ 17 ♘xe4 ♖e8, as long as he meets 18 ♗d3 with 18...f5! 19 ♗c4+ ♔f8 20 ♗d5 ♘c6, rather than 18...d5? (originally recommended by Gurevich), which allows White to turn the tables with 19 0-0-0!.

b) One of the main tactical justifications of Black's 11th is seen after 14 ♕e4 ♕e7!.

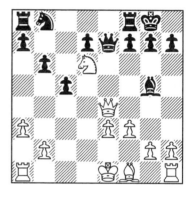

Here the greedy 15 ♕xa8? brings White nothing but grief after 15...♕e3+ 16 ♗e2 ♘c6 17 ♕b7 (or 17 ♘c4 ♕e6 18 ♕b7 d5 19 0-0 ♘d4) 17...♕d2+ 18 ♔f1 ♕xd6 19 ♖d1 ♘d4, as analysed by Aagaard. Instead White must bail out to an ending a pawn down with 15 ♕xe7 ♗xe7 16 0-0-0, but there is only one side trying to win from here.

Returning to the position after 14 ♗c4, we have thus far been following the game L.Janjgava-A.Chernin, Lviv 1987 (and a couple of others). All these games have continued 14...♘c6 and although Black is doing well, I agree with Aagaard that Black's most precise continuation is 14...♕e7!.

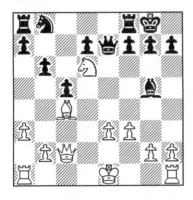

Now 15 ♕e4? ♕xd6 16 ♕xa8 ♘c6 17 ♕b7 ♗xe3 is a disaster for White, while 15 ♘f5 ♕e5 16 e4 g6 also brings Black the advantage. Aagaard concludes his analysis here, but extending things a little further the game might see either 17 ♘g3 ♗e3! (preventing White from castling) 18 ♖d1 ♕f4 with both a material and a positional advantage, or 17 h4 ♗f4 18 g3 ♗xg3+ 19 ♘xg3 ♕xg3+ 20 ♕f2 ♕xf2+ 21 ♔xf2 ♘c6 when Black's two extra pawns should ensure a relatively easy endgame conversion.

It seems that the pawn sacrifice with 7 d5?! can only be recommended as a surprise weapon or in games played with a fast time limit. If Black is well prepared then he will have good chances to either consolidate his extra pawn or, in certain cases, execute a devastating attack.

B) 7 dxc5 bxc5

This structure is usually quite comfortable for Black thanks to his extra central pawn. White's typical plan will involve doubling rooks on the d-file,

but we will see that the d-pawn can easily and conveniently be defended.

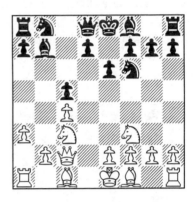

Certain side-variations of Chapter 1 (reached after the opening moves 4 ♗f4 ♗b7 5 e3 ♗e7 6 h3 c5 7 dxc5 bxc5 and 4 ♗g5 ♗b7 5 ♘c3 h6 6 ♗h4 ♗e7 7 e3 c5 8 dxc5 bxc5 respectively) lead to almost identical positions as those found in the present variation, so I decided not to cover them in any detail because I would just end up repeating the same advice in different sections of the book. Instead the present section is intended to provide a one-stop, 'three for the price of one' solution!

From the above diagram White will usually place his e-pawn on e3 (to cover d4) and bishop on e2, having first developed his queen's bishop actively. Thus we consider two principal options:

B1: 8 ♗g5
B2: 8 ♗f4

These are by far the most common moves, which also happen to correspond to the two aforementioned lines beginning with 4 ♗g5 and 4 ♗f4. There is one final point which should be addressed regarding the comparisons between these and the present variation beginning with 4 a3, which is that the move a2-a3 may itself be regarded as a slight weakening of the white queenside, especially when one considers the half-open b-file at Black's disposal.

Before considering the two main moves, we should briefly note that the immediate 8 e3 makes less sense, as the bishop will have to settle for a less appealing home on d2 or b2. Occasionally White tries 8 e4, but this leaves d4 as a permanent weakness and Black obtains a good game after 8...♘c6 9 ♗d3 ♕b8 10 h3 ♗e7 (10...♗d6!?) 11 ♗e3 d6. M.Braude-J.Arnason, New York 1992, continued 12 0-0 ♘d7 13 ♖ab1 a5 14 b3 ♘de5 15 ♘d2 0-0 (15...g5!?) 16 f4 ♘xd3 17 ♕xd3 ♖d8 18 ♖fd1 ♗a6 19 ♘f3 and now 19...♗f6 looks best with a full share of the chances.

A) 8 ♗g5 ♗e7 9 e3

White can shuffle his move order with 9 ♖d1 either here or at any time over the next few moves, but the great majority of games will end up reaching the same position after subsequent short castling and doubling on the d-file from White.

9...0-0 10 ♗e2 d6

Black should normally settle for a small centre, rather than become over-excited and play an early ...d5, which could see his central pawns come under fire. For the time being, he should develop solidly and only consider a further central advance once the rest of his army has been fully mobilized.

11 0-0

In L.Johannessen-B.Ostenstad, Asker 1997, White tried a more creative but ultimately less sound approach with 11 0-0-0?! and soon wound up in trouble after 11...♘bd7 12 h3 ♕b6 13 e4 ♖ab8 14 g4 ♗c6 15 ♗d3 ♖b7 16 ♖he1 ♖fb8, as Black enjoyed a ready-made attack along the open b-file. After the further 17 ♖d2 ♕a5 18 ♖e3 Black could have obtained a near-winning position with the simple 18...♖xb2 19 ♕xb2 ♖xb2 20 ♔xb2 ♘b6. Material is equal here, but White's rooks are doing nothing useful and his queenside is looking extremely shaky with ...♕a6 on the agenda.

11...♘bd7

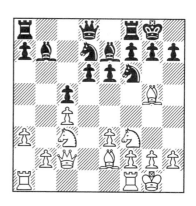

11...♘c6?! would not fit the demands of the position as well. The d4-square is unavailable, so the knight is better off supporting its brother on f6 while keeping the long diagonal clear.

12 ♖fd1

12 ♖ad1 makes no real difference;

the usual result being a transposition after 12...♕b6 13 ♖d2 ♖fd8 14 ♖fd1 ♘f8.

12...♕b6

Black has also enjoyed considerable success with 12...a6!?, the point of which is to post the queen on c7 without fearing harassment from a knight on b5. The game A.Anastasian-L.Van Wely, Dresden 2007, was a model performance from Black, who gradually took over the initiative after 13 ♘d2 ♕c7 14 ♗f3 ♖ab8 15 ♗f4 ♗xf3 16 ♘xf3 ♘h5 17 ♖d2 ♘xf4 18 exf4 g6 19 h4 ♘f6 20 ♖e1 ♖fd8 21 ♘g5 ♗f8 22 ♕d1 ♗g7 23 ♖e3 d5! when the long-term value of the central pawn majority was starting to become apparent.

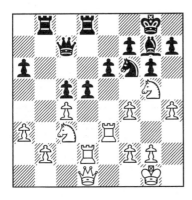

The remaining moves were 24 cxd5 exd5 25 ♘xd5 ♘xd5 26 ♖xd5 ♗d4 27 ♖xd8+ ♕xd8 28 ♖d3 ♖xb2 29 ♘f3 ♕b8! 30 ♖xd4 cxd4 31 ♕xd4 ♕b6 0-1.

13 ♖d2

13 b4!? cxb4 (13...a5!? 14 b5 ♖ad8 looks interesting) 14 axb4 ♖fc8 15 ♘d2 a5 16 bxa5 ♖xa5 17 ♖ab1 ♕a7 18 ♗f4 ♕a8 19 ♗f1 d5 20 ♕b2 ♗c6 21 cxd5 was agreed drawn in J.Plaskett-M.Adams,

British Championship, Eastbourne 1990.

13...♖fd8 14 ♖ad1

White is utilizing the semi-open file to the best of his ability, but Black can easy summon enough resources to defend d6.

14...♘f8

White must now consider the positional threat of ...♘g6 followed by ...h6, forcing the exchange of his bishop for a knight.

15 ♗d3

15 ♗h4 ♘g6 16 ♗g3 did not save the bishop after 16...♘h5! in J.Mazet-M.Palac, Geneva 2005.

15...h6 16 ♗h4 ♖ab8 17 h3 ♗c6 18 ♗g3 ♕b7 19 ♗e2 ♘e4 20 ♘xe4 ♗xe4 21 ♕c1 e5!? 22 ♗h4 g5 23 ♗g3

We have been following the game A.Gupta-D.Bocharov, Abu Dhabi 2005. Black has been steadily improving his position, and at this point could have cemented his advantage with 23...f5!.

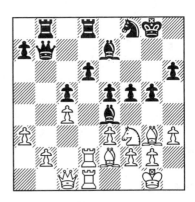

White's position looks distinctly unenviable.

B2) 8 ♗f4

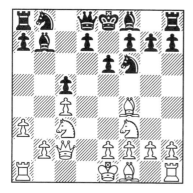

This is slightly more popular than 8 ♗g5. White hopes that the bishop will prove more effective on the h2-b8 diagonal, but in all honesty I doubt that it makes any significant difference to the evaluation of the position.

8...♗e7

Black can also play 8...♘h5!?, intending 9 ♗g3 ♗e7 or 9 ♗g5 ♗e7 10 ♗xe7 ♕xe7, while if he wishes to mix things up he can try 8...♗xf3!? 9 gxf3 ♘c6 10 e3 ♘h5 11 ♗g3 ♘xg3 12 hxg3 ♖b8 with balanced chances.

9 ♖d1

The immediate 9 e3 might tempt Black into playing 9...♘h5!?. Naturally 9...0-0 is also fine when the game will almost certainly end up transposing to the main line, as White will almost always put his rooks on the d-file.

9...0-0 10 e3 ♕b6 11 ♗e2 d6 12 0-0 ♖d8 13 ♖d2

In the case of 13 b4 (M.Cebalo-J.Arnason, Cannes 1993) it looks interesting for Black to try 13...cxb4!? 14 axb4 ♘a6 with good counterplay.

13...♘bd7 14 ♖fd1 ♘f8

The position remains identical to

Line B1, except for the position of White's dark-squared bishop.

15 ♘g5!?

White attempts to exploit the position of the f4-bishop by utilizing the vacant g5-square. In E.Lobron-L.Polugaevsky, Biel 1986, he instead elected to expand on the queenside with 15 b4. However, following 15...cxb4 16 axb4 Black could have obtained an excellent game with 16...♘g6 17 ♗g3 ♘h5!.

This eliminates a valuable enemy bishop and eases the pressure against d6. Now Black's dark-squared bishop could become a significant asset.

15...♘g6

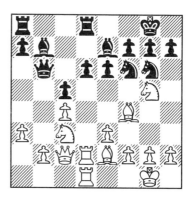

15...♖d7 was a solid alternative. From this point the game I.Khenkin-N.Kalesis, Iraklion 1992, continued:

16 ♗g3 ♘e8 17 h4!?

White looks to gain some kingside territory, although there is always a possibility that moves such as this will end up leaving weaknesses.

17...♖ab8 18 ♘ce4 ♘f8

Black must avoid 18...h6? 19 ♘xf7! ♔xf7 20 ♗h5.

19 ♗h5 g6 20 ♗f3

Now instead of the game's 20...f5, I think that it would have been worthwhile for Black to insert the move...

20...f6! 21 ♘h3

before proceeding with...

21...f5

Play might continue:

22 ♘c3

22 ♘eg5? h6 the knight is trapped.

22...♗xf3 23 gxf3 a6

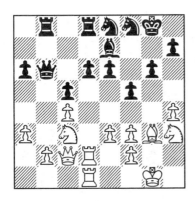

Black stands well here; as usual, his central pawns make a positive impression. White's kingside weaknesses are not causing him any immediate problems, but they certainly do not help his long-term chances.

C) 7 e4

This is the main line, and leads to positions reminiscent of the Sicilian so any readers who also play that opening should feel very much at home.

7...cxd4

Obviously Black must not delay this capture as otherwise d4-d5 would make the bishop on b7 look ridiculous.

8 ♘xd4 ♗c5

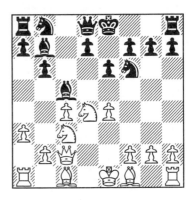

The alternatives are 8...d6 with a Hedgehog formation and 8...♘c6 9 ♘xc6 ♗xc6, which resembles the game continuation although some differences remain. The choice is largely a matter of personal taste, but I feel that the text gives Black the most interesting prospects. Similar ideas can be found in the Kan and Taimanov variations of the Sicilian where Black often develops this bishop actively, especially in response to an early c2-c4.

9 ♘b3

9 ♗e3? is never played on account of 9...♘g4. On the other hand, 9 ♘f3!? is ignored by most sources, but is nowhere near as bad as it looks and has even been used by such strong

Grandmasters as Timman, Nikolic and Krasenkow:

a) 9...♘c6 has been the most popular response, but in I.Rajlich-N.Dzagnidze, Turin Olympiad 2006, White obtained quite an active position after the forcing sequence 10 b4 ♘d4 11 ♕d3 ♘xf3+ 12 gxf3 ♗e7 13 ♖g1 0-0 14 ♗b2 with decent attacking chances, although Black later got the better of this encounter.

b) 9...♘g4 works out very well for Black after 10 ♘d1?! (S.Korotkjevich-J.Markos, Pardubice 2002) 10...♕f6!, but White can do much better with 10 h3! ♘xf2 11 ♖h2, trapping the knight. Play may continue 11...f5 12 b4 ♘xe4 13 bxc5 ♕c7 14 ♗e3 bxc5 15 0-0-0 when I prefer White's piece over Black's three pawns, although the position remains rather complicated.

c) Considering that the main advantage of White's 9th was to avoid blocking the b-pawn, it makes quite good sense for Black to consider the untested 9...a5!?. Then ...♘g4 ideas really are in the air and meanwhile the other knight can come to c6 without the bishop being driven away. I think that Black should have enough active prospects to maintain the balance, but 9 ♘f3 may well warrant a closer investigation than it has hitherto received.

9...♘c6

With this dynamic move Black emphasizes that he does not fear an exchange of bishop for knight and instead concentrates on developing rapidly while aiming at the sensitive d4-square. Now the main lines of 10 ♗f4

and 10 ♗g5 will be discussed in the next chapter. In the remainder of this chapter we will focus on two of White's less popular but still quite respectable options:

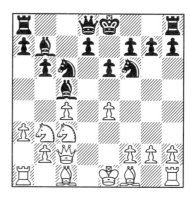

C1: 10 ♗d3
C2: 10 ♘xc5

Instead 10 ♗e2 is too timid. Black obtains easy play after 10...♘d4 11 ♘xd4 ♗xd4 and now:

a) 12 ♗f4 (A.Ushenina-V.Jakovljevic, Ljubljana 2005) can be met by 12...0-0 when 13 ♗d6? loses a pawn to 13...♗xc3+ 14 bxc3 ♗xe4.

b) 12 0-0 0-0 13 ♗d3 (White has already lost a tempo compared with normal lines) 13...♗xc3 14 bxc3 ♕c7 15 ♕e2 d6 16 f4 ♘d7 17 a4 ♖ac8 gave White no compensation for his chronic structural defects in M.Tupy-S.Kristjansson, Olomouc 2001.

c) 12 ♗f3 ♕b8 13 0-0 (Chan Peng Kong-T.Thamtavatvorn, Ho Chi Minh City 2003) 13...♗e5 with nice control over the dark squares.

d) 12 ♘b5 ♗e5 13 f3 (White also

achieves nothing with either 13 ♗f3 a6 14 ♘c3 ♕c7 or 13 ♗d3 ♕b8 14 g3 a6 15 ♘c3 0-0) 13...a6 14 ♘c3 was played in the game H.Fuerlinger-A.Kranz, Austrian League 2002, when 14...0-0 would have given Black at least equal chances.

C1) 10 ♗d3

This is a perfectly reasonable move, although the drawback is that, unlike the two main lines of 10 ♗f4 and 10 ♗g5, it does not put the black position under any immediate scrutiny.

10...d6!?

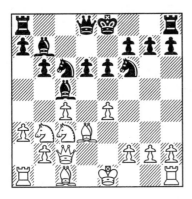

Black has no reason to fear the exchange on c5, and in some variations he may even consider recapturing with the d-pawn.

11 0-0 0-0 12 ♗g5

In case of the more restrained 12 ♗d2 (O.Cvitan-I.Farago, Neuchâtel 1993), Black might try the active 12...♘g4!?: for example, 13 ♗f4 (both 13 h3 ♘ge5 and 13 ♘xc5 dxc5 are also fine for Black) 13...♘ge5 14 ♗e2 f5!? with interesting counterplay.

12...h6 13 ♗h4 g5!

Black can get away with this

slightly weakening move as most of the enemy forces are situated far away on the opposite flank. Now he can activate his pieces to the greatest extent possible.

14 ♗g3 ♘h5!

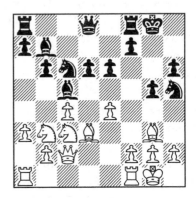

14...e5 has been more common, but I find the text more appealing; Black prepares to eliminate the more dangerous of the opponent's bishops while maintaining the fluidity of his pawn structure. The game G.Gerhards-R.Kurylo, correspondence 2003, proceeded 15 ♔h1!? ♘xg3+ 16 fxg3 (White obviously wanted to utilize the open file, but the drawback is that his ability to fight for the centre has been permanently diminished) 16...♘d4 17 ♘xd4 ♗xd4 when Black had an excellent position; the dark-squared bishop being an especially powerful asset.

C2) 10 ♘xc5 bxc5

In return for relinquishing the bishop-pair Black has obtained a firm grip over the d4-square. We should also note that, just as in Line B, the presence of the pawn on a3 exerts a slight but permanent destabilizing effect over the white queenside pawns.

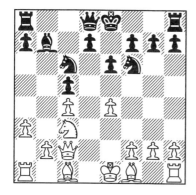

From this point Black will often follow up with moves like ...d6 and perhaps ...h6, increasing his control over the dark squares in order to compensate for the loss of the bishop. It is worth noting, however, that he should not necessarily rush to play ...e5 as this would leave his central pawns a little too static. He will often play the move eventually, but only after suitable preparation or if there is a particularly pressing reason.

11 ♗d3

This is the typical continuation. 11 ♗e3 ♕e7 should normally lead to broadly the same type of position, although occasionally White unwisely tries to be a bit more creative:

a) In S.Khazhomia-K.Tsatsalashvili, Sibenik 2007, the careless 12 0-0-0?! was punished by 12...♘g4! 13 ♘b5 ♘xe3 14 fxe3 0-0 15 ♕c3 f6 when White had no real compensation for his pawn weaknesses.

b) 12 ♖d1 meets with the same punishment of 12...♘g4!. In H.Skoien-

A.Olsen, Molde 2004, White tried to complicate the game with 13 ♗f4 ♘d4 14 ♖xd4 cxd4 15 ♘b5, but after 15...e5 16 ♗d2 d6 17 ♗b4 ♖d8 18 c5 0-0 19 ♘xd6 ♗c6 he did not have enough for the exchange.

c) White's best is probably 12 ♕d1 0-0 13 ♗e2 (H. Koneru-Xu Yuhua, Elista 2004) when 13...d6 leads to a conceptually very similar position to the main line below.

11...d6

Black lays another brick in his dark-squared pawn wall.

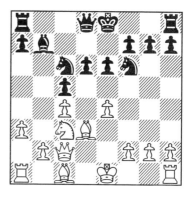

12 0-0

The most accurate reply to 12 ♖b1 (H.Kallio-A.Greet, Budapest 2005) may well be 12...0-0!?, as 13 b4 seems premature in view of 13...cxb4! 14 axb4 ♘e5! intending ...♖c8 with strong counterplay. In the game I preferred 12...a5 and obtained a decent position which was unfortunately ruined by a subsequent blunder.

12...0-0

When learning how to handle non-forcing positions such as this, it is much more important to focus on positional understanding than concrete variations. So in this case, rather than conduct a detailed theoretical survey, we will concentrate our attention on a small number of particularly instructive examples. For our main line we will focus on the game T.Radjabov-M.Adams, Prague (rapid) 2002 – regardless of the fast time limit, players of this calibre can demonstrate a wealth of instructive ideas from which the rest of us may learn:

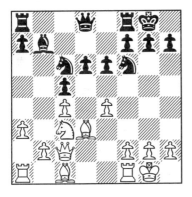

13 f4

White can also develop the bishop actively with 13 &g5 before pushing the f-pawn, although this approach has its own drawbacks. A.Vyzmanavin-V.Salov, Irkutsk 1986, proceeded with 13...h6 14 &h4 g5!? 15 &g3 e5 (15...♘h5!? also deserves serious consideration) when the bishop had been well and truly shut out of the game, at least for the time being. Play continued 16 ♕d1 a5 17 ♖b1 ♖b8 18 ♖e1 &g7 19 f3 &c8 (Salov improves his bishop, although another way to fulfil that objective would have been 19...♘d4!?, intending ...&c6) 20 &f2 &e6 21 &f1 ♖b7

22 ♘b5 (Salov mentions the line 22 ♘d5 ♕b8 23 ♘xf6 &xf6 24 ♕d2 &g7 25 h4 f6 when only Black has been helped by the knight exchange) 22...♘d4 23 b4!? (Vyzmanavin wants to open the position to free his bishops) 23...axb4 24 axb4 ♘xb5 25 cxb5 c4! 26 b6 ♕b8 27 ♖e2 (27 ♕d2 ♖c8 is evaluated as slightly better for Black by Salov) 27...♖c8 28 ♖d2 (Salov considers White's best to be 28 &h1!, which might lead to equality after a sequence like 28...♘d7 29 ♖d2 ♘xb6 30 ♖xd6 c3 31 ♖c1! – 31 &g3 f6 does not help White, as the threat of ...c2 means that there is no time for him to capture the bishop on e6 – 31...&b3 32 ♕xb3 ♕xd6 33 &a6 ♕d2 34 ♕c2 ♖cc7 35 &xb7 ♖xb7 36 &xb6 ♖xb6 37 ♕xc3) 28...c3 29 ♖c2 when White seemed to have everything under control, but the truth was revealed after the powerful exchange sacrifice 29...♖xb6! 30 &xb6 ♕xb6+ 31 &h1 d5!.

This saw Black seize the initiative and he soon went on to win after 32 exd5 ♘xd5 33 ♕d3 ♕d4 34 ♖cc1 ♘e3 35 ♕xd4 (or 35 ♖a1 &c4!, winning easily)

35...exd4 36 ♗a6 ♖d8 37 ♗d3 ♗c4 38 ♗xc4 ♘xc4 39 ♔g1 ♘d2 40 ♖a1 ♘b3 41 ♔f2 0-1; a model game which perfectly demonstrates Black's chances.

We now return to the no-less instructive Radjabov-Adams and 13 f4:

13...h6

With this prophylactic move, Adams safeguards himself against any potential threats to the h7-pawn involving e4-e5, as well as against any future ♗g5 pins. Neither of these are threatened at the moment, but it does no harm to anticipate such possibilities. One must, of course, take care not to weaken one's kingside unnecessarily, but Adams has evidently judged this not to be an issue here.

14 ♕d1 ♖b8 15 ♗e3 ♖e8!

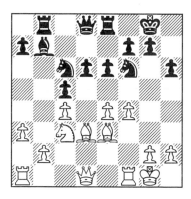

Further prophylaxis, this time directed against the sequence e5 dxe5; ♗xc5, after which the rook will no longer be hanging. It is interesting that Adams does not rush with ...e5, preferring to maximum flexibility with his central pawns for as long as possible.

16 ♖b1 a5

Preventing any b2-b4 ideas. A pre-

vious game from the same rapid match had continued 16...♗a8 with a draw in 46 moves. Evidently Britain's number one decided that the text was slightly more accurate.

17 ♘b5

Presumably this was designed to provoke Black's next.

17...e5

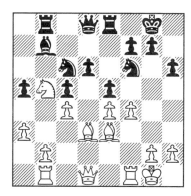

White was threatening 18 ♘xd6, meeting 18...♕xd6 with 19 e5 when 19...♘xe5?? would lose the queen after 20 ♗h7+.

18 f5

Radjabov decides to close the centre and pins his hopes on a kingside attack. Instead 18 b3 exf4 19 ♗xf4 ♘e5 20 ♗c2 ♖e6 (Ftacnik) leaves all of Black's pieces on good squares.

18...♘d4 19 ♘c3

The e-pawn needed protecting; besides the knight had little else to do on b5.

19...♗c6 20 ♖f2

20 b3 ♖b6 21 ♘d5 ♗xd5 22 cxd5 ♕b8 23 ♗c2 is equal according to Ftacnik, but I am not sure what White is doing after 23...♕b7, intending to fol-

low up ...♖b8.

20...♖b6 21 g4 ♘h7

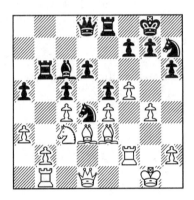

Fortifying the kingside; Black certainly does not want the g-file to become open.

22 ♖g2

White might have done well to consider 22 f6!?: for example, 22...♘xf6 (perhaps 22...g5!? 23 h4 ♕d7 can be considered) 23 g5 hxg5 24 ♗xg5 ♘e6 25 ♗xf6 gxf6 26 ♕f3 ♔f8 with unclear play.

22...♘g5?!

Threatening 23...♘h3+ and later ...♘f4, but White can easily prevent this. The problem is that unless the knight can achieve something definitive on g5, it will soon be driven away by h2-h4 when White's kingside offensive begins to gather momentum. Thus I prefer Ftacnik's suggestion of 22...♕h4! 23 ♘d5 ♗xd5 24 cxd5 and now 24...♖eb8 looks preferable for Black.

23 ♖g3 ♕a8

This was Adams' idea, making use of the knight to menace the white e-pawn.

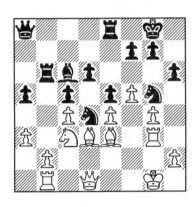

24 ♗xg5?

I don't like this move at all and fail to comprehend why White did not prefer 24 ♘d5 ♗xd5 25 cxd5, intending h4 and g5. It is worth mentioning that 25...♖eb8 26 h4 ♘gf3+ does not work after 27 ♖xf3 ♘xf3+ 28 ♕xf3 ♖xb2 29 ♖d1 with a big advantage.

24...hxg5

Black's questionable 22nd has been made to look like an excellent move. Now his kingside is more or less secure and both of his minor pieces are superior to their white counterparts. The next job will be to increase the pressure along the b-file.

25 ♕d2 ♕d8 26 ♖h3 ♕e7 27 ♘e2 ♖b3!?

Was this a slip-up or a clever trap? The simpler 27...♖eb8 would have cemented Black's advantage.

28 ♘c1

28 ♘xd4? exd4 leave White positionally lost.

28...♖b6

The rook has been forced to retreat. From a purist's perspective this may reek of imperfection, but ironically it leads to swift success in the game.

29 ♕xa5?

Radjabov falls for the trap. We should, of course, remember that this was only a rapid game and thus the players should not be judged too harshly, especially this far into the game when time pressure must have been looming.

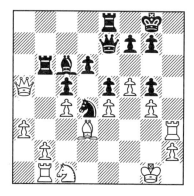

29...♕b7!

Attacking both b2 and e4.

30 ♕d2 f6!?

Black could in fact have played 30...♗xe4!?, but the position becomes rather complicated and in the circumstances Adams' choice looks more pragmatic. Ftacnik analyses 31 ♕xg5 ♗h1! 32 ♗f1 ♘f3+ 33 ♖xf3 ♕xf3 34 ♘d3 (no better is 34 f6 g6 35 ♘e2 d5 36 ♘g3 ♖xf6 37 ♘xh1 ♖f4) 34...f6 35 ♕g6 ♕a8, with a big advantage to Black.

31 ♖e3?

Ftacnik gives 31 ♘e2 as the best chance, but White is still not out of the woods after 31...♗xe4 32 ♘xd4 cxd4 (32...exd4!? 33 b4 ♖e5) 33 b4 ♖a8 or 33...♖c8.

31...♗xe4!

Evidently White had overlooked

this tactical shot, after which his position quickly crumbles.

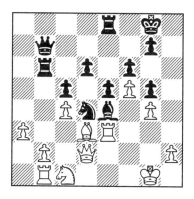

32 ♕f2

The point, of course, is that 32 ♗xe4 can be met by 32...♕xe4! 33 ♖xe4 (or 33 ♕d3 ♕xg4+) 33...♘f3+with huge material gains.

32...♗c6 33 h4

After 33 b3 ♖a8 34 a4 ♗xa4 35 ♗e4 ♗c6 Black dominates the board.

33...♘f3+ 34 ♖xf3 ♗xf3 35 hxg5 fxg5 36 ♕e3 e4 37 ♗f1

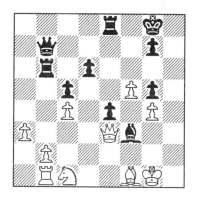

37...♕e7

37...♖xb2 would have won even more quickly, as shown by 38 ♖xb2 ♕xb2 39 ♕xg5 ♕d4+ 40 ♔h2 ♕f2+, but the text does not spoil anything.

38 b4 ♕e5 39 b5?

This is a blunder in a hopeless position.

39...♕g3+ 0-1

A fine performance from Britain's number one, notwithstanding a few minor errors. Along with Vyzmanavin-Salov, this game illustrates quite convincingly how, with skilful and patient play, Black can gradually build upon his positional assets; namely the d4-square, his extra central pawn and the half-open b-file.

Summary

The move 5 ♕c2 is both natural and strong, and fully deserves its status as the main line against 4...♗a6. After the further 5...♗b7! 6 ♘c3 c5 we have considered three main options. The sacrifice 7 d5?! is known to be less than sound here, although the second player must react with great precision in order to obtain the better game. Instead 7 dxc5 bxc5 leads to a pawn structure that can arise in several variations of the Queen's Indian. Generally there is not much need for any dense theoretical knowledge, and I hope that the material presented here will provide the reader with enough ideas to handle these positions with confidence.

We ended this chapter by considering the main line of 7 e4 cxd4 8 ♘xd4 ♗c5 9 ♘b3 ♘c6, examining White's early deviations along with the relatively uncommon but still quite respectable options of 10 ♗d3 and 10 ♘xc5. In general I would say that the black position contains sufficient resources in all these lines, although a good level of positional understanding is essential for success and thus I hope that the featured games have provided considerable food for thought.

Chapter Eleven

The Petrosian Main Line: 10 ♗f4 and 10 ♗g5

---

1 d4 ♘f6 2 c4 e6 3 ♘f3 b6 4 a3 ♗a6 5 ♕c2 ♗b7 6 ♘c3 c5 7 e4 cxd4 8 ♘xd4 ♗c5 9 ♘b3 ♘c6

Having dealt with all of White's minor possibilities after 4 a3 ♗a6 5 ♕c2 ♗b7, we now move on to the two most critical variations:

A: 10 ♗f4
B: 10 ♗g5

A) 10 ♗f4

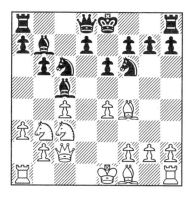

With this logical move White takes

aim at the sensitive d6-square. He will usually proceed by exchanging on c5 followed by occupying that square with his own bishop or occasionally even the other knight by means of ♘b5-d6.

10...0-0

The main alternative is 10...e5. This is perhaps Black's most solid move, but after analysing it in some detail I believe that White can obtain a small edge after 11 ♗g5 h6 12 ♗h4 0-0 13 f3. Instead I recommend that Black continues developing as rapidly as possible. This approach yields a far greater range of dynamic possibilities as well as being, in this writer's opinion, objectively stronger. It is true that the theoretical burden is somewhat heavier, but I am confident that after perusing the content of this chapter the reader will consider the extra time and effort to be thoroughly worthwhile.

We now consider in detail the following possibilities:

A1: 11 0-0-0
A2: 11 ♖d1
A3: 11 ♘xc5

Instead 11 ♗e2 (P.Dziadyk-V.Grinev, Kiev 2004) can be well met by 11...♘d4!? 12 ♘xd4 ♗xd4. In S.Lputian-M.Adams, Wijk aan Zee 2000, White preferred the sensible though rarely played 11 ♗d3 and after 11...e5 12 ♗g5 h6 13 ♗h4 ♗e7 14 0-0 ♘h5 15 ♗xe7 ♕xe7 16 ♖ad1 ♘f4 17 ♘d5 ♕g5 18 ♘xf4 exf4 19 f3 ♖ac8 20 ♕f2 ♘e5 the chances were balanced. It also looks interesting for Black to try either 11...d6!? or 11...♘g4!?.

A1) 11 0-0-0

This is not seen too often, but is quite ambitious and it is important for Black to react with precision and vigour.

11...e5!

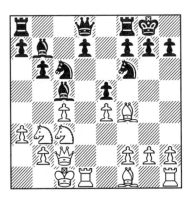

Comparing the situation with one move ago, it turns out that a small change in the position – the inclusion of castling by both sides – greatly improves the effectiveness of this move.

12 ♗g5

The alternatives are no better:

a) The best reaction to 12 ♗g3 (P.Cramling-M.Illescas Cordoba, Ponferrada 1997) would have been the consistent 12...♘d4! 13 ♘xd4 exd4! (13...♗xd4 14 f3 is solid enough for White) 14 ♘d5 ♘xd5 15 exd5 (15 cxd5 ♖c8 is also promising for Black) 15...b5! with the initiative.

b) In R.Bagirov-E.Alekseev, Tula 2002, White preferred to cover the sensitive d4-square even at the expense of his pawn structure with 12 ♗e3 ♗xe3+ 13 fxe3. The game continued 13...♖c8 14 ♗d3 a6 15 ♘d5 ♘a7 16 ♔b1 and now 16...b5! 17 c5 d6 would have brought Black a clear advantage.

12...♘d4! 13 ♘xd4 ♗xd4

Now White will have a hard time dealing with the pressure against c3 and e4.

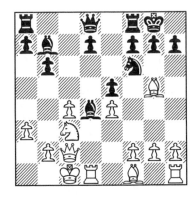

14 ♘d5

The alternatives also fail to provide a satisfactory solution to White's problems:

a) After 14 ♗d3? ♗xc3 15 bxc3 (15 ♕xc3 ♘xe4 16 ♗xd8 ♘xc3 gives Black a winning endgame) 15...h6 16 ♗h4 ♕e7 17 ♔b2 ♖ac8 18 f4 ♖c5 19 f5 ♖fc8 Black soon converted his advantage to victory in A.Pliasunov-S.Ionov, St Petersburg 2001.

b) 14 f3 (D.Adla-M.Olazarri, Montevideo 1994) should also be met by 14...♗xc3! 15 ♕xc3 (15 bxc3 would wreck White's structure, resulting in something similar to variation 'a') 15...♘xe4 16 ♗xd8 ♘xc3 17 ♖xd7 ♖fxd8 18 ♖xb7, at which point the splendid move 18...♘d1! maintains some initiative in the ending. Note that White is unable to complete development with 19 ♗e2?! on account of 19...♘xb2!.

c) 14 ♘b5 ♗xe4 15 ♕e2 d5 is evaluated as unclear by Yrjölä and Tella, but after the further 16 ♘xd4 exd4 17 ♖xd4 ♖c8 White has considerable difficulties connected with his retarded development and unsafe king.

14...♗xd5 15 exd5 b5 16 ♖xd4 exd4 17 c5 h6 18 ♗h4

We have been following the game P.Soln-D.Polajzer, Ljubljana 2002. At this point Black could have obtained the advantage with the energetic

18...b4!, intending 19 axb4 ♕b8 20 ♗xf6 ♕f4+, etc.

Armed with the considerable ammunition presented here, I believe that Black has every reason to feel confident after 11 0-0-0.

A2) 11 ♖d1 e5! 12 ♗g5 ♘d4

Black reacts in a similar fashion to Line A, although the impact is not quite as forceful here.

13 ♘xd4 ♗xd4

13...exd4 is also playable, but the text is more reliable here.

14 ♗d3 ♗c6

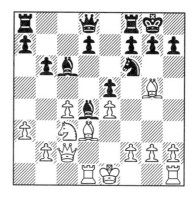

The alternative is 14...h6 when P.Jaracz-E.Berg, Stockholm 2006, continued 15 ♗h4 ♗xc3+ 16 ♕xc3 d6 and here 17 ♕c2 may give White chances for an advantage: for example, 17...b5!? (trying to obtain counterplay before White completes development) 18 cxb5 g5 19 ♗g3 ♕a5+ 20 ♔f1 ♖ac8 21 ♕e2 ♕a4 22 f3.

15 0-0

This has been the only move played, although 15 ♘d5!? is a logical alternative. Then after 15...♗xd5 16 cxd5 h6 17 ♗h4 b5!? (17...g5 18 ♗g3 ♘h5 looks close to equal, although Black will have a few light-square holes) 18 0-0 (White must, of course, avoid 18 ♗xb5?? ♕a5+) 18...a6, intending ...♕b6, the chances are balanced.

15...♗xc3 16 ♗xf6

This is forced as 16 ♕xc3? ♘xe4 wins a pawn.

16...♕xf6 17 ♕xc3 ♕g5

We have been following the game A.Lauber-E.Agrest, German League 2001. Black went on to win this game, but he was the higher rated player and objectively I would evaluate the chances as about equal; Black may have the better bishop, but he is hampered by his backward d-pawn. In any case, the game continued 18 ♗c2 ♖ac8 19 ♖d6 ♖fe8 20 ♖fd1 h5 21 ♕d2 ♕xd2 22 ♖6xd2 ♖c7 23 f3 ♔f8 24 ♔f2 ♔e7 25 b4 ♖d8 26 ♖d6?! (26 ♗b3 was better) 26...♗b5! 27 ♖6d5 ♗xc4 28 ♖xe5+ ♗e6 29 ♗d3 g6 30 a4 f6 31 ♖b5 ♗b3 32 ♖a1 ♖c3 33 ♔e2 ♖dc8 (also strong was 33...d5!? 34 exd5 ♗xd5) 34 ♔d2 ♖3c6 35 ♖a3 a6 36 ♖xb6 ♖xb6 37 ♖xb3 a5 38 b5 ♖c5 and Agrest went on to convert his material advantage.

In both Lines A and B we have seen that under the right conditions Black can obtain a good game with the delayed 11...e5, compared to 10...e5 which reveals his hand a little too soon and so presents the opponent with some additional opportunities. We must now address the critical line in which White attempts to exploit his opponent's refusal to advance the e-pawn.

A3) 11 ♘xc5 bxc5

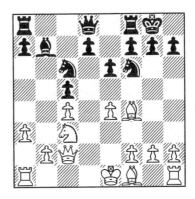

12 ♗d6

This is the only consistent move and nothing else is ever played. After this critical continuation the game can become extremely sharp, with the evaluation frequently hinging on whether the bishop on d6 turns out to be a strength or a liability.

12...♘d4

I will keep this tried and tested move as my main recommendation, although the reader may also wish to investigate 12...♕b6!?, an interesting and as yet untested suggestion from Jeroen Piket. Black offers a positional exchange sacrifice, which White can choose to accept or decline:

a) 13 ♗xf8 ♘d4 with two main queen moves:

a1) 14 ♕b1 ♖xf8 15 ♗d3 d5 gives Black excellent compensation: for example, 16 cxd5 exd5 17 0-0 c4!? (17...♘b3 was fine, but Black is playing even more ambitiously) 18 ♗c2 dxe4 19 ♘xe4 (no better is 19 ♗xe4 ♘xe4 20 ♘xe4 ♘b3 21 ♘g5 g6) 19...♗xe4 20 ♗xe4 ♘b3, regaining the material with a clear advantage.

a2) 14 ♕d3 ♖xf8 15 ♗e2?! (15 ♖d1 ♕xb2 16 ♖b1 ♕xa3 17 ♖xb7 ♕c1+ 18 ♘d1 ♘c2+ 19 ♔e2 ♘d4+ 20 ♔e1 ♘c2+ is perpetual, but perhaps White should already be looking to equalize) 15...d5! gives Black excellent chances.

White is in trouble) 14...♘e8 15 ♘a4 ♕a5 (15...♕d8!? is possible) 16 ♕xa5 ♘xa5 17 ♗e7! (not 17 ♗xc5?? ♘b3) 17...♘b3 18 ♖d1 ♗c6 19 ♘xc5 ♘xc5 20 ♗xc5 ♗a4 21 ♗d4 ♗xd1 22 ♔xd1, leading to an unclear endgame in which, perhaps somewhat ironically given the intent behind Black's 12th, it is now White who has good compensation for the exchange.

13 ♕d3

Instead 13 ♕d1? (R.Bagirov-V.Dobrov, Abu Dhabi 2002) can be refuted by the tactical strike 13...♘xe4! 14 ♘xe4 (14 ♗xf8? ♕h4! 15 g3 – 15 ♘xe4 ♕xe4+ 16 ♔d2 ♕f4+ followed by 17...♖xf8 is even worse – 15...♕f6 leaves White unable to cope with the numerous threats) 14...♗xe4.

Play might continue 16 exd5 exd5 17 0-0 ♗a6! with a powerful initiative.

b) Perhaps 13 e5 is a sterner test, refusing the bait and maintaining the bishop's powerful position. Best play then looks like 13...♖fc8! (13...♘d4 14 ♕d3 ♘h5 15 0-0-0! appears better for White) 14 ♕d2 (after 14 exf6? ♘d4 15 ♕d3 ♕xd6 16 fxg7 ♕e5+ 17 ♘e2 d5

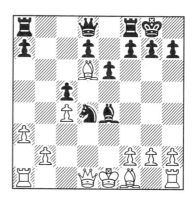

White's position is on the verge of collapse, as illustrated by the following brief variations:

a) 15 ♗xf8? ♘c2+ 16 ♔e2 (16 ♔d2? ♕g5+) 16...♘d4+!? (16...♔xf8) 17 ♔e3 ♗c2 followed by recapturing on f8 with a winning position.

b) After 15 f3 ♗c2 16 ♕d2 ♖e8 17 ♗e5 ♗b3 18 ♗xd4 (18 ♖c1 d5) 18...cxd4

19 ♕xd4 ♖c8 Black's advantage is already close to decisive.

c) 15 ♖c1 ♕f6 16 ♗xc5 (or 16 ♗xf8 ♖xf8 17 ♖c3 ♖b8 18 b3 ♕e5) 16...♘f3+! 17 gxf3 ♗xf3 and Black should win without too many problems.

13...♖e8

The alternative 13...e5 has also been played, but I think that the text is better.

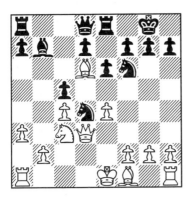

This whole variation encompasses a fascinating blend of strategy and tactics. The long-term chances lie with White's bishop-pair, but for the time being he suffers from a serious lag in development. The bishop on d6 is a potential match winner, but can also prove tactically vulnerable. On the whole I feel quite confident about Black's chances; the one caveat being that a certain degree of theoretical knowledge is necessary if one is to navigate the ensuing complications successfully.

Here 14 ♗xc5? is a blunder due to 14...♘b3, and so White normally chooses between either an ultra-ambitious or a more solid course:

A31: 14 b4?!
A32: 14 e5

Instead 14 ♖d1 does not appear to have been tried. Black can obtain a good game with 14...e5!, as after 15 ♗xc5 d6! 16 ♗xd4 exd4 17 ♕xd4 ♘xe4 18 ♗e2 ♕g5! 19 ♖g1 ♘xc3 20 ♕xc3 d5 White's extra pawn in no way makes up for his inability to castle.

A31) 14 b4?!

This has been overwhelmingly the most popular choice, but the whole concept of expanding on the queenside seems excessively ambitious when the king is still rooted to its starting square. Moreover, the text neglects development while presenting Black with an ideal opportunity to improve his pieces with...

14...e5!

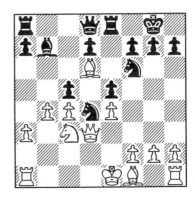

This excellent move enables Black to stabilize his knight and to fix the weak e4-pawn, while simultaneously increasing the scope of the rook on e8. Though I would not go so far as to claim a definite advantage for Black, practice has demonstrated quite conclusively that it is White who must tread the more carefully. We will now focus on three responses:

A311: 15 ♗xc5
A312: 15 ♖b1
A313: 15 ♖a2

The alternatives lead to even greater problems for White:

a) 15 ♗e2? overlooks the main threat of 15...cxb4! 16 axb4 ♖e6 when the bishop is short of squares. Following 17 c5 (17 ♗c5 is met by 17...a5!) Black has a choice of promising lines:

a1) 17...♘e8 18 ♗g4 ♖g6 19 ♗h5 ♖g5 20 ♗xe5 ♖xe5 21 ♗xf7+ ♔xf7 22 ♕xd4 (L.Van Wely-J.Granda Zuniga, Wijk aan Zee 1997) 22...♕e7 is good for Black.

a2) 17...♘xe2!? may be even stronger: 18 ♕xe2 ♘e8 19 ♕d2 ♘xd6 20 cxd6 ♕b6 21 ♖d1 ♗c6 22 0-0 ♕xb4 23 ♘d5 ♕xe4 24 ♖fe1 ♕xd5 25 ♕xd5 ♗xd5 26 ♖xd5 was seen in I.Thomas-P.Jaracz, Schwaebisch Gmuend 2005, and now 26...a5!? 27 ♖a1 a4 28 ♔f1 f5 29 ♔e2 ♔f7 is an easy win.

b) 15 bxc5?! is also dubious in view of 15...♕a5 16 f3 ♗xe4! 17 fxe4 ♘xe4 18 ♖c1 ♕xa3 and now:

b1) 19 ♕e3 ♘f5 20 ♕xe4 ♕xc1+ 21 ♘d1 ♘xd6 22 cxd6 ♕a3 23 ♗d3 g6 with a clear advantage.

b2) 19 ♘a2 is relatively best, although even here 19...♕a5+ 20 ♘c3 ♘xc5 21 ♗xc5 ♕xc5 leaves Black with three pawns and a lead in development for the piece.

A311) 15 ♗xc5 a5!

This is much stronger than 15...♘b3 16 ♖b1 ♘xc5 17 bxc5 ♗c6 18 ♗e2 ♕a5 19 0-0 ♕xc5 (or 19...♕xa3 20 ♘d5 ♕xc5 21 ♘xf6+ gxf6 22 ♖fd1) 20 ♘d5 when the position is about equal. We now follow the model game E.Miciak-M.Maros, correspondence 2001:

16 bxa5??

This is already a losing blunder, although the position was by now becoming extremely dangerous for White:

a) 16 ♖d1? is very risky due to 16...d6! 17 ♗xd4 exd4 18 ♕xd4 axb4 19 axb4 ♘xe4 when it is doubtful that White will survive for long.

b) 16 ♗d6 is his only chance, but even here Black obtains a strong initiative with 16...♖e6! 17 ♗xe5 ♘xe4!? (17...♘c2+ 18 ♕xc2 ♖xe5 is also playable).

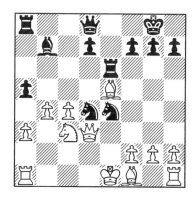

Then 18 ♕xd4 ♘xc3 19 ♗d3 (or 19 ♕xc3 ♕g5!) 19...♗xg2 20 ♖g1 axb4 21 ♔d2 f6 leaves Black excellently placed. Even so, this was the lesser evil as after the move played in the game Black swiftly obtains a winning position.

16...♕xa5 17 ♗b4 ♕xb4! 18 axb4 ♖xa1+ 19 ♔d2 ♖ea8 20 f3 ♖8a3 21 ♕e3 ♖b3

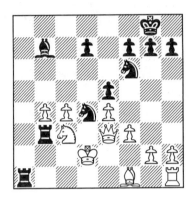

After a forcing sequence we can see that Black's rook and knight easily outclass the white queen, and the game is soon over:

22 b5

22 ♕g5 ♖b2+ 23 ♔d3 d6 would not alter the result.

22...♖aa3 23 h3

White is not helped by either 23 ♗d3 ♖xc3 or 23 ♗e2 ♖b2+ 24 ♔c1 ♖c2+.

23...d6!

White is almost completely paralysed, so Black calmly prepares to improve another piece.

24 ♕d3 ♘d7! 25 ♘d5 ♗xd5 26 cxd5 ♘c5! 0-1

Just to add insult to injury, Black emphasizes the fact that he does not yet need to capture the queen! Faced with this utter humiliation, White resigned.

A312) 15 ♖b1 cxb4 16 axb4

It should hardly need stating that the alternative recaptures would not improve White's chances:

a) 16 ♗xb4?! ♕c7! threatens 17...a5 winning the bishop, and so practically forces the time-wasting 17 a4.

b) 16 ♖xb4?! ♗c6 17 f3 (or 17 ♖b2 ♖e6 18 ♗b4 a5 19 ♗c5 ♖b8) 17...♘h5!? 18 ♗xe5 (18 g3? ♕f6) 18...♘xf3+ 19 ♕xf3 ♖xe5 gives Black the advantage.

16...♖e6 17 c5

17 ♗xe5? is practically suicidal in view of 17...♘xe4!, but now White's bishop has been immobilized and could well become a target.

17...♖c8 18 f3 ♖xd6!

This is the most ambitious and interesting treatment. Instead the game A.Delchev-P.Jaracz, Nova Gorica 2004, was soon agreed drawn after 18...♘e8 19 ♗xe5 ♘xf3+ 20 ♕xf3 ♖xe5 21 ♗d3 (21 ♗c4!? ♕h4+ 22 g3 ♕e7 23 0-0 ♘f6 24 ♘d5 ♗xd5 25 exd5 a5 26 d6 ♕e8 27 ♗a6 ♖b8 28 bxa5 ♖xc5 29 ♕a3 ♖xa5 30 ♕xa5 ♕e3+ 31 ♔g2 ♕e4+ looks like a perpetual) 21...♕h4+.

19 cxd6 ♘e8

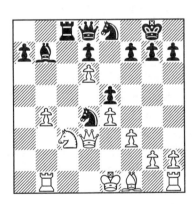

Black will shortly pick up the pawn on d6, thereby reaching something close to material parity. Meanwhile his knight is a tower of strength on d4, while the rest of his pieces are much more active than their white counterparts. We now follow the game M.Bosboom-E.Alekseev, Wijk aan Zee 2005:

20 ♗e2 ♘xd6 21 ♗d1

21 0-0?? allows 21...♖xc3 and 21 ♔f2 f5 22 exf5 ♘6xf5 would also be problematic for White.

21...♕h4+! 22 g3 ♕h3

Alekseev ensures that the white king will have to remain in the centre for the foreseeable future.

23 ♖b2 f5!?

23...h5!? also deserved consideration.

24 ♖f1 ♕h6

24...♘c4 25 ♖a2 a6 26 exf5 d5 27 ♖ff2 seems to keep everything defended.

25 ♖a2 a6 26 ♖ff2

At this point the game continued with 26...♔h8 and although Black's position remained more than satisfactory, White was able to consolidate his position and eventually came away with a draw. Instead I would recommend the more forcing 26...fxe4!, leading to a position in which White's e4-pawn will remain a chronic weakness after both 27 fxe4 ♕g6 and 27 ♘xe4 ♘xe4 28 fxe4 ♕g6. In both cases the superb activity of all Black's pieces, combined with the weakness on e4 and the general disarray of the opposing forces, leads me to assess his chances as favourable.

A313) 15 ♖a2!?

This looks like White's best chance, relatively speaking.

15...cxb4! 16 axb4 ♕b6

Once again Black targets the bishop on d6.

17 ♗c5

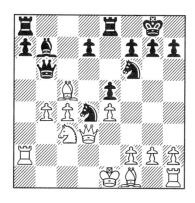

Now Black faces a difficult choice between two quite promising moves.

17...♕c6

In U.Hueser-H.Burger, correspondence 2002, Black was also successful after 17...♕c7 18 f3 a5! 19 ♗xd4 exd4 20 ♘b5 ♕f4 (20...♕e5 was also possible) 21 ♕d2 ♕h4+ 22 ♕f2?! (in N.Vitiugov-S.Ionov, Saint Petersburg 2005, White improved with 22 g3, although

22...♕h5 23 ♗e2 axb4 still left Black with some initiative) 22...♕g5 23 ♕d2 ♘xe4! 24 fxe4 (24 ♕xg5 ♘xg5+ 25 ♔f2 axb4 leaves White in trouble) 24...♕h4+ 25 ♔d1 axb4 26 ♖xa8 ♖xa8 27 ♕xd4 ♗xe4 with an ongoing attack.

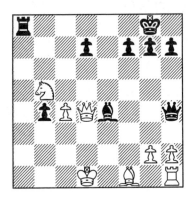

Eventually he regained the sacrificed material while retaining an extra pawn after 28 h3 ♕h5+ 29 ♔c1 ♕f5 30 ♔b2 ♗b1 31 ♔b3 ♕c2+ 32 ♔xb4 ♕a4+ 33 ♔c3 ♕a5+ 34 ♔b3 d5! 35 ♗d3 ♗xd3 36 ♕xd3 dxc4+ 37 ♕xc4 ♖b8 38 ♔c2 ♕xb5 39 ♕xb5 ♖xb5 40 ♔d3 ♖e5! Black's last move ensured that the enemy king remained cut off, thus guaranteeing an easy win.

18 ♘d5?

This is the only move to have been played, but I think it is asking far too much of the white position. Instead he should definitely prefer one of the following alternatives:

a) Perhaps the safest course of action would have been 18 f3 a5 19 ♗xd4 axb4 20 ♖xa8 ♗xa8 21 ♗e3 bxc3 22 ♗e2 with equality, although White must be careful to avoid 22 ♕xc3? d5! with a strong attack.

b) 18 ♗xa7!? looks risky, but I have not been able to find more than equality for Black after 18...♕c7! 19 ♗e2 ♘xe2 20 ♕xe2 ♗c6 21 ♗e3 ♘xe4 22 ♘xe4 ♖xa2 23 ♕xa2 ♗xe4 24 0-0 ♕b7 25 ♕a7 ♗xg2 26 ♕xb7 ♗xb7 27 ♖d1 d5 28 cxd5 ♖d8 29 d6 f6.

18...a5! 19 ♘e7+ ♖xe7 20 ♗xe7

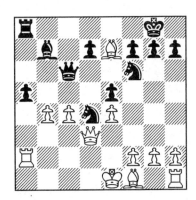

We have been following the game O.Tuka-A.Nosenko, Chernigov 2005, in which 20...axb4 21 ♖xa8+ ♗xa8 22 f3 b3 gave Black decent compensation for the exchange, although he later went wrong and lost. Although that is quite acceptable, I consider it even more promising to play:

20...♘xe4! 21 bxa5

21 f3 is an alternative, but after 21...♕e6 (Ionov) Black has a strong initiative.

21...d6!

The immediate 21...d5 22 f3 is not so clear, not least because 22...dxc4? 23 ♕xe4 ♕b5? 24 ♗xc4! wins for White.

22 ♗h4

This is more or less forced, as otherwise a subsequent ...f6 would trap the bishop.

22...d5!

This excellent move brings Black a huge attack. We will soon see why it was so important to drive the bishop back to h4 before opening up the centre.

23 f3 dxc4! 24 ♕xc4

The point of Black's 21st is seen after 24 ♕xe4 ♕b5! when 25 ♗xc4? loses to 25...♕b4+!, as the bishop is no longer covering that square from e7.

24...♕h6! 25 fxe4

There is nothing better.

25...♖c8!?

25...♕xh4+ should also win, but the text seems even more precise.

26 ♕d3 ♕xh4+ 27 g3 ♖c1+ 28 ♔f2

28 ♔d2? ♕g5+ wins even more quickly.

28...♕f6+ 29 ♔g2 ♕g6 30 ♖e2 h6

But not 30...♘xe2?? 31 ♕d8 mate!

31 ♖e3 ♘c2 32 ♖e2 ♘e1+ 33 ♖xe1 ♖xe1

Black wins. There is no doubt, though, that White should have preferred one of the alternatives on move 18. However, if Black does not wish to allow such a course, he can investigate 17...♕c7 which also looks promising.

A32) 14 e5

We have seen how effective Black's counterplay becomes when he is allowed to play ...e5 himself. Although the text has been played less frequently than 14 b4, its appeal is self-evident; the bishop on d6 receives some much needed support, while the rook on e8 is less likely to find an active role. The only drawback from White's point of view is that the Queen's Indian bishop now enjoys a greatly enhanced view of the long diagonal.

14...♘g4

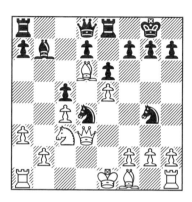

14...♘h5?! looks worse; a possible continuation being 15 ♘e2 ♘xe2 16 ♕xe2 ♕h4 17 ♕e3 ♘f4 18 ♕g3 ♘xg2+ 19 ♗xg2 ♕xg3 20 hxg3 ♗xg2. Black may be able to hold this ending, but White's beautifully-placed bishop ensures that there will only be one side trying to win.

After the text, we face a final division in the material:

A321: 15 ♘e4
A322: 15 b4!?
A323: 15 ♗xc5!?

Instead 15 h3 ♕h4! (Piket) is awkward for White, while 15 ♖d1 ♕g5!? targets e5. Play might continue 16 ♘e4 ♗xe4 17 ♕xe4 f5! 18 exf6 ♘xf6 with some initiative, or 16 h4 ♕f5! 17 ♕xf5 exf5! when the rook on e8 enters the game with powerful effect.

A321) 15 ♘e4

This was played in G.Miniboeck-I.Farago, Austrian League 1998, which we will now follow:

15...♗xe4!

Black 'sacrifices' his remaining bishop in order to disrupt the enemy king.

16 ♕xe4 ♘b3 17 ♖d1 ♕a5+

This is the point – the king has to move.

18 ♔e2 f5! 19 ♕f4

White endeavours to keep the position closed. Instead 19 exf6 ♘xf6 20 ♕e5 enables Black to choose between 20...♖f8!?, 20...♕b6 and 20...♕a4, with active prospects in all cases.

19...♘d4+ 20 ♖xd4

White has no real choice, as 20 ♔d3? ♕a4 would be suicidal.

20...cxd4 21 ♕xd4

White certainly has some positional compensation for the exchange, but one must also take into consideration his retarded development.

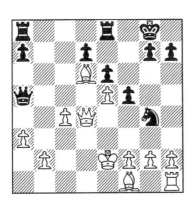

At this point Black played 21...♕a4 and although he went on to win, I think I would prefer the immediate 21...♘h6!, intending ...♘f7 to exchange

the opponent's best piece. In that case I do not believe that White could claim sufficient compensation, especially as it will take him a good few moves to develop his kingside pieces.

A322) 15 b4!?

This was suggested by Yrjölä and Tella, who remark that the position is 'very murky'. So far the idea has not been tested in practice, but I would suggest...

15...f6!

as a suitable antidote. Play might continue:

16 bxc5

16 ♗xc5? ♘b3 is certainly not an improvement for White.

16...♘f5 17 ♘b5

No better is 17 ♗e2 ♘xe5.

17...♘xe5 18 ♕c3 ♖c8

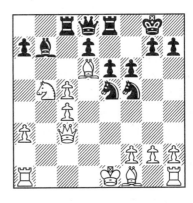

Black's superior development and powerful knights give him excellent chances: for example, 19 ♘xa7 ♘xd6 20 cxd6 ♖c5 (20...♗xg2!? is interesting, but hardly necessary) 21 ♘b5 ♕b6 22 a4 (the threat was 22...♕xb5) 22...♖ec8 when White is in big trouble; he is lagging in development and his queenside is about to collapse.

A323) 15 ♗xc5!?

This amazing idea was tried in H.Banikas-M.Roiz, Istanbul 2003. After many subsequent adventures White's ingenuity was eventually rewarded with a full point, but we will soon see how Black could have improved.

15...♘b3 16 ♕d1

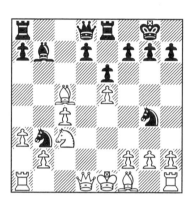

Now instead of the game's 16...♕a5?!, I agree with Roiz that Black should prefer...

16...♘xa1! 17 ♕xg4 ♖c8!

Roiz also analyses 17...♘b3!?, but I think that the text is even better.

18 ♗xa7

The alternative is 18 ♗d6 ♕b6 19 ♗d3 (19 b4 ♘c2+ is awkward) 19...♕xb2 and now:

a) 20 ♘e4 does not work after 20...♘c2+ 21 ♗xc2 (21 ♔d1? ♘d4 22 ♘f6+ ♔h8 is winning for Black) 21...♕xc2 22 ♘f6+ ♔h8 23 ♘xe8 ♕c3+ 24 ♔e2 ♕c2+ 25 ♔e3 ♖xe8. Material is level here, but the exposed position of White's king will create difficulties for him.

b) 20 ♘d1 looks better, but even here after 20...♘c2+! (20...♕b3 21 ♕e2 ♗xg2 22 ♖g1 allows White to become a bit more active) 21 ♔d2 ♕d4! I do not believe that White has enough for the exchange, although I must admit that the bishop on d6 is rather well placed.

18...♕a5 19 ♗d4 ♘c2+ 20 ♔d2 ♘xd4 21 ♕xd4

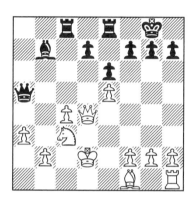

If White were given a few tempi to coordinate his pieces then he would gain the advantage. However, as things stand his situation is rendered highly precarious by his centralized king and lagging development. Black can best exploit these factors with a temporary sacrifice:

21...d6!

21...♖ed8 is given by Roiz, but the text seems more energetic.

22 exd6 e5 23 ♕e3

It is hard to say whether White should prefer this to 23 ♕d3 ♖ed8 24 ♔c1 when Black can create awkward problems with 24...♗a6!. The most likely outcome appears to be some sort of endgame in which Black, after winning the c- and d-pawns, will enjoy a material advantage of the exchange for a pawn. This ought to provide some winning chances, although if White manages to get his queenside pawns rolling then any result could be possible.

23...♖ed8 24 c5 ♕xc5

The alternative is 24...♖xc5!? 25 b4 ♖d5+! (not 25...♖xd6+? 26 ♗d3) 26 ♘xd5 ♕xd5+ 27 ♔e1 ♖xd6 28 f3! ♕a2 29 ♗e2! ♕a1+ 30 ♔f2 ♕xh1 31 ♕xe5 ♖d8 32 ♕c7 (this is the point; White regains one of the black pieces) 32...♖e8 33 ♕xb7 ♕xh2 when Black has slightly the better chances.

25 ♕xc5 ♖xc5

Black has quite good chances to convert his material advantage.

B) 10 ♗g5

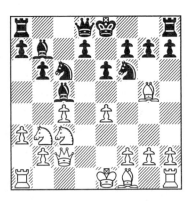

This may be regarded as the ultimate main line of the 4 a3 ♗a6 system. White establishes what he hopes will be a troubling pin on the enemy knight and in many variations he will follow up with long castling. Now the most frequently played continuation is 10...h6 11 ♗h4 ♘d4 12 ♘xd4 ♗xd4.

Although this is an absolutely valid method of playing the position, not to mention one that I myself have used on more than one occasion, I eventually decided to recommend something different.

10...♘d4!?

Essentially this is the same idea, except that Black is hoping to benefit from the omission of the moves ...h6 and ♗h4. As we will soon see, there are arguments for and against each approach and there is still no clear consensus as to which should be preferred. The statistics are encouraging, though; according to my database the text has scored an impressive 55% for Black, compared with 43% for 10...h6.

11 ♘xd4 ♗xd4

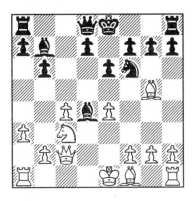

The bishop takes up an influential central position while incidentally threatening to take on c3. Once again in the 5 ♕c2 variation, one can already sense that the battle for the dark squares will be a prevailing theme. Here White has two serious options to consider:

B1: 12 ♗d3
B2: 12 ♘b5

The former is the calm approach, especially when compared with the more aggressive latter. The alternatives are only occasionally seen:

a) 12 0-0-0? can be more or less refuted by 12...♗xc3! when 13 bxc3 ♗xe4 14 ♕d2 (C.Tunge-A.Aaberg, Gausdal 1991) 14...♕e7 15 ♔b2 ♗c6 leaves White with very little to show for his pawn, and 13 ♕xc3 ♘xe4 14 ♗xd8 ♘xc3 15 ♖d3 ♘a2+ 16 ♔b1 ♖xd8 17 ♔xa2 ♔e7 was nothing more than a technical exercise for Black in A.Stamenkovic-P.Bodiroga, Herceg Novi 2005.

b) 12 f3 does not appear to have been tried. The response 12...h6 works well after 13 ♗h4? ♗xc3+! 14 ♕xc3 (14 bxc3 would ruin White's structure) 14...♘xe4!, but 13 ♗f4! looks better. Instead I would suggest 12...♗e5, keeping a firm hold over the dark squares.

B1) 12 ♗d3 ♕b8!

This is a highly thematic move for this variation. Black unpins the knight while improving his control over the central dark squares. Note that 12...♕c7?! would have been less suitable, as the queen would have been vulnerable to ♘b5 ideas. Now after a subsequent ...0-0 the king's rook may slot over to c8, occupying an ideal spot on the semi-open file while also menacing the enemy queen.

13 ♘e2!?

This is the only really challenging move, fighting for the dark squares.

a) It is worth considering the conse-

quences of 13 ♗h4 0-0 14 ♗g3 ♗e5. At this point we have actually reached something closely resembling the main line of the 10...h6 variation (the actual sequence would be 10...h6 11 ♗h4 ♘d4 12 ♘xd4 ♗xd4 13 ♗d3 ♕b8 14 ♗g3 ♗e5), except that Black has virtually saved a tempo by omitting the move ...h6, which contributes very little to his position. The game A.Dreev-E.Lobron, Internet 2004, continued 15 0-0-0 ♖c8 16 ♔b1 a6 17 ♕e2 b5 18 f3 and here 18...bxc4 19 ♗xc4 ♕c7 followed by ...♖ab8 would have given Black a very active position.

b) 13 0-0-0 can be met by 13...h6 (13...♕e5!? may also be a good move, intending 14 ♗d2 ♗xf2 or 14 f4 ♗e3+) 14 ♗xf6 ♗xf6 when I prefer Black's chances thanks to the tremendous potential of his unopposed dark-squared bishop. Two practical examples:

b1) After 15 ♔b1 0-0 16 g3 ♖c8 17 f4 ♗xc3 18 ♕xc3 d5 Black was better in M.Mishkoski-M.Mitkov, Struga 2005.

b2) 15 g3 0-0 16 f4 was L.Van Wely-B.Gelfand, Monaco (rapid) 2002.

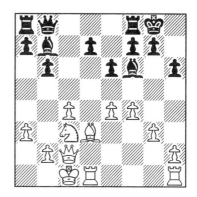

Here I think that Black should have

played 16...d6, preventing any e4-e5 ideas and maintaining the better chances. Instead the game continuation of 16...a6 allowed Van Wely to initiate complications with 17 e5!? ♗xh1 18 exf6 ♗c6 19 ♕e2 when he had some compensation for the exchange and eventually emerged victorious.

13...♗c5

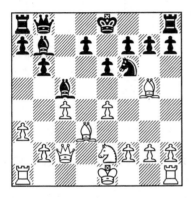

13...h6?! has been played, but after 14 ♗d2 ♗c5 15 b4 ♗e7 16 0-0 0-0 17 f4 White was better in P.Tregubov-J.Lipka, Cappelle la Grande 1995.

14 b4

This is White's most energetic continuation. Others give Black nothing to worry about:

a) The immediate 14 0-0 can be met by 14...♘g4!? 15 ♗f4 ♗d6 16 ♗g3 h5! with counterplay. Now after the natural 17 ♕c3 (R.Alvarez-E.Pileckis, Yerevan 2007) Black should have played 17...♗xg3 18 hxg3 ♕e5 with a comfortable position.

b) 14 ♕c3 ♗e7 (14...♘g4!? has also been played) 15 e5 soon led to simplification in I.Khenkin-C.Lutz, German League 2002, after 15...♘e4 16 ♗xe4

♗xg5 17 ♕f3 ♗xe4 18 ♕xe4 0-0. Following the natural 19 ♖d1 ♕c7 White decided to activate his rook in a creative fashion with 20 h4!? ♗e7 21 ♖h3, at which point 21...♖ad8!? deserved consideration, intending ...d6 or even ...f6!? with a fair share of the chances.

c) 14 ♗f4 has also been played, but Black equalizes easily with 14...♗d6, for example:

c1) 15 ♗d2 ♘g4 16 h3 ♘e5 17 f4 ♘xd3+ 18 ♕xd3 0-0 19 0-0 ♕c7 20 ♗b4 ♗c5+ was equal in K.Miton-B.Lalic, British League 2006.

c2) 15 ♗xd6 ♕xd6 16 f4 ♕c5 17 ♖f1 was H.Pilaj-V.Babula, Austrian League 2006. Here it looks interesting for Black to try 17...♘g4!? and 17...♖c8 is another good move.

c3) 15 ♗g3 ♕c7 16 0-0-0 ♗xg3 17 hxg3 ♖c8 18 ♔b1 b5! 19 cxb5 ♕xc2+ 20 ♗xc2 ♘xe4 21 ♖d4 ♘f6 (21...♖c4!?) 22 f3 ♔e7 23 ♖a4 ♖a8 was agreed drawn in B.Avrukh-B.Gelfand, Ashdod 2004.

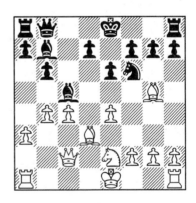

14...♗e7

This is very solid, although some players have preferred the more enterprising 14...♗d6!? when White has tried:

a) 15 ♗d2 ♘h5 16 g3 f5 17 f3 fxe4 18 ♗xe4 ♘f6 19 ♗xb7 ♕xb7 20 0-0 0-0 21 ♕d3 (M.Dziuba-P.Liwak, Lubniewice 2003) 21...♗e7 with approximate equality.

b) With 15 h3 White prepares to castle. After 15...a5 16 c5!? the game M.Cebalo-I.Zaja, Montecatini Terme 2002, continued 16...♗e5 17 ♖b1 axb4 18 axb4 ♖a3 at which point 19 f4 would have been good for White. Instead 16...♗e7!? looks like a possible improvement, placing the bishop on a less vulnerable location.

15 ♖b1

15 0-0 is a sensible alternative when 15...a5 16 ♕c3 d6 17 ♖fd1 is given as slightly better for White by Ftacnik. Instead I would suggest the more active 15...♘g4! 16 ♗f4 ♗d6.

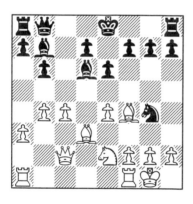

Now after 17 ♗g3 ♗xg3 18 ♘xg3 (or 18 hxg3?! ♕e5! intending to swing to h5) 18...h5! 19 ♖fd1 h4 20 ♘f1 ♕f4 Black is doing very nicely. Similarly after 17 ♗xd6 ♕xd6 18 ♘g3, again 18...h5! is a good move, intending 19 c5 ♕f4!, while 19 ♖fd1 h4 20 ♘f1 can be

met by 20...♕f4 or even 20...h3!? 21 g3 ♕d4!.

15...0-0 16 f4 h6 17 ♗h4

So far we have been following the game P.Acs-Z.Almasi, Paks 2005. Almasi chose 17...♕d8 and eventually won, although White stood slightly better out of the opening. Instead I would propose Ftacnik's suggestion of a central counterattack with 17...d5!? as an improvement.

Now 18 e5 dxc4 19 ♗xc4 (19 ♕xc4 ♖c8) 19...♘d5 20 ♗xe7 ♘xe7 is equal according to Ftacnik, while 18 cxd5 can be met by 18...♘xd5! 19 ♗xe7 ♘xe7 20 0-0 ♖d8 again with approximately balanced chances.

B2) 12 ♘b5

This is the most critical continuation, with which White attempts to highlight the downside to his opponent's refusal to play ...h6. The point is that White will get to force through the move e4-e5, although it is far from clear which side will actually benefit from this. Is White punishing his adversary with this uncompromising approach, or merely weakening his own position?

12...♗e5

12...♗c5 is also playable, but I have chosen to concentrate on the text.

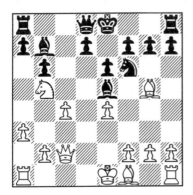

13 f4

Once White has started down the aggressive path he should continue in the same vein. A few players have bottled out with 13 ♗d3, but after 13...a6 (13...♕b8!? also looks good) 14 ♘c3 it is clear that White has only succeeded in wasted time. Following 14...♕c7 the following examples will illustrate Black's chances:

a) After 15 ♕e2 b5! 16 0-0 bxc4 17 ♗xc4 ♗xc3 18 bxc3 ♘xe4 Black was a pawn up for nothing in H.Valgmaee-N.Wikman, correspondence 1990.

b) 15 0-0-0 could also be met by 15...b5!? (15...0-0 is fine too) 16 cxb5 0-0!, intending ...♖fc8 with more than enough compensation.

c) In I.Naumkin-V.Tukmakov, USSR 1988, Black whipped up a vicious attack in wonderfully creative fashion after 15 h3 0-0 16 0-0 ♘h5!? (the more conventional 16...♖ac8 was a decent

alternative) 17 ♘e2 f5!.

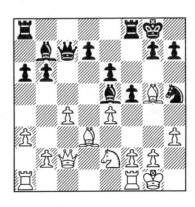

Amazingly the game was over in just eight more moves: 18 exf5 exf5 19 ♗xf5 (the lines 19 ♗e3 f4 and 19 f4 ♗d6! are mentioned by Tukmakov) 19...♕c6 20 f3 (20 ♗xh7+ ♔h8 21 f3 ♕c5+ 22 ♔h1 ♗c7! 23 ♗h4 ♕e5 reaches the note to White's 23rd, below) 20...♕c5+ 21 ♔h1 (21 ♖f2? allows 21...♖xf5 22 ♕xf5 ♗h2+ 23 ♔xh2 ♕xf5) 21...♗c7! 22 ♗xh7+ (after 22 g4 ♕e5 23 ♖f2 Black crashes through with 23...♗xf3+! 24 ♔g1 ♘g3) 22...♔h8 23 f4 (23 ♗h4 ♕e5 24 f4 ♘xf4 25 ♖xf4 ♖xf4 26 ♗g3 ♕e3! wins for Black, as 27 ♘xf4 ♕xg3 is curtains and 27 ♗xf4?? allows 27...♕xh3+! 28 ♔g1 ♕xg2 mate) 23...♖ae8! (Black brings his final piece into the attack) 24 b4 ♕e3 25 ♘g1 ♘g3+ 0-1. White resigned in view of 26 ♔h2 ♘xf1+ 27 ♖xf1 ♖xf4 28 ♗xf4 ♗xf4+ 29 ♔h1 ♕g3 30 ♖xf4 ♕xf4 31 ♗g6 ♖e5 when Black keeps a material advantage along with a devastating attack.

13...♗b8 14 e5

Once again this is the only consistent move.

14...h6

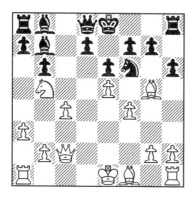

In this critical position White must choose between:

B21: 15 exf6
B22: 15 ♗xf6

Instead 15 ♗h4 is never played, as 15...g5 works out well for Black.

B21) 15 exf6 hxg5 16 fxg7 ♖g8 17 ♕h7 ♔e7

We have reached a highly irregular position, but one in which Black has good reason to feel confident. For the time being he is a pawn down, but he enjoys long-term compensation cour-

tesy of his splendid pair of bishops combined with his central pawn majority. The king on e7 is nowhere near as exposed as it may appear. Overall, tournament practice has indicated that White's task is the more difficult.

18 fxg5

The most obvious, although Black should certainly pay attention to the second of the following alternatives:

a) 18 ♗d3?! is inaccurate and after 18...♗xf4 19 ♕h6? (19 0-0 is better, although 19...♕b8 20 ♖ae1 ♗e5 followed by ...♖xg7 still looks good for Black; please note, however, that 19...♗e5? would be a blunder due to 20 ♖xf7+! ♔xf7 21 ♖f1+ ♔e7 22 ♗g6 ♗f6 23 ♕h6! with a decisive attack) 19...♕b8! 20 0-0 ♕e5 21 ♖ae1 ♕xb2 22 ♗e4 ♗xe4 23 ♖xe4 ♕xg7 Black was already winning in R.Tuominen-H.Salo, Finland 2004.

b) 18 ♗e2!? is somewhat better as the bishop can later jump to h5. The game P.Toulzac-M.Palac, Cap d'Agde 2003, proceeded 18...♗xf4 19 0-0 a6 20 ♘c3 ♗e5 21 ♗h5 f5. It looks as though White's attack has reached a dead end, but to his credit he now came up with 22 ♖xf5! (22 ♖ae1 ♖xg7 23 ♕h6 ♕h8! 24 ♕xh8 ♗d4+ 25 ♔h1 ♖xh8 is winning for Black – Emms) 22...exf5 23 ♕xf5 ♗xc3 24 ♖e1+ ♔d6 (24...♗xe1?? allows mate in one with 25 ♕e5) 25 c5+ (25 bxc3? ♔c7) 25...♔c7.

Despite appearances to the contrary, White's attack is not too dangerous here. The black king is not, and has never been, in any danger of being mated and the most that White can realistically hope for is a draw.

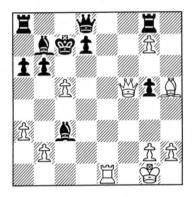

After the further continuation 26 bxc3 (26 cxb6+? ♔c8 27 bxc3 ♕xb6+ 28 ♔h1 ♗c6 sees Black consolidating) 26...♗c6 (26...♖c8!? is one possible winning attempt) 27 ♗f7 ♔b7 28 ♗xg8 ♕xg8 29 ♕xg5 ♕c4 30 h4 ♕xc3 31 ♖e7 ♕d4+ 32 ♔h2 bxc5 33 h5 ♕d6+ 34 ♔g1 ♕d4+ 35 ♔h2 ♕d6+ 36 ♔g1 ♗b5 37 h6 ♗d3 White could have forced a draw with 38 g8♕! ♖xg8 39 ♕xg8 ♕d4+ (39...♕xe7 allows 40 ♕d5+!) 40 ♔h2 ♕h4+ 41 ♔g1 ♕d4+ with perpetual check, as pointed out by Emms. Instead Toulzac faltered with 38 ♕e5? and after 38...♕xe5 39 ♖xe5 c4 40 ♖d5 ♗h7 41 ♖xd7+ ♔c6 42 ♖e7 c3 43 ♔f2 c2 44 ♖e1 ♔d5 Black went on to win the ending.

Summing up, the rook sacrifice might appear superficially dangerous, but in reality it seems to be White who is fighting for a draw. We now return to 18 fxg5:

18...♗e5 19 ♕d3 a6!

This seems to be the correct time to expel the knight. Instead 19...♖xg7 20 h4 ♕h8 21 ♖h3! (21 0-0-0 ♗f4+ 22 ♔c2 ♕h7 intending ...♖h8 gives Black good compensation in the ensuing ending)

brings White the advantage, as shown by 21...♕h7 22 ♖d1 ♕xd3 23 ♖hxd3 ♗c6 24 ♘d4.

20 ♘c3 ♕c7 21 0-0-0 ♖xg7 22 h4 b5 23 cxb5

If White tries to keep the queenside closed with 23 c5!? there could follow 23...♖d8 24 ♕c2 ♖c8! 25 b4 d6 26 cxd6+ ♗xd6 27 ♖h3 ♗e5 28 ♔b2 f6! 29 gxf6+ ♗xf6 with excellent chances for Black.

23...axb5 24 ♔b1

We have been following the game D.Lemos-K.Mekhitarian, Buenos Aires 2007. The first point to note is that 24...♗xc3 can be met safely by 25 ♖c1!. In the game Black played 24...♗c6?!, at which point White missed an ideal opportunity to block the queenside with 25 ♘a2! followed by ♘b4 with a clear advantage. Instead I propose that Black breaks open the queenside immediately:

24...b4! 25 axb4 d6

I believe that Black has good compensation for the two pawns. His structure is far superior, his king is the safer and the bishop on e5 is the best placed piece on the board.

B22) 15 ♗xf6 gxf6 16 ♘d6+ ♗xd6 17 exd6

We now reach an entirely different type of position. The only real danger for Black is connected with the inability of his forces to switch between opposing flanks. On the other hand, his structure is very sound and the doubled f-pawns are not at all weak, whereas White's c-, d- and occasionally g-pawns could all become long-term targets. Overall, I would rate the chances as approximately equal and the following analysis will demonstrate some of the typical ideas for both sides.

17...f5

This is a standard move, establishing a solid chain of pawns and restricting the enemy bishop.

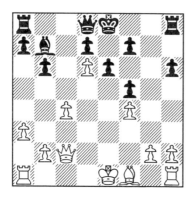

17...♖c8 is equally playable. Indeed, I doubt that there are any major reasons to prefer one move over the other, and in some cases transpositions can occur as both moves are likely to figure in Black's plans. Following 17...♖c8 the game S.Lputian-K.Nikolaidis, Panormo 1998, was a fairly instructive example demonstrating quite accurate play

from both sides: 18 ♗e2 f5 (18...♗xg2?? would have led to disaster after 19 ♖g1 ♗b7 20 ♕h7! ♖f8 21 ♕xf7+! and mates) 19 ♕c3 ♖g8 20 0-0-0 ♔f8 21 ♗f3 ♗xf3 22 gxf3 ♕h4 23 ♕d4 f6 24 ♔b1 ♔f7 25 ♖d2 ♕h3 26 ♕d3 ♕h4 (if Black wanted to continue the fight, he might have considered 26...a6!?, intending ...♖c5 and ...b5 to open up the queenside; White could, of course, meet ...♖c5 with b4, but this would create plenty of holes which might later be exploited) 27 ♕d4 ♕h3 28 ♕d3 ♕h4 29 ♕d4 ½-½.

18 ♕c3 ♖g8 19 0-0-0

The actual move order used in our main game was 19 h4 ♔f8 20 0-0-0 ♖c8, but immediate castling seems more logical to me.

19...♖c8 20 h4!?

This is the only move to have been tried, although alternatives may well be playable. Still, the remainder of the present game combined with the earlier reference (Lputian-Nikolaidis) should demonstrate enough typical ways for Black to handle the position.

20...♔f8 21 ♖h2

A few other possibilities:

a) After 21 ♖h3 ♗e4 22 ♖e1 ♖c6 (Skembris) the position remains approximately equal.

b) 21 ♔b1 ♖g7 22 ♗e2 ♔g8 23 ♗f3 ♗c6 24 ♗xc6 ♖xc6 25 ♖d2 was J.Markos-V.Babula, Czech League 2006, and now 25...♖g4 26 g3 ♕f8 (26...♖c5!?) 27 ♖hd1 ♕g7 28 ♖d3 ♕xc3 29 ♖xc3 f6 once again looks fairly level.

21...♗e4

21...♗d5!? is an interesting alternative. We now follow I.Khenkin-

S.Skembris, Lido Estensi 2003:

22 g3 ♖g7 23 ♖e2 ♔g8 24 ♗g2 ♗xg2 25 ♖xg2

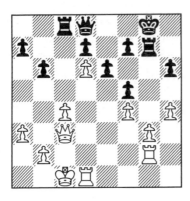

25...♔h7

25...♖c5!? was also possible, hoping that the threat of ...b5 might provoke a queenside weakness.

26 h5 ♖g4 27 ♖d3 ♖c6

27...♖c5!? deserved consideration.

28 b3 f6 29 ♔b2 ♕f8 30 ♕d4 ♕f7 31 ♖h2 ♕g7 32 ♕e3 ♕f8 33 ♕d4 ♕g7 34 ♕e3 ♕f8 35 ♖hd2

After repeating the position once White decides to continue the fight. However, he has no advantage and the game soon ended in a natural conclusion after 35...♕f7 36 ♕d4 ♔g7 37 ♖h2 ♕f8 38 ♖h4 ♕e8 39 ♖xg4+ fxg4 40 f5 exf5 41 ♖e3 ♖xd6 42 ♕xd6 (42 ♕xb6? axb6 43 ♖xe8 ♖d3 is not what White wants) 42...♕xe3 43 ♕xd7+ ♔f8 44 ♕xf5 ♔e7 45 ♕xg4 ♕d2+ 46 ♔b1 ♕d3+ 47 ♔b2 ½-½.

Summary

10 ♗f4 can lead to some fascinating variations after 10...0-0. We have seen that after most of White's non-forcing responses, the delayed 11...e5 intending ...♘d4 should give Black a decent position. Without a doubt White's most ambitious and principled continuation is 11 ♘xc5 bxc5 12 ♗d6, although I believe I have demonstrated that Black's tactical resources, based on his lead in development and the instability of the bishop on d6, should always provide at least sufficient counterchances.

As far as this writer has been able to ascertain, the system with 10 ♗g5 ♘d4 11 ♘xd4 ♗xd4 seems to be in good health at present. In Line B1 we saw how the calm 12 ♗d3 can be neutralized with the aid of a few solid moves combined with Ftacnik's 17...d5!?. Variation B2 with 12 ♘b5 is more ambitious but also riskier for White, especially in Line B21 with 15 exf6 hxg5 16 hxg7 ♖g8 when Black's pair of bishops and central majority give him excellent chances. White's best is probably 15 ♗xf6 gxf6 16 ♘d6+ ♗xd6 17 exd6 (Line B22), leading to roughly equal chances for both sides.

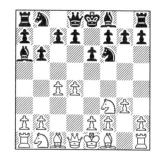

Chapter Twelve

The Fianchetto Variation: 4 g3 ♗a6

1 d4 ♘f6 2 c4 e6 3 ♘f3 b6 4 g3

Finally we arrive at what has for several decades been regarded as White's foremost weapon in his quest for an opening advantage against the Queen's Indian. True, there will doubtless be many who would argue in favour of one of the alternative approaches, but when we take into consideration the fact that 4 g3 has accounted for approximately 50% of all games in the Queen's Indian, it becomes difficult to dispute this variation's status as the main line.

The rationale behind White's fourth move is not hard to comprehend. In very simple terms, he anticipates the arrival of the enemy bishop on b7 and deploys his own bishop in preparation to fight for the crucial long diagonal.

4...♗a6

Both this and the more traditional 4...♗b7 are equally playable, and I certainly have no intention of attempting to show that the latter is in any way

inferior. I do, however, believe that the more modern text move offers somewhat more chances for Black to play for a win by unbalancing the game through methods that will be revealed in due course.

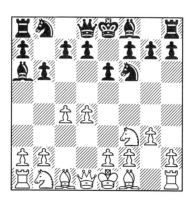

Newcomers to the Queen's Indian may find a6 to be a strange choice for the bishop, although we have already seen in Chapters 8-11 that such a development can bring certain unique advantages. In fact, at a rudimentary level the justification for the move is much the same as it was against 4 a3 – Black immediately attacks the c4-pawn, knowing that each possible reply carries its own unique drawback.

A summary of White's options

There are several ways in which White may defend his c-pawn, most notably:

1) 5 ♘bd2 is popular, but the drawback is that, just as in the Petrosian system, in most variations this piece would be more actively placed on c3.

2) 5 ♕a4 looks sensible, but White's problem is that after 5...♗b7! the queen has been diverted from the centre, thus enabling Black to follow up with ...c5, striking back without fearing the response d4-d5.

3) For many years 5 ♕c2 was considered innocuous for the same reason until the discovery of a dangerous pawn sacrifice caused a dramatic re-evaluation. Full details can be found in Chapter 14, in which I recommend a no-nonsense approach beginning with 5...♗b4+!?.

4) Finally, the main line of 5 b3 will be covered in Chapters 15 and 16. In response Black has tested numerous systems, the most popular being 5...♗b4+ 6 ♗d2 ♗e7 which can lead to some exceptionally deep theoretical waters. After much deliberation I decided to eschew these heavily-trodden paths in favour of something altogether fresher, and at the start of Chapter 15 you can find out how I came to regard 5...b5!? as an ideal repertoire choice.

Before we move on to the main lines (options 2-4), the remainder of the present chapter will be devoted to White's less common fifth-move alternatives:

A: 5 ♕b3!?
B: 5 ♘bd2

Others can be discarded quickly:

a) Attempts to sacrifice the c-pawn result in, at best, nebulous compensation for White. Thus 5 ♗g2?! ♗xc4 6 ♘e5 ♗d5 defends comfortably, while after the slightly better 6 ♘c3 d5 7 ♘e5 (V.Ovchinnikov-Y.Kipriyanov, Novosibirsk 2007) 7...♗a6 White has a slight lead in development, but no open lines and very little else to show for the pawn.

b) 5 e3?! combines poorly with g2-g3, and after 5...d5 Black is already at least equal.

A) 5 ♕b3!? ♘c6!?

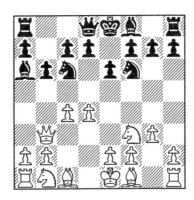

Black develops while forcing his opponent to deal with the threat of ...♘a5. White almost always reacts with either:

A1: 6 ♗d2 or
A2: 6 ♘bd2

The alternatives are either harmless or plain inferior, for example:

a) 6 ♗g2? (V.Lehoczki-J.Rigo, Hungary 1997) just loses a pawn after 6...♘a5 7 ♕c2 ♘xc4 8 0-0 c6.

b) 6 d5? was the same story after 6...♘a5 7 ♕a4 ♗xc4 8 dxe6 fxe6 9 ♘c3 ♘d5 in A.Czerwonski-P.Stempin, Bytom 1986.

c) 6 ♕a4?! ♗b7! threatens 7...♘xd4 and in L.Wilton-J.Nielsen, Esbjerg 1989, White only made matters worse with 7 d5?! exd5 8 cxd5 ♗b4+ 9 ♗d2 ♘xd5 when he had no compensation whatsoever for the pawn.

d) 6 e3 (T.Karolyi-V.Bolzoni, Belgian League 1990) does not lose any material, but Black is very comfortably placed after 6...♗e7.

A1) 6 ♗d2

This is generally considered to be the less challenging of White's two main options.

6...♗b7!

The bishop drops back to its traditional post, conveniently threatening 7...♘xd4 in the process.

7 ♗c3

7 d5 has yielded a plus score for White, something I find bizarre as it does not appear at all threatening. After the strongest reply 7...♘e7! (7...exd5 8 cxd5 ♘e7 9 d6 cxd6 10 ♗g2 gives White compensation), White is more or less forced into 8 dxe6 fxe6 when Black's central majority and half-open f-file should assure him of excellent prospects in the middlegame. A good example was A.Fominyh-K.Sakaev, Moscow 1999, which continued 9 ♗g2 ♘f5 10 0-0 ♗c5 11 ♘c3 (Black should not be worried by 11 ♗b4 ♕e7 12 ♗xc5 ♕xc5 13 ♘bd2 0-0 14 ♕d3 ♘d6 15 ♖ac1, as in D.Bunzmann-V.Kunin, Griesheim 2004, and now 15...♘de4, or 11 ♗c3 ♘e4 12 ♘bd2 0-0 13 ♘xe4 ♗xe4 14 ♖ad1 a5 15 ♕a4 d6 16 a3, which was seen in A.Fominyh-A.Poluljahov, Samara 2000, and here 16...♕e7, with a slight edge to Black in both cases) 11...0-0 12 ♕c2 ♕e8!, intending ...♕h5 with excellent prospects on the kingside.

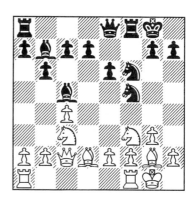

After the further 13 ♗g5 (13 e4 can be met by 13...♕h5! – Gershon)

13...♘g4!? (another good option is
13...♕h5 14 ♗xf6 ♖xf6 15 ♘e4 ♗xe4 16
♕xe4 ♖af8 17 ♖ad1; Gershon evaluates
this position as equal, but after
17...♘d6 Black's kingside pressure
must surely count for something) 14 h3
♘xf2! 15 ♖xf2 ♘xg3 the defensive burden proved too much for White to
handle.

7...♘e4!

Black guarantees himself the advantage of the bishop-pair. Note that after
the imminent exchange on c3, White
will be unable to recapture with his
knight because of the threatened
...♘xd4.

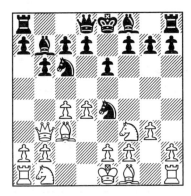

8 a3

In A.Shneider-V.Iordachescu, Bastia
(rapid) 2000, White decided that it was
worth retreating his queen to its original square with 8 ♕d1 in order to recapture with the knight on c3. Rather
than fall in with his opponent's idea,
Black sensibly switched plans with
8...d5!, maintaining the active knight in
the centre. After the further 9 cxd5
exd5 10 ♗g2 ♗d6 11 0-0 0-0 White decided to improve his bishop with 12

♗d2, at which point I rather like the
idea of attacking d4 with 12...♕f6!.
Now 13 e3 would block the bishop, but
13 ♗e3 would be strongly met by
13...♘e7!, improving Black's worst-
placed piece and intending ...♘f5.

8...♘xc3 9 ♕xc3 ♗e7

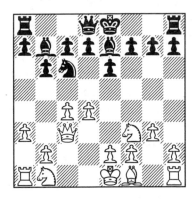

10 ♗g2

White has nothing better:

a) In case of 10 e4 (A.Fominyh-
A.Kunte, Kelamabakkam 2000), I rather
like Aagaard's energetic suggestion of
10...f5!? (Black can also prepare this
with 10...0-0) when the Danish-Scot
goes on to analyse 11 d5 ♗f6 12 ♕e3
exd5 (another idea is 12...♘e5 13 ♘xe5
♗xe5 14 exf5 ♕f6, intending 15 fxe6
dxe6 16 ♘c3 ♗xc3+ 17 ♕xc3 ♕xc3+ 18
bxc3 exd5 with advantage to Black) 13
exd5+ ♔f7!? with dangerous threats.
Extending this a little further, play
might continue 14 dxc6 ♗xc6 15 ♗e2
♖e8 16 ♕d3 ♕e7 17 ♘bd2 ♗xb2 18 ♖b1
(after 18 ♖a2 ♕xe2+! 19 ♕xe2 ♗c3!
Black regains the knight on f3 with advantage) 18...♗c3! 19 ♔f1 ♗xd2 20
♕xd2 ♕xa3 21 ♔g2 with unclear play.

b) 10 ♕d3?! seems a little sluggish,

and after 10...d5 11 cxd5 ♕xd5 Black is already mobilized and ready for action. In J.Timman-J.Polgar, Malmö 2000, White soon got into trouble after 12 e4 ♕a5+ 13 ♘bd2 (no better is 13 ♘c3 0-0-0 14 ♕c4 f5!? 15 ♗d3 ♘b4 – Stohl) 13...0-0-0 14 ♖c1, at which point 14...♗f6! would have been very unpleasant for White.

10...♗f6 11 e3 ♘e7! 12 ♕d3 c5!

With his last two moves Black has ensured an active role for his unopposed dark-squared bishop.

13 ♘c3 cxd4 14 exd4 ♖c8

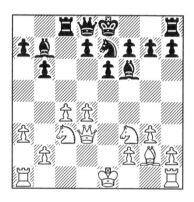

This position simply looks better for Black. The plan is ...d5 with a probable transition to a favourable IQP position; Black will have two bishops, active pieces and firm control over the crucial d5-square.

15 ♘b5

In F.Grube-N.Poesch, Internet 2004, White varied with 15 0-0 ♗a6 (15...d5 16 cxd5 ♘xd5 17 ♘e4 0-0 also looks good for Black) 16 ♘b5 d5 17 cxd5 ♘xd5 18 ♘e5 0-0 19 ♖fe1 ♘c7 20 a4 ♗xe5 21 ♖xe5 ♕d7 22 ♕b3 and here 22...♗xb5 23 axb5 ♕xd4 would have

won a pawn. We will now follow the game J.Ehlvest-V.Ivanchuk, Elista Olympiad 1998:

15...d5! 16 cxd5 a6!

With this neat *zwischenzug* Black forces the enemy knight away from its active post.

17 ♘c3

17 d6!? ♘d5 18 ♘c3 ♕xd6 19 ♘e4 ♕e7 20 ♘xf6+ ♕xf6 would not alter the evaluation: Black stands better, bishop-pair or not.

17...♘xd5 18 ♘e4 ♗e7

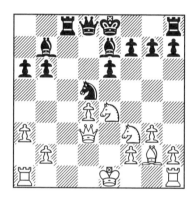

18...0-0 was also possible, as in the previous note. Either way Black's position is preferable, and Ivanchuk went on to win with 19 0-0 ♕c7 20 ♘e5 f6 21 ♘f3 ♕c2 22 ♕xc2 ♖xc2 23 ♖ab1 ♔f7 24 ♖fe1 ♖hc8 25 ♗f1 h6 26 h4 b5 27 ♗d3 ♖2c7 28 h5 ♘b6 29 ♘ed2 ♗d5 30 ♘h4 f5 31 ♘df3 ♗f6 32 ♘e5+ ♗xe5 33 ♖xe5 ♖c1+ 34 ♖e1 ♖xe1+ 35 ♖xe1 ♘a4 36 b4 ♖c3 37 ♘g6 ♖xa3 38 ♘f4 ♘c3 39 ♗f1 ♗e4 40 f3 ♗xf3 41 ♖xe6 ♘e4 42 d5 ♖a1 43 d6 ♘d2 44 ♖e7+ ♔g8 and 0-1.

A2) 6 ♘bd2 ♘a5

6...d5 and 6...♗b7 are the main alternatives, but after studying both in some detail I believe the text to be the most promising for Black. Now we should consider:

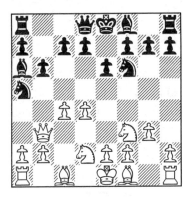

A21: 7 ♕a4
A22: 7 ♕c3!

Instead 7 ♕c2 is not dangerous after 7...c5 when White has tried:

a) 8 dxc5 ♗xc5 9 e3 ♖c8 10 ♕a4 ♗b7 11 b4 ♗c6 (11...♘e4!?) 12 b5 was J.Bellon Lopez-S.Ivanov, Stockholm 2005, and now after 12...♗b7 13 ♗g2 ♘e4! 14 ♘xe4 ♗xe4 15 ♗b2 (15 0-0?? ♗xf3 16 ♗xf3 ♕f6 wins) 15...0-0 16 0-0 d5 Black is clearly better.

b) 8 e4 cxd4 9 e5 ♘g8 10 ♗d3 (10 ♘xd4 is no better after 10...♕c7 11 f4 ♖c8 12 b3 b5!) 10...♖c8 11 0-0 runs into 11...♘xc4! 12 ♘xc4 ♗xc4 13 ♗xc4 b5 when White was in danger of losing a pawn in S.Bjarnason-W.Browne, Reykjavik 1988.

A21) 7 ♕a4
This used to be quite popular, but has now been superseded by Line A22.

7...♗b7!
White was threatening to win a piece with 8 b4, so please do not forget this move!

8 ♗g2
White has experimented with 8 ♗h3 in a few games, but Black gets easy play after 8...c5 9 0-0 cxd4 10 ♘xd4 ♖c8 11 ♖e1 ♗c5 12 ♘4f3 ♗c6 13 ♕d1 (S.Peric-Y.Razuvaev, Geneva 1994) 13...d5! with the better chances.

8...c5 9 dxc5
It is in White's interests to create a static pawn structure. Instead 9 0-0?! cxd4 10 ♘xd4 ♗xg2 11 ♔xg2 (A.Sygulski-E.Kengis, Albena 1986) 11...♕c7 gives Black an easy game.

9...bxc5 10 0-0
After 10 ♘b3 ♘xb3 11 axb3 ♗e7 12 0-0 0-0 13 ♖d1 ♗c6 14 ♕a6 ♕b6 15 ♕xb6 axb6 Black's superior structure gave him a slight edge in A.Fominyh-B.Lalic, Calcutta 2002.

10...♗e7

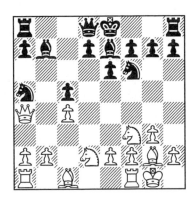

White has tried several moves here, without coming close to demonstrating an advantage.

11 ♘e5

This is probably best; White is slightly cramped and needs to find a useful role for his knights. The alternatives are even less threatening:

a) 11 e4? just blunders a pawn and after 11...♘xe4 12 ♘xe4 ♗xe4 13 ♘e5 ♗xg2 14 ♔xg2 ♕c7 15 ♗f4 f6 16 ♘f3 e5 17 ♗e3 ♘c6 18 ♖fe1 ♘d4 19 ♗xd4 cxd4 Black was already winning in E.Heyken-H.Schussler, Malmo 1987.

b) 11 ♕c2 0-0 12 b3 ♘c6 was harmless in T.Gareev-P.Gnusarev, Mallorca 2004.

c) 11 ♖e1 0-0 12 e4 d6 13 e5 ♗c6 14 ♕c2 dxe5 15 ♘xe5 ♗xg2 16 ♔xg2 ♕b6 17 ♘df3 ♘c6 saw Black take over the initiative in D.Barlov-I.Csom, Bern 1992.

11...♗xg2 12 ♔xg2 ♕b6 13 ♘df3 ♕b4 14 ♕c2

14 ♕xb4 cxb4 15 ♗d2 ♘e4 16 ♗e1 ♖c8 is at least equal for Black.

14...♕b7

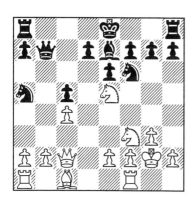

Chances were balanced here in L.Ftacnik-I.Farago, Warsaw 1987.

A22) 7 ♕c3!

This seems to be White's only realis-tic try for an advantage.

7...c5

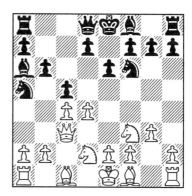

At present this seems to be Black's most respected defence. At the time of writing there are over 40 games with it on my database, almost all of them fea-turing IMs and GMs, including many of the world's best. I was also struck by the absence of a single game prior to 2002; clearly this is very much a mod-ern battleground.

8 dxc5

Nothing else is ever played, with good reason; for instance, after 8 ♗g2 cxd4 9 ♘xd4 ♖c8 10 b3 d5 Black al-ready has a great position.

8...bxc5 9 e4!

This is the only challenging move. In L.Van Wely-P.Lerch, Kuppenheim 2005, White tried 9 ♗g2 and though he eventually won the game, I have a feel-ing this had more to do with the near 400-point rating chasm than the strength of his opening play. After 9...♗b7 10 0-0 ♗e7 11 b3 0-0 12 ♗b2 ♕b6 13 ♖ad1 Black could have utilized his central majority to good effect with 13...d5!?, and 13...♘c6 was another sensible option, improving Black's worst-placed piece.

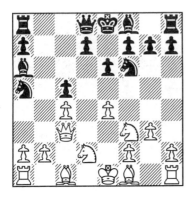

9...♗b7!?

This is the most dynamic move, as well as the most popular amongst the world's elite. 9...d6 is possible, but after 10 a3 ♗b7 11 b4 ♞c6 12 ♗g2 White should be a little better.

10 e5

In I.Lysyj-P.Anisimov, Krasnoyarsk 2007, White opted for the somewhat inconsistent 10 ♗d3 and after 10...♞c6 11 a3 (11 e5 ♞d4 12 exf6 ♗xf3 13 ♞xf3 ♞xf3+ 14 ♔f1 ♞d4 15 ♗e4 ♖b8 16 ♔g2 ♕xf6 is better for Black), Black could have obtained a comfortable game with 11...♗e7, intending 12 0-0 d6 13 b4 ♞d7! 14 ♖b1 0-0.

10...♞e4 11 ♞xe4

In the game A.Morozevich-L.Aronian, Monaco (rapid) 2007, White experimented with 11 ♕e3. The Russian GM is rightly renowned for his stupendous creativity, but on this occasion his original play brought him no advantage after 11...♞xd2 12 ♗xd2 ♞c6 13 ♗g2 ♞d4 14 0-0 ♗xf3 15 ♗xf3 ♖b8 16 ♖ab1 ♕c7. He then erred with 17

♗c3?, which allowed 17...♕xe5! and after 18 ♗xd4 ♕xd4 19 ♕a3 ♕xc4 20 ♕xa7 ♖d8 he was a pawn down for nothing, although he eventually managed to hold the draw.

11...♗xe4

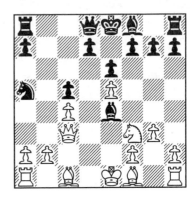

The position holds chances for both sides. Given some time White would like to pile up on the d-file to exploit his adversary's backward pawn. Meanwhile Black will generally look to counter this plan with ...♞c6 followed by ...♗xf3 and ...♞d4, installing the knight on an ideal outpost while conveniently masking his only real weakness. Let us see how these ideas play out in practice:

12 ♗g2 ♞c6 13 0-0

13 ♕e3 achieves nothing after 13...♗xf3 14 ♗xf3 ♞d4!.

13...♖b8

Sensibly removing the rook from the watchful eye of White's bishop.

14 ♖e1

14 ♞g5 ♗xg2 15 ♔xg2 turned out well for Black in L.Van Wely-B.Gelfand, Monaco (rapid) 2005, after 15...♕c7 16 ♖e1 ♗e7 17 ♞f3 ♕b7 18

♔g1 0-0 19 b3 d6 20 ♗b2 dxe5 21 ♘xe5 ♘d4 22 ♕d3 ♖fd8. He could also have considered fighting for the initiative with 15...f6!? 16 exf6 ♕xf6 when his central pawn majority could become an important asset.

14...♗xf3 15 ♕xf3

15 ♗xf3 ♘d4 does not alter the position in any significant way.

15...♘d4 16 ♕d3

We have been following the game E.Bareev-A.Grischuk, Moscow (blitz) 2007. Here it looks quite interesting for Black to try 16...d6!?.

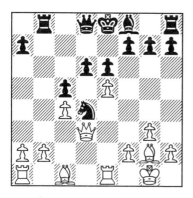

The idea is to eliminate the e-pawn, thus enabling Black to provide full support to the important knight. I do not see any real problems for Black here – true, it may appear risky to allow the opening of the e-file before castling, but I have not been able to find any way in which this can be exploited. As far as strategic factors are concerned, White may have the two bishops, but Black enjoys a preponderance of central pawns and with most of his pieces occupying dark squares, it seems unlikely that White's unopposed

bishop will be able to inflict much harm.

B) 5 ♘bd2

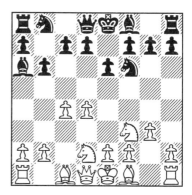

This is a natural reaction, defending the c-pawn while continuing to develop. The drawback is, of course, that in many positions this knight would be more usefully placed on c3. There are several ways in which Black can attempt to utilize its inferior positioning, but I believe...

5...♗b4

...to be the most suitable option for our repertoire. The alternatives 5...♗b7, 5...c5 and 5...d5 are all equally playable, and the choice between them will largely be determined by an individual's personal tastes. Ultimately the choice of the text was influenced more by compatibility issues than any illusions of objective superiority over the alternatives. The point is that when planning Chapter 14, I decided that it would be best to advocate the solid 5...♗b4+ in response to 5 ♕c2. Considering that the response 6 ♘bd2 would have to be covered anyway, and that the resulting position is more commonly reached via the move order of the present chapter, the decision to meet 5 ♘bd2 with 5...♗b4 became a no-brainer.

So what are the pros and cons of our chosen system? Immediately we can see that Black develops a piece and prepares to castle while renewing the threat to the c-pawn. The drawback is that he will quite often have to resort to exchanging his potentially valuable dark-squared bishop for the knight on d2. Fortunately in the system I have in mind he should be able to obtain a useful lead in development as compensation.

6 ♕c2

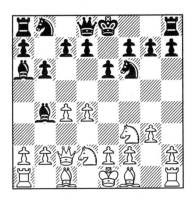

This natural move is by far the most common response. Once again, please note that the present position can also arise via the move order 5 ♕c2 ♗b4+ 6 ♘bd2 (6 ♗d2 is the main line, as we will see in Chapter 14).

Here is a summary of White's alternatives:

a) 6 b3? is a mistake in view of 6...♗c3! (this position has been more commonly reached via the main line of 5 b3 ♗b4+ and now 6 ♘bd2? ♗c3!) 7 ♖b1 ♗b7 when White is already in severe difficulties, as shown by 8 ♗b2 ♘e4 9 ♖g1? (going from bad to worse) 9...♕f6! 10 ♗c1 ♘c6 11 e3 ♘b4 when Black was already winning in K.Shirazi-J.Benjamin, Berkeley 1984.

b) 6 e3 was once tried by Tregubov, but the idea does not impress after the logical 6...0-0 7 a3 ♗xd2+ 8 ♕xd2 (P.Tregubov-L.Ravi, Ubeda 2000) 8...d5 9 b3 c5 with active play.

c) 6 a3 ♗xd2+ 7 ♘xd2 ♗b7! is awkward and after 8 ♘f3 (8 f3 d5 also gives White nothing), Black can seriously consider 8...♗xf3!? (8...0-0 is also fine) 9 exf3 d5: for example, 10 b3 ♘c6 11 ♗b2 0-0 12 ♗g2 ♕d6 13 0-0 dxc4 14 bxc4 ♖ad8 saw Black win a pawn in S.Krivoshey-V.Belikov, Alushta 1999.

d) 6 ♕b3 is one of two semi-serious alternatives to the main line. Play continues 6...c5 7 ♗g2 ♘c6.

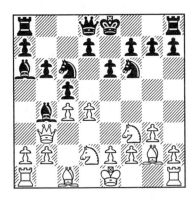

Black's approach is absolutely logical and easy to understand – he just continues developing and attacking the enemy centre. White has tried a few different moves here, but without coming close to an advantage:

d1) V.Tukmakov-Y.Balashov, Moscow 1983, saw Black equalize fairly effortlessly after 8 a3 &xd2+ 9 &xd2 cxd4 10 ♕a4 ♕c8 11 0-0 0-0 12 b4 &b7 13 b5 ♘e7 14 ♘xd4 &xg2 15 ♔xg2 ♕c5 16 ♘f3 ♖fc8.

d2) 8 dxc5 &xc5 9 0-0 0-0 10 a3 (for 10 ♕a4 &b7 see variation 'd3') 10...♖c8 11 ♕a4 &b7 12 b4 &e7 13 &b2 ♕c7 14 ♖ac1 d6 was a comfortable Hedgehog for Black in F.Chin-J.Rodgaard, Thessaloniki Olympiad 1988.

d3) 8 0-0 0-0 9 ♕a4 &b7 10 dxc5 &xc5 11 ♘b3 &e7 12 ♘e5 ♖c8 13 ♘xc6 &xc6 14 &xc6 ♖xc6 15 &f4 ♕a8 16 ♖ac1 ♖fc8 17 ♖fd1 was agreed drawn in E.Solozhenkin-M.Agopov, Helsinki 2001. Here White has also tried keeping more pieces on with 12 ♖d1 (V.Frias Pablaza-Liang Jinrong, Lucerne 1982), although this does leave his queen looking rather oddly placed. Indeed, I wonder if Black might try to exploit this with 12...♘b8!?, threatening ...&c6 and intending to re-route the knight either via a6 to c5, or to d7 as is customary in the Hedgehog formation. I think that Black is at least equal after both 13 ♘bd4 d6 and 13 ♘fd4 &xg2 14 ♔xg2 a6.

e) 6 ♕a4 is the only other sensible move, to which Black should once again respond by challenging in the centre with the logical 6...c5! when there might follow:

e1) The safest response to 7 dxc5 is 7...&xc5 (although 7...bxc5 is also quite playable). Then after 8 &g2 &b7 9 0-0

0-0 10 b4 &e7 11 &b2 Black can choose between the safe and solid 11...d6, and the more double-edged 11...a5!? 12 b5 d6 13 ♘d4 &xg2 14 ♔xg2 when it is unclear which outpost (c6 for White or c5 for Black) will prove more relevant, B.Gulko-I.Ibragimov, New York 2006.

e2) 7 a3 &xd2+ 8 &xd2 cxd4 9 &g2 (9 ♘xd4 &b7 is awkward) 9...&b7 10 0-0 enables Black to equalize fairly effortlessly with 10...&c6! 11 ♕d1 &xf3! 12 &xf3 ♘c6, as White will be forced to exchange on c6 in order to regain his pawn.

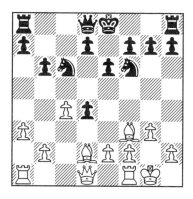

Several games have proceeded with 13 &f4 0-0 14 &d6 ♖e8 15 &xc6 (15 b4? led to trouble for White in P.Murdzia-E.Solozhenkin, Lublin 1993, after 15...e5 16 &d5?! – 16 b5 could be met by 16...e4!, although this would still have been preferable to the game – 16...♘xd5 17 cxd5 ♕f6 18 dxc6 ♕xd6 19 cxd7 ♕xd7 with a clear extra pawn) 15...dxc6 16 ♕xd4 c5 17 ♕f4 (after 17 ♕e5 ♕d7 18 ♖fd1, as in R.Mascarinas-A.Huss, Bad Ragaz 1989, Black can try the active 18...♕a4!?, intending 19 b4 ♖ac8 20 bxc5 ♘d7!) 17...♘h5 18 ♕e5 f6

19 ♕xh5 ♕xd6 20 ♖fd1 ♕e7 followed by a swift handshake.

We now return to White's main choice, 6 ♕c2:

6...0-0!?

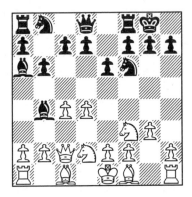

This is an important moment, as the text is slightly unusual. The main line is regarded as 6...♗b7 7 ♗g2 ♗e4 8 ♕b3 ♗xd2+ 9 ♗xd2 0-0 10 0-0 d6. Here Black is very flexibly placed and can aim to challenge the white centre in a number of different ways. This reliable system has been used by many top class players, although personally I cannot help but feel that White's two bishops ought to count for something if he plays precisely. The text is not so well investigated, but I have been unable to find any reason to regard it as inferior.

So what are the advantages of my chosen recommendation? For starters, Black refuses to waste time moving the light-squared bishop for a second and third time in quick succession. In fact one could argue that this piece is already perfectly placed on a6, exerting pressure against the white pawns on c4

and e2. Black already enjoys a lead in development, and to my mind it makes perfect sense to castle quickly and open up the queenside. The immediate plan will usually be to play ...d5, attacking c4. Depending on how White responds, the move ...c5 may also figure in our plans. This will be all the more effective if followed by a quick ...♖c8, gaining more time by harassing the white queen.

Let us now see how these concepts translate into practice. Before we move on, please note that the immediate 6...d5?? would lose a piece after 7 ♕a4+.

7 ♗g2

7 e4?! does not appear to have been tried here, perhaps with good reason as after 7...d5 8 e5 ♘e4 Black is very active. 7 a3 is worth considering, though, when Black should probably exchange with 7...♗xd2+, now that White has spent a tempo on a2-a3 and because 7...♗e7 should leave White a little better after the solid 8 ♗g2 or the more ambitious 8 e4!?. Following the natural 8 ♗xd2 the game P.Nikolic-C.Balogh, German League 2006, continued 8...♗b7 (Black could also try to make use of the bishop's placement on a6 with 8...d6!? 9 ♗g2 ♘bd7, intending ...♖c8 and ...c5) 9 ♗g2 ♗e4 10 ♕a4 d6.

The position resembles a Classical Nimzo-Indian. Black went on to obtain a nice game after 11 0-0 a5 12 ♖ac1 ♕d7 13 ♕d1 a4 14 ♗g5 ♕e7 15 ♘d2 ♗xg2 16 ♔xg2 ♘bd7 17 ♘e4, at which point 17...e5! looks very logical, hoping to secure a future outpost on c5.

7...d5

Black's next job will usually be to play ...c5, develop the queen's knight to c6 or d7, and place a rook on the c-file. White's two principal responses are:

B1: 8 a3!?
B2: 8 0-0

Others are rather feeble:

a) 8 b3 is slow and in M.Molinaroli-B.Donner, Muenster 1997, Black soon took over the initiative after 8...c5 9 dxc5 ♗xc5 10 0-0 ♘c6 (10...♘bd7 followed by ...♖c8 looks equally good) 11 ♗b2 ♖c8 12 ♖ac1 ♕e7 13 ♕b1 d4 14 ♕a1 e5 15 a3 ♗b7 16 b4 ♗d6.

b) 8 ♘e5 should also be met by 8...c5, aiming to open files and exploit Black's lead in development. A.Nabil-A.Dyce, Elista Olympiad 1998, continued 9 dxc5 ♕c7!? (9...♗xc5 also looks good) 10 ♘d3 ♗xc5 11 ♘xc5 ♕xc5 12 0-0 ♘c6 13 ♕a4?! ♗xc4! 14 ♘xc4 b5 and Black was already winning material.

B1) 8 a3!? ♗xd2+ 9 ♘xd2 c5!

Black should waste no time in striking at White's centre.

10 dxc5 bxc5

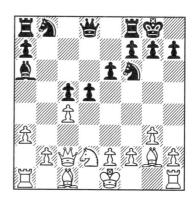

11 0-0

This is the most natural, although it is worth checking the alternatives:

a) The pawn grab 11 cxd5 exd5 12 ♕xc5 is inadvisable as Black can immediately regain the material while maintaining the initiative after 12...♖e8 13 0-0 (13 e3?! ♘bd7 is too risky for White) 13...♘bd7.

b) 11 b4!? ♘bd7 12 0-0 cxb4 13 axb4 ♗xc4 14 ♘xc4 ♖c8 15 ♕a4 ♖xc4 16 ♕xa7 was double-edged but approximately equal in V.Korchnoi-B.Parma, Yerevan 1971.

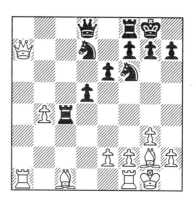

White has the advantage of two bishops against two knights, but Black is better developed and controls the centre, while it remains to be seen whether the b-pawn will turn out to be a strength or a weakness.

11...♕b6 12 b3

12 b4?! cxb4 works out well for Black after either 13 axb4 ♖c8 or 13 ♖b1 ♘c6 14 axb4 ♘d4 (Pelletier).

12...♘c6 13 e3

13 cxd5? ♘d4 is inadvisable, and 13 ♗b2 d4 is also pleasant for Black.

13...♖ad8 14 ♖d1! d4 15 ♘f3

We have been following the game H.Stefansson-Y.Pelletier, European Team Championship, Crete 2007. Now instead of the immediate 15...e5 16 exd4, Pelletier suggests the more precise regrouping of the bishop with 15...♗b7! 16 exd4 ♘xd4 17 ♘xd4 ♗xg2 18 ♔xg2 cxd4 when Black's central superiority and safer king should fully compensate White's passed queenside pawns and alleged advantage of bishop over knight.

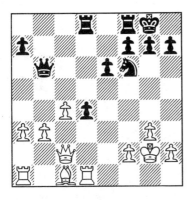

A few sample continuations include 19 f3 e5, 19 ♗f4 ♖fe8, 19 ♗g5 e5, and 19

♗b2 e5 20 b4 ♕c6+ 21 f3 ♘d5! with a good position in each case.

B2) 8 0-0 c5!

Once again Black should not delay this active move.

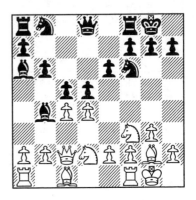

9 dxc5

The alternatives are no better:

a) 9 b3 is playable, but is hardly likely to threaten Black. It should be sufficient to point out that the game S.Mamedyarov-G.Kamsky, Kemer 2007, actually reached this position with *White* to move, via the move order 5 b3 c6 6 ♗g2 ♗b4+ 7 ♘bd2 d5 8 0-0 0-0 9 ♕c2 c5 (moving the c-pawn for the second time). In that game White obtained an opening advantage, but it is safe to say that the extra tempo will make things more than acceptable for Black and both 9...♘bd7 and 9...♘c6 should be fine.

b) 9 cxd5 invites complications with 9...♗xe2!? (9...exd5 is a safe alternative): for example, 10 dxe6 ♘c6! or 10 ♖e1 ♗xf3 11 ♗xf3 exd5 12 dxc5 (T.Kononenko-N.Bojkovic, Antalya 2002) 12...♘c6! with good play for

Black in both cases.

9...♗xc5

Black recaptures this way to keep the a3-f8 diagonal clear for his bishop, as well as the c-file for a rook.

10 a3

Intending to expand on the queenside. Others are less threatening:

a) As usual 10 b3?! is too timid and 10...♘bd7 11 ♗b2 ♖c8 was already more comfortable for Black in R.Dautov-*Comp P ConNers*, Lippstadt 2000.

b) 10 ♘e5 ♕c7 11 ♘d3 was seen in E.Durenko-R.Yusupov, Moscow 1996. Here instead of 11...♗d6, I would prefer 11...♗e7 as there the bishop is less exposed and keeps the d-file clear for the rooks. Play may continue 12 b3 ♘bd7 13 ♗b2 when Black has a pleasant choice between 13...♖ac8 and 13...b5!?.

10...♘bd7

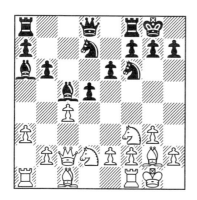

11 ♕a4

After 11 cxd5 ♘xd5 (11...♖c8!?) 12 ♘b3 ♗e7 13 ♘bd4 ♖c8 Black was the more active in P.Nikolic-M.Palac, Bled 2000.

11...♕c8!?

Attempting to maintain the bishop's active position, although 11...♗b7 is also fine.

12 b4

Instead G.Scholz Solis-R.Cruz, Santiago 1971, saw 12 cxd5 ♘xd5 (both 12...exd5!? and 12...♗xe2!? can also be considered) 13 ♖e1 ♗e7 14 ♘b3 ♖d8 15 ♗g5 ♕c4 16 ♕xc4 ♗xc4 17 ♘bd2 ♗a6 18 e4, and here 18...♗xg5 19 ♘xg5 ♘e7 or 19...♘c7 would have been equal.

12...♗d6!

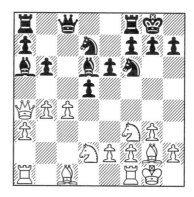

Here 12...♗e7 is less accurate due to 13 ♘d4! when the threat of 14 ♘c6 would probably force the somewhat undesirable 13...♗b7. However, after the text Black is fully developed and enjoys at least an equal share of the chances. The game I.Ivanisevic-B.Socko, European Team Championship, Crete 2007, continued with the lame 13 ♘d4?! (13 b5!? would have avoided material loss, although I would definitely prefer Black after 13...♘c5 followed by ...♗b7) 13...♗xc4 14 ♗b2 ♕a6 15 ♕c6 ♗e5 16 ♘xc4 ♗xd4 17 b5 (or 17 ♗xd4 ♖ac8!) 17...♕a4 18

♗xd4 ♖ac8 19 ♕d6 ♕xc4 20 e3 ♕xb5 21 a4 ♕c6 and Black went on to convert his material advantage.

Summary

5 ♕b3 is not to be taken lightly. Before researching this chapter I had never paid too much attention to it, but if you want proof that it should be taken seriously, you need only scan the listed game references to see names like Bareev, Morozevich and Van Wely on the White side. I have advocated an active, dynamic and reliable antidote which has found favour with many of the top players in the world. At present Black seems to be holding his own, although if this line continues to be de-bated at elite level the future may reveal further refinements on either side.

After 5 ♘bd2 ♗b4, 6 ♕c2 is the only serious try for an advantage. Then 6...♗b7 is the most popular move, but I hope to have convinced the reader of the merits of rapid development with 6...0-0!?, which I believe to be every bit as promising as the main line. Black will follow up with the simple and absolutely logical plan of opening the queenside, usually by means of ...d5 and ...c5, followed by a rapid development of the knight to d7 or c6, and the rook to c8. The ideas are crystal clear and we have seen that in many cases it is White who needs to be the more careful.

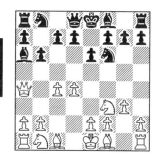

Chapter Thirteen

The Fianchetto Variation: 5 ♕a4

1 d4 ♘f6 2 c4 e6 3 ♘f3 b6 4 g3 ♗a6 5 ♕a4

This move should not worry the second player unduly, but it remains a popular choice at all levels so we should definitely be ready for it. White protects the c-pawn by deploying his queen on what he hopes will be an active location. The drawback is that on a4 her influence over the centre, specifically the crucial d5-square, is diminished. This enables Black to strike in the centre with ...c5 without fearing the response d4-d5.

5...♗b7!

The bishop has done its work on a6. Having drawn the white queen away from the centre, it returns to its traditional post in preparation for ...c5. It should also be noted that 5...c5 is an equally valid move order which usually leads to the same position after 6 ♗g2 ♗b7!.

6 ♗g2 c5

Black continues with his plan. At this point White almost always chooses between:

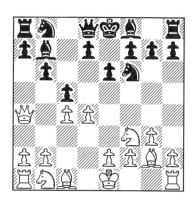

A: 7 0-0

B: 7 dxc5

Alternatives are extremely rare:

a) Compared with the dangerous pawn sacrifice mentioned in the introduction to our next chapter, 7 d5?! would be inadvisable here as the queen is clearly misplaced on a4. This can be most graphically illustrated after

7...exd5 8 cxd5 (8 ♘h4? ♗c6 allowed Black to break the pin on the d-pawn with gain of tempo in E.Donaldson Akhmilovskaya-I.Kulish, Moscow Olympiad 1994) 8...♗xd5!? 9 ♘c3 ♗c6.

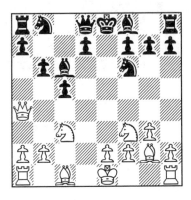

In the 5 ♕c2 variation it is extremely risky for Black to capture on d5 with the bishop, but an extra tempo makes a world of difference and here the second player is at least equal after 10 ♕b3 (10 ♕c2 should be met by 10...♗e7, rather than 10...d5? 11 ♘e5 ♗b7 12 ♕a4+ ♘bd7 13 ♗g5 with awkward pressure) 10...♗e7 11 ♘e5 0-0 12 ♘xc6 ♘xc6 13 0-0 (A.Karlsson-B.Jonsson, Reykjavik 1993) 13...♖e8, or 13 ♗g5 (C.Chellstorp-E.Haag, Birmingham 1975) 13...♘d4 14 ♕d1 ♖c8 15 0-0 ♘e6 and White's compensation is questionable in both cases.

b) 7 e3 can hardly threaten Black after 7...♗e7 8 ♘c3 (8 0-0 0-0 9 ♘c3 reaches the same position) 8...0-0 9 0-0 (after the 9 d5?! exd5 10 cxd5 of C.Cubek-A.Postojev, Baden 2003, Black can take the pawn with 10...♘xd5! 11 ♕e4, at which point the simplest solution is probably 11...f5 12 ♕c4 b5! 13 ♘xb5 ♔h8, intending ...♘b6 with advantage; there may also be a second good option in 11...♘b4!? 12 ♕xb7 ♘8c6 when White will have a hard time extricating his queen) when Black obtains a good game with 9...♕c8 (or 9...♘e4!?) 10 ♖d1 cxd4 11 exd4 d5.

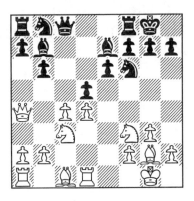

A couple of examples:

b1) After 12 ♘e5 dxc4 13 ♗xb7 ♕xb7 14 ♕xc4 ♖c8 15 ♕b3 (M.Mueller-V.Chuchelov, Goch 1991) 15...♘c6 Black enjoys quite a favourable IQP position.

b2) 12 cxd5 ♘xd5 13 ♘xd5 ♗xd5 14 ♗f4 (N.Litvinov-V.Kachar, Saratov 2006) 14...♕b7 also leaves him with at least equal chances.

A) 7 0-0

This enables Black to force an immediate trade of the light-squared bishops and is generally viewed as less ambitious than 7 dxc5.

7...cxd4 8 ♘xd4 ♗xg2 9 ♔xg2 ♕c8!

Other moves are playable, but the text looks like the most logical continuation to me. The queen fulfils three purposes on c8:

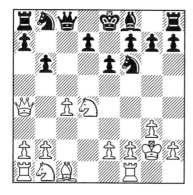

1) It eyes the vulnerable c4-pawn.

2) It facilitates ...♘c6.

3) In some variations it may come to b7, replacing the bishop on the long diagonal while also supporting a future ...b5 break.

10 ♗f4

This is the most ambitious move, although now that I have written those words I realize that they are bordering on oxymoronic, as the 7 0-0 variation must rank as one of the most timid anti-Queen's Indian lines at White's disposal. Perhaps it would be more appropriate to remark that the text is the only move to prevent wholesale exchanges after 10...♘c6, which would now meet with the retort 11 ♘b5!, forcing the weakening 11...e5. Still, judging by the positions reached in the main line, perhaps White's best policy would be to head for an equal position, as seen in the following two branches:

a) 10 ♘c3 ♘c6 11 ♘xc6 ♕xc6+ 12 ♕xc6 dxc6 leads to dry equality. 10...♗e7 is also playable, although it should be noted that, by comparison with the main line, White should be

marginally better off as his dark-squared bishop has the option of moving to a square other than f4. Nevertheless this should not make too big a difference, so if you do not wish to grant your opponent an easy path to a totally level ending then you may wish to play this way.

b) 10 ♖d1 ♘c6 is once again an easy equalizer when White has tried:

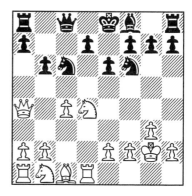

b1) 11 ♘b5 a6 12 ♘d6+ ♗xd6 13 ♖xd6 brought White an eventual victory in Z.Ilincic-W.Paschall, Budapest 2005, although the position at this stage is nothing special for him. Indeed, if Black had reacted with 13...♕b7 14 f3 b5! 15 cxb5 axb5 his superior structure (courtesy of the extra central pawn) and lead in development would have more than compensated White's supposed advantage of bishop over knight.

b2) 11 ♘xc6 ♕xc6+ 12 ♕xc6 dxc6 is absolutely equal, although I am ashamed to say that I once went on to lose this position with Black against the Hungarian GM and 5 ♕a4 specialist Zlatko Ilincic.

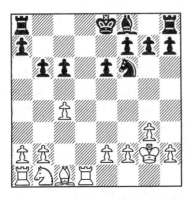

This game came at the end of a long and pretty dismal tournament for me, and judging by the way I handled the endgame I think it is likely that he would have beaten me from either side of the position! The game continued 13 ♗f4 ♖d8 (13...♗e7 is also fine) 14 ♘c3 ♗b4 15 ♗e5 ♔e7 16 a3 ♗d6 17 ♗xd6+ ♖xd6 18 ♖xd6 ♔xd6 19 b4 ♔c7 20 ♖d1 ♖d8 21 ♖xd8 ♔xd8 22 ♔f3 ♔e7 23 ♔f4

and here 23...♘d7 would have been simplest, intending 24 g4 f6 with ideas of ...c5 and/or ...♘e5. It is conceivable that a stronger player may try to win this position with either colour, but there is certainly no reason to prefer

White over Black.

Instead I played 23...♘e8 and after a long series of micro-errors topped off by a final, excruciating blunder, I ended up losing. To show you how *not* to play this endgame, I leave you with the remaining moves of Z.Ilincic-A.Greet, Budapest 2005: 24 c5 bxc5 25 bxc5 ♘c7 26 ♔e4 f6 27 f4 ♘b5 28 ♘b1 g6 29 g4 f5+ 30 gxf5 exf5+ 31 ♔e5 ♘c7 32 ♘d2 ♘b5 33 ♘c4 ♘c3 34 e3 ♘e4 35 ♔d4 ♔d7 36 ♘e5+ ♔c7 37 ♘f3 ♔d7 38 ♘g5 ♘xg5?? (the position after 38...♘f6 should still be tenable) 39 fxg5 ♔e6 40 a4 a5 41 h3 1-0. Funnily enough, in retrospect this game was of fantastic benefit to my chess development, as it made me appreciate just how much scope exists to outplay an opponent from a 'completely drawn' position. Though well beyond the scope of the present book, it is worth mentioning that in the subsequent game A.Greet-T.Eggleston, British Championship, Douglas 2005, my eventual victory was in a large part due to the lessons learnt from the aforementioned disaster against Ilincic.

Before returning to the main line, I would like to say a few words about playing for a win from an equal position, with particular reference to the above variations. Although easy equality after twelve moves must rank as a clear theoretical success for Black, such an outcome may not be so desirable if he desperately needs to play for a win. For players who may be concerned about this, I propose one of two solutions:

1) Play the endgame anyway. I remember reading somewhere the following wise words (I don't have the exact quotation to hand, so will have to paraphrase): 'It is a whole lot easier to play for a win from an equal position that from an inferior one.' There is a world of difference between a *drawn* position and an *equal* position which still contains plenty of play, as I discovered to my cost against Ilincic. If your opponent is looking for an easy draw, sometimes you just have to role your sleeves up and grind away.

2) Alternatively, if you really prefer to keep more pieces on the board, then you can, of course, meet either of the above moves with 10...♗e7 and ...0-0, leading to positions similar to those found in the main line. The only slight drawback is that White's bishop is not yet committed to f4, and could perhaps find a more useful role on a different square, although this should not matter too much. I will not analyse this in any depth, though, as the positions after 10 ♗f4 ♗e7 are so conceptually similar that you can learn more or less everything you need to know by studying that section.

We now return to the main line of 10 ♗f4, against which Black should complete the development of his kingside:

10...♗e7

Remember that 10...♘c6?! can be met by 11 ♘b5!, as mentioned above. The text, on the other hand, allows Black to count on a very comfortable version of the well-known Hedgehog

formation. The exchange of light-squared bishops has taken some of the tension out of the position and, more importantly, given him some extra breathing space on the queenside. The queen will find an ideal home on b7, conveniently gaining a tempo due to the check along the diagonal and supporting the thematic ...b5 break. Meanwhile it is by no means clear that the white bishop will be optimally placed on f4. Before moving on, I will briefly mention that 10...a6 has often been played and will often end up transposing. Personally I do not consider 11 ♘b5 to be a threat worth preventing, and thus believe developing the kingside to be a slightly higher priority at this stage of the game.

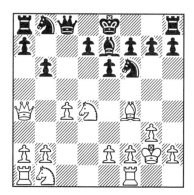

11 ♘c3

As indicated in the previous note, 11 ♘b5 is not dangerous after 11...♕c6+ 12 f3 0-0 13 ♘1c3 (13 ♘d2?! is almost self-evidently inferior and in M.Matlak-H.Korhonen, Kiljava 1984, Black soon gained the advantage after 13...d5 14 ♖fc1?! a6 15 ♘c3 d4 16 ♕xc6 ♘xc6 17 ♘a4 e5 18 ♗g5 ♖ab8) 13...♖c8

14 ♖fd1 (the feeble 14 ♗xb8? ♖cxb8 15 ♘d4 of T.Assmann-W.Ploetz, Kitzingen 1980, could have been most convincingly refuted by 15...♕c5! 16 ♖fd1 ♖c8 17 b3 d5 with a clear advantage to Black) 14...♘e8 15 ♖ac1 a6 (the knight is forced to retreat) 16 ♘d4 ♕b7 with a very comfortable position for Black in M.Diesen-J.Vilela, Alicante 1978.

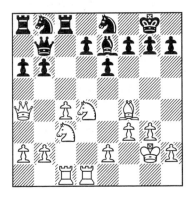

It seems safe to conclude that 11 Nb5 is premature, so White should instead focus on completing development.

11...0-0

Black can insert the move ...♕b7+ either here or any time over the next few moves. Usually we will arrive at the same position regardless, although to my mind it feels correct to postpone the check for a few moves in order to maintain the slight pressure against c4, thereby preventing White from recentralizing his wayward queen with ♕c2.

12 ♖fd1

From time to time White tries an alternative such as 12 e4, but the rook will almost always end up coming to d1 over the next few moves.

12...a6 13 e4

In such a non-forcing position it would be impractical to catalogue all the possible move orders, so I will restrict myself to a brief discussion of a few noteworthy examples in order to illustrate both sides' ideas.

a) The game A.Greet-A.Shabalov, Port Erin 2005, soon turned into a miserable experience for your author, and I hope that Shabalov's example will prove useful in demonstrating how Black may seize the initiative in such positions. The game proceeded 13 ♘c2?! (this is a bit too passive) 13...♕b7+ 14 f3 ♖c8 15 ♖d2, at which point Black unleashed the excellent 15...b5!.

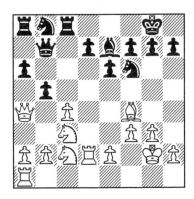

After the forced 16 cxb5 d5! his terrific central control and active pieces gave him more than enough for the pawn, and I soon went down after 17 ♘d4?! (17 ♕b3 would have been better, although 17...♘bd7 18 bxa6 ♕xa6 is still very pleasant for Black) 17...♘bd7 18 ♘c6?! ♗f8 (White is probably already beyond salvation) 19 ♘e5 ♘xe5 20 ♗xe5 ♘d7 21 ♗d4 e5 22 ♗f2 d4 23 bxa6 ♖xa6 24 ♕d1 ♘c5 25 ♘e4 ♘xe4 26 fxe4 ♕xe4+ 27 ♔g1 g6 28 ♖d3 ♖ac6 29 ♕b3 ♕xe2 30 ♖f1 ♖f6 0-1.

b) 13 ♖d2 leads after 13...♕b7+ 14 f3 ♖c8 15 ♖ad1 (for 15 e4 d6 see the main line) to a position that has been reached numerous times, via several different move orders.

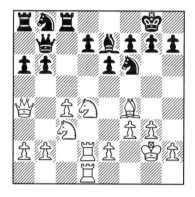

From here F.Hegeler-A.Von Gleich, Hamburg 1987, continued 15...d6 (threatening 16...e5) 16 ♘c2, at which point 16...b5!? 17 cxb5 d5! would have given Black fine compensation, much as in Shabalov-Greet above.

13...♕b7 14 f3 d6

My opinion concerning the respective merits of the text and the alternative 14...♖c8!? has fluctuated in both directions. The evaluation hinges on whether or not e4-e5 is a move worth preventing. The drawback to 14...d6 is that, following a knight retreat to c2 or e2, Black will be more or less forced to consign his rook – at least temporarily – to a defensive role on d8. In an ideal world he would prefer to meet an attack on the d-pawn with ...♘e8, keeping the more powerful rook for active

duties along the c-file. But, of course, in order for the knight retreat to be viable the rook must already be on c8. Thus after 14...♖c8, the natural though indolent move 15 ♖d2 (which has actually been White's most common choice) allows Black to have his cake and eat it after 15...d6 16 ♘de2 (or 16 ♘c2 ♘e8 17 ♖ad1 ♘c6 18 g4?!, as in Z.Sturua-A.Chernin, Dnipropetrovsk 1980, and now 18...♖ab8 threatens ...b5 with a fine position) 16...♘e8 17 ♖ad1 ♘d7 (17...♘c6 also looks fine; it is tough for White to prevent the plan of ...♖ab8 and ...b5) 18 e5 when Black is rather spoilt for choice:

a) If he wishes to play ambitiously then 18...g5!? could well be worth a look, intending 19 exd6 ♗f6 20 ♗e3 ♘e5 with a dangerous initiative.

b) Alternatively, 18...b5 should lead to an advantage with minimal risk. The position after 19 cxb5 d5 20 bxa6 ♖xa6 was reached twice by the Swedish IM Lars Ake Schneider in the 1980s:

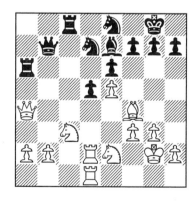

b1) The first game, Y.Kraidman-L.Schneider, Gausdal 1981, continued 21 ♕d4 g5! 22 ♗xg5 ♗xg5 23 ♕g4 h6 24 f4 d4+ 25 ♔f2 at which point 25...♘xe5! (in the game 25...dxc3? 26 ♖xd7 enabled White to escape with an eventual draw) 26 fxe5 dxc3 should win easily.

b2) The second, T.Welin-L.Schneider, Malmo 1986. instead saw 21 ♕c2 g5! 22 ♗e3 ♘xe5 23 ♘d4 ♘c4 24 ♖e2, and now the simplest solution looks to be 24...♘xe3+ 25 ♖xe3 ♖xa2 26 ♖e2 ♘d6, intending ...♗f6 when Black should win comfortably.

After witnessing these variations, it follows that White's only principled response to 14...♖c8 must be 15 e5, although I see no reason for Black to worry here either. The game P.Kruglikov-O.Averkin, Krasnodar 1997, continued 15...♘h5! 16 ♘e4 (in the case of 16 ♗e3, as in V.Ivanov-A.Yunusov, correspondence 1991, 16...♖c5! targets the e5-pawn) 16...♘c6 17 ♘xc6 ♘xf4+ 18 gxf4 ♖xc6 19 ♖d4 and now 19...♖ac8 20 ♖ad1 ♖8c7 looks fine for Black.

The d-pawn can easily be defended and the ...b5 break is on the cards. Meanwhile White's doubled f-pawns, while not too vulnerable at present,

could become a telling factor later in the endgame.

So which move is better – 14...d6 or 14...♖c8? Perhaps it boils down to personal taste, but here is my own opinion. Overall I consider the 7 0-0 variation to be harmless at best. Once the light-squared bishops are exchanged, I would tend to regard these Hedgehog positions as somewhat easier to play for Black; an assessment vindicated both by practical statistics and analysis. In my mind, therefore, the real question is which variation gives *White* the best chance of equalizing. And it seems to me that the aforementioned line with 14...♖c8 15 e5 gives him decent chances of doing just that. Looking objectively at the last diagram, I see no problems for Black but nor would I claim any real advantage. Therefore, having weighed everything up, I consider it worthwhile to stabilize the centre with 14...d6, preventing e4-e5 and guaranteeing a favourable Hedgehog, even if this means losing a tempo with ...♖fd8, ...♘e8 and later ...♖dc8.

15 ♘de2

If White refrains from attacking d6 then Black follows with ...♖c8, achieving his ideal position much as in the line 14...♖c8 15 ♖d2 d6 above. The alternative 15 ♘c2 ♖d8 16 ♘b4 was seen in W.Unzicker-K.Langeweg, Wijk aan Zee 1981, and here 16...♘h5!? 17 ♗e3 (17 ♗xd6?? ♖xd6 18 ♕e8+ ♗f8 19 ♖xd6 ♘f6 20 ♕d8 ♘bd7 21 ♖xd7 ♘xd7 wins for Black as the knight on b4 is hanging) 17...♖c8 looks very pleasant for Black.

15...♖d8

Obviously 15...♘e8? makes no sense when the rook is still on f8.

16 ♖d2

16 b4?! (V.Dydyshko-K.Lerner, Ivano Frankovsk 1982) 16...♘c6 just leaves the c-pawn looking weak.

16...♘c6 17 ♖ad1 ♘e8

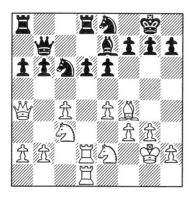

Compared with the line 14...♖c8 15 ♖d2 d6, Black's rook is slightly less active on d8, and in certain lines he may even lose a tempo to bring it to c8. Fortunately this is not the kind of position in which such a small detail is likely to matter too much, and if Black can successfully carry out the thematic ...b5 break he will more than likely obtain the advantage. In fact, it is not at all easy for White to prevent this as you can see from the following examples:

a) 18 b4? leaves the c-pawn horribly weak and Black has a pleasant choice between 18...♖dc8 19 ♖c1 g5! 20 ♗e3 ♘e5 21 c5 ♘c4 22 ♘d1 b5 23 ♕c2 (Z.Lang-H.Dobosz, German League 1997) 23...g4! when White's position is falling apart, and the immediate 18...g5!? when M.Oliwa-A.Pieniazek,

Krynica 1997, continued 19 ♗e3 ♘e5 20 ♖d4 ♘xc4 21 ♖xc4 b5 22 ♕a5 bxc4 23 ♗xg5 f6 24 ♗e3 d5 and White's compensation was nowhere near sufficient.

b) 18 ♘d4?! is a tactical oversight and in S.Emelyanov-G.Haese, correspondence 1994, Black soon won a pawn after 18...♘xd4 19 ♖xd4 b5! (but not 19...e5? 20 ♗xe5!; the text on the other hand blocks the path of the white queen to e8) 20 ♕a5 (20 cxb5? e5 21 ♗xe5 dxe5 22 ♖xd8 ♗xd8 23 bxa6 ♕xb2+ wins for Black) 20...bxc4 21 ♖xc4 ♕xb2+ 22 ♖d2 ♕b7, which he later converted to victory.

c) 18 a3 betrayed White's difficulty in finding a constructive plan in W.Browne-U.Andersson, Buenos Aires 1978. Against this or any similarly non-committal move, Black's simplest and most direct response is 18...♖ab8, threatening ...b5.

Summing up, 7 0-0 is not in the least bit threatening to Black and in many lines it seems to be White who stands a greater risk of becoming worse.

B) 7 dxc5 bxc5!?

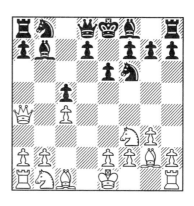

This move sends a clear message: 'If you don't want to permit an exchange of light-squared bishops, you will have to pay by allowing me to improve my pawn structure.' It must be said that 7...♗xc5 is also perfectly playable and has in fact been the more popular choice, outnumbering the pawn recapture by approximately two games to one. Many games have proceeded with the long theoretical line 8 0-0 0-0 9 ♘c3 ♗e7 10 ♖d1 ♘a6 11 ♗f4 ♘c5 12 ♕c2 ♕c8 13 ♖ac1 ♘ce4 14 ♘d4 ♘xc3 15 ♕xc3 a6 16 ♕b3 ♗xg2 17 ♔xg2 ♕b7+ 18 ♕f3 ♖a7 19 ♕xb7 ♖xb7 20 f3 ♖c8 21 e4.

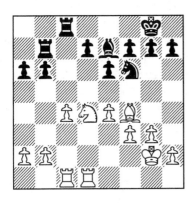

This leads to a simplified position in which White stands marginally better, but Black should have little difficulty in holding the draw.

I have chosen to advocate the pawn recapture mainly in order to unbalance the position. Black gains a central majority which can often become an important asset as the game progresses. Before we continue I would like to emphasize a couple of pertinent themes:

1) Firstly, a point of caution: Black should take care not to play ...d5 too hastily as after cxd5 exd5 his hanging d- and c-pawns could come under heavy fire. Usually he will be better advised to settle for a small centre with ...d6, only contemplating a further central advance after the rest of his pieces have been fully mobilized.

2) White's natural plan will be to exert pressure along the d-file with moves like ♗f4 and doubling rooks. Although Black can easily summon enough defenders, it is also worth knowing that there are times at which certain tactical features may enable him to leave the d6-pawn *en prise*. This can be an extremely useful weapon to have in your arsenal, although we will also see that under the wrong conditions it can backfire. Over the course of our analysis you will discover exactly when this idea should and should not be essayed.

8 0-0

Occasionally White shuffles the move order with 8 ♘c3, but the king will always castle short, so we will assume that he plays this first.

8...♗e7 9 ♘c3

Again other moves have been seen, but the knight can hardly have a better square than c3.

9...0-0

Black should also carry out the essential task of castling before worrying about any of his other pieces. At this point White must decide which rook to bring to the d-file. This may seem like a trivial decision, but we will see that it can affect certain variations in rather a drastic way. We now analyse:

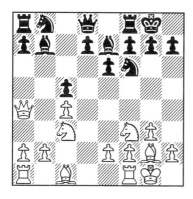

B1: 10 ♖d1
B2: 10 ♗f4

The alternatives are rare and harmless:

a) In S.Kristjansson-H.Stefansson, Strandgotu 2001, Black reacted to the slow 10 ♖e1 with the active 10...d5!? (10...d6 11 e4 ♘c6 should also be fine). The game continued 11 ♕b3 ♕b6 12 ♘e5 ♖d8 13 ♗f4 ♘bd7 14 cxd5 ♘xe5 15 d6 (White gains nothing from either 15 ♕xb6 axb6 16 ♗xe5 ♘xd5, or 15 ♗xe5 ♕xb3 16 axb3 ♘xd5) 15...♗xd6 16 ♗xb7 ♖ab8 17 ♕xb6 axb6 18 ♖ed1 (18 ♗g2 ♘c4 is pleasant for Black) 18...♘c4 (also possible was 18...♖xb7 19 ♗xe5 ♖bd7) 19 ♗xd6 ♘xd6 20 ♗c6 ♔f8 leading to approximate equality, although I have a slight preference for Black on account of his superior central control.

b) 10 ♗g5 d6 11 ♖fd1 ♘bd7 12 ♕c2 a6 (12...♕b6 is a sensible alternative) 13 ♖d2 ♕c7 14 ♖ad1 ♖fd8 15 b3 h6 16 ♗xf6 ♘xf6 was comfortable for Black in A.Vidarte Morales-H.Urday Caceres, Lima 1999.

c) 10 ♕c2 leads to a position more commonly reached via the move order 4...♗b7 5 ♗g2 ♗e7 6 ♘c3 0-0 7 ♕c2 c5 8 dxc5 bxc5 9 0-0 (in the present version Black has lost a tempo with ...♗a6-b7 and White on ♕a4-c2). The queen retreat is a little premature here, and we will subsequently see that there are certain positions in which it would prefer to move to b5 or b3. Black should just play 10...♘c6 or 10...♕b6 with similar play to the main lines.

B1) 10 ♖d1 ♕b6 11 ♗f4

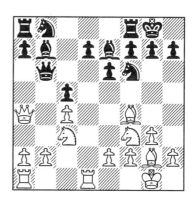

11...d6

Black should settle for a modest centre for the time being. On his 2006 DVD Jacob Aagaard recommends the more spirited 11...♖d8 12 ♖d2 d5?!. The intention is most admirable, but as far as I can see the idea falls down after 13 cxd5 exd5 14 ♘e5! ♘a6 15 ♖ad1 ♕e6 16 ♘c4 ♘b4. So far we have been following V.Tukmakov-K.Aseev, Odessa 1989. Now instead of the game's 17 a3 ♗c6 18 ♕a5 d4 19 axb4 ♗xg2 20 ♔xg2 cxb4 21 ♖xd4 ♖xd4 22 ♖xd4 bxc3 23 bxc3 ♕xe2 with equality, the improvement 17 ♘a5!, as advocated by Yrjölä and Tella, puts Black under serious pressure after 17...♗c8 18 ♕b3 ♗d7 (or 18...♗f8 19 a3 c4 20 ♕xc4!! dxc4 21 ♖xd8 and White wins) 19 ♘xd5 ♘fxd5 20 ♗xd5 ♘xd5 21 ♖xd5 ♗e8 22 ♖xd8 ♖xd8 23 ♖xd8 ♗xd8 24 ♕xe6 fxe6, reaching an endgame in which White has good chances to convert his extra pawn. Therefore it seems that the plan with an early ...d5 cannot quite be justified.

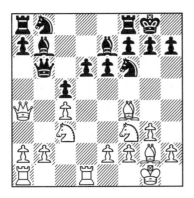

White has three main ideas here. He can prepare to double rooks, offer a queen exchange or attempt to open a queenside file:

B11: 12 ♖d2
B12: 12 ♕b3
B13: 12 ♖ab1

B11) 12 ♖d2

This has been White's most popular choice, but it allows a clever riposte.
12...♘c6!

This is the best known case where Black can successfully leave his d-pawn unguarded. The idea is that if White goes ahead and captures then the b2-pawn will drop. *It is very important that when this happens Black will be attacking the rook on a1.*

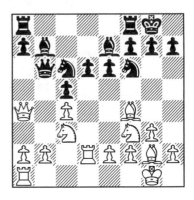

Before moving on, it should be noted that the text is not forced and players wishing to simplify their preparation can consider 12...h6!?, inviting a transposition to Line B2 after, for example, 13 ♖ad1 e5. I had actually been intending to recommend this in order to simplify the reader's workload, until it occurred to me that White may be able to derive some small benefit from the positioning of his 'spare' rook on a1 instead of f1, such as with 13 ♕b3, when capturing on b3 (which is not, of course, obligatory) would open the a-file. The black position remains playable of course, but given that this minute difference may slightly favour White, I felt it more principled to recommend the text.

Calling Black's bluff

Naturally our first order of business should be to find out what happens if White takes the d-pawn:

13 ♗xd6?! ♗xd6 14 ♖xd6 ♕xb2 15 ♖b1 ♕xc3 16 ♖xb7 ♘d4!

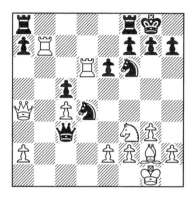

This is Black's idea. The first crucial point to recognise is that White must avoid the diabolical trap 17 ♘xd4?? ♕e1+ 18 ♗f1 ♘e4! when he was forced to resign in R.Dautov-M.Palac, Vienna 1996, as well as in three subsequent games! For anyone who does not know, Rustem Dautov is an experienced Grandmaster rated 2615 at the time of this game, so if this sort of thing can happen to him it can happen to anyone!

Instead 17 ♕d1! is the only move, when play continues 17...♖ad8 18 ♖xd8 ♖xd8 19 ♘xd4 cxd4 20 ♖xa7 ♕xc4. This ending should probably lead to a draw, but practice has demonstrated that it is White who stands the greater risk of losing. He may have an outside passed pawn and a nice bishop, but Black controls the centre and has the safer king. A good example was the game M.Hoffmann-C.Horvath, Budapest 1992, which continued 21 ♕a4 ♕c1+ 22 ♗f1 g6 23 ♕a5 ♖b8 24 ♖a8 ♖xa8 25 ♕xa8+ ♔g7 26 a4 e5!.

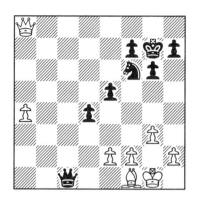

It turns out that Black can break through to the enemy king before White queens the a-pawn! The game continued 27 a5 e4 28 ♕d8 d3! 29 exd3 e3! 30 fxe3 (30 ♕e7 was more stubborn, but after 30...♘g4 31 ♕e4 ♕e1! 32 ♕d4+ f6 33 ♕b2 exf2+ 34 ♔g2 ♘e3+ 35 ♔f3 ♘xf1 36 ♕xf2 ♘d2+ Black should win fairly comfortably) 30...♕xe3+ 31 ♔g2 ♘g4 32 ♕b6 ♕d2+ 33 ♔h3 h5 34 ♗g2 ♘f2+ 35 ♔h4 g5+ and White resigned in view of 36 ♔xh5 ♕e2+ 37 ♔xg5 ♕g4 mate. I should mention that *MegaBase* lists the result of this game as '1-0', but as White is about to be mated I will assume that this is a data error, although I suppose it is just about conceivable that Black could have overstepped the time limit.

In any case, you can see that taking on d6 can only lead to problems for White.

Refusing the bait

If White is not going to take the pawn, then...
13 ♖ad1

...is the most obvious candidate. A few other examples:

a) 13 ♖b1 ♖fd8 14 ♕d1 ♘d4 reaches variation 'd', below.

b) 13 ♕b3 is well met by 13...♘a5! 14 ♕b5 (after 14 ♕xb6 axb6 White cannot defend c4 as 15 b3?? loses to 15...♘xb3) 14...♖fd8 (14...♕c7!?) 15 ♖ad1 ♕xb5 16 cxb5 ♘c4 17 ♖c2 (J.Borges Mateos-P.Dias, Albacete 2003) and here 17...a6 is better for Black.

c) 13 ♘e1 ♖fd8 14 ♖ad1 ♘d4 15 ♗xb7 ♕xb7 16 e3 ♘f5 17 ♗g5 was V.Ikonnikov-I.Farago, Deizisau 1997, and now 17...♖ab8 looks fine for Black.

d) 13 ♕d1 ♖fd8 and now both 14 ♖b1 ♘d4 15 e3 ♘xf3+ 16 ♗xf3 (M.Mraz-A.Brenke, correspondence 1999) 16...♘e8, and 14 b3 ♘d4 15 e3 ♘xf3+ 16 ♗xf3 (M.Dlugy-L.Portisch, London 1986) 16...♘e8 are about equal.

e) 13 ♕b5 ♕c7 14 ♖ad1 a6 15 ♕a4 ♘d4! and now:

e1) 16 ♘xd4 cxd4 17 c5 e5 18 cxd6 ♗xd6 19 ♗xb7? (19 ♖xd4 exd4 20 ♗xd6 ♕xd6 21 ♗xb7 was the last chance, although White is still struggling after 21...♕b6 22 ♗xa8 dxc3 23 ♗f3 ♕xb2) 19...♕xb7 20 ♗g5 ♘e8 21 ♘b1 h6 22 ♗e3 dxe3 23 ♖xd6 ♘xd6 24 ♖xd6 exf2+ 25 ♔xf2 ♕h1 and Black won easily in M.Djurkovic-I.Kragelj, Bled 1993.

e2) 16 ♘e1 ♗xg2 17 ♘xg2 ♖fb8 18 b3 h6 and Black was at least equal in V.Salov-M.Chandler, Manila Interzonal 1990.

13...♘d4!

This possibility might be considered the secondary tactical point which vindicates Black's 11th move.

14 ♘e1

There is nothing better, especially as 14 ♘xd4 cxd4 15 ♗xb7 ♕xb7 16 ♖xd4? e5 is obviously no good for White.

14...♗xg2 15 ♔xg2 ♕b7+

The game J.Sriram-H.Koneru, Visakhapatnam 2006, also turned out successfully for Black after 15...h6 16 f3 ♖fd8 17 g4 ♕b7 18 h3 ♘d7 19 b3 ♘b6 20 ♕a3 d5 21 cxd5 exd5 22 ♗g3 ♘e6 23 ♘c2 c4 24 ♕a5 ♗g5 25 e3 d4 26 ♘e4 d3 27 ♘xg5 dxc2 28 ♖xd8+ ♘xd8 29 ♖c1 hxg5 30 ♖xc2 cxb3 31 axb3 ♘e6 0-1.

16 ♔g1 h6

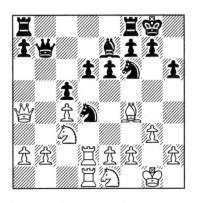

We have been following the game P.Skatchkov-S.Ionov, Cappelle la Grande 2006. Black has a comfortable position, and later went on to take over the initiative: 17 ♘c2 (if White drives the knight away with 17 e3 ♘f5, then his bishop would suffer from a lack of available squares) 17...♖ad8 18 b3 a6 19 ♕a5 ♘c6 20 ♕a4 ♘d4 21 ♗e3 ♘f5 22 f3 d5 23 cxd5 exd5 24 ♘xd5 ♘xd5 25 ♕e4 ♘d4 26 ♘xd4 cxd4 27 ♗xd4 ♗b4 28 ♖d3 ♖fe8 29 ♕g4 ♗f8 30 e4 ♘b4 31 ♖3d2 ♖xd4 32 ♖xd4 ♗c5 33 ♔g2 ♗xd4 34 ♖xd4 ♘xa2 35 ♖d6 g6 36 ♕f4 h5 37 h4 ♘c3 38 ♕f6 ♕xb3 39 ♖xa6 ♕c2+ 40 ♔h3 ♕d1 0-1.

Overall we have seen that the primitive attempt to attack the d-pawn by means of 12 ♖d2 can be more than adequately countered by 12...♘c6!. We now consider White's slightly more subtle alternatives.

B12) 12 ♕b3

Offering a queen exchange. 12 ♕b5 is less popular and not particularly challenging in view of 12...♕c7! when the white queen is misplaced and will have to waste time retreating. Play may continue 13 ♖d2 (the sacrifice 13 ♗xd6 ♗xd6 14 ♖xd6 ♕xd6 15 ♕xb7 ♘bd7 does not give White enough) 13...a6 14 ♕a4 ♘c6 15 ♘e1 (15 ♖ad1 ♘d4! reaches variation 'e' in the notes to 12 ♖d2 ♘c6 13 ♖ad1, above) 15...h6 with comfortable play for Black in M.Nezar-A.Istratescu, Nancy 2005.

12...♖d8

Black must not forget to protect the d-pawn, as White was threatening to capture it after exchanging queens.

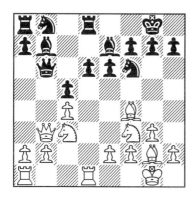

13 ♖d2

This is the most natural move, although it may not be best. The alternatives are hardly very inspiring though:

a) 13 ♘b5 achieves nothing for White after 13...♘e8: for example, 14 ♖d2 ♘c6 15 ♖ad1 ♘a5! 16 ♕c2 a6 17 ♘a3 ♘f6 18 ♗g5 ♗e4 19 ♕c1 h6 20 ♗xf6 ♗xf6 and Black was slightly better in G.Kallai-P.Genov, Dresden 2000, although a draw was soon agreed. Later, in G.Kallai-V.Chuchelov, French League 2003, the Hungarian GM tried to 'improve' with 15 ♘c3?, but after 15...♘a5 16 ♕c2 ♘xc4 17 ♘a4 ♕b5 18 ♘c3 ♕a6 19 ♖dd1 ♖ab8 he was simply a pawn down for no compensation.

b) 13 ♕xb6 axb6 14 ♘b5 ♘e8 is also nothing for Black to worry about. For the time being White has an outpost on b5, but the knight can eventually be exchanged and in the long run Black's central majority (which was further strengthened by the exchange on b6) may become the dominant factor. The top-class encounter F.Vallejo Pons-V.Anand, Linares 2005, continued 15 a3 h6 (I am not altogether sure why Anand felt the need to play this, and the straightforward 15...♘c6 looks perfectly fine) 16 ♖ac1 ♘c6 17 ♘e1 ♘a5 18 ♗d2 ♗xg2 19 ♔xg2 ♘c6 (19...d5!?) 20 e4 ♘a7 21 ♘c3 ♘c7 when the position was about equal and a draw was agreed twenty moves later.

Returning to the main line, and now in H.Olafsson-J.Lautier, Antwerp 1998, Black took an ambitious but in my opinion fully justified decision to exchange the queens:

13...♕xb3!

Instead 13...♘a6 or 13...♘bd7 would have been approximately equal.

14 axb3 ♘c6

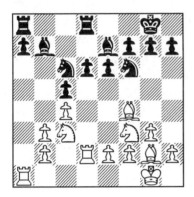

The change in the pawn structure brings both positive and negative repercussions for both players. On balance, however, it seems to me that the b3-pawn is more likely to become weak than Black's a-pawn, which is not so easy to attack. The course of the game supported that assessment: 15 ♖ad1 ♘e8 16 ♘e1 ♖db8 17 ♘d3 ♘d4 18 b4 cxb4 19 ♘a4 ♗xg2 20 ♔xg2 ♘b3 21 ♖c2 ♘d4 22 ♖cd2 g5 23 ♗e3 ♘f5 and Black was just a pawn up for nothing, although White eventually managed to salvage a draw.

B13) 12 ♖ab1

This is White's latest attempt, with which he intends to open the b-file.

12...♘bd7

12...♘a6 is a valid alternative, but the knight could turn out to be misplaced here and it soon transpires that White's intended b2-b4 is hardly worth preventing.

13 b4

This is the consistent move. In P.Dias-M.Chandler, Santo Antonio 2001, White changed his mind with 13 ♖d2 ♖fd8 14 ♖bd1, but after 14...♘f8 15 h3?! (floundering without a plan) 15...♘g6 16 ♗e3 h6 (16...d5!?) 17 ♕c2 ♗c6 18 ♘e1 ♖ac8 19 b3 ♕b7 20 ♘a4?? (this is a blunder, but even after the superior 20 ♗xc6 ♕xc6 21 ♘g2 d5 22 ♘b5 ♕b7 Black is clearly for choice) 20...♗xg2 21 ♘xg2 ♘e4 he was losing the exchange and shortly after the game.

13...cxb4

13...♗c6?! 14 b5 ♗b7 15 ♕c2 ♖fd8 16 e4 gave White the makings of a nice positional bind in P.Nikolic-H.Stefansson, Selfoss 2002, although there was certainly no need for Black to exacerbate his problems here with 16...e5? 17 ♗d2 ♘f8 18 ♘d5 ♘xd5 19 cxd5 ♗c8 20 a4.

14 ♖xb4 ♗c6!

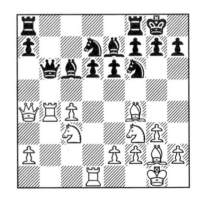

First played by Boris Gelfand, this excellent *zwischenzug* ensures Black of a comfortable game.

15 ♕a3

15 ♖xb6? ♗xa4 16 ♖bxd6 ♗xd1 17

♖xd1 ♖ac8 is just better for Black. In A.Voinov-E.Shaposhnikov, Saratov 2006, White tried to improve with 15 ♕b3 ♕c5 16 ♗e3 and now 16...♕a5 looks simplest, intending 17 ♘b5 d5 when Black is fine. Going back, 15...♕d8!? looks very interesting too as 16 ♗xd6 a5! traps the rook, and after 17 ♖b5 ♗xd6 18 ♖xd6 ♗xb5 19 ♘xb5 ♘e4 I doubt that White has quite enough for the exchange.

15...♕c5 16 ♗e3

16 ♖b3 ♕xa3 17 ♖xa3 ♘b6 is equal according to Gershon, but the weakness of the c4-pawn leads me to prefer Black.

16...♕h5

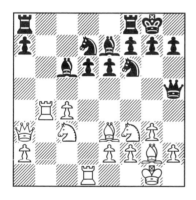

17 h3

White must tread carefully as 17...♘g4 was a serious threat. Now in J.Lautier-B.Gelfand, Enghien les Bains 2003, Black decided to force a draw:

17...♗xf3

17...d5 was possible, but White can maintain the balance with 18 g4! ♕g6 19 ♘h4 ♕c2 (but not 19...♗xb4? 20 ♕xb4 ♕c2 21 ♖c1 – Gershon) 20 ♖c1 ♕xc1+ 21 ♗xc1 a5 22 cxd5 axb4 23 ♕b3

♘xd5 24 ♘xd5 ♗xh4 (after 24...exd5 25 ♘f5 White is better according to Gershon) 25 ♘xb4. Gershon evaluates this endgame as slightly better for White, but 25...♗xg2 26 ♔xg2 ♖fc8 looks roughly equal to me, although either side might try to outplay the other.

18 ♗xf3

After 18 exf3? d5 Black wins material.

18...♕xh3

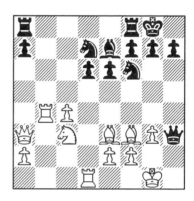

19 ♗g2

19 ♗xa8?! ♖xa8 20 c5 ♘xc5 (inferior is 20...♘g4? 21 ♖xg4 ♕xg4 22 cxd6) 21 ♖h4 ♕f5 (Gershon) is better for Black, who has two pawns for the exchange and a safer king.

19...♕h5 20 ♗f3 ♕h3

Neither player can profitably avoid the repetition.

21 ♗g2 ♕h5 22 ♗f3 ½-½

Summing up, it seems that Black is in excellent shape in all lines after 10 ♖fd1. We will now consider those lines in which White arranges to occupy the d-file with his queen's rook.

B2) 10 ♗f4 ♕b6 11 ♖ad1

Obviously White can still transpose to Line B1 with 11 ♖fd1 d6, but after the text we will see how a seemingly trivial choice of one rook over the other can have a profound impact over the ensuing struggle.

11...d6 12 ♖d2

This is where the positioning of White's other rook can make a big difference.

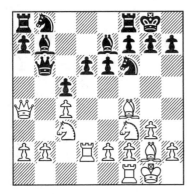

12...h6!

It is at this point that Black requires a completely different handling compared with Line B11. The point is that the sacrifice 12...♘c6?! is less effective here because after 13 ♗xd6 ♗xd6 14 ♖xd6 ♕xb2 there is no rook hanging on a1, which means that White has time for 15 ♕b3! ♕xb3 16 axb3 with a marginally better ending.

The point of the text is to prepare ...e5, relieving the pressure against d6 and securing a powerful outpost for a knight on d4. Please note that the immediate 12...e5?! can be strongly met by 13 ♗g5, eliminating the knight and obtaining control over d5 (hence the need for the text).

Black sometimes plays 12...♖d8 13 ♖fd1 h6, but if he is planning to play ...e5 and ...♘c6-d4 anyway, he often has no need to spend an extra tempo defending the d-pawn. It should also be noted that 13...♘c6? is even less advisable here than it was on the previous move in view of 14 ♗xd6 ♗xd6 15 ♖xd6 ♕xb2 16 ♕b5! ♕xb5 17 cxb5 ♖xd6 18 ♖xd6 ♘b4 19 ♘e5 ♗xg2 20 ♔xg2 ♔f8 21 e4 when Black faced a miserable endgame in B.Lalic-J.Emms, Southend 2001.

13 ♖fd1 e5! 14 ♗e3 ♘c6

After 14...♘g4 15 ♘e1!? ♘xe3 16 fxe3 White's dominance over the central light squares looks more relevant than his compromised structure.

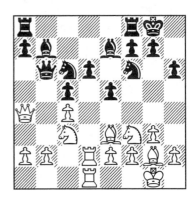

Before we consider any specific variations after 14...♘c6, it is worth taking some time to reflect upon the change in pawn structure and how it affects the plans for both sides. The most obvious point is that the d5-square has been permanently weakened. White's plan is usually pretty clear; he will look to exchange pieces and gradually aim for positional domination based upon his control over d5 and the static nature of Black's central pawn wedge. If, by magic, we could remove all minor pieces except for White's queen's knight and Black's dark-squared bishop then we would more or less arrive at White's dream scenario. Fortunately from Black's perspective, this grotesque fantasy need never become a reality.

Positive features of Black's position

Firstly, let us note that Black currently controls more space and his pieces enjoy a greater freedom. In the short- to mid-term, his queen's knight will take up a wonderful outpost on d4 from where it influences the entire board. It is, of course, conceivable that this piece will eventually be evicted by e2-e3, but this is not always easy for White to arrange. To begin with there is a bishop blocking that pawn from advancing, and even after it has been relocated White may have to worry about the weakness of the f3-square.

Furthermore, the asymmetry of the pawn structure rather favours Black. His extra central pawn on d6 may not be advancing any time soon, but it provides constant support for its colleagues on c5 and e5, thus ensuring that the rest of Black's pieces will enjoy maximum freedom for more important tasks. Looking across to the queenside, the open b-file and potential pawn lever ...a5-a4 could provide plenty of headaches for White, a good example being the main game below.

We will now see how these con-

cepts have played out in practice.

15 ♘e1!?

White anticipates ...♘d4 and prepares for a bishop exchange. Considering his lack of space and the fact that his long-term strategy is centred on the light squares, his reasoning is easy to understand. The alternatives illustrate White's problems quite convincingly:

a) 15 ♕b5?! achieves nothing after 15...♕c7! as the queen will soon be targeted by a black rook.

b) 15 ♘h4?! ♘d4 16 ♗xb7 ♕xb7 17 f3 (L.Seres-N.Lakos, Hungary 1999) 17...♘d7! leaves White facing the dual threats of ...♘b6, winning the c4-pawn, and ....♗xh4, ruining his kingside structure.

c) With 15 ♖b1 White makes abundantly clear his intention to open the queenside.

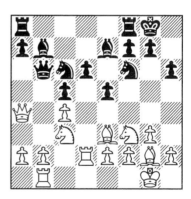

Therefore 15...a5 is more or less obligatory (15...♖fd8? allows 16 b4! – Bareev). The high-class encounter P.Nikolic-E.Bareev, Bled 1991, continued 16 ♕b5 ♕c7 17 ♕b3 ♖fd8 18 ♘h4 ♖ab8 19 ♘f5 ♘d4 20 ♘xe7+ ♕xe7 21 ♕d1 ♗xg2 22 ♔xg2 ♕e6 23 b3 d5!

(Black exploits his dynamic potential before White can complete his intended regrouping) 24 cxd5 ♘xd5 25 ♖c1 f5! 26 ♘xd5 ♖xd5 27 ♖c4 and here 27...f4! would have been very strong.

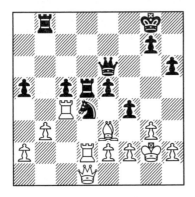

In his annotations Bareev modestly evaluates the position as equal, but it seems to me that White is in considerable trouble after 28 ♗xd4 (28 gxf4?? exf4 wins after either 29 ♗xf4 ♕e4+ or 29 ♗xd4 ♖g5+ 30 ♔h1 ♕h3) 28...exd4 29 ♖d3 ♖f8 with a strong initiative.

Going back to an earlier point in this game, it also looks promising for Black to play 17...a4!?, taking the opportunity to expand on the queenside.

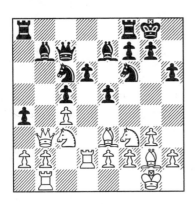

Now 18 ♘xa4?! loses material after 18...♘a5! 19 ♕c2 (or 19 ♕c3 ♘e4) 19...♗e4 20 ♖d3 ♘c6, while both 18 ♕c2 ♘d4 and 18 ♕a3 ♘d4 are also not much fun for White. 18 ♕d1 is probably best, but after 18...♘d4 Black is very comfortably placed.

Let us now return to the main line of 15 ♘e1!?, as we follow the instructive game R.Dautov-L.Schandorff, German League 2002:

15...♖fd8 16 ♘d5

If White plays too ambitiously with 16 g4!? ♘d4 (Black must avoid 16...♘xg4? 17 ♘d5 ♕a6 18 ♕xa6 ♗xa6 19 ♘xe7+ ♘xe7 20 ♖xd6) 17 g5, he risks becoming worse after 17...hxg5 18 ♗xg5 ♗xg2 19 ♘xg2 ♕b7, intending 20 ♗xf6 ♗xf6 21 ♘d5 ♗g5, as analysed by Finkel.

16...♘xd5 17 ♗xd5 ♖ab8

Black already has a comfortable position, and the further course of the game provides a textbook illustration of how to improve it.

18 ♘d3?!

The knight has very little to do here. Instead Finkel proposes 18 f3 ♘d4 19 ♗xb7 ♕xb7 20 ♘g2 f5 (20...a5!? intending ...♕b4 looks very tempting) 21 ♗f2 ♗f6, which he evaluates as unclear. Note that 22 ♘e3 can always be met by 22...♗g5!, exchanging the powerful knight before it can get to d5.

18...a5! 19 b3 ♕c7 20 f3 ♘d4 21 ♗xb7 ♖xb7 22 ♗f2

Alternatively, 22 ♔g2 f5 23 ♗g1 ♗g5 24 e3 ♘xf3 25 ♔xf3 e4+ 26 ♔g2 exd3 27 ♖xd3 ♖b4 (Finkel) 28 ♕a3 a4 is better for Black.

22...♗g5 23 ♖b2 f5 24 ♘e1 e4 25 f4

25 ♔g2 ♖b4 26 ♕a3 ♖db8 maintains the pressure.

25...♗f6 26 ♖bd2 ♘c6

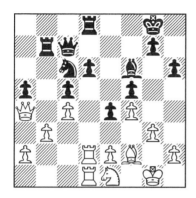

Schandorff is methodically preparing ...a5-a4, and White soon crumbles under the pressure.

27 ♖c1

White would ideally like to play 27 ♘c2 in order to install the steed on d5, but unfortunately for him this loses an exchange after 27...♗c3 28 ♖d5 ♘e7. True, the first player can obtain some compensation after 29 ♘e3, but in the long run Black should eventually prevail. The alternative 27 ♘g2 ♗c3 leads to a similar result, unless White tries to save his material with 28 ♖c2, after which there follows 28...♘d4! 29 ♗xd4 cxd4 30 e3 ♖b4! 31 ♕a3 d5! with a near-decisive advantage, as shown by 32 cxd5 ♖xd5 or 32 exd4 ♗xd4+! 33 ♖xd4 ♕c5 34 ♖cd2 dxc4, winning easily.

27...♖b4 28 ♕a3 a4 29 ♘c2 ♖a8 30

♖cd1 ♖bb8 31 ♕c1 axb3 32 axb3 ♘a5 33 ♖xd6 ♘xb3 34 ♕e3 ♗d4

This wins an exchange and the game. The remaining moves were 35 ♖6xd4 (35 ♘xd4? ♕xd6 is even worse) 35...cxd4 36 ♘xd4 ♘xd4 37 ♖xd4 (37 ♕xd4 ♖d8 wins) 37...♖b2 38 ♕c3 ♖aa2 39 ♖d5 ♖xe2 40 ♗d4 ♖g2+ 0-1.

Summary

We have examined 5 ♕a4 in considerable detail, but I think the effort has been worthwhile. According to my database this move accounts for almost one in every six games after 4 g3 ♗a6, so it is important for Black to learn the correct countermeasures. We have seen that after 5 ♕a4 ♗b7 6 ♗g2 c5 7 0-0 cxd4 8 ♘xd4 ♗xg2 9 ♔xg2 ♕c8! Black equalizes effortlessly, and in many of the ensuing Hedgehog positions it seems to be White who comes under some pressure.

7 dxc5 is a bit more challenging, but after my recommendation of 7...bxc5 Black's central majority offers him excellent long-term chances, a fact which is perhaps best illustrated in the final part of the chapter in which we examined the plan of ...d6 and later ...e5. Overall, I believe that if the reader takes the time to study thoroughly the contents of the present chapter, he will enjoy excellent chances of success against the white queen's early flank excursion.

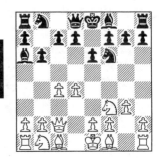

Chapter Fourteen

The Fianchetto Variation: 5 ♕c2!?

1 d4 ♘f6 2 c4 e6 3 ♘f3 b6 4 g3 ♗a6 5 ♕c2!?

Over the past couple of years the popularity of this variation has positively skyrocketed! For those readers who may be unfamiliar with the latest theoretical trends, a brief historical recap should help to set the scene.

For several decades 5 ♕c2 was considered thoroughly innocuous in view of the thematic central strike 5...c5. The point being that after 6 d5 (which is, in principle, the move that White would like to play) 6...exd5 7 cxd5 ♗b7 (7...♘xd5?? is, of course, a blunder due to 8 ♕e4+), White is unable to save his d-pawn, as shown by both 8 ♘c3 ♘xd5 9 ♕e4+ ♕e7 and 8 e4 ♕e7!. Thus 5 ♕c2 advocates were forced to settle for the tame 6 ♗g2 ♗b7 7 dxc5, which was obviously never going to worry Black.

Until very recently theoreticians believed that this was the end of the story and the entire variation was consigned to the conceptual scrap-heap. In the

middle of 2006, however, 5 ♕c2 stormed back into the limelight when it actually transpired that White could simply sacrifice the d-pawn with 6 d5 exd5 7 cxd5 ♗b7 8 ♗g2!.

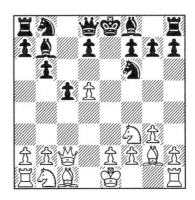

Funnily enough the idea was not a new one, the earliest example on my database being D.Fuhrmann-T.Doering, German League 1995, as well as a couple of subsequent games from 2001. Presumably the world's top players and theoreticians had seen these games without ever taking

White's idea seriously. Indeed, the Bibliography mentions three sources dating from 2006, of which not a single one even mentions the pawn sacrifice. This all changed, however, when Vallejo Pons utilized the sacrifice to defeat Macieja at the Turin Olympiad in June 2006 before Gelfand followed up by trouncing Aronian at the Dortmund super-tournament two months later. 5 ♕c2 had finally hit the big time!

In the early days of the resurgence just about everyone reacted to the sacrifice with 8...♗xd5? 9 ♘c3 ♗c6 10 e4, but after several crushing defeats for Black (including one at the expense of your author, courtesy of Pavel Tregubov in October 2006), the superiority of 8...♘xd5 became universally accepted. At the time of writing this line is still being hotly debated, with new developments occurring practically every week.

After extensive research I decided that the best policy with regard to the present book would be to avoid the pawn sacrifice. There are two main arguments in favour of doing so:

1) I doubt that many readers would be enamoured by the prospect of having to learn the myriad of theoretical lines required just to survive the opening, all for the sake of a meagre pawn. Even assuming perfect defence, it is still an open question whether Black can fully extinguish his opponent's combustible initiative.

2) Compared with more traditional lines in which the majority of theoretical assessments have been refined by decades of analysis and practical testing, the theoretical status of this variation is exceedingly volatile. Indeed, future refinements will inevitably cause existing verdicts to be overturned. Even a cutting edge black repertoire, based upon the best available information at the time of writing, could very easily be rendered obsolete by the discovery of one key improvement.

All things considered, I believe that for our purposes the most pragmatic approach will be to avoid this treacherous territory. I recommend that you do so by playing the less common, but fully sound and respectable...

5...♗b4+!?

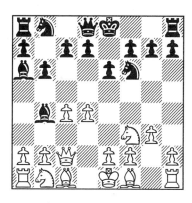

Aside from being a perfectly decent move, the text could also prove to be an ideal psychological weapon. Remember that anyone who plays 5 ♕c2 nowadays will more than likely be hoping to blow you away with the aforementioned pawn sacrifice, and for that reason alone it makes perfect sense to steer the game into relatively tranquil waters.

6 ♗d2

This is probably White's best chance for an advantage. The alternative 6 ♘bd2 0-0 leads directly to back to Line B of Chapter 12.

6...♗e7

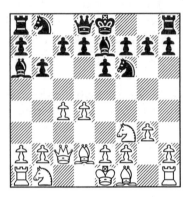

Just as in many other lines of the Queen's Indian as well as a few other openings, the insertion of the 'free' move ♗d2 is in fact slightly detrimental to White's chances. This point is best illustrated if we follow the analogous variation 5...♗e7 6 ♗g2 0-0 7 0-0 c6 8 b3 d5 9 ♗b2 when the bishop is ideally placed. Then after 9...♘bd7 10 ♘bd2 we reach a highly theoretical position technically classified as a Catalan, in which White's chances are to be preferred slightly. However, now if the game follows that analogous path, the bishop will be unable to take up its best position on b2. Here White must make a fundamental choice between a calm and a more aggressive approach:

A: 7 ♗g2
B: 7 e4!?

Instead 7 b4?! is obviously premature, and Black has good chances to seize the initiative after 7...c5 8 dxc5 bxc5 9 a3 (B.Leclercq-A.Sasu Ducsoara, Nantes 2004) 9...♗b7 10 ♗g2 ♘c6.

A) 7 ♗g2

Covering this variation has proven to be rather a tricky task. The point is that after a few logical moves by both sides the game will almost invariably transpose to a highly theoretical variation from either the Catalan or the main line Queen's Indian. Both have featured in hundreds of games on the database, many of which have involved some of the top players in the world. On the other hand, we must remember that the actual probability of reaching these positions through our recommended move order is very low indeed. After 4 g3 ♗a6, 5 ♕c2 is only one of a handful of options. Then after 5...♗b4+ a certain percentage of games will continue with 6 ♘bd2, and even after 6 ♗d2 ♗e7 a lot of players will prefer 7 e4 over 7 ♗g2. Given the circumstances, it would seem ludicrous to subject the present variation to the same level of scrutiny as I have the most popular main lines. Instead I hope to strike a suitable balance by offering concise summaries and recommendations against White's major options, without devoting too much space to the sidelines.

7...0-0

Occasionally Black delays castling, but having researched the different move orders I have not been able to find any compelling reason to do so. For instance, 7...c6 does not eliminate any of White's options as if he wants a set-up with ♗f4 and ♘bd2. he can just play 8 ♗f4 before castling. Then 8...0-0 is more or less forced anyway when 9 0-0 reaches the main line below. Instead 8...d5? would lose material after 9 cxd5 ♘xd5 (9...cxd5?? 10 ♗xb8 wins a piece due to the queen check on a4) 10 ♗xb8 ♖xb8 11 ♕xc6+.

8 0-0 c6

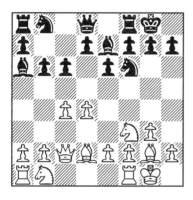

Black prepares ...d5 and stakes a claim to the centre, while making full use of the bishop on a6. The text is an important preparatory move, ensuring that a subsequent cxd5 can be met by ...cxd5 to avoid a backward c-pawn. A symmetrical structure with an open c-file can often favour Black, as the bishop on g2 would be misplaced, while its counterpart on a6 would play an important role on the queenside. Therefore White should generally seek to maintain the central tension by reinforcing his c-pawn, typically with b2-b3 or ♘bd2 (after moving the bishop from d2). After that he will usually

look to gain space in the centre with e2-e4. Black, for his part, can follow a standard scheme of development with ...d5, ...♘bd7, ...♖c8 and ...c5, after which the white queen could begin to feel uncomfortable.

9 ♗f4

The bishop will normally come to this square sooner or later. Most others are less immediately challenging, although I would advise the reader to pay particular attention to variation 'b2' below:

a) 9 ♖c1 d5 10 cxd5 cxd5 11 ♘c3 should be met by 11...♗b7!, temporarily retreating the bishop in order to facilitate the active development of the knight. A.Onischuk-M.Gurevich, Cap d'Agde 2000, continued 12 ♘e5 ♘fd7 13 ♘xd7 ♕xd7 14 e4 dxe4 15 ♗xe4, and here 15...♗xe4 would have brought Black a superior position after 16 ♘xe4? ♕xd4 or 16 ♕xe4 ♘c6 17 d5 exd5 18 ♘xd5 ♗c5.

b) Some strong players have attempted to make a positive virtue out of the bishop's supposed misplacement on d2 by using it to support a queenside offensive with a4-a5, viz. 9 b3 d5 and now:

b1) 10 a4 ♘bd7 11 a5 c5 (it would be illogical for Black to prepare this with ...♖c8 when the a-file is liable to become open at any moment) 12 ♖d1 dxc4 13 bxc4 (in L.Cernousek-R.Cvek, Strmilov 2004, White erred with 13 ♘e5? cxb3 14 ♕xb3 ♘xe5 15 ♗xa8? cxd4 16 ♗f4, at which point 16...♗xe2 would have been the most convincing route to victory) 13...♗b7 14 dxc5 ♗xc5

15 ♘c3 ♕e7 16 a6 ♗c6 17 h3 (J.Jirka-D.Arutunian, Olomouc 2005) and now 17...♖ac8 looks very comfortable for Black.

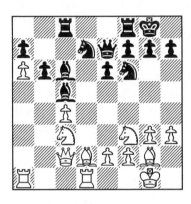

b2) Whilst I was in the process of refining the final version of this book, I picked up what turned out to be a very high-class White repertoire book written by Boris Avrukh. More than half of that tome is devoted to the Catalan, so I was eager (as well as a little apprehensive!) to see where our respective works crossed paths. The relevant position occurs after 10 ♖d1 ♘bd7, at which point the Israeli Grandmaster recommends 11 a4!? (11 ♗f4 ♖c8 reaches Line A1, while 11 ♗e1 is rather sluggish and Black soon obtains an active position with the standard plan of 11...♖c8 12 ♘bd2 c5) 11...c5 12 ♘a3 (other moves have been played, but the text has been the habitual choice of the experts) 12...♗b7 13 ♕b2 (13 a5 dxc4! 14 ♘xc4 was V.Korchnoi-K.Lerner, Muenster 1996, and here 14...b5! 15 ♘ce5 ♗e4 16 ♕b2 ♘xe5 17 dxe5 ♘d5 gives Black an advantage – Avrukh) 13...♘e4 (13...♖c8 is the other main

move, but I slightly prefer the text) 14 ♗e1 (14 ♗f4 should be met by 14...♗f6) 14...♗f6 15 e3.

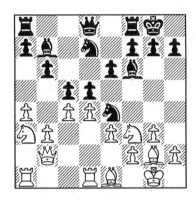

At this point Avrukh quotes the game J.Piket-V.Kramnik, Monaco (rapid) 1997, which continued with 15...cxd4?! (this is my punctuation) 16 ♘xd4 ♕b8 17 ♖ac1 ♖d8 18 ♕b1 a6 19 a5 ♗e7 20 ♘ac2 bxa5 21 ♗xa5 ♖c8 22 ♘b4 ♘ef6 23 cxd5 ♗xb4 24 ♗xb4 ♗xd5 25 ♖xc8+ ♕xc8 26 e4 ♗b7 27 f3 when White's space advantage and bishop pair gave him a pleasant advantage.

Instead I think it would have been more promising for Black to maintain the central tension for a few more moves, perhaps with 15...♕e7 16 b4 ♖ab8, intending to swing the king's rook across to c8 or d8. The position is complex and full of tension, but at this stage I see no reason to rate Black's chances as inferior.

Returning to 9 ♗f4:

9...d5

At this moment White must make an important decision regarding the development of his queen's knight. His main options are:

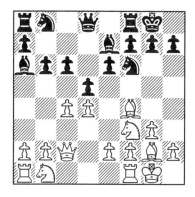

A1: 10 b3
A2: 10 ♘bd2

A brief perusal of the alternatives will demonstrate some of the resources contained within the black position:

a) 10 ♘e5 should be met by the typical 10...♘fd7!.

b) 10 cxd5 cxd5 11 ♖c1 (both 11 ♘c3 ♘c6 and 11 ♘e5 ♘fd7! are less challenging) 11...♘bd7 12 ♘c3 (the 12 ♗c7?! ♕c8 13 e3 of K.Tsatsalashvili-G.Hitter, Heraklio 2004, meets with the convincing retort 13...♘c5!) 12...♕c8! (the queen intends to slot in to b7, after which the knight will be developed to its most active square of c6; instead 12...b5 13 a4! gives White good chances for an edge) with a choice for White:

b1) 13 ♘d2 ♘h5 14 e4!? ♘xf4 15 gxf4 dxe4 16 ♗xe4 ♘f6!? 17 ♗xa8 ♕xa8 18 ♕d1 ♗d6 19 ♘e2 ♕d5 gave Black very attractive compensation for the exchange in D.Guerra Bastida-F.Canabate Carmona, Almeria 1989.

b2) 13 a4 ♕b7 14 ♘b5 ♖ac8 15 ♕d1 ♘e4 16 ♘d2 ♘df6 17 ♘xe4 ♘xe4 18 f3

♘f6 was equal in K.Urban-K.Landa, Cappelle la Grande 2000.

b3) 13 ♘e5 ♕b7 14 e4 ♖ac8 15 exd5 ♘xe5 16 ♗xe5 ♘xd5 17 ♕d2 ♕d7 18 ♘xd5 exd5 19 h4 ♖xc1+ 20 ♖xc1 ♖c8 21 ♖xc8+ ♗xc8 22 ♕c3 ♗b7 was very drawish in A.Khalifman-L.Janjgava, Riga 1988.

A1) 10 b3 ♘bd7 11 ♖d1

White almost always plays this at some point over the next few moves. The centre is liable to open up at any time, so it makes perfect sense to place a rook opposite the enemy queen.

11...♖c8

Black responds in kind!

12 ♘c3

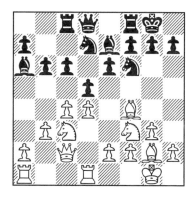

This position has been reached in hundreds of games through various different move orders. Black can consider taking on c4, but White may have some chances for an edge after 13 bxc4 (13 ♘d2 and 13 e4!? are also possible, with some compensation in both cases) 13...♗xc4 14 ♘d2 ♗a6 15 ♕a4 ♗b7 16 ♕xa7. Therefore I suggest that Black refrains from the immediate capture in favour of the more sophisticated...

12...♕e8!?

This has proven to be one of Black's most reliable moves, and has been tested repeatedly at the highest level. That being said, the reader may also wish to investigate the waiting move 12...h6!?, a relatively new idea which was first introduced in 2002 by Sasikiran and which has also scored quite highly. Following the natural 13 e4 dxc4 14 ♘d2 b5 15 bxc4 bxc4 White can try:

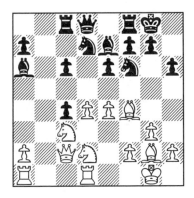

a) 16 ♗f1 ♘b6 17 a4 ♗b4 18 a5 ♘bd7 19 ♖a4 ♕e7 20 ♘xc4 ♗xc4 21 ♗xc4 ♗xc3 22 ♕xc3 ♘xe4 23 ♕b4 ♕xb4 24 ♖xb4 g5 25 ♖b7 gxf4 26 ♖xd7 ♖a8 27 gxf4 was agreed drawn in P.Schlosser-A.Grischuk, French League 2004.

b) 16 ♕a4 ♗b5! 17 ♘xb5 ♘b6! gives Black a fine position after both 18 ♕xa7 cxb5 and 18 ♕a6 cxb5 19 ♕xb5 (V.Mikhalevski-A.Goldin, Ashdod 2003) 19...♕xd4 20 ♗e3 (20 e5 ♕d7!) 20...♕d7 21 a4 ♕xb5 22 axb5 ♘g4!? with an extra pawn and a dangerous passed c-pawn.

c) After 16 ♘a4 c5 17 d5, the natural

looking 17...exd5 18 exd5 (18 e5? ♘h5 19 ♗xd5 ♘xf4 20 gxf4 ♘xe5 was very bad for White in A.Tsybulnik-N.Maiorov, St Petersburg 2003) 18...♘h5 19 ♗e3 ♗f6 20 ♖ab1 ♗d4 21 ♘xc4 ♗xc4 22 ♕xc4 ♗xe3 23 fxe3 ♕g5 gave Black a fine position and led to eventual victory in P.Nielsen-K.Sasikiran, Hastings 2002/03. However, in his notes Sasikiran suggested 21 ♘e4! ♗xe3 22 fxe3 intending ♘ac3 as slightly better for White, as occurred in the subsequent game D.Yevseev-A.Lugovoi, Saint Petersburg 2004.

Therefore it looks preferable for Black to block the centre with 17...e5! 18 ♗e3 ♘g4, as recommended by Sasikiran, who goes on to analyse 19 ♘xc4 ♗xc4 20 ♕xc4 ♘xe3 21 fxe3 ♗d6 22 ♕a6 ♘b6 and 22 ♗h3 ♖b8 with equality in both cases. In V.Filippov-A.Goldin, Las Vegas 2003, White tried to improve with 19 ♗f1!? ♘xe3 20 fxe3 ♗g5 21 ♕c3 ♖b8 22 ♗xc4 and although he eventually prevailed after 22...♗xc4 23 ♘xc4, I think that Black could have improved with 22...♕f6!, defending a6 laterally while eyeing the kingside.

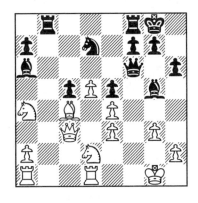

Now 23 ♖f1 ♕g6 looks okay, while the attempt to trap the bishop with 23 h4?! allows 23...♗xc4 24 ♘xc4 ♕f3 25 hxg5 ♕xg3+ when Black has at least a draw, as 26 ♔f1?? f5! wins. To conclude, 13...h6!? is a very interesting move, although we must remember that White is not obliged to open the centre immediately and may also consider a quiet move of his own.

We now return to 12...♕e8!?:

13 e4

The main alternative 13 a4 seems to have been defused after 13...dxc4 14 bxc4 ♗xc4 15 ♘e4 (this is the only challenging move, hoping to exploit the advantage of the bishops) 15...♘xe4 16 ♕xc4 ♗d6 17 ♘e5 f5! when White can probably regain his pawn but has little chance of achieving anything more.

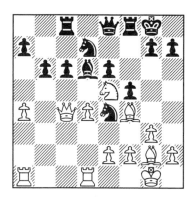

Practice has seen:

a) In V.Anand-V.Kramnik, Leon 2002, White, perhaps concerned about the possibility of ...g5, opted for 18 h4, but achieved nothing after 18...c5 19 ♗xe4 (19 ♖ac1 should be met by 19...♖c7!, rather than 19...cxd4? 20 ♕xc8 ♕xc8 21 ♖xc8 ♖xc8 22 ♘xd7 ♘c3 23 ♖d2 ♗xf4 24 gxf4, as analysed by Gershon) 19...cxd4 20 ♕xd4 ½-½.

b) 18 ♖ac1 is a slight improvement, but Black should still be fine after 18...♘xe5 (18...g5?! looks premature in view of 19 ♗xe4 fxe4 20 ♗xg5) 19 dxe5 ♗a3 20 ♖c2 ♗c5 21 ♗xe4 fxe4 22 ♕xe4 ♖d8 23 ♖xd8 ♕xd8 24 ♖d2 ♕c7 with equality in T.Osbahr-P.Valent, correspondence 2003.

13...dxc4

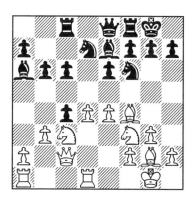

This is the correct time for the capture. We will soon see that Black has a specific follow-up in mind...

14 ♘d2

This has been White's most common choice, although it is doubtful whether it is sufficient for any advantage. The following have been tested too at a high level:

a) 14 bxc4 ♗xc4 15 ♘d2 ♗a6 16 ♕a4 ♗d3 17 ♘db1 b5 18 ♕xa7 ♗xb1 (18...♗c4!?) 19 ♖axb1 b4 20 ♘e2 ♖a8 21 ♕c7 ♖xa2 (21...c5!?) 22 ♘c1 ♖c2 was very double-edged in A.Grischuk-R.Ponomariov, Khanty-Mansiysk 2005.

b) 14 h3 ♗b4 15 ♘d2 (after the 15 ♖e1 of A.Beliavsky-Z.Izoria, Minneapolis 2005, Izoria's suggestion of 15...♕e7 looks sensible, while the Georgian GM also mentions the possibility of 15 e5 ♘d5! 16 ♘g5 f5 17 exf6 ♘7xf6 with an edge to Black) 15...e5 16 ♗e3 was seen in O.Gritsak-Z.Izoria, Warsaw 2005, and here Izoria recommends 16...♕e6! when Black simply intends to keep his extra pawn: 17 bxc4 ♗xc4 18 ♘xc4 ♕xc4 19 ♖ac1 ♗a3 or 19...♕e6, although it is true that White's pair of bishops offers him a modicum of compensation. Note that White is not helped by 17 f4 exf4 18 ♗xf4 (18 gxf4?! ♘d5! 19 ♘xd5 cxd5 is even worse) 18...♘h5.

14...e5!

This excellent move is one of the main points behind Black's twelfth.

15 dxe5

15 ♗xe5?! ♘xe5 16 dxe5 ♘g4 17 ♗h3 h5 18 ♘xc4 ♗xc4 19 bxc4 ♗c5 20 ♗xg4 hxg4 21 ♘a4 ♕xe5 22 ♘xc5 ♕xc5 23 ♖d7 ♖cd8 24 ♖xa7 b5 25 ♖a5 ♖d4 26 ♖c1 ♕b6 27 ♕b2 ♖xe4 was clearly better for Black in A.Baryshpolets-E.Miroshnichenko, Alushta 2007.

15...♘g4

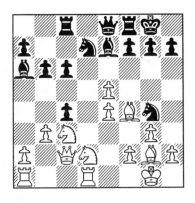

16 ♘xc4

White achieves nothing with 16 ♗h3 h5 17 ♘xc4 ♗xc4 18 bxc4 ♗c5 19 ♗xg4 hxg4 20 ♘a4 ♘xe5 21 ♘xc5 bxc5 22 ♔g2 ♕e6 23 ♗xe5 ♕xe5...

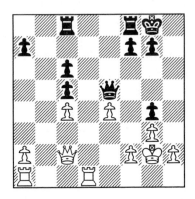

...when Black had equalized and was perhaps even slightly the more comfortably placed in L.Ftacnik-D.Gross, Baden 2007.

16...♗xc4 17 bxc4 ♗c5 18 ♖d2 ♘gxe5 19 ♖ad1 ♕e6 20 ♘a4 ♗b4 21 ♖d4 ♗e7

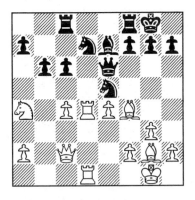

White has a pair of bishops, but his queenside pawns are compromised and Black has a ready-made outpost on c5. The game A.Beliavsky-Z.Almasi, Groningen 1994 soon resulted in a draw after 22 ♕e2 ♘c5 23 ♘b2 ♖cd8 24 ♖xd8 ♖xd8 25 ♖xd8+ ♗xd8 26 ♗e3 ♘ed7! 27 ♕c2.

A2) 10 ♘bd2 ♘bd7

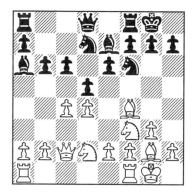

We have now transposed to one of the main lines of the closed Catalan, usually reached via the move order 3 g3 d5 4 ♘f3 ♗b4+ 5 ♗d2 ♗e7 6 ♗g2 0-0 7 0-0 c6 8 ♕c2 b6 9 ♗f4 ♗a6 10 ♘bd2 (10 b3 would reach Line A1, above) 10...♘bd7.

From this point Black has a couple of key ideas. The typical motif of ...♖c8 and ...c5 is, of course, a recurring theme, while in many positions the move ...♘h5 may play a role, targeting the bishop which is now rather short of escape squares. If White retreats to e3 then the Dutch-like ...f5 can sometimes prove attractive, especially as the further ...f4 may prove difficult to stop. On a cautionary note, this move must be timed carefully and the subsequent analysis will feature some examples illustrating when it should or should not be played.

11 ♖fd1

Several different moves have been tried here. 11 ♖ac1 usually just transposes to our main line after 11...♖c8 12 ♖fd1. Aside from that, the following two deserve our attention.

a) 11 e4 leads by force to an equal endgame after 11...♘xe4! 12 ♘xe4 dxe4 13 ♘e5 ♘xe5 14 dxe5 ♕d3 15 ♖ac1 ♕xc2 16 ♖xc2 ♖ad8 17 ♗e3 c5 18 ♗xe4 ♖d7, as seen in a few different games.

b) 11 ♖fe1 is a major alternative when most games have proceeded with 11...♘h5!?, putting an immediate question to the bishop. A few possible developments:

b1) The course of G.Kaidanov-A.Ivanov, Chicago 1995, was rather instructive, as the provocative 12 ♗e5!? was met by the calm 12...♖c8! (12...♘xe5? 13 dxe5 would leave the knight on h5 looking ridiculous, and 12...f6 13 cxd5! would have been slightly awkward). Play continued 13 cxd5 cxd5 (13...exd5 14 ♗h3! is slightly annoying) 14 ♕a4 ♗b7 15 ♕xa7 ♗c6 16 ♕a6 f6

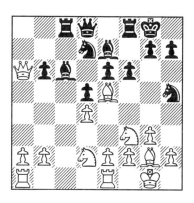

17 ♗f4 e5! 18 dxe5 ♘c5 19 ♕a3 ♘e6 20 ♕b3 ♘hxf4 21 gxf4 ♘xf4 with a clear

advantage for Black. In his notes Kaidanov says that White could have improved with 17 ♗h3, but after 17...♖a8 18 ♕d3 fxe5 19 ♗xe6+ ♔h8 20 ♘xe5 ♘xe5 21 dxe5 ♕e8! White's compensation for the piece seems questionable.

b2) In O.Lehner-V.Atlas, Austrian League 2000, White preferred 12 cxd5 ♘xf4 13 gxf4 cxd5 14 f5!? (the slow 14 ♕a4 ♗b7 15 e3 a6 16 ♕b3 ♘f6 17 ♖ac1 ♕d6 18 ♖c2 ♖fc8 19 ♖ec1 ♘e8 20 ♖xc8 ♖xc8 21 ♖xc8 ♗xc8 22 ♕c2 ♕c7 23 ♕xc7 ♘xc7 gave Black the better endgame in R.Marszalek-A.Kharitonov, Moscow 1992), but achieved nothing after 14...♕c8! 15 ♕b3?! (according to Atlas, White should have preferred 15 ♕xc8!? ♖axc8 16 fxe6 fxe6 17 ♗h3 ♔f7 18 e4 ♗b7 or 16 ♗h3 exf5 17 ♗xf5 ♖c7, with approximately equal chances in both cases) 15...exf5 16 ♕xd5 ♘f6 17 ♕e5 ♕d7 18 e4 (18 ♘h4 is strongly met by 18...♖ae8!) 18...fxe4 19 ♘xe4, at which point Black's most straightforward route to an advantage would have been Atlas' suggestion of 19...♗b7!.

b3) 12 ♗e3 is a sensible move, preserving the bishop and questioning the usefulness of the black knight on h5. Now 12...f5? would be premature in view of 13 cxd5 cxd5 14 ♕c6! forcing the awkward-looking 14...♔f7, as 14...♖f6? 15 ♗g5 is no good. Therefore Black should prefer 12...♖c8!, improving his position while covering the c6-square and thus facilitating the idea of ...f5. In L.Psakhis-R.Ovetchkin, Moscow 2002, White tried to fight on the queenside with 13 cxd5 cxd5 14 ♕a4

♘b8 15 ♘e5, but got nowhere after 15...♕e8! 16 ♕xe8 ♖fxe8 17 ♗f3 ♘f6 18 ♖ec1 ♘fd7 19 ♘xd7 ½-½.

11...♖c8 12 ♖ac1

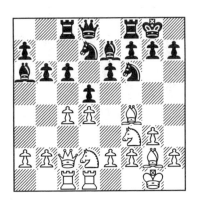

In J.Horvath-A.Kiss, Zalakaros 1995, White attempted to do without this preparation, instead preferring the immediate 12 e4?!. Personally I think this a little overzealous, and if Black had reacted with 12...♘xe4! 13 ♘xe4 dxe4 White might have had trouble regaining his pawn: 14 ♘e5 (White dare not recapture immediately with c4 hanging) 14...g5!? (Black is playing ambitiously!) 15 ♗e3 f5 16 ♕a4 ♘b8! and the onus is on White to demonstrate compensation.

12...♘h5

We have reached a critical position in which White must decide whether or not to preserve his bishop.

13 ♗e3

13 e4?! is not a great move, but is worth investigating as it was played at the highest level in the game T.Radjabov-V.Topalov, Wijk aan Zee 2003, which continued 13...♘xf4 14 gxf4 ♘f6!? (the most ambitious;

14...dxe4 15 ♘xe4 ♕c7 would have been equal according to Ribli) 15 ♘e5 (15 e5 ♘h5 16 f5 ♘f4 is good for Black – Ribli) 15...♘h5! 16 ♕a4 ♗xc4 17 ♘xc6 (17 ♘dxc4 b5 18 ♕a6 bxc4 19 ♘xc6 ♖xc6 20 ♕xc6 ♘xf4 would transpose to the game) 17...b5 18 ♕a6 ♖xc6! 19 ♕xc6 ♘xf4 when Topalov had succeeded in obtaining excellent compensation for the exchange.

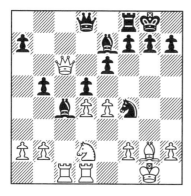

Play continued 20 ♘xc4 bxc4! (it is too early to regain material with 20...♘e2+ 21 ♔f1 ♘xc1 22 exd5 ♘xa2 23 ♕xb5 ♘b4 when the position remains unclear, as analysed by Ribli) 21 exd5 exd5 22 ♖c3 ♗h4! 23 ♖g3, at which point 23...♗xg3 24 hxg3 ♘xg2 25 ♔xg2 ♖e8 would have left Black a clear pawn up in the endgame.

b) 13 ♘e5 ♘xf4 14 gxf4 ♘xe5 15 dxe5 (15 fxe5 ♗b4!?) 15...♗b4 16 b3 f6 17 a3 ♗xd2 18 ♕xd2 fxe5 19 cxd5 (perhaps White did not like the look of 19 fxe5 ♕h4!?) 19...cxd5 20 ♖xc8? (20 fxe5 would have kept White in the game) 20...♕xc8 21 fxe5 ♕c5 with a clear advantage to Black in ·S.Giemsa-F.Doettling, Baden 2007.

13...♘hf6!?

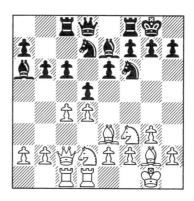

Ideally I would have preferred to avoid resorting to an immediate retreat, but in this case it seems to be the soundest course of action. The obvious alternative is 13...f5 and if Black is not happy to repeat the position then he can, of course, play this way. Nevertheless in S.Lputian-M.Thejkumar, Kolkata 2008, White was able to obtain an edge with 14 ♕a4 ♗xc4 (14...♘b8 15 ♘e5 f4 16 gxf4 ♘xf4 is mentioned by Ribli, after which 17 ♗xf4 ♖xf4 18 e3 looks a bit better for White) 15 ♘xc4 b5 16 ♕xa7 bxc4 17 b3 cxb3 18 axb3 when his bishop-pair was a useful asset.

14 ♗g5

This is the only move to have been tested. White's natural plan is to aim for e2-e4, so if he is unwilling to settle for a repetition with 14 ♗f4 ♘h5 then this is clearly the most obvious choice. Note that here 14 ♕a4? can be met by the typical trick 14...♗xc4! 15 ♘xc4 b5 16 ♕xa7 bxc4 when Black stands better. The position is identical to Lputian-Thejkumar above, except that Black has substituted the useful ...♘hf6 for the weakening ...f5. Play may continue 17 b3 ♖a8 18 ♕b7 ♕a5! 19 ♗d2 ♕xa2 20 bxc4 ♖fb8 21 ♕c7 (21 ♕xc6? ♖a6) 21...♗a3 22 ♖a1 ♕xc4 with an extra pawn.

14...h6 15 ♗xf6 ♘xf6 16 e4

White has proceeded in a logical manner, although based on the available practical examples it seems that Black may have two routes to a satisfactory position:

a) 16...♗b7 17 c5 ♘d7 18 b4 a5 19 a3 ♖a8 was agreed drawn in A.Khalifman-Z.Efimenko, Moscow 2007.

b) 16...dxc4 17 ♘xc4 ♕c7 18 ♘e3 ♕b8 19 ♗f1 ♗b7 20 e5 ♘d5 21 ♘xd5 cxd5 was D.Andreikin-S.Sjugirov, St Petersburg 2008.

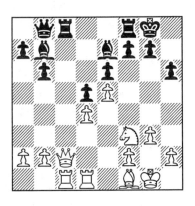

The position was about equal, although Black's bishop-pair gives him some chances to be better and he did in fact prevail eventually after a long endgame grind.

Both Lines A1 and A2 have been tested extensively and the final words undoubtedly are yet to be said. Nevertheless on the basis of what we have seen, I do not see any major problems

for Black at this time. We now move on to what is arguably the more critical continuation.

B) 7 e4!?

I would tend to regard this as White's most strategically consistent continuation. Nowadays most players who opt for 5 ♕c2 do so with aggressive intentions, and the text continues in the same vein.

7...d5!

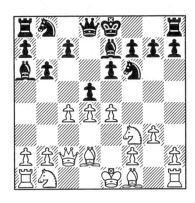

Black should not hesitate to establish a foothold in the centre.

8 cxd5

This is the typical reaction, intending to gain space with e4-e5. The alternatives are rare:

a) White gains nothing from attempting to omit this exchange with 8 e5 ♘e4 9 ♗d3 (9 cxd5 ♗xf1 10 ♔xf1 exd5 reaches the main line) 9...0-0. The game A.Vuilleumier-M.Oleksienko, Dresden 2007, continued 10 0-0 (after 10 ♗xe4? dxe4 11 ♕xe4 ♗xc4 12 ♕xa8 ♗d5 13 ♕xa7 ♗xf3 14 0-0 ♘c6 15 ♕a6 ♘xd4 16 ♘c3 ♗b4! White is in big trouble) 10...c5 11 ♗xe4 dxe4 12 ♕xe4

♕d7 13 d5?! exd5 14 cxd5 f5! 15 exf6 ♗xf6 16 ♖e1, at which point 16...♗xb2 would have won material for insufficient compensation.

b) The pawn sacrifice 8 ♘c3 ♗xc4 9 ♗xc4 dxc4 10 0-0-0 led to double-edged play in L.Nisipeanu-P.Eljanov, Foros 2007, although the power of Eljanov's subsequent play seemed to cast doubts over the soundness of White's pawn sacrifice. The game continued 10...c6 11 ♗f4 ♘a6! (threatening ...♘b4-d3 and thus provoking the following weakening) 12 a3 b5! (now it is only a matter of time before Black smashes through with ...b4) 13 ♘e5 ♕c8 14 ♗g5 0-0 15 h4 ♖b8 16 ♕e2 ♕b7 17 h5 h6 18 ♗f4 c5! 19 d5 b4 20 ♘a4 bxa3 21 ♕xc4 exd5 22 exd5 ♘b4 23 bxa3 ♘bxd5 24 ♔c2 ♘xf4 25 gxf4 ♕c8 and Black soon triumphed.

8...♗xf1 9 ♔xf1 exd5 10 e5 ♘e4

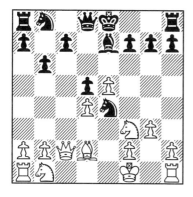

Before going any further, a brief comparison will aid our evaluation of the situation. The position after Black's 10th bears a strong resemblance with the rather better known line 5 b3 ♗b4+ 6 ♗d2 ♗e7 7 ♘c3 (aiming for an immediate central expansion; instead 7

♗g2 is the main line) 0-0 8 e4 d5 9 cxd5 ♗xf1 10 ♔xf1 exd5 11 e5 ♘e4.

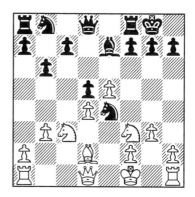

Structurally things are identical, except for the position of the white b-pawn. White enjoys a preponderance of central pawns, but these can sometimes be undermined by ...c5 and/or ...f6, although sometimes Black will prefer the blocking ...f5, especially in conjunction with a transfer of the queen's knight to e6. Finally, we should note that White's central pawns are fixed on the same colour squares as his bishop, although at the same time they also restrict Black's own bishop quite effectively.

So how do these two slightly different positions compare with one another? The bad news is that the present variation represents a definite improvement for White due to the absence of the useless move b2-b3. Aside from saving himself a full tempo, there are some players who have attempted to extract an even greater benefit by meeting a subsequent exchange of knights on c3 with bxc3, supporting the centre.

Despite all of that, it turns out – perhaps slightly surprisingly – that the black position is still quite playable. Nowadays the latter of the above variations is not considered at all dangerous for Black, so what we are essentially left with is White having an improved version of a harmless variation. The question is whether or not the undeniable improvements will prove sufficient for him to claim an opening advantage. As far as I have been able to discern Black seems to be holding his own, although the whole line has not yet been tested exhaustively. In fact, the growing popularity of this variation is directly attributable to the success of White's pawn sacrifice as more and more Black players are looking for ways to avoid it. At the moment the theory is not too well established and there remains plenty of scope for new ideas on both sides. Unlike the pawn sacrifice variation, however, there is considerably less danger of Black being blasted off the board here!

11 ♘c3

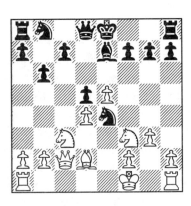

White needs to develop his queen-

side and challenge the powerful knight on e4.

11...♘xc3

11...f5?! has not yet been tried, perhaps with good reason as 12 exf6 ♘xf6 13 ♖e1 is clearly better for White. On the other hand, 11...♘xd2+ has been played in several games, although in principle I prefer to leave that piece on the board in hopeful anticipation of a favourable bad bishop endgame. Now White must make a major decision between:

B1: 12 ♗xc3
B2: 12 bxc3!

B1) 12 ♗xc3

With this recapture White keeps the c-file open while hoping to obtain a few additional active prospects for his bishop.

12...♕d7 13 ♔g2

Preventing a check on h3 while connecting the rooks. In M.Rodshtein-M.Lushenkov, Dagomys 2008, White attempted to do without this move and instead preferred 13 h4 ♘c6 (another possibility was 13...h6!?, preparing to castle without allowing ♘g5, while also preventing the ♗d2-g5 manoeuvre used by White in the game) 14 ♗d2 ♘d8 (14...h6? 15 ♖c1 wins a pawn) 15 ♗g5 ♖c8 (15...f6!? 16 exf6 gxf6) 16 ♔g2 ♘e6 17 ♗xe7 ♕xe7 18 ♖ad1 h6 19 ♕a4+ c6 20 b4 0-0 with a comfortable position for Black. After the game continuation of 21 ♖d3, it looks quite tempting to try 21...f6!? 22 ♖e1 ♕f7.

13...♘c6

13...0-0 has been played, but I would prefer not to commit the king earlier than necessary.

14 h4 ♘d8

This looks like the most consistent, although in A.Ushenina-Zhao Xue, Dagomys 2008, Black was successful with 14...a5!? 15 ♖he1 ♘d8 16 ♖e2 ♘e6 17 ♕d2 0-0 (Black finally castles, safe in the knowledge that ♘g5 ideas are no longer a threat) 18 ♖ae1 c5 19 a3 c4 20 ♘h2 b5 21 ♖d1 ♕a7!, intending to strike on the queenside with ...b4 before White manages to achieve anything on the opposite flank.

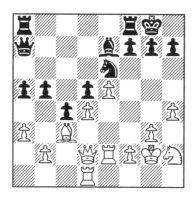

The game continued 22 f4 b4 23 axb4 axb4 24 ♗xb4 ♗xb4 25 ♕xb4 ♘xd4 26 ♖ed2 ♘f5 27 ♘f1 and now instead of 27...♖fb8?! 28 ♖xd5!, Black should have preferred 27...♖ab8 or 27...♘e7 with some advantage in both cases.

15 ♘h2 0-0 16 f4 f5!

This is a typical reaction to the advance of the f-pawn. We now follow the game S.Williams-F.Jenni, European Club Cup, Fuegen 2006:

17 exf6 gxf6!

17...♗xf6 and 17...♖xf6 are both possible, but the text is more ambitious. Black compromises his pawn structure, but takes control of the crucial e5- and g5-squares.

18 ♖he1

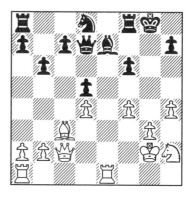

18...♘f7

18...♗d6!? is another possibility. Jenni's intention was obviously to utilize this square for his knight, but in the game he never had a chance to do so effectively. The advantage of preferring 18...♗d6 is that the bishop is removed from its unstable position while clearing the second rank for the queen. Furthermore, White's ♗c3-b4 idea is prevented. Some possible developments include:

a) 19 f5? secures a potential outpost on e6, but the drawback is the weakening of g3 and the general improvement of the black bishop. After 19...♔h8 20 ♖e3 ♘b7 (20...♘f7 is also playable, but only because of the tactical trick 21 ♘g4! ♘h6! 22 ♘xh6 ♕g7, regaining the piece with advantage) 21 ♖ae1 ♖g8 Black is clearly on top, the plan being to double on the g-file.

b) 19 ♕e2 looks better. Now after 19...♔h8 20 ♕h5 c6 21 ♖e3 ♖g8 22 ♖ae1 Black must avoid 22...♗xf4?? 23 ♖e7 ♕h3+! 24 ♔h1! h6 25 ♖e8 when White is first to break through. Instead 22...♕g7 is better, with chances for both sides.

19 ♕e2!

Williams transfers his heavy artillery to the danger zone.

19...♖ae8 20 ♕h5

20 ♕g4+!? ♕xg4 21 ♘xg4 ♘d6 22 ♘e3 c6 23 ♗b4 ♘e4 24 ♗xe7 ♖xe7 25 ♖ac1 ♖e6 looks approximately equal. Black could even consider the pawn sacrifice 25...♘d6!? 26 ♖xc6 ♘f5 27 ♔f2 ♖fe8 28 ♖c3 h5 29 ♖d3 ♘h6 when White has no advantage whatsoever.

After the move played in the game, Black should have responded with 20...♔h8! with a full share of the chances.

Instead he faltered with 20...♗d8?, overlooking the strong riposte 21 ♗b4!. The remainder of the game is of no importance to us from a theoretical perspective, but it is worth playing through in order to appreciate what to avoid as Black. The remaining moves were 21...♗e7 22 ♕g4+ ♕xg4 23 ♘xg4 ♘d6 24 ♗xd6 cxd6 25 ♘h6+ ♔h8 26 ♘f5 ♗d8 27 ♖xe8 ♖xe8 28 ♖c1 (*see diagram*) and in this humiliating position Black resigned.

The turning point of this game came when White was given the opportunity to activate his bishop. As this piece would traditionally be viewed as bad, it would not surprise me if Jenni literally forgot that it could play an active role in the game, as he clearly had not planned for White's 21st. Despite the unfavourable outcome to this game, we have seen that with correct play Black can obtain a fine position against 12 ♗xc3.

B2) 12 bxc3!

With this move White attempts to extract the absolute maximum benefit from the omission of b2-b3. This pawn may prove useful in supporting White's centre, while in other cases he may even attempt to wrest the initiative with c3-c4.

12...♕d7

This has been the most popular choice, although one could certainly make an argument for 12...c5!?. The game D.Smerdon-M.Oleksienko, Pardubice 2007, continued 13 ♔g2 ♘c6 14 h4 ♕d7 (14...0-0? 15 ♘g5 g6 16 ♘xh7! ♔xh7 17 h5 gives White a strong attack – Emms) 15 ♖ae1 ♕e6 (not 15...h6? 16 e6 fxe6 17 ♕g6+) 16 ♘g5 ♗xg5 (16...♕g6!?) 17 hxg5 cxd4, at which point 18 ♖xh7 (Emms) would have brought White the advantage.

Instead I would propose the improvement 15...cxd4!? 16 cxd4 ♖c8.

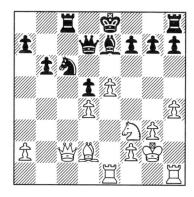

Play might continue 17 ♕d3 ♕e6 (once again 17...h6? 18 e6 fxe6 19 ♕g6+ is inadvisable, although 17...♘d8!? looks playable) 18 ♘g5 (other moves are possible, but this is the most forcing) 18...♕g6 19 ♕xg6 hxg6 (19...fxg6!? may also be playable) 20 e6 ♗xg5 21 exf7+ ♔xf7 22 ♗xg5 which looks about equal, or perhaps even slightly preferable to Black. Based on the (admittedly limited) evidence available, it seems to me that 12...c5 is fully viable and it would be interesting to see more tests in the future.

13 ♔g2

In K.Sakaev-E.Tomashevsky, Serpukhov 2007, White attempted to do without this move, favouring the more aggressive 13 h4 although this brought him little joy after 13...♘c6 (Black can also consider 13...c5!? or 13...h6!?) 14 h5 0-0 15 ♖e1 ♖ae8 16 ♔g2 ♘d8 17 ♗g5 ♘e6 18 ♗xe7 ♕xe7 19 ♘h4 ♕g5 20 ♘f5 f6! when Black had taken over the initiative and went on to win.

13...♘c6 14 c4!?

This energetic move has been the most popular choice, although in R.Ris-S.Bakker, Dutch League, 2007 White demonstrated that it is equally possible to adopt a more measured approach with 14 h4 h6 15 ♖ae1, reaching a critical position in which Black must consider his options very carefully:

a) 15...0-0?? loses immediately to 16 ♘g5! hxg5 (or 16...g6 17 e6 winning easily) 17 hxg5 g6 18 e6 ♕e8 19 ♖h6 ♔g7 20 ♖eh1.

b) 15...♘d8 would be an excellent move, were it not for the fact that 16 e6! ♘xe6 17 ♘e5 ♕d6 18 f4! gives White quite a potent initiative.

c) 15...♕e6 can be met by 16 ♘h2 or 16 ♘g1, intending to advance the f-pawn (or, in the latter case, perhaps to prepare a knight transfer to f4).

d) In the game Bakker opted for 15...0-0-0, which may well be best. The game continued 16 h5 ♕e6 17 ♘g1!, intending to oust the queen with a knight transfer to f4 (it is important for both sides to remember this possibility). Black reacted badly with 17...f6? and soon lost after 18 ♕g6! ♗f8 19 ♘h3

♘e7 20 exf6 ♕xf6 21 ♕xf6 gxf6 22 ♖e6 ♖d6 23 ♖xd6 cxd6 24 ♘f4 ♔d7 25 ♔f3 ♗g7 26 ♖e1 ♖h7 27 ♘e6 1-0. Instead 16...♔b7 should have been preferred, improving the king and maintaining a solid position, although objectively White can probably claim a slight edge.

14...♘d8!

This is a key move, aiming for a light-square blockade with the knight on e6 and queen on d5.

15 e6!?

This is White's sharpest and most ambitious attempt, although the following possibilities should also be considered.

a) After the timid 15 ♖ac1 ♘e6 everything is in order for Black.

b) 15 ♗e3 (E.Atalik-Zhao Xue, Kallithea 2008) should probably be met by 15...♘e6.

c) 15 ♕b3 was tested in K.Sakaev-E.Tomashevsky, Serpukhov 2007, which continued 15...c6 16 ♖hc1 ♘e6 17 ♖ab1 0-0 (the computer suggests the radical 17...g5!?, intending 18 cxd5 ♕xd5 19 ♕xd5 cxd5 or 18 ♗e3 g4 19 ♘d2 h5) 18 cxd5 ♕xd5 19 ♕xd5 cxd5 20 ♖b5 ♖fd8 21 a4 ♖d7 with an approximately equal endgame.

d) The game A.Huzman-M.Carlsen, European Club Cup, Kallithea 2008, took rather a radical course after 15 cxd5 ♕xd5 16 ♕a4+ (so far no-one has grabbed the pawn with 16 ♕xc7!? ♘c6 17 ♗e3 0-0 when Black clearly has compensation, but nothing conclusive after 18 ♖ac1 or 18 ♖hc1) 16...c6 17 ♖hc1 ♔d7!? (17...0-0?! leaves Black awkwardly tied to the defence of the c-pawn; however, if the reader is uncomfortable with the text he may also wish to consider the active 17...g5!? or the less adventurous 17...b5!?, intending 18 ♕b3 ♘e6 19 ♖ab1 a6 with a solid position).

At first glance this move appears crazy, but Carlsen evidently judged that His Majesty would not be in too great a danger with the centre closed and ...♘e6 on the way. The game continued 18 ♗b4 (it is important that after 18 e6+? ♘xe6 the knight on f3 is pinned, otherwise ♘e5+ would be horrible) 18...b5 (another approach was 18...♗xb4 19 ♕xb4 g5!?) 19 ♕a3 ♗xb4

20 ♕xb4 a5 21 ♕b3 ♘e6, at which point Huzman decided to embark on a sacrificial attack with 22 ♖xc6!? ♕xc6 23 d5 ♕c4 24 dxe6+ ♔xe6. At this critical juncture White faltered with 25 ♘d4+? (he could have retained reasonable compensation with 25 ♕e3 ♖hd8 26 ♖c1 ♕d5 27 ♖c5 ♕b7 28 ♕b3+ ♔e7 29 ♖xb5) 25...♔d5! 26 ♕f3+ ♔xd4 27 ♕e3+ ♔d5 28 ♖d1+ ♔e6 29 ♖d6+ ♔e7 30 ♕g5+ ♔e8 31 e6 ♖c8 32 exf7+ ♕xf7 33 ♖d3 ♕b7+ 34 ♔h3 ♖f8, after which Black easily converted his material advantage.

We now return to 15 e6:

15...fxe6 16 ♘e5 ♕d6!

The stem game Ni Hua-E.Tomashevsky, Nizhniy Novgorod 2007, had seen Black falter with 16...♕c8? 17 ♕a4+ b5 (17...♔f8 18 ♖he1 gives White a huge initiative, and 17...c6 is not much better after 18 cxd5 exd5 19 ♗b4! ♗xb4 20 ♕xb4 ♕c7 21 ♖he1 ♘e6 22 ♖ac1 c5 23 ♕b5+ ♔f8 24 ♕d3 – Emms) 18 cxb5 0-0 19 ♖hc1.

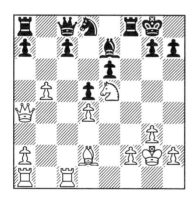

Black's king had reached a safe haven safe, but the rest of his position was a sorry sight and Ni Hua went on to win convincingly.

The improvement on move 16 was noted by Krasenkow, and subsequently used by Tomashevsky himself in the game E.Kourousis-E.Tomashevsky, European Championship, Plovdiv 2008:

17 ♕a4+ c6 18 c5!?

White is playing very energetically, but it appears that Black can negotiate the complications to reach a favourable endgame.

18...bxc5 19 ♗f4 0-0!

The computer suggests 19...g5!?, but 20 ♗e3 0-0 21 ♖ac1 is not so clear.

20 dxc5 ♕xc5 21 ♘d7

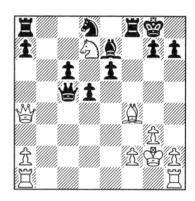

21...♖xf4!

Emms noted 21...♕b4 22 ♕xb4 ♗xb4 23 ♘xf8 ♔xf8 as roughly equal. The point of the text is to aim for a similar ending, but with White having a knight instead of the more useful bishop.

22 ♕xf4

22 gxf4 also favours Black after 22...♕b4 (or 22...♕d6 23 ♘e5 ♗f6) 23 ♕xb4 ♗xb4.

22...♕d6 23 ♕xd6 ♗xd6 24 ♖hc1 ♔f7

25 f4 ♔e7 26 ♘e5 c5

By now Tomashevsky was clearly better and White soon resigned after a few further inaccuracies: 27 ♖ab1 ♗xe5 28 fxe5 ♖c8 29 ♔f3 ♖c7 30 ♔e2 ♘f7 31 ♖b8 ♘xe5 32 a4 ♘c6 0-1.

Summary

At the time of writing the popularity of 5 ♕c2 shows no sign of abating, and the coming months and years will doubtless bear witness to a whole host of new ideas and refinements on both sides of the debate. It is hard to anticipate how the pawn sacrifice will be regarded in five or ten years' time. If I ever write a second edition to this book then, who knows, perhaps it will be possible to prove that with precise play Black can consolidate his extra pawn and emerge with a clear advantage, although right now I wouldn't bet any money on it!

Regardless of such speculation, I hope to have convinced you that, at the start of 2009 at least, 5...♗b4+ represents a more stable foundation upon which to base one's repertoire.

After 6 ♗d2 ♗e7, Line A soon transposed to a major branch of either the Catalan or the main line Queen's Indian in which Black does not appear to have too many worries. Line B is more challenging and further testing will be required before a definite verdict can be made. 12 bxc3! appears critical, but for the time being Black seems to be holding his own both with the main line of 12...♘c6 and the less common 12...c5!?. The other good news is that, even if White does find some clever new ideas, the black position appears relatively stable and he should usually be able to avoid any serious opening problems.

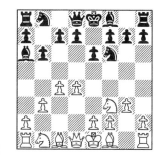

Chapter Fifteen

The Fianchetto Variation: 5 b3

1 d4 ♘f6 2 c4 e6 3 ♘f3 b6 4 g3 ♗a6 5 b3

Finally we come to the main line, which accounts for close to 60% of all games after 4 g3 ♗a6. The decision over which of Black's numerous set-ups to recommend was probably the most difficult and important problem with which I was confronted over the course of this entire project. In assessing the pros and cons of the different systems, I took into consideration a variety of factors, aside from the obvious issue of theoretical soundness.

I wanted to advocate a system that would not require an excessive amount of theoretical preparation; a variation which – at the risk of expressing what has become something of a cliché amongst chess authors and publishers – enables the practitioner to apply positional understanding and principles without needing to memorize a plethora of analysis. Moreover, it needed to offer realistic prospects for Black to

play for a win and, ideally, would be something which has hitherto received comparatively little attention in most other theoretical works.

Ladies and gentlemen, without further ado, I present to you...

5...b5!?

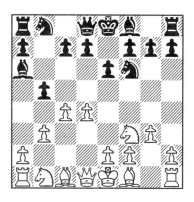

This is far from new, but by the standard of the main lines is relatively unexplored and ticks all the relevant boxes in terms of the aforementioned selection criteria. For any readers who may have been expecting a lengthy treatise dealing with the ultra-theoretical main lines beginning with 5...♗b4+ 6 ♗d2 ♗e7, I hope that the sight of the less common though still highly respectable text move will make for a pleasant surprise. 5...b5 has only been the fourth most frequently played move in the position (the top three being 5...♗b4+, 5...♗b7 and 5...d5), but according to my database it has been the highest scorer with an encouraging 53% for Black.

So what are the ideas behind moving the b-pawn for the second time? Primarily Black wishes to exchange a wing pawn for a central one, which makes extremely good sense from a strategic point of view. By far the most common response is 6 cxb5 ♗xb5 leading to a significant structural change, the implications of which will be discussed in the next chapter. For the time being we will consider three less common alternatives:

A: 6 ♕c2
B: 6 ♘bd2
C: 6 ♗g2

Others can be dealt with quickly:

a) 6 e3 unsurprisingly proved to be completely harmless after 6...bxc4 7 bxc4 c5 8 ♗e2 (8 d5 allows 8...♘xd5! 9 cxd5 ♕f6) 8...cxd4 9 exd4 ♗e7 10 0-0 0-0 in M.Kosovac-N.Ostojic, Belgrade 2006.

b) With 6 c5 White attempts to keep the game closed, but in doing so he overextends his position and reduces his control over the light squares. In N.Ristic-A.Goldin, Krynica 1997, Black equalized easily with 6...d6! 7 cxd6 (or 7 b4 ♘c6 8 a3 ♗b7 with comfortable play) 7...cxd6 8 ♗g2 ♘bd7 9 0-0 ♗e7 at which point White, perhaps dissatisfied with the outcome of the opening, tried a dubious sacrifice with 10 d5?! and went on to lose.

A) 6 ♕c2!?

This is a curious echo of Chapter Fourteen's 5 ♕c2!?, especially when you consider games such as A.Gamundi Salamanca-M.Rivas Pastor, Ponferrada 1992, which continued...

6...bxc4 7 bxc4 c5 8 d5!?

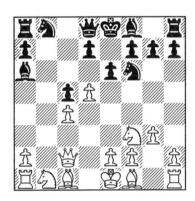

Other moves have been tried, but the text is the only remotely challenging one as far as I can see: for example, 8 ♗g2 ♘c6 9 0-0 (J.Toman-A.Vuckovic, Schwaebisch Gmuend 2005, saw instead 9 e3? cxd4 10 exd4, at which point Black could have won a pawn with 10...♘b4! 11 ♕b3 ♗xc4!, intending 12 ♕xc4 ♖c8) 9...cxd4 10 ♖d1 ♖c8 11 ♘xd4 ♘xd4 12 ♖xd4 ♗c5 was already more comfortable for Black in M.Geldyeva-Zhao Xue, Doha 2006.

8...exd5 9 cxd5 ♗b7

In Chapter 14 I explained the reasons for my reluctance to enter the 5 ♕c2 pawn sacrifice variation, but with the b-pawns absent from the board it is a different story for reasons that will become apparent.

10 ♗g2

At this point Rivas Pastor should have played:

10...♘xd5!

This is superior to the bishop capture, just as in the analogous position after 5 ♕c2. Now after the natural...

11 0-0 ♗e7

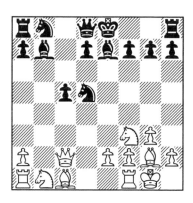

...Black is doing absolutely fine, as the absence of pawns on b2 and b6 helps him for a number of reasons: his c-pawn is now passed, and thus more influential; his knight has the opportunity to retreat to b6 if attacked; and the open b-file and a1-h8 diagonal provide additional opportunities for counterplay. Thus, in the unlikely event that you ever reach this position, you have every reason to feel confident as you will have obtained a considerably improved version of a topical variation.

B) 6 ♘bd2 c5!?

Black can also exchange on c4, but I rather like the idea of retaining the tension for the moment, thereby cutting out certain resources for White, such as a timely ♕a4.

7 ♗g2 ♘c6 8 d5!?

This ambitious pawn sacrifice was used with success in the high-level blitz game R.Ponomariov-M.Carlsen, Moscow 2007.

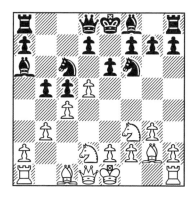

Instead 8 ♘e5 ♖c8 9 ♘xc6 dxc6 10 dxc5 ♗xc5 11 0-0 0-0 was equal in G.Sargissian-H.Odeev, Dubai 2006, although earlier on I would have been tempted to sacrifice an exchange with 8...♘xd4!? 9 ♗xa8 (9 e3 would be met by 9...♘f5) 9...♕xa8, obtaining excellent compensation.

8...exd5 9 cxd5 ♘xd5 10 ♗b2

We have reached a crossroads. In the game the Norwegian sensation played 10...♘f6 11 0-0 ♗e7, but after 12 e4 d6 13 ♘h4 ♖c8 14 ♘f5 0-0 15 f4 White had decent compensation and went on to win. It seems to me that retreating the knight to f6 rather invites the white e-pawn to lunge forwards.

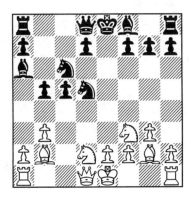

Therefore I propose 10...♘b6!? as a sensible alternative, after which 11 0-0 d5 looks quite acceptable for Black. True, White does have a lead in development, but it is difficult for him to open any files as e2-e4 can always be met by ...d4. Moreover, Black might even consider long castling in certain variations. To summarize, White can probably claim a measure of compensation but I doubt that it can be enough for an advantage.

C) 6 ♗g2!?

With this move White gambits a pawn. The idea is interesting, but with accurate play Black has absolutely nothing to fear.

6...bxc4 7 ♘e5

7 bxc4?! ♗xc4 can hardly give White enough compensation, and 7 ♘fd2 ♘c6 8 ♘xc4 d5 9 0-0 ♗e7 10 ♗b2 0-0 11 ♘e3 ♘b8!? was comfortable for Black in Bui Vinh-G.Timoshenko, Budapest 2003.

7...♗b4+! 8 ♗d2

8 ♔f1? d5 9 bxc4 regains the pawn, but after 9...0-0 we simply arrive at a

normal-looking position with the white king on a stupid square.

8...cxb3!

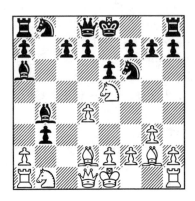

It is this tactical finesse which enables Black to retain his extra pawn.

9 axb3

The justification of Black's last is, of course, seen after 9 ♗xb4 b2! when White will lose material for insufficient compensation. The alternatives are also uninspiring:

a) After 9 ♕xb3?! ♗xd2+ 10 ♘xd2 c6 White has a slight lead in development, but hardly enough to offset the missing pawn.

b) 9 ♘c3 d5 10 ♕xb3 ♗d6 11 0-0 (11 ♕a4+ ♘fd7 12 ♘xd5 exd5 13 ♗xd5 0-0 14 ♗xa8 ♘b6 is also good for Black – Emms) 11...0-0 was a similar story in M.Serik-A.Grekh, Lvov 2007.

9...♗xd2+ 10 ♕xd2

10 ♘xd2 is occasionally seen, but does nothing to improve White's prospects.

10...d5

10...c6 is also fine.

11 0-0

Instead 11 ♕b4? ♕d6 12 ♕a4+ c6 13

♘c3 0-0 14 0-0 (J.Maiko-O.Vozovic, Kharkov 2005) 14...c5! sees Black exchanging off one of his weak pawns to obtain a clear advantage.

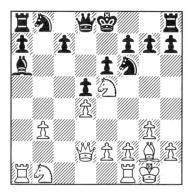

Due to the half-open a- and c-files and his slight lead in development, White certainly has a degree of compensation. At the same time Black is very solid and to me it seems almost inconceivable that he could stand worse here.

11...0-0

This has been the only move played, although I see nothing wrong with Emms' suggestion of 11...♘fd7!?. The English Grandmaster goes on to analyse 12 ♘xd7 ♕xd7 13 ♘c3 0-0 14 ♖fc1 c6 when Black should be fine, the principal plan being ...♕b7 and ...♘d7.

White may be able to equalize by regaining one of the queenside pawns, but I doubt that he can realistically hope for any advantage.

12 ♖c1

This position was first reached in S.Shipov-E.Lobron, Moscow (rapid) 1994. From here the game continuation of 12...♕d6 may not have been the most accurate, as White could have availed himself of an interesting tactical opportunity with 13 ♖c6!? ♘xc6 14 ♖xa6, leading to very unclear complications. Instead I would suggest that Black takes a leaf out of Emms' book with 12...♘fd7!, especially because 13 ♘xd7 ♕xd7 14 ♘c3 c6 (14...♖c8!? is also possible) reaches the same position as seen in the previous note.

Summary

At the start of this chapter we became acquainted with our repertoire choice against 5 b3: the ambitious 5...b5!?. None of White's rare sixth moves need overly concern us, but it was necessary to analyse them all the same. We will shortly move on to the rather more interesting subject of 6 cxb5, White's most popular and, indeed, most challenging move.

Chapter Sixteen

The Fianchetto Variation: 5 b3 b5!? 6 cxb5

1 d4 ♘f6 2 c4 e6 3 ♘f3 b6 4 g3 ♗a6 5 b3 b5 6 cxb5 ♗xb5

In this chapter we address the main lines of the 5...b5 system. We can already see that Black has achieved what he hopes will prove to be a strategically favourable pawn exchange. On the other hand, the exchanging operation has come at the expense of some time; both in terms of the tempo which might have been spent developing another piece, and the fact that Black's light-squared bishop will often have to retreat when attacked by the enemy knight which will usually be destined for c3.

Strategic guidelines

Black has a few different ways of handling this variation. One popular method involves a classic light-square strategy with moves like ...♗c6 and ...♕c8-b7 in order to obtain a firm grip over the e4- and d5-squares. The effect can be even greater if Black is able to exchange his dark-squared bishop for a white knight, such as on c3. Although this approach is perfectly valid, I have instead decided to concentrate on what might be termed a central strategy. The idea, very simply, is to play an early ...d5 followed by a subsequent ...c5, eroding White's centre in a manner fully in keeping with Black's fifth move.

The specific advantages of this approach are:

1) The pawn on d5 secures a firm foothold in the centre and blunts the diagonal of White's soon to be fianchettoed king's bishop.

2) If Black can execute his plan successfully then he will remain with an extra central pawn – a definite strategic boon which enables him to aspire to a full point rather than mere equality.

3) This central strategy is simple and easy to understand, making it a convenient choice for players of all levels. This clarity of purpose means that

even if you forget the precise theoretical recommendation in a particular position, you will always know roughly what it is that you should be looking to achieve.

General principles

Before we consider any concrete variations, I would like to highlight a number of common themes and rules of thumb which I believe will prove useful:

1) In the likely event of a white knight appearing on c3, either immediately or during the next few moves, the b5-bishop should retreat to a6 in order to avoid blocking the c-pawn. The pinning ...♗b4 is also inconsistent with our central strategy; if we are intending to open the game with ...c5 then it makes no sense to exchange this bishop for an enemy knight.

2) Some White players have attempted to prevent the ...c5 break by playing b3-b4, which may be supported by a3 or ♖b1. This prevents our normal method of counterplay involving ...c5, but the pawn on b4 becomes a new target which can and should be attacked by ...a5!.

3) From time to time White offers a bishop exchange with ♗a3. In such cases our most effective reaction will almost always be ...♗d6!, allowing the exchange but only on our own terms. If White proceeds to exchange on d6, we should have no qualms about recapturing with the c-pawn, as the doubled d-pawns will control a lot of key central squares.

4) If a position appears with the black d-pawn on d5 and a white knight on e5, the move ...♘fd7! is often a useful resource, intending to exchange the enemy's powerful beast while keeping the other knight on b8 to guard c6.

5) Occasionally Black will have reason to move his king's knight, either to the e4-square or perhaps to d7 to exchange a white knight on e5. Whatever the reason, as soon as this knight has moved Black may well be able to consider the idea of ...f5 which, if timed correctly, could lead to quite a comfortable version of a Stonewall Dutch.

6) Very often Black will delay castling in favour of developing his queenside pieces and perhaps carrying out an early ...c5 break. The point is that the extra tempo required for castling can, in certain positions, make it difficult or even impossible to carry out the pawn break.

7) On a cautionary note, the decision to open the centre should never be taken lightly when one has yet to castle. *In the present variation there are two specific tactical motifs which Black must always keep in mind for as long as his king remains centralized*:

7a) If White's queen's knight is still on c3, then he can occasionally break through with a ♘xd5 piece sacrifice. (See the notes to Line B3 for a few examples of this theme.)

7b) In some variations we will see White moving his queen's knight to a4. If he does this then a premature ...c5 can allow the sequence dxc5 ♘xc5; ♘xc5 ♗xc5; b4!. That wins a piece by attacking the bishop on c5 while simultaneously threatening ♕a4+, picking up the bishop on a6 – definitely something to avoid!

In the following analysis we will see some specific examples of both of these themes. For the time being, please remember: *whenever you delay castling, you should always be on the lookout for both of these tricks.*

I am sure that you are itching to find out how these numerous concepts can be applied over the board, so without further ado we will begin to explore some specifics.

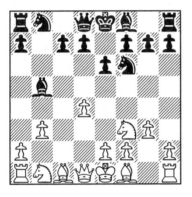

7 ♗g2

This natural move is by far the most popular choice. For our purposes 7 ♘c3 has no independent significance as after 7...♗a6 White will almost certainly proceed with 8 ♗g2, after which 8...d5 reaches Line A, below.

7 ♗a3!? is an unusual alternative, but not a bad one. White intends to inhibit ...c5 while also engineering what he hopes will be a favourable exchange of bishops. Various responses have been seen, but I rather like Black's

idea in R.Cifuentes Parada-D.Campora, Ciudad Real 2004, which continued 7...♗d6!? (7...♗xa3 8 ♘xa3 ♗c6 has been seen in a few games and is also fine for Black)

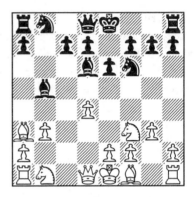

8 ♗g2 (after 8 ♗xd6 cxd6 Black's improved central control should fully compensate for his compromised structure, while White's soon to be fianchettoed bishop will not have much of a future after a timely ...d5) 8...♗c6 9 0-0 0-0 10 ♘e5 ♗xg2 11 ♔xg2, at which point the simple 11...♕e7 would have given Black a nice position.

After the text move we arrive at an important crossroads.

Despite having established a general plan for the opening and early middlegame, we still face a difficult choice between two distinct sequences. I spent a lot of time analysing 7...♗b4+!? 8 ♗d2 a5, followed by a subsequent ...d5. There are various arguments for and against this option, but overall I consider it to be a fully viable alternative to 7...d5. The only real problem with this move order is that Black will have to come up with something completely different against 7 ♘c3, as 7...♗b4 8 ♗d2 leads to quite distinct positions. My recommended system, on the other hand, has the advantage of being equally applicable against both the 7 ♗g2 and 7 ♘c3 move orders.

7...d5

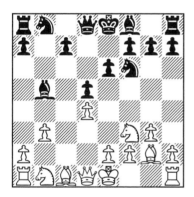

With this move Black establishes control over the centre, while questioning the usefulness of the bishop on g2. White will usually castle either here or on the next move, but occasionally he postpones it in favour of immediate queenside action. Thus we now consider:

A: 8 ♘c3
B: 8 0-0

From time to time White tries 8 ♗a3!? when G.Kallai-A.Khalifman, German League 2002, proceeded with the typical 8...♗d6 (this is not the only playable move and 8...♗xa3 has also been used successfully; after 9 ♘xa3 ♗a6 10 b4 0-0 11 ♕a4 ♕d7 12 ♕a5 – White is playing very ambitiously, but his plan soon backfires – 12...c6 13 ♘e5 ♕b7 14 ♖b1 ♘bd7 15 ♘xc6 ♕xc6 16 b5 ♕b6 17 ♕xa6 ♕xd4 18 0-0 ♕d2 Black won a pawn in T.Gruskovnjak-L.Lenic, Ljubljana 2006) 9 ♗xd6 cxd6 10 ♘c3 ♗d7 11 0-0 ♘c6 12 a3 a5 13 ♕d3 0-0 14 ♖fc1 ♖b8 15 ♖ab1 when a draw was agreed. In the final position 15...♘a7!? looks quite attractive for Black, intending ...♘b5 with an active position.

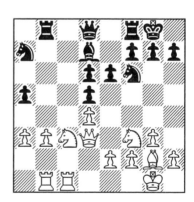

A) 8 ♘c3 ♗a6 9 b4!?

Several games have featured 9 0-0 ♘bd7 with an instant transposition to Line B. However, the text has been the highest-scoring move, yielding 59% for the first player. White takes time out from developing in order to establish a queenside bind and prevent ...c5, and obviously the pawn cannot be taken on account of 10 ♕a4+.

The alternatives are less challenging:

a) After 9 ♘e5 ♘bd7 (9...♘fd7 also looks fine) 10 ♘c6 ♕c8 11 0-0 ♕b7 12 ♘a5 ♕b4 13 ♗d2 ♕xd4 White did not have enough for the pawn in M.Becker-A.Litwak, Duisburg 2006.

b) 9 ♘a4 ♘bd7 10 ♕c2 (10 0-0 reaches variation 'e' in the notes to White's 10th in Line B) fails to achieve the desired effect after 10...c5! 11 ♘xc5 ♘xc5! 12 dxc5 ♕a5+ 13 ♗d2 ♕xc5 when Black was already at least equal in G.Sarakauskas-Z.Gyimesi, Liverpool 2006.

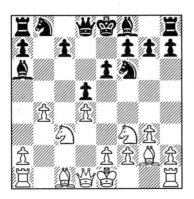

9...c6

This is one of Black's most solid responses, preventing b4-b5 and threatening to capture on b4. His next objective will be to finish developing and then prepare a queenside attack with ...a5.

10 ♖b1 ♘bd7 11 0-0 ♗d6 12 ♖e1

In A.Matthiesen-S.Brady, Saint Vincent 2005, the move order was 12 ♗f4

♗xf4 13 gxf4 0-0 14 ♖e1, leading to the same position.

12...0-0 13 ♗f4 ♗xf4 14 gxf4 ♗c4

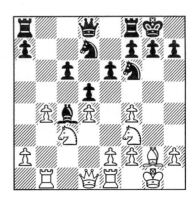

We have been following the game Z.Gyimesi-R.Dautov, German League 1997, which continued 15 a3 (after 15 ♘e5!? ♘xe5 both 16 dxe5 ♘d7 and 16 fxe5 ♘d7 intending ...a5 look fine for Black) 15...a5 16 e3 axb4 17 axb4 ♕e7 (also promising is 17...♘e8!? followed by ...♘d6) 18 b5 cxb5 19 ♘xb5 ♘e4 20 ♘d2 ♘xd2 (another tempting continuation was 20...♗xb5 21 ♗xe4 ♗a4 22 ♗c2 ♗xc2 23 ♕xc2 ♖fc8 with an edge for Black) 21 ♕xd2 ♖a2 when Black's position was slightly preferable, although White managed to equalize with careful play after 22 ♕d1 ♕h4 23 ♕f3 ♘f6 24 ♕g3 ♕xg3 25 hxg3 ♗d3 26 ♖b3 ♖b8 27 ♖xd3 ♖xb5 28 ♖dd1 g6 and ½-½.

B) 8 0-0

Castling will sooner or later prove indispensable, and the majority of White players have opted to do so at the earliest convenience.

8...♘bd7

Black prioritizes his queenside development in preparation for a quick ...c5, just as prescribed in the introductory guidelines.

9 ♘c3

This natural move requires no explanation. Occasionally White tries 9 ♗a3!?, which should as usual be met by 9...♗d6, as prescribed in the chapter introduction. Play continues 10 ♗xd6 (White gains little from delaying the exchange; if the bishop remains on a3 then the knight on b1 and rook on a1 will be unable to move) 10...cxd6 11 ♘c3 ♗a6 when I would evaluate the position as dynamically equal. If White were magically able to simplify down to a king and pawn ending then he would, of course, be winning, but so long as Black keeps enough pieces on the board, his doubled central pawns will prove very useful as they control so many important squares.

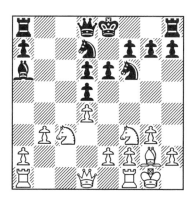

One example was K.Chernyshov-Z.Medvegy, Salgatarjan 2003, which continued 12 ♘d2 ♕b6 13 ♘db1 0-0 14 ♘a4 ♕b4 15 ♘bc3 ♖fc8 16 a3 ♕b7 17 ♖b1 ♘b6 18 ♕d2 ♘xa4 19 bxa4 (or 19 ♘xa4 ♖c6) 19...♕d7 when Black stood

slightly better; both sides have doubled pawns, but Black's d-pawns control far more important squares than White's a-pawns.

9...♗a6

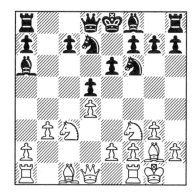

Up to this point both sides have proceeded in eminently logical fashion. We now reach a critical juncture at which White must choose between a large number of alternatives. I consider the following three to be worthy of special consideration:

B1: 10 ♗b2
B2: 10 ♖e1
B3: 10 ♘e5!?

At this point we should also pay attention to the numerous alternatives available:

a) With 10 a3 ♗d6 11 b4 White hurries to prevent the freeing ...c5 break. Fortunately for us, the old adage 'when one door closes another one opens' rings true here as Black can now play to attack the b-pawn with a timely ...a5. After the natural moves 11...0-0 12 ♖e1 ♗b7! (making way for the a-pawn) 13

♘a4 a5 14 ♘c5 ♗c6 15 ♖b1 axb4 16 axb4 ♗b5 Black had equalized in E.Bacrot-M.Carlsen, Moscow (blitz) 2007.

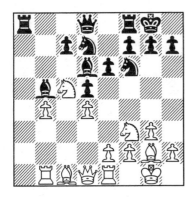

Indeed, his sounder pawn structure may even give him a minute advantage and in the end the Norwegian *wunderkind* prevailed.

b) With 10 ♖b1 White hints at a possible b3-b4 advance and hopes, by comparison with our last variation, that his rook will be more usefully placed on the b-file. The one drawback is that the b4-square is currently not under White's control; a fact which can be exploited with 10...♗b4!, conveniently developing with gain of tempo. After the further 11 ♘a4 0-0 12 a3 ♗e7 (12...♗d6 13 b4 ♕e8 14 ♖e1 ♘e4 15 ♗b2 ♗b5 16 ♘c3 ♘xc3 17 ♗xc3 ♘b6 18 e4 dxe4 19 ♖xe4 ♘d5 was also balanced in M.Lorenzi-W.Mueller, correspondence 2003) 13 b4 ♘e4 14 ♗b2 ♘d6 15 ♖e1 ♘c4 16 ♘d2 ♘xd2 17 ♕xd2 ♗b5 18 ♘c5 ♘xc5 19 bxc5 ♕d7 chances were roughly equal in P.Nikolic-V.Anand, Monaco (rapid) 1997.

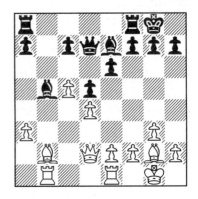

c) 10 ♗g5 allows Black to choose between two promising lines:

c1) 10...c5!? is arguably the most principled reaction. Now in H.Boskova-P.Vavra, Liberec 2007, White reacted with the strange 11 dxc5?! ♗xc5 which only aided Black's development. Of course, 11 ♖c1 would have been better, but after 11...♖c8 I still see no problems for Black.

c2) Black can also complete the development of his kingside with 10...♗d6 (10...♗e7 is also quite playable) 11 ♖c1 0-0 12 ♘a4 h6 (12...♕e7!?) 13 ♗xf6 (13 ♗f4?! ♗xf4 14 gxf4 allows the nice tactical trick 14...♘h5! 15 ♕d2 ♕f6! 16 ♖xc7 ♖fd8 when Black regains the pawn with advantage) 13...♕xf6 14 ♕d2 ♖fb8, with balanced chances in D.Antic-N.Ostojic, Jahorina 2000; Black can easily defend c5 and c7, and in the long run his bishop-pair could become a real asset.

d) 10 ♗f4 has been criticized by some commentators, but I think the bishop is quite well placed here. Play continues 10...c5 (10...♗d6!? is untested, but White may be able to claim a slight edge after 11 ♘e5 0-0 12 ♘c6 ♕e8 13 ♖c1) 11 ♖c1 ♖c8 and now:

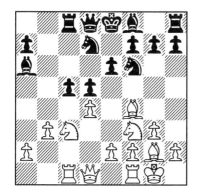

d1) 12 dxc5?! ♗xc5 13 ♘a4 ♗a3 14 ♖xc8 ♕xc8 is slightly better for Black, as pointed out by Gershon.

d2) 12 ♘a4 (V.Grabliauskas-V.Epishin, Olomouc 1996) should probably be met by 12...cxd4! (the game continuation of 12...c4 looks less convincing after 13 bxc4 ♖xc4 14 ♖xc4 dxc4 when 15 ♕c2 would have been pleasant for White) 13 ♘xd4 ♗b7 (14 ♘c6 was threatened and 13...e5?! looks premature in view of 14 ♘c6 ♖xc6 15 ♖xc6 ♗b7 16 ♖xf6!) 14 ♖xc8 ♕xc8 with a double-edged position. White is slightly the better developed, but Black controls the centre and may soon threaten ...e5. The critical continuation looks like 15 ♕d2! ♗e7 16 ♖c1 ♕a8 17 ♘b5 0-0 when White's pieces are active, but Black's central majority is a useful long-term asset. Before moving on, it should be noted that in that final variation 15...e5?! would have been risky in view of 16 ♖c1 ♕b8 17 ♘b5 exf4 (or 17...♗e7 18 ♘c7+ ♔f8 19 ♗g5 ♗a3 20 ♖c2 d4 21 ♗xb7 ♕xb7 22 ♗xf6

♘xf6 23 ♘c5!) 18 ♘c7+ ♔d8 19 ♕a5 ♔e7 20 gxf4 (20 ♕b4+ ♔d8 21 ♕a5 ♔e7 repeats) 20...♘e8 21 ♘xd5+ ♗xd5 22 ♗xd5 with dangerous compensation for the piece; Black's king is exposed and it will take some time to coordinate his forces.

d3) In H.Banikas-R.Hübner, Corfu 1999, White preferred 12 ♘e5 ♘xe5 (12...cxd4!? also deserves consideration: 13 ♕xd4 ♗a3 14 ♖c2 ♘b6! prevents ♕a4 and prepares to castle with a good position, while 14 ♘xd7 ♕xd7 15 ♖c2 0-0 is equal – Gershon) 13 ♗xe5 ♘d7 (this is the safe continuation, although 13...♘g4!? 14 ♗f4 g5!? is very interesting) 14 ♗f4 ♗e7 15 dxc5, at which point I would suggest 15...♗xc5!? (in the game 15...♖xc5 16 b4 ♖c4 17 ♕a4 ♕b6 18 a3 ♗f6 19 ♗xd5! led to unclear complications).

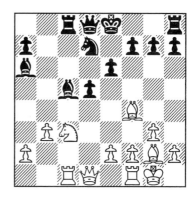

Play might continue 16 ♘a4 ♗a3 17 ♖xc8 ♕xc8 18 ♕d4 0-0 19 ♖e1 (19 ♕xa7?! ♗xe2 20 ♖e1 ♗b5 is a good trade for Black), and now 19...♕b7 20 e4 ♕b4 21 ♕xb4 ♗xb4 22 ♖d1 favours White (Gershon), but Black should prefer 19...♘c5 with approximate equality.

e) 10 ♘a4 should not be dangerous. White tries to control c5, but the rest of his pieces are currently in no position to assist the knight. If nothing else Black can always just play 10...♗b5 when it is not clear whether White has anything better than repeating with 11 ♘c3 ♗a6, as has occurred in a couple of games. If Black wishes to play more ambitiously then 10...♗d6 is the logical choice. Now 11 ♗b2 0-0 12 ♖c1 was seen in S.Lputian-T.Gelashvili, Yerevan 2000, and here instead of the game's 12...♕e7 13 ♕c2 when White stood slightly better, Gelashvili suggests 12...♕b8!? without further comment.

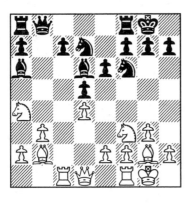

Some practical tests would be useful, but on the whole it looks to me like the ideas of ...♕b5 and/or ...♖fc8 should give Black enough chances. Here are a couple of speculative sample variations:

e1) After 13 ♕c2 ♕b5 14 ♖fe1 ♘e4!? Black controls the crucial c5-square while preparing to meet 15 ♘d2 with 15...f5!, reaching a very pleasant-looking Dutch.

e2) 13 ♘c5 ♘xc5 14 dxc5 ♗e7 leads

to a complex strategic situation. For the time being White's pieces are quite active, but in the long run Black's central majority may prove to be a more significant factor. Aside from exchanging on c5, 13...♕b5!? is also worth considering. After 14 ♘xa6 ♕xa6 Black has relinquished the bishop-pair, but on the other hand the e6 and d5 pawn tandem is currently doing a nice job of controlling the light squares. Black intends to free his position with ...♖fc8 and ...c5, and if White tries to prevent this with 15 a3 ♖fc8 16 b4, there follows 16...♕b5 intending ...a5.

After that lengthy but necessary diversion, we now move on to the three principal continuations.

B1) 10 ♗b2

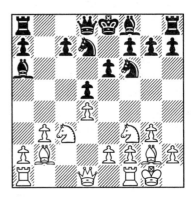

This is probably White's most obvious developing move. The first player prepares to occupy the c-file while anticipating the opening of the long diagonal which could result from Black's intended ...c5.

10...♗e7

Most players have preferred to

complete development and castle before opening the centre. The immediate 10...c5 is playable, but White has some chances for a slight edge after either 11 &c1 or 11 &e1!? intending a quick e4.

11 &c1

This is White's most natural follow-up. Others are less dangerous:

a) 11 ♘e5?! ♘xe5 12 dxe5 ♘d7 13 ♘xd5? is way too optimistic here and in H.Luther-A.Seyb, German League 2005, a few accurate defensive moves led to a swift rebuttal of White's attack after 13...exd5 14 ♕xd5 &b8 15 e6 fxe6 16 ♕xe6 &b6 17 &c6 &b5.

b) M.Roeder-V.Epishin, Groningen 1996, saw the somewhat better 11 &e1 (this is a sensible move, although if White wants to play like this he might be better off doing so on the previous move, as in Line B2, below) 11...0-0 12 e4 ♘xe4 13 ♘xe4 dxe4 14 ♘d2 (14 &xe4 is nothing to worry about after 14...&b7), after which 14...f5!? looks critical: for example, 15 f3 &b4! 16 fxe4 &b7 17 a3 &xd2 18 ♕xd2 fxe4 19 &xe4 &d5 when Black has a decent position as the b2-bishop is well and truly stifled.

11...0-0 12 ♘a4

This certainly feels consistent with White's previous play, although a few alternative approaches have also been tried:

a) With 12 &e1 White hopes to activate his pieces with the help of the pawn thrust e2-e4. Play continues 12...c5 (the immediate central break seems simplest to me, although 12...&c8 is also perfectly fine) and now:

a1) In S.Turna-V.Babula, Slovakian League 2002, White erred with 13 &a3?! &c8 14 e4 ♕a5 15 &b2 cxd4 16 ♘xd4 ♘e5! (aiming at d3) 17 &f1 &xf1 18 ♔xf1, at which point 18...♕a6+! would have been extremely strong: 19 ♕e2 (after 19 ♔g1 ♘d3 20 ♕e2 dxe4 Black is winning) 19...♕xe2+ 20 ♘cxe2 (all of 20 ♘dxe2 ♘d3, 20 &xe2 ♘d3 and 20 ♔xe2 dxe4 are no better) 20...♘d3 and White is in big trouble.

a2) 13 e4 is the consistent move, although White gains no advantage after 13...♘xe4 14 ♘xe4 dxe4 15 &xe4 &b7 16 &e2 &c8 17 ♘e5 &xg2 18 ♔xg2 cxd4 19 &xc8 ♕xc8 20 ♘xd7 ♕xd7 21 ♕xd4 ♕c6+ 22 ♕e4 &c8 with equality in W.Koch-A.Lauber, Budapest 1997, although Black eventually managed to grind out a victory.

b) 12 &c2 is a playable but slightly slow continuation, and Black has no problems after 12...&c8:

b1) 13 h3 looks slow and 13...c5 14 dxc5 ♘xc5 15 ♕a1 ♕b6 16 &fc1 &fd8 17 ♘d1 ♘ce4 (17...♘fe4!?) 18 &d4 ♕a5 (18...&c5 also looks fine) was about equal in Y.Pelletier-R.Damaso, European Championship, Plovdiv 2008.

b2) 13 ♘a4 appears consistent, but White achieves nothing after 13...c5 14 ♘xc5 ♘xc5 15 dxc5 ♗xc5 16 a3 ♕e7 17 b4 ♗b6 18 ♘e5 (S.Temirbaev-T.Likavsky, Mallorca 2004) and here 18...♖xc2 19 ♕xc2 ♖c8 looks simplest, when I prefer Black.

12...♖c8 13 ♘c5

After 13 ♘e1 c5 14 dxc5 ♘xc5 15 ♘xc5 ♖xc5 16 ♖xc5 ♗xc5 17 ♘d3 (M.Tosic-A.Kovacevic, Herceg Novi 2001) 17...♗e7 Black is at least equal.

13...♘xc5 14 dxc5 c6

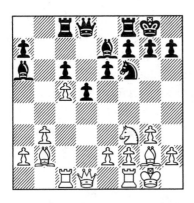

We have arrived at position with the same structure as variation 'e2' in the notes to White's 10th move, above. Once again the chances are approximately equal, although the strategically unbalanced nature of the position means that both sides may strive for the full point.

15 b4

In A.Stickler-V.Meier, German League 1991, White found himself outplayed after 15 ♖e1 ♘e4 16 ♕d4 f6! 17 ♗h3 e5 18 ♕e3 ♕a5 19 ♗xc8 ♖xc8 20 ♗c3 ♕xc5 21 ♘d2 ♘xc3 (21...♕xe3 22

fxe3 ♘xc3 23 ♖xc3 f5 also leaves Black firmly in control) 22 ♕xc5 ♘xe2+ 23 ♔g2 ♗xc5 24 ♖xc5 ♗d3; with two pawns for the exchange and a dominant centre, Black was clearly better and went on to win.

15...♘d7 16 ♘d4

We have reached a critical position in which Black must consider his options with great care. The game T.Polak-A.Sofrigin, Schwarzach 1998, continued 16...♗f6?! 17 f4 ♗c4? 18 ♘xc6! ♖xc6 19 ♗xf6 ♗xe2 20 ♗xd8 ♗xd1 21 ♗e7 ♖e8 22 ♗d6 ♗a4 23 f5 with a clear advantage to White. Here 17...♕c7 looks better, although Black must still be careful, as shown by 18 ♖f2 e5 19 fxe5 ♘xe5?! 20 ♖xf6! gxf6 21 e4 with a strong initiative.

The last variation highlights quite convincingly the potential drawbacks to having a bishop on f6. With that in mind, I think that Black should have preferred 16...♕c7!, connecting the rooks and retaining the option of playing on the queenside as well as in the centre. A sample continuation might be 17 f4 ♖b8 18 ♕d2 (18 a3?! allows 18...♗xc5) 18...♕b7 19 ♗c3 (after 19 a3?! ♗xc5 20 bxc5 ♕xb2 21 ♕xb2 ♖xb2 22 ♘xc6 ♖xe2 Black is better) 19...♗c4, intending ...a5 with good counterplay.

B2) 10 ♖e1

The intention behind this move is clear: White is preparing to open the centre with e2-e4.

10...♗b4!

Black develops with gain of tempo, conveniently holding up e2-e4 by threatening to remove a defender of that square.

11 ♗d2

11 ♗b2 is almost never played. After 11...0-0 12 a3 (A.Schmidlechner-N.Kelecevic, Austria 2002), 12...♗d6 looks like the most active square for the bishop and following 13 e4 dxe4 14 ♘xe4 ♘xe4 15 ♖xe4 ♗b7 Black has no problems.

11...c5!

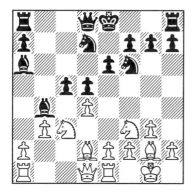

11...0-0 has been played more frequently, but in this position I can see nothing wrong with the immediate central strike.

12 dxc5

12 a3 should not be a cause of concern to Black after 12...♗xc3! 13 ♗xc3 ♘e4 14 ♗b2 c4!, ensuring that the centre remains closed. B.Ostenstad-E.Agrest, Bergen 2001, continued 15 bxc4 ♗xc4 16 ♘d2 ♘xd2 17 ♕xd2 0-0 with equality, as it is hard to see any way in which the two bishops will realistically be able to hurt Black. As a matter of fact Black may even be able to improve upon this slightly with the zwischenzug 15...♖b8!, forcing White

to take time out to defend b2 before recapturing on c4.

12...♗xc5 13 b4!?

Attempting to seize the initiative by means of a temporary sacrifice. Instead 13 ♘a4 ♗e7 14 ♘d4 ♖c8 15 ♖c1 ♗b7 16 ♖xc8 ♕xc8 17 ♕b1 0-0 was agreed drawn in Xu Jun-D.Campora, Seville 2003, but I prefer Black in the final position as the extra central pawn is an advantage provided that he avoids too many exchanges.

13...♗xb4

This seems fine although I have also not been able to find anything wrong with 13...♗e7!?: for example, 14 e4 dxe4 15 ♘xe4 ♘xe4 16 ♖xe4 ♗b7 17 ♖d4 ♗d5 with a solid position. In fact once Black has castled, the splendid outpost on d5 may even make his position a little easier to play.

14 ♕a4

White can try the combination 14 ♘xd5!? ♘xd5 15 ♗xb4 ♘xb4 16 ♕a4 which regains the piece, but he will achieve no more than equality after 16...♖b8!? (16...0-0 17 ♕xb4 is perhaps just fractionally better for White) 17 a3 ♗b5 18 ♕xb4 ♗xe2 19 ♕d4 (19 ♕c3 ♗xf3 20 ♕xg7 ♕f6 transposes) 19...♗xf3 20 ♕xg7 (White risks becoming worse after 20 ♗xf3?! ♕f6) 20...♕f6 21 ♕xf6 ♘xf6 22 ♗xf3 ♔e7.

14...♕a5 15 ♕xa5 ♗xa5 16 ♘xd5 ♗xd2 17 ♘xf6+ ♘xf6 18 ♘xd2 *(see diagram)*

White's pieces are marginally the more active, but Black is in no real danger and the game V.Anand-A.Karpov, Monaco (blindfold) 1997, was soon agreed drawn after 18...♖c8

19 ♘b3 0-0 20 ♘d4 ♖c7 (20...♖fd8 21 e3 ♔f8 also looks fine) 21 a4 ♖d8 22 e3 ♔f8 23 h3 ♖dc8 24 ♘b5 ♗xb5 25 axb5.

B3) 10 ♘e5!?

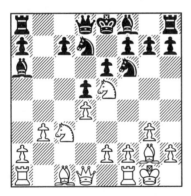

Finally we come to what I believe to be the most critical continuation. After examining Black's various responses with a fine toothcomb, I came to realize that this position is deceptively dangerous, although I believe that I have succeeded in carving out a rather creative route to safety. I consider my recommendation to be fully sound, but must admit that it is the kind of move about which some players may instinc-

tively feel suspicious. Thus before we investigate this new idea, I invite the reader to join me in retracing the analytical steps of my investigation into Black's tenth-move alternatives. I hope that by doing so you will come to appreciate why I felt that such a radical new approach was required! Here is my analysis of Black's three most natural moves:

a) Firstly, we must recognise that the obvious 10...♘xe5?! is risky in view of 11 dxe5 ♘d7 12 ♘xd5! exd5 13 ♕xd5 with a very dangerous initiative in P.Kiss-M.Menacher, Balatonlelle 2005. White won this game very convincingly and although improvements do exist for Black, I would not recommend that you follow this path. It is worth noting that 11...♗b4!? may render this line just about playable, but according to my analysis White still has at least a couple of routes to an advantage.

b) 10...♗d6 is the most popular move when White can choose between:

b1) 11 ♘c6 ♕c8 12 a3 0-0 13 ♗g5 ♕e8 was complex, but probably slightly better for White in A.Beliavsky-V.Topalov, Madrid 1997. Personally I would not feel completely comfortable with the knight entrenched on c6, although if Black manoeuvres carefully then he should probably be okay. In passing it is worth mentioning Avrukh's proposed improvement of 13 ♗f4, intending 13...♕e8 14 ♘b4! ♗b7 15 ♘d3! with advantage; an assessment echoed by Wells. However, it seems to me that Black can improve with 13...♕b7! 14

♘a5 ♕b6. According to Avrukh White can obtain a clear advantage with 15 b4, but Black can in fact free his game with 15...♗xf4 16 gxf4 c5! 17 ♘a4 (or 17 dxc5 ♘xc5) 17...♕c7 18 ♘xc5 (18 dxc5 would be met by 18...♕xf4) 18...♘xc5 19 dxc5 ♕xf4, reaching a position in which White's queenside pawns are certainly a long-term threat, but his kingside could prove to be a cause for concern. To evaluate this position definitively would take extensive analysis, but my gut feeling is that Black is at least equal and so Beliavsky's treatment may have been best after all.

b2) 11 ♗f4!? is even more promising in my opinion.

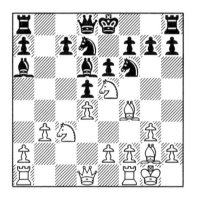

The game A.Karpov-M.Carlsen, Moscow (blitz) 2007, proceeded 11...0-0 12 ♖c1 ♗xe5 13 dxe5 ♘g4 (13...♘h5 14 ♘a4 ♘xf4 15 gxf4 gives White a nice queenside bind) and here the legendary former World Champion executed the familiar tactical breakthrough 14 ♘xd5! exd5 15 ♕xd5 ♘b6 16 ♕a5 ♗xe2 17 ♖fe1 ♗d3. The Norwegian prodigy eventually prevailed, but at this point 18 h3! would have put Black

under serious pressure. It is not so easy to suggest improvements for Black here, as all of his earlier moves were very logical. 15...g5!? is one idea, but overall I still do not trust the black position.

c) For some time I believed 10...c5!? to be the perfect solution to Black's problems. This move seems absolutely logical, averting the positional threat of 11 ♘c6 while striking at the very central pawn whose protection the knight has just abandoned. In J.Sriram-T.Bakre, Visakhapatnam 2004, things worked out well for Black after 11 ♗f4 ♖c8 12 ♘a4 ♘xe5 13 ♗xe5 (13 dxe5 ♘d7 leaves the e5-pawn in constant need of protection, and White must even worry about ideas like ...g5!?) 13...cxd4 (13...♘d7!?) 14 ♕xd4 ♗d6. Unfortunately the real problem arises after 11 ♘xd7! and now:

c1) 11...♕xd7 is dubious in view of 12 ♗a3 when White exerts strong pressure against c5 while making it difficult for Black to castle. A sample continuation is 12...♖c8 (12...cxd4?! 13 ♗xf8 ♔xf8 14 ♕xd4 ♔e7 15 ♖fd1 ♖hd8 16 e4 can hardly be recommended for Black) 13 ♖c1 ♗e7 (13...cxd4 14 ♗xf8 ♔xf8 15 ♕xd4 is also unsatisfactory; in the time it takes Black to castle artificially, White will open the centre with e2-e4) 14 dxc5 ♗xc5 15 ♗xc5 ♖xc5 16 ♕d4 ♖c6 (16...♕c8? 17 ♘b5! would be embarrassing) 17 ♖fd1 ♕c7 (17...0-0 18 e4 is pleasant for White) 18 e4 dxe4 19 ♕b4 ♕b6 20 ♕a4 0-0 21 ♘xe4 ♖xc1 22 ♘xf6+ gxf6 23 ♖xc1 and Black falls some way short of equality.

c2) Black should therefore prefer 11...♘xd7. Now O.Salama-J.Jurek, Olomouc 2006, continued 12 ♖e1, at which point Black could have obtained a comfortable position with either 12...cxd4 13 ♕xd4 ♕b6 or 12...♖c8 13 ♗b2 cxd4 14 ♕xd4 ♕b6. So far everything appears to be in order for Black. His 10th move makes perfect sense from the perspective of general principles, while all the available game references lead to positions in which Black either obtained or had the opportunity to obtain at least an equal position. I was all set to recommend this course of action when it occurred to me that White can set far greater problems with the hitherto untested though palpably superior 12 ♗b2!.

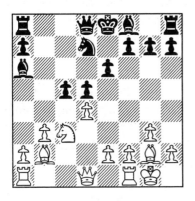

The more I studied this position, the more I came to realize the extent of Black's difficulties. Some exemplary variations:

c21) 12...♗e7?! 13 dxc5! ♘xc5 (13...♗xc5 14 ♘a4! more or less forces the bishop back to f8) 14 ♕d4! ♖c8 15 ♕xg7 ♗f6 16 ♕h6 ♗xe2 17 ♖fe1 is extremely dangerous for Black.

c22) 12...♖c8 can also be met by 13 dxc5!? ♗xc5 (or 13...♘xc5 14 b4 ♘d7 15 b5 ♗b7 16 e4 with a strong initiative) 14 ♘a4 ♗f8 15 ♖c1 ♘f6 (15...♖xc1 16 ♕xc1 ♘f6?? loses after 17 ♕c6+) 16 ♕d2 ♗e7 17 ♕e3 ♖xc1 18 ♖xc1 0-0 19 ♘c5 (19 ♕xa7 ♗xe2) 19...♗c8 20 b4 with a clear advantage.

c23) 12...♘b6 (preventing any ♘c3-a4 ideas) 13 ♖e1! (13 dxc5? ♗xc5 would justify Black's last) prepares to open the centre: for example, 13...c4 14 e4 ♗b4 15 exd5 ♗xc3 16 ♗xc3 ♘xd5 17 ♗xd5 ♕xd5 18 ♖e5 ♕d7 19 d5 and Black has big problems.

c24) 12...♘f6 13 dxc5 ♕a5 (13...♗xc5?? loses immediately after 14 b4!) 14 ♘a4 and at the very least Black will have to relinquish the bishop-pair.

c25) 12...cxd4 13 ♕xd4 ♕b6 may be relatively the best chance, but after 14 ♕d2 (14 ♕f4 is also promising) 14...♘f6 15 ♖ac1 ♗e7 16 ♖fe1 0-0 17 e4 dxe4 18 ♘xe4 ♖ad8 19 ♕f4 ♘xe4 20 ♗xe4 ♗d3 21 ♖c7 White maintains some initiative.

Try as I might, I have still not been able to find a satisfactory continuation for Black after 11 ♘xd7!.

For some time I felt rather dismayed and even wondered if I might have to ditch 5...b5!? altogether. Fortunately I happened to mention my predicament in a telephone conversation with John Emms and after a few minutes of bouncing ideas around, the Grandmaster's mind produced a moment of inspiration in suggesting...

10...c6!?

It is hardly surprising that nobody has tested this move up to now. On first impressions the move may appear at best to be a loss of a tempo in the event of a subsequent ...c5. On the other hand, White's last move introduced a number of specific positional and tactical motifs. In response to such a direct challenge, I would argue that it is not enough for Black to let himself simply be guided by general principles. Instead a more concrete approach is needed, and the text contains two very specific ideas:

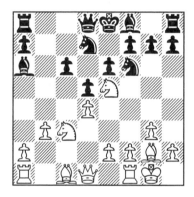

1) Somewhat ironically, Black prevents the positional threat of 11 ♘c6 by placing a pawn on that very square. As the reader will doubtlessly have noticed, 11 ♘xc6?? is impossible due to 11...♕c7 winning a piece.

2) Black prepares to exchange knights on e5 when the secure fortification of the d5-square will enable him to avoid the kind of sacrifice that we witnessed in Kiss-Menacher and Karpov-Carlsen.

This is a completely original idea and in the absence of any game references I instead offer the following analysis of White's principal candidate moves.

a) The simplest response to 11 f4 is 11...♗d6! intending ...c5,

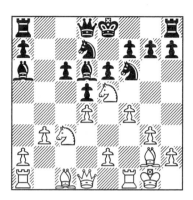

when the usefulness of White's last becomes highly questionable. The immediate 11...c5 is also possible, although White now has the opportunity to launch an attack with 12 f5!?. This may or may not be good, but at least it allows him to make sense of his previous move. Play may continue 12...cxd4 13 ♘xf7! (13 ♘xd7?! ♕xd7 is less dangerous after both 14 ♕xd4 ♖c8 and 14 fxe6 fxe6 15 ♕xd4 ♖c8) 13...♔xf7 14 fxe6+ ♔xe6 15 ♘xd5 ♘xd5 (15...♖c8!?) 16 ♕c2 and even here Black's position should contain enough defensive resources after either 16...♘5f6 or 16...♘7f6!?.

b) 11 ♗b2 ♘xe5 12 dxe5 ♘d7 reaches a structure which should be fine for Black as long as White does not succeed in establishing a dark-square blockade on the d4- and c5-squares; an event which indeed appears rather unlikely in the present position.

c) 11 ♗g5 can be met by 11...♘xe5! 12 dxe5 h6 when Black is fine.

d) 11 &f4 罝c8 (Black can also exchange on e5 immediately, but I would just as soon retain the tension) 12 ♘a4 ♘xe5 13 &xe5 ♘d7 14 &f4 &a3!? looks like a good move, preventing White from obtaining a queenside clamp with 罝c1.

Play may continue 15 ♕d2 ♕e7! (White was threatening to embarrass the bishop, such as with 15...0-0?! 16 b4!), after which Black will follow up with ...c5, either before or after castling.

e) 11 ♘d3!? is one of White's more interesting moves, hoping to exploit the slowness of Black's last move to establish control over the crucial c5-square. Black must be careful here as 11...c5? 12 dxc5 ♘xc5?? loses a piece to 13 ♘xc5 &xc5 14 b4!. Instead 11...罝c8! looks best: for example, 12 ♘a4 &b5 13 ♘ac5 ♘xc5 14 ♘xc5 &xc5 15 dxc5 ♕e7 reaching an interesting and double-edged position.

though rather less dangerous than in the analogous position with a black pawn on c5. After 11...♘xd7 White arrives at a further crossroads:

f1) 12 &f4 c5 (12...罝c8!? also looks good) 13 罝e1!? (or 13 罝c1 罝c8) 13...cxd4 14 ♕xd4 ♕b6 looks safe for Black.

f2) 12 ♘a4 can be safely met by 12...罝c8 (or 12...&b5!?), intending 13 &b2 &e7 or 13 罝e1 &d6 14 e4 0-0.

f3) 12 &b2 &d6 looks safe enough, intending to delay ...c5 until the king has been safely tucked away. If Black is feeling more adventurous then *Fritz's* cheeky suggestion of 12...h5!? is not as ridiculous as it may at first appear.

f4) 12 罝e1 looks quite sensible, intending e2-e4 against which Black can react in one of two ways:

f41) The most straightforward would be to complete development with 12...&b4 13 &d2 0-0, allowing White to carry out his plan with 14 e4.

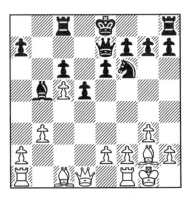

This confers certain advantages upon both sides: White has the two bishops; Black can point to his central majority.

f) Finally 11 ♘xd7!? is playable, al-

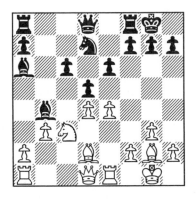

White probably stands a little better here, although the black position remains extremely solid. His only problem is that as long as the central tension remains it will be difficult to arrange ...c5. Still, by centralizing his pieces he should be able to arrange a timely ...dxe4 followed by ...c5. Meanwhile it is not easy to find a really effective plan for White. The obvious idea would be to play on the c-file, but this is not so easy as ♘c3-a4 might run into ...♝b5, forcing the knight back.

f42) If Black is feeling more ambitious then 12...f5!? is possible. For instance, after 13 ♝f4 (13 f3 is not dangerous in view of 13...♝b4 14 ♝d2 0-0 when Black succeeds in evacuating his king before the centre has opened) 13...♖c8!? Black can decide, according to circumstances and personal taste, whether to play ...c5 on the next move or to play ...♝e7 and ...0-0 first.

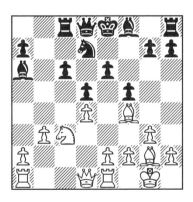

His Stonewall pawn formation provides excellent control over the central squares while completely nullifying White's fianchettoed bishop.

Summary

This has been one of the most theoretically critical chapters in the entire book. My recommended response to White's ever-popular 4 g3 ♝a6 5 b3 was designed to provide realistic prospects for Black to unbalance the game without demanding an encyclopaedic level of theoretical preparation. After absorbing the contents of the past two chapters, I hope you will agree that the recommended system of 5...b5!? in conjunction with a central strategy involving ...d5 and ...c5 meets these criteria.

At the present time, I believe that the theoretical status of 5...b5 makes it an ideal repertoire choice. It is sufficiently well established for its theoretical soundness not to be in question, while remaining unusual enough for us to assume that a significant proportion of White players will not have acquired much experience of playing against it. According to my analysis, Line B3 with 10 ♘e5 seems to be the critical test at present. Time and practice will tell whether 10...c6!? will prove a fully reliable antidote, but as far as I have been able to discern, the black position seems to be resilient enough.

We have reached the end of our journey. I thank you for taking the time to read this book, and wish you all the best.

Index of Variations

1 d4 ♘f6 2 c4 e6 3 ♘f3 b6 and now:

A: 4 ♘c3 and lesser 4th-moves

B: 4 a3

C: 4 g3

A) 4 ♘c3 – *36*

4 ♗f4 – *7*

4 ♗g5 ♗b7 (4...h6 5 ♗h4 ♗b7 6 ♘c3 c5 – *12*) 5 ♘c3 h6 6 ♗h4 ♗e7 7 e3 c5

8 ♗d3 – *15*

8 ♗e2 – *17*

4 e3 ♗b7 5 ♗d3 (5 ♘c3 d5 6 cxd5 exd5 7 ♗b5+ – *19*) 5...d5 6 0-0 ♗d6 7 ♘c3 (7 b3 0-0 8 ♗b2 ♘bd7 9 ♘bd2 – *23*) 7...0-0 8 b3 ♘bd7 9 ♗b2 a6 10 ♖c1 (10 cxd5 exd5 11 ♖c1 ♘e4 – *28*) 10...♕e7 – *32*

4...♗b4

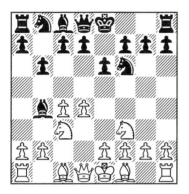

5 ♗g5 – *79*

5 ♗d2 – *36*

5 g3 – *39*

5 ♕c2 – *42*

5 e3 ♘e4 6 ♕c2 ♗xc3+ 7 bxc3 ♗b7 8 ♗d3 f5 9 0-0 0-0

   10 ♘e1 – *51*

   10 ♘d2 – *54*

5 ♕b3 c5 6 ♗g5 (6 ♗f4 – *61*; 6 a3 ♗a5 7 ♗f4 – *62*) 6...♗b7 7 a3 (7 dxc5 – *65*; 7 0-0-0 – *66*; 7 e3 – *75*) 7...♗a5

8 dxc5 – *68*

8 e3 – *73*

5...h6 6 ♗h4 g5 7 ♗g3 ♘e4 8 ♕c2 ♗b7

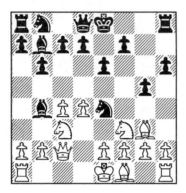

9 e3 – *90*

9 ♗e5 ♗xc3+ 10 bxc3 ♖g8

11 d5 – *83*

11 ♘d2 – *85*

9 ♘d2 – *86*

9...d6 10 ♗d3 – *93*

10 ♘d2 – *91*

10...♗xc3+ 11 bxc3 f5

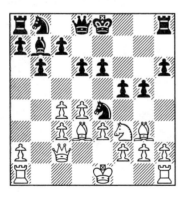

12 d5 – *95*

12 c5 – *93*

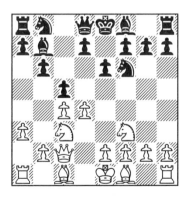

8 ♗f4 –*136*

7...cxd4 8 ♘xd4 ♗c5 9 ♘b3 ♘c6

10 ♗f4 – *147*

10 ♗d3 – *140*

10 ♘xc5 – *140*

10 ♗g5 ♘d4 11 ♘xd4 ♗xd4 12 ♘b5 (12 ♗d3 – *161*) 12...♗e5 13 f4 ♗b8 14 e5 h6

      15 exf6 – *166*

      15 ♗xf6 – *167*

10...0-0 11 ♘xc5 – *150*

11 0-0-0 – *148*

11 ♖d1 – *149*

11...bxc5 12 ♗d6 ♘d4 13 ♕d3 ♖e8

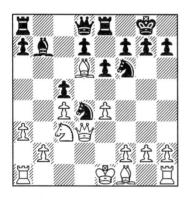

14 b4

14 e5 ♘g4

    15 ♘e4 – *157*

    15 b4 – *158*

    15 ♗xc5 – *159*

14...e5 15 ♗xc5 – *153*

15 ♖b1 – *154*

15 ♖a2 – *155*

C) 4 g3 ♗a6 5 b3 – *169*

5 ♕b3 ♘c6 6 ♘bd2 (6 ♗d2 – *171*) 6...♘a5

    7 ♕a4 – *174*

    7 ♕c3 – *175*

5 ♘bd2 ♗b4 6 ♕c2 0-0 7 ♗g2 d5

    8 a3 – *181*

    8 0-0 – *182*

5 ♕a4 ♗b7 6 ♗g2 c5 7 dxc5 (7 0-0 – *186*) 7...bxc5 8 0-0 ♗e7 9 ♘c3 0-0 10 ♖d1 (10 ♗f4 – *201*) 10...♕b6 11 ♗f4 d6

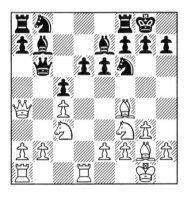

    12 ♖d2 – *196*

    12 ♕b3 – *199*

    12 ♖ab1 – *201*

5 ♕c2 ♗b4+ 6 ♗d2 ♗e7

    7 ♗g2 0-0 8 0-0 c6 9 ♗f4 d5

        10 b3 – *211*

10 ♘bd2 – *215*

7 e4 d5 8 cxd5 ♗xf1 9 ♔xf1 exd5 10 e5 ♘e4 11 ♘c3 ♘xc3

12 ♗xc3 – *220*

12 bxc3 – *222*

5...b5

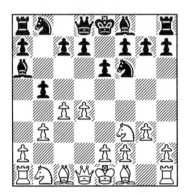

6 cxb5 – *232*

6 ♕c2 – *228*

6 ♘bd2 – *229*

6 ♗g2 – *230*

6...♗xb5 7 ♗g2 d5 8 0-0 – *236*

8 ♘c3 – *235*

8...♘bd7 9 ♘c3 ♗a6 – *237*

10 ♗b2 – *240*

10 ♖e1 – *242*

10 ♘e5 – *244*